PSYCHOLOGICAL PERSPECTIVES IN ENVIRONMENTAL AND DEVELOPMENTAL ISSUES

About the Editors

Adesh Agarwal is Professor and Head of the Department of Psychology at D.D.U. Gorakhpur University, Gorakhpur. She started her University teaching career in 1963 at Lucknow University, but later moved to Gorakhpur University. She was also research associate at Florida State University, Tallahassee, U.S.A., and, Ottawa University, Ottawa, Canada. She has published extensively in foreign and Indian journals in the areas of human motivation, time perspective, personality, human development, applied social and health psychology. Research students have done doctoral work under her guidance in all these areas. She has contributed to edited volumes like *Cognition and Culture: A Cross-cultural Approach to Cognitive Psychology* (Ed. J. Altariba), *Motivation and Affective Processes* (Ed. A.K. Srivastava), *Contemporary Games* (Ed. C.H. Adair). She is also author of several books like—*Achievement Motivation and Time Perspective, Two Simulated Enquiry Environments: A Social Simulation. Game and a CAI Based Information Retrieval System.* She is also Member of Executive Committee of National Academy of Psychology, India. Under her leadership, Department of Psychology has received the coveted Special Assistance grant from, University Grants Commission and is running the D.S.A. programme very successfully.

Ashok Kumar Saxena (*b.* 1948), M.A. (1967, Gorakhpur, First Position), Ph.D. (1979, Gorakhpur) studied the problems of Hostility and Alienation in University students, delinquents and prisoners. In an I.C.S.S.R. project formulated Alienation-Aggression hypothesis which is a better explanation than Frustration-Aggression hypothesis. Constructed Saxena Hostility scale, Co-author of text books and member editorial board of journals, has made research contributions in the areas of verbal learning, Psycholinguistics, creativity, self-disclosure, self-evaluation, perception of authority and social responsibility. As an Applied Psychologist did Radio-counselling and Brainstorming sessions. The problem of distress in widows and rural poor received his exploratory attention. Distress by natural disasters is his current concern. A committed advocate of Indian Indigenous Psychology is busy developing "Parasuram Syndrome".

PSYCHOLOGICAL PERSPECTIVES IN ENVIRONMENTAL AND DEVELOPMENTAL ISSUES

Editors

ADESH AGARWAL

ASHOK KUMAR SAXENA

Department of Psychology, D.S.A.
Deen Dayal Upadhyaya Gorakhpur University
Gorakhpur

CONCEPT PUBLISHING COMPANY, NEW DELHI-110059

ISBN : 81-8069-012-1

First Published 2003

Published and Printed by
Ashok Kumar Mittal
Concept Publishing Company
A/15-16, Commercial Block, Mohan Garden,
New Delhi-110059 (INDIA)

Phone : 5351460, 5351794
Fax : 091-11-5357103
Email : publishing@conceptpub.com

FOREWORD

The present volume by Professors Adesh Agarwal and A.K. Saxena contains the papers presented and deliberated at seminars on Environmental Psychology and on Human Development organized under the U.G.C's D.S.A. programme, Department of Psychology, University of Gorakhpur, Gorakhpur. The papers reflect the concerns of the participants and their approaches. The following paragraphs attempt to identify the basic psychological issues in the general framework of the scopes of the two seminars, and in one instance, indicate an alternative paradigm for viewing the problems.

The relationship of man to his environment, the subject matter of environmental psychology, is vast as it spans the entire gamut of the biotic and abiotic environment. It touches almost all disciplines: natural, biological, social, humanities, education, business, law, practical affairs like planning and management and even international affairs. However, the term environment has been limited to man's natural and built physical environment. This is not unique, for comparative psychology has similarly been equated with animal psychology, leaving anthropological and cross-cultural psychology to social psychologists.

Man has taken liberties with his environment in the name of "development" and "quality of life" which have been defined largely in physical and economic terms. The fall-out has acquired political overtones so that the developing nations are being advised to strive for "sustainable development", after the advisors have themselves already plundered the natural resources, and considerably polluted the environment.

Like other organisms are responsive to their natural environment and they also fashion the environment according to their needs and desires. The psychologist is interested in knowing as to how the natural and built environment is represented in man's cognition. For instance, man experiences and structures the space around him in different ways inviting varied reactions. Privacy, personal space and crowding, territoriality, life in a mega-city, desert, jungle, in confined space like workplace, jail, inside submarine, on the ocean floor or on the mountain top or in the outer space are all differently experienced. In varied settings there is sometimes information overload and at other times there is attenuation, deprivation of distortion. All this influence man's perception of his environment. His experience of the built environment like apartments in multistoried structures, factories, shopping arcades, park and garden vary. A tourist in a new city makes and retains mental maps of routes he takes by noting landmarks to find his way about it. Man must devise strategies to orient himself and learn to cope with the various spatial dispositions in his environment even in planning transport systems, road layouts, highways and expressways to function effectively.

Equally important are man's feelings and attitudes toward his environment. What and how we feel colour our emotional reactions. An environment may be pleasing or neighbourhood annoying. The feeling of crowding is a psychological response to the physical presence of others. But the physical and the psychological do not covary, nor are they always in the same direction for different people at different times. The feeling of loneliness may haunt a person even in a crowded place, just as another may feel suffocated in a sparsely populated place. Inmates in a prison, those living in condominiums or as neighbours in housing complexes or in exclusive locality feel and react differently.

The features of the physical environment influence the nature of social bonds among the residents. Social distancing, isolation, social intrusion, integration and assimilation are varied forms of social reactions. Change in the housing patterns may threaten the identity of a community. Conversely, the social environment—the kind of pressure for modelling the physical environment to its requirements neighbourhood community—may exert and wishes, e.g., construction of roads, highways and other institutions (for instance, hospitals, schools, multistoried apartment buildings, entertainment areas, like shops, cinema or amusement parks.) Sometimes the environment or its modification may induce stress and call for adjustment or coping reactions. Thus the interaction between social and physical is reciprocal; it could be facilitating or restraining.

It would be evident that such cognitive and affective responses would be learned, retained and employed in future problem solving. The cognitive map of the growing child consists of objects and people and it is gradually built during the course of its development. Information concerning environment is not only directly acquired, it is also filtered through the affective reactions of the significant others in the child's life. Education, media and other agencies also help in fashioning the attitudes and values towards the environment.

Most human strivings are in the service of needs. Motivational foundations of behaviour are of concern to the environmental psychologist. Seeking satisfaction of various needs requires a continuous commerce with the environment. And since needs have a tendency to multiply and grow, it implies an ever increasing interaction with environment. Modern business philosophers have exploited this tendency. Pressure selling makes us buy first then we begin feeling (as if to justify our purchase) that we needed it; we buy a thing so we must have needed it, although we generally buy what we need!

Theoretically speaking it has been proposed by some psychologists that cognitive discrepancy (e.g. Festinger's Dissonance theory or Hadley Cntril's Transactional theory) initiates a motivational state. When disturbed balance must be restored (Fritz Heider). But it is surprising that often cognitive discrepancy does not result in conative behaviour. So often one is awáre of the polluting consequences of one's actions (cognitive discrepancy); yet it does not always insulated from others, perhaps from our own larger interests. The nexus between cognition and motivation does not always appear to be potent enough to lead to the appropriate behaviour.

Apart from such holistic features of the environment, there are specific aspects of the physical environment to which humans respond in various ways. The intensity and quality of lighting, air, water, temperature and other sensory inputs, it is well known, affect human efficiency.

One of the consequences of development through industrialization, urbanization and modernization is the degradation of the physical environment both at the level of sensory inputs and at holistic level. Toxic exhausts, affluent, other wastes as well as the manner of their disposal pose health hazards through their direct as well as indirect impact via changes in flora and fauna which tie at the basis of human life support system. The entire field of behaviour toxicology deals with problems of the behaviour consequences of pollution.

Management of environment, therefore, is of crucial importance in environmental planning. The environmental psychologist assists the environmentalist in dealing with the behavioural consequences of any insult to the natural environment that may be the result of his planning. It may be remembered here that a given ecology has evolved through millennia of evolution away processes and to which man's biological system, like that of other living species, has tuned itself. Any violence to a given ecology such as through deforestation, mining or through creation of fresh structures like dams and bridges, setting up hazardous industries is bound to vitiate the balance in nature. Environmental management, therefore, is crucial to living; it may be so manipulated as to cause minimal damage to the environment without retarding development. Furthermore, people have to be educated in the proper use of the environmental resources. Environmental education is the prophylactic measure to properly deal with the environment—how thoughtless actions damage it—and that they must learn to lead a responsible civic life. Environmental education, thus, is required for healthy living and a good social life.

Sometimes natural calamities strike communities resulting in considerable damage to natural environment, such as floods, landslides, draught, fire, cyclone or blizzard. Accidental happenings like leakage of poisonous gas, explosion and fire may occur. Even intentional acts cause damage such as during hostilities and war such as chemical, biological or nuclear pollution. All such eventualities require human intervention; and here psychological intervention. Through inoculation as prop hylacxis and counselling techniques are found helpful.

In sum, the goal of the environmental psychologist is to research into the man—environment relationship and to devise strategies, which minimize, damage, promote pro-life values and optimize human happiness. Paradoxically though, all development involves interference with natural environment.

As noted earlier the terms "development" and "Quality of life" are defined essentially in terms of material prosperity (e.g., GND) and in terms of comforts which environment is expected to provide. The human relations aspect is limited to; the social relations consequences of environmental manipulation. Peace of mind, feeling of well-being and happiness are regarded as products of economic prosperity. This particular mode of thinking seems linked to assumptions, perhaps drawn from a distorted interpretation of Judeocristian thought, concerning the nature of man and his destiny. These are (i) man is cream of creation and (ii) there is a dichotomy between man and nature. It follows therefrom that (a) man has a (moral) right and authority (power); (b) to use (exploit) nature (utilitarianism) with; (c) the means (technology) at his command for the satisfaction of his needs and desires. A distorted interpretation of Max Weber and of rise of capitalism from Calvinism are marshalled in its support. Just as Marxist thesis is based upon economic determinism.

The logical consequence of this kind of thinking is that since needs proliferate; unrestrained consumption (consumerism) puts an ever increasing demand on nature. Once regarded a model of development the Achieving Society (McLeand) as held out before the developing nations to emulate. It showed that ingenuity and entrepreneurship promised almost an infinite growth, where excellence and not merely success mattered and enough was not enough. In this attempt to outbid, the effort got profaned resulting in achievement anxiety and depression. Science and technology put tools of exploitation of nature in man's hands. This produced an abandoned supply of goods and services; but the cost was heavy. Man became a victim of the trap he set himself because he counterfeited the concepts of "development" and "quality of life" in purely economic and amoral sense. It is lately that he has begun to think of cost—benefit analysis of human intervention (e.ġ., depletion of ozone). This has made him realize that nature has to be judiciously used and not indiscriminately exploited without damaging his own interests. Sustainability of development indicates this awareness.

It appears that this attitude of "control over nature" promotes a feeling of assertion and aggression rather than of acceptance, respect and even reverence for nature. The man-environment aymbiotic relationship is overlooked.

The early anthropologists uncharitably interpreted reverence for nature among the primitive people as born of fear of the elemental forces of nature (air/wind for cyclone; water/rain for floods; fire for devastation etc.) and occasionally he is supposed to have deified them. Accordingly propitiating the deities by prayers and offerings was supposed to have come about. But it may be argued that the preliterate man could also have realized the pro-life values of those very elements (sun for light and heat; water for good harvest, washing and cleaning; fire for cooking and incineration; wind for drying etc.) Even the philosopher Tharus regarded water to be source of all life. The primitive man must have appreciated the intimate relationship between his needs and the benign powers of nature. Many of the socio-religious practices and rituals in the preliterate and even in the civilized survive till today. Reflecting sensitivity to ecology.

Abram (1997) the ecologist has forcefully argued with evidence from the everyday rituals of the Bali islanders (Chapter 1: The Ecology of Magic) for the relatedness of human awareness to larger ecology (p. 261). Abram stresses the need for becoming ever more aware of the other lives and other forms of sentience and sensibility that surround our live (p. 272). Elaborating on the nexus of man and his environment, adds: "By acknowledging such links between the inner psychological world and the perceptual terrain that surrounds us, we begin to turn inside out (code), loosening the psyche from its confinement within a strictly human sphere freeing sentience to rerun to the sensible world that contains it. And indeed each terrain, each ecology, seems to have its own particular intelligence, its unique vernacular of soil and leaf and sky)" (p. 262).

Focusing upon the concept of lebenswelt (life world) in Husserl's phenomenology and Merleau-Ponty's modification thereof Abram (1997) examines the sensorial dimension of experience. He feels that: "... our sensory perceptions (are) simply our part of vast interpenetrating web work of our perceptions and sensations borne countless other bodies-supported, that is not just by ourselves, but by icy streams rumbling down granite slopes, by owl wings and lichens, and by the unseen, imperturbable wind," (p. 65) And further their," The intertwined web of experience is, of course, the life world to which Husserl alluded in his final writings, yet now the life world has been disclosed as a profoundly canal field....... Yet this is not the biosphere as it is conceived by an abstract and objectifying science, ...it is, rather the biosphere as it is experienced and lived from within, by the intelligent body—by the attentive human animal who is entirely a part of the world that he, or she, experiences." (p. 55). Abram concludes: "For it is only at the scale of our direct, sensory interaction with the land around us that we can appropriately notice and respond to the immediate needs of the living world" (p. 268).

It may be instructive to examine the attitude of harmony with nature rather than control and exploitation of nature in the context of our culture. Most of the socio-religious practices in our society commence with invocation (in prayers) to the presiding gods and goddesses in the Hindu pantheon (Varuna, Agni, etc.). Consider also in this context the worship of blora and fauna and the status they enjoy in our daily life (e.g., *Tulsi, Neem, Bargad,* Mango etc.) in social and religious rituals; damages to them is resented, cutting forbidden and even regarded a "sin". The fauna too are similarly regarded and likewise associated with deities (e.g., serpent Sheshanag with Vishnu; bull Nandi with Shiva; tiger with Durga; peacock with Saraswati; owl with Lakshmi and mouse with Ganapati). Hanuman, Garuda and Jatayu are similarly venerated. Even the inanimate nature is similarly regarded: Mount Kailash, Nanda Devi, Gunga Mata, Narmada, Godavari, Brahmaputra etc. Nature is not perceived as subservient to man, for after all, man is only one form of existents among many others in nature. Nature is respected, even venerated; the attitude towards nature is one of seeking from it and not that of demanding from it. Can we, therefore, not look for an alternative paradigm for understanding this man-environment symbiosis? Such an alternative would be based upon an attitude towards environment, which promises as much respect, and dignity to nature as man claims for himself. This will serve to humanize the technological society and promise a healthier relationship with the environment.

In this context it is refreshing to look at what the economist James Eggert (1999) has to say. Traditional and modern economics are concerned with growth, expansion and acceleration. In this enterprise economics has been enormously successful. But Eggert questions if this has made for happiness or adequately answered the question: what one wants from life? Although a thoroughbred economist he pleads for an enlargement of the economic concept of value that future development becomes sustainable and life worth living. Metaphorically he finds in the Song of the Meadowlark (1999) an incentive to view holistically the economic activity in the context of man environment relation. As a Thoreauan he is painfully aware of what science, technology, and modern business interests have done to environment and he wants to retrieve the situation for a sustainable future.

Philosophers too have been concerned with man's relation to the cosmos and with the problem of values. In recent times the post-modern philosophers like Levinas (1981) and Derrida (1967) have raised the issue of ethical responsibility in a novel way. The term "ethical responsibility". However, is not used in the conventional sense of prescriptive morality. They feel that the very presence of the "other", everything other than self, makes a demand on the self. Following Levinas and Derrida, Kurukkal (1997) places the thematization to the other in the ethical domain. Saya hw: "It is an ethical imperative and acknowledgement of the demand of the other that creates a responsibility toward the other. It is this responsibility which fills the nation of the other in Levinas (p. 1406)". The other deserves to be treated with respect and dignity.

Reference has been made to the view of an economist and a modern philosopher to highlight the point that the "other", in this context the environment, needs to be treated in a somewhat different way than what we have been accustomed to. This means that "not-self", in the context of man-environment relationship must be accorded the same significance as to our own "self". It means that a change in our attitude toward nature and technology is required. Environment must not be exploited for man's greed. From a limited concern of economics with growth, expansion and acceleration there seems to be a need for a holistic approach to development. The terms "utility" and "value" have to be redefined in terms of man's happiness and well-being. That is likely to produce a more harmonious relationship between man and environment and also serve man better. Technology will be humanized rather than man turned into a robot and at the mercy of science and technology.

The other set of paper included in this volume are form the

proceedings of seminar on human development. Early developmental psychology dealt with ontogenetic development of behaviour; physiological (sensory, motor and maturational processes), Social, linguistic, psychological (intellectual, affective and thought processes), moral development and the like. General psychology concerned itself with normal adult behaviour. From the point of view of the comparative method human development was compared with the development of behaviour in other species, such as that of the sub-human primates (researches on chimpanzees by Wolfgang Kóhler and of the apes by Kelloggs). Some others went down to investigate development of behaviour at still lower phylogenetic levels, because it was believed that humans were endowed with a more complex nervous system both in terms of structure and function of what was found in the lower specifies. "Man is only bigger and better than rat!" At the other end was a growing interest in the declining years of the living being; education in mortality, better living conditions and health care system having increased longevity. Gerontology grew as a full-fledged discipline in the field of human development. The entire course of human development got subsumed under "life span study".

Many studies reported in this volume deal with various aspects of human development. Some of them deal with ecological and cross-cultural factors also. However, there is a greater concern with the products of development than with the processes of development. Although this distinction between product and process is important, it is not easy to separate the two. But the more important is to uncover the process of development rather than the end-result of the process Early psychologists investigating the developmental process investigated for instance as to how the sensors-motor processes lead to the development of the formal abstract thought through concrete operations, such studies were concerned with both the product, as well as, with the processes of development. (Piaget). In his later writings Piaget, like Chomsky, conceived of structures as innate which unfurl themselves and differentiate into various mental processes. There is no "yesterday" or "tomorrow" for an infant. Jaensch, for instance, conceives an eidetic undifferentiated state, from which differentiation takes place (if one ignores the distortion of the idea into a political monstrosity of the Aryan myth under Hitler). Heinz Werner too postulated the process of development as one of differentiation from undifferentiated homogeneity to differentiated heterogeneity. The global undifferentiated experience in the first stage differentiates itself and crystallizes in forms of perceptual responsiveness, almost like a new branch of a growing tree. At a later stage of development the sensory-perceptual reactivity separates itself from mnemonic processes. For a child has no past or future; only the present exists. Memory of past and idea of a future develops from the perceptual present. This represents yet another branching out. Imaginal functions emerge still later. Next to appear is the fantasy activity as yet another branching. Still later thinking activity separates itself from fantasy activity. This is the process of gradual differentiation from initial global undifferentiated experiences, almost like the growth of branches from a growing tree. Werner arrives at this hypothesis of mental development from his study of child, animal and primitive mentality. Later in their brilliant observations and experiments. Luria and Vyogotsky find an intimate relationship between the development of thought and acquisition of language reminding one of Bibot, Washburn and Watson. They stress role of ecology in development of mental processes.

Some of the papers presented at the two seminars may be read with interest in the framework of the scopes of environmental psychology and human development discussed above. They reflect the concerns of the researchers, their orientation, the different approaches they use, and the findings they arrive at which have been faithfully summarized in the Preface. The editors have done an admirable job and make the two symposia proceedings available to a wider audience. Psychologists, educationists and ecologists in particular and social scientists and lay readers in general will find reading rewarding.

H.S. Asthana
Former Head, Department of Psychology
and
Ex-Vice Chancellor, M.J.S.J. Saugar University,
Saugar

255/79, Kundri
Rakabganj,
Lucknow

ACKNOWLEDGEMENTS

We hope that the readers will like the fruit of our labour. We wish to acknowledge the contributions and thank all the authors. Special thanks are extended to Professor H.S. Asthana, our teacher, and former Head of this department and Vice Chancellor of Saugar University, who very kindly agreed to write the Foreword, inspite of great personal inconvenience due to his health. Professors Udai Jain and Qamar Hasan are duly thanked for having gone through the manuscripts and giving their valuable suggestions. We wish to thank the former Vice Chancellor, Professor R.K. Misra for his continuous encouragement, and the present Vice Chancellor who not only gave encouragement but also the financial assistance from the UGC publication grant, without which this dream would not have come true. We will be failing in our duty if we do not thank our coleagues and students who made tireless efforts to make this possible, special thanks are expressed towards Prof. N.K.M. Tripathi who was the organizing secretary of the seminar on human development. Our staff members and specially Mrs. Mannu Dubey deserve thanks for their untiring assistance during the hosting of seminars and for providing the secretarial help. We thank Mr. J.K. Bose for his typing.

ADESH AGARWAL
&
ASHOK K. SAXENA
(Editors)
DDU Gorakhpur University, Gorakhpur

CONTENTS

SECTION B

DEVELOPMENTAL ISSUES

LIST OF CONTRIBUTORS

Nazish Bano is lecturer in Psychology at P.G. College at Deoria. She has worked in the area of memory. The title of her Ph.D. thesis is "An Experiment on Reconstructive Memory for Stories".

Anubhuti Dubey is a lecturer in the department of Psychology, D.D.U., Gorakhpur University, Gorakhpur. She is working in the area of Health Psychology and Applied Social Psychology and has published a number of research papers in these areas. She has also contributed one Chapter in a book. At present, she is working on her doctoral thesis. Her thesis is on the "Role of some psychosocial variables in coping with chronic illness".

Chandra Bhal Dwivedi is a professor and chairman of the Department of Psychology, Banaras Hindu University. He has published extensively in the area of cognition, stress, affective processes, and indigenous psychology (Add. Department of Psychology, Banaras Hindu University, Varanasi-221005)

Satya Gopal Jee is a research fellow at Department of Psychology, Banaras Hindu University. He is presently working in the area of Dementia and Dementia of Alzheimer's type.

Uday Jain is Professor and Head, Department of Psychology, Barkatullah University, Bhopal. He has also taught earlier at the Universities of Rajasthan, Allahabad, Sagar and North Eastern Hills. He was Fulbright Fellow at the University of Chicago and Swarthmore College, and later the Principal Co-investigator of CIDA—Shastri Indo-Canadian Project on Community and Regions, Overcoming Ecological Crisis. He has authored *Psychological Consequences of Crowding* and has contributed many articles in reputed journals. He has also edited: *Perspectives on Psychology and Social Development.*

Lila Krishnan is a Professor (Psychology) in the Department of

Humanities and Social Sciences, at the Indian Institute of Technology, Kanpur. She holds a Master's degree in Applied Psychology from the University of Jabalpur, and a Ph.D. from McMaster University, Hamilton, Ontario, Canada. Seriously committed to both teaching and research, she believes that the two are mutually enriching. Her research experience includes a study of attitude change (M.A. level), recipient reactions to helping in Canada (Ph.D. Dissertation), helping behaviour and recipient reactions among Indian subjects (ICSSR-sponsored project), and reward allocation and distributive justice in Indian settings (ICSSR-sponsored project). In addition, she has published on cognitive-developmental issues, child rearing, and other aspects of social behaviour in the Indian cultural context.

Babban Mishra is Reader in Psychology at D.D.U. Gorakhpur University. He got his M.Phil and Ph.D. Degree from the Centre of Advanced Study in Psychology, Utkal University, Bhubaneshwar. He is a Psycholinguist interested in language acquisition and processing. He is the author of a number of publications including books in Hindi and English on a variety of topics in Psychology. He has translated two books in Hindi i.e. *Experimental Designs in Behavioural Researches* as Vyavharparak Anushandhan Ke Prayogik Abhikalp by K.D. Broota and *Bilinguisticism in a Multilingual Society : Theoretical and Pedagogical Applications* as Bahubhashi Samaj Meny Dvibhashikta: Sedhantik Aur Shiskchha Shastriya Nihitartha, by Ajit Mohanty (in Press). His review of 'Naming the Mind' by Kurt Danziger has been published in B.N. Puhan (Ed.) *Indian Psychological Abstracts and Reviews*. He has completed three Research Projects.

Manju Mishra is senior lecturer in Psychology at P.G. College at Khalilabad, Sant Kabir Nagar. She has worked in the area of Psychology of women as is evident from the title of her Ph.D. thesis—"Future Orientation, Optimism, Social Skills and Well-Being in Working Women".

R.C. Mishra is Professor of Psychology at Banaras Hindu University since 1992. He joined the University in 1974 as a Lecturer, and was promoted as a Reader in 1984. A D.Phil. from Allahabad University, he has been a Post-doctoral Research Fellow, a Shastri Research Fellow, and a Visiting Fellow at Queen's University, Kingston, Canada. He has also been a Visiting Professor at the University of Geneva. His principal research interest is in cultural influence on human development. he has published extensively in professional journal in the fields of cognition, acculturation, schooling and cross-cultural studies, and contributed articles to nearly two dozen edited volumes including the Handbook of Cross-Cultural Psychology (Editors: J.W. Berry, P.R. Dasen and T.S. Saraswathi) and Handbook of Culture and Psychology (Ed. D. Matsumoto). He has coauthored (with D. Sinha and J.W. Berry) Ecology, acculturation and psychological adaptation, and coedited (with J.W. Berry and R.C. Tripathi) Psychology in human and social development.

Rajendra Mishra is professor and Head of the Department of Psychology, B.R.A. Bihar University, Muzafarpur. He has guided research and published in the areas of social and developmental psychology. (Add. Department of Psychology, B.R.A. Bihar University, Muzafarpur)

Girishwar Misra, is Professor of Psychology at Delhi University. Earlier, he has done teaching and research at Universities of Gorakhpur, Allahabad and Bhopal. He was Chairman of the Department of Psychology and Dean, Faculty of Arts at Bhopal and Delhi. He is a prolific writer and has written many research articles in various Journals. He has written and edited many books e.g. *Psychological Consequences of Prolonged Deprivation, Deprivation: Its Social Roots and Psychological Consequences, Psychology of Poverty and Disadvantage, Applied Social Psychology in India, Psychological Perspectives on Stress and Health.* He was a Fulbright Fellow at Michigan University and Swarthmore College. He is Editor of *Psychological Studies*, and is a member of Executive Committee of International Association of Cross-culture Psychology. He was also elected President of National Academy of Psychology, India.

Pushpa Misra is Professor of Psychology at Lucknow University. She has done extensive work in the area of Psychology of Perception and Developmental Psychology. She has published research articles, psychological tests and books in these areas.

Neelima Misra is presently Professor of Psychology and Head at the Department of Psychology, Lucknow University. For the last few years her major area of research has been stress and health. Currently she is engaged in research work on family relationships, especially the built environment. She is member of various academic bodies such as Indian Science Congress, Indian Academy of Applied Psychology, National Academy of Psychology, and member of the editorial board of Indian Journal of Clinical Psychology.

R. Murlidharan was Professor. and head of educational psychology department at the prestigious institution of National Council of Research and Training, and she worked and published extensively in the area of child development.

Sushma Pandey is senior lecturer in the Department of Psychology at D.D.U. Gorakhpur University. She is currently Principal investigator of two U.G.C. Projects viz. (1) Psycho-Social Study of Population Control, Women Health and Empowerment (under D.S.A.) and (2) Social Dynamics of Child Abuse and its Psychological consequences in Eastern Districts of U.P. (Independent Project, funded by U.G.C.). She has published several research articles on coping with (Work/crowding) stress, correlates of future orientation, and Reproductive Health and also she has been co-author in six books. Her area of interest includes Community Psychology, Experimental and Social Psychology.

Rakesh Pandey is a Lecturer in Psychology at D.D.U. Gorakhpur University. He was formerly a Lecturer in Yoga Psychology at Bihar Yoga Bharati, Munger. He has contributed many papers in reputed national and International Journals and published more than 20 research papers in conferences and symposia. He is a recipient of Young Scientist Award of Indian Academy of Applied Psychology and has also published several psychological tests and scales. He has referred many research articles submitted to the journal *Personality and Individed Differences* and is an editorial consultant to the *Journal of Projective Psychology and Mental Health*. His area of research interest includes experimental clinical psychology, emotion, stress, and health psychology, (Add. Department of Psychology, D.D.U. Gorakhpur University, Gorakhpur); e-mail:rpan_in@yahoo.com

Sheetla Prasad was exposed to the excitement of research soon after doing his M.A. in 1983 from Gorakhpur University. He became a research assistant in a project on Learning Disabilities. After completing his doctoral thesis in the area of learning disabilities he started teaching psychology at St. Andrew's Degree College, and also kept up with his research programmes. In 1993, he joined Ewing Christian College, Allahabad, a premier institution of learning, and also an autonomous college of Allahabad University. Besides learning disabilities his other major interest area is health psychology.

Sheela Singh is Reader in Psychology at D.N.P.G. College, Gorakhpur. She has done research in the areas of experimental, environmental and Personality psychology, and has published research articles in these areas. The title of her Ph.D. thesis is—Experimental Study of the Role of Materials in Verbal Learning.

Namita Srivastava is a research scholar in Psychology Department in Lucknow University.

Shalini Srivastava is a teacher and has done Ph.D. in Psychology. She has worked in the area of Environmental Psychology. The title of her Ph.D. thesis reflects this, it is An Empirical Study of Environmental Needs, Family Atmosphere and Competence Among Children.

Achal Nandini Srivastava started her teaching career in 1974 at St. Andrew's Degree College, Gorakhpur. While there, she completed her doctoral work on religious personality in which she has investigated the depths of the persons known as 'religious'. In 1982, she joined the faculty at Gorakhpur University. There she started to peel the layers off the problems of learning disabled and hyperactive children and her interest in this area continues.

Tara Singh is a senior lecturer of psychology at Barkatulla University, Bhopal. He has contributed research papers in the area of cognitive development. He was also engaged in research on ecological crisis under the partnership programme of Shashtri Indo Canadian Institution.

Ashok Kumar Saxena (*b.* 1948), M.A. (1967, Gorakhpur, First Position), Ph.D. (1979, Gorakhpur) studied the problems of Hostility and Alienation in University students, delinquents and prisoners. In an I.C.S.S.R. project formulated Alienation- Aggression hypothesis which is a better explanation than Frustration-Aggression hypothesis. Constructed Saxena Hostility scale, Co-author of text books and member editorial board of journals, has made research contributions in the areas of verbal learning, Psycholinguistics, creativity, self-disclosure, self-evaluation, perception of authority and social responsibility. As an Applied Psychologist did Radio-counselling and Brainstorming sessions. The problem of distress in widows and rural poor received his exploratory attention. Distress by natural disasters is his current concern. A committed advocate of Indian Indigenous Psychology is busy developing "Parasuram Syndrome".

Ashok Kumar Srivastava is Reader at National Council of Educational Research and Training, New Delhi. He has worked extensively in the areas of developmental and educational psychology and has published in Indian and foreign journals. He has edited *Child Development : The Indian Perspective*. He has done work on indigenous concepts of intelligence.

Prem Sagar Nath Tiwari is Reader in Psychology at D.D.U. Gorakhpur

University. He has worked extensively in the area of Rural Development and Environmental Psychology. Earlier he has worked as JRF under the DSA Programme of Psychology Department, Allahabad University. He did Ph.D. in Psychology with Professor Durganand Sinha in the area of motivation and change proneness among farmers. He joined as lecturer in Psychology Department of D.D.U. Gorakhpur University in 1980. Apart from 14 articles in Journals and more than 25 in various Seminars and Conferences, he has written the first Indian book on Environmental Psychology in Hindi and has contributed chapter in Modern Social Psychology. His recent book on Psychology of Successful and Unsuccessful villagers (in Press) is coming shortly. He has supervised 3 Ph.D. and 4 M.Phil Dissertations and completed three research projects. He is also working in the areas of Disaster Management and Development of Competence among Children. He served on the executive committee of National Academy of Psychology, India.

Ira Tripathi is senior research fellow in Psychology at D.D.U. Gorakhpur University. The title of her Ph.D. thesis is "Development of Health Behaviour in Children Relation to Mother's Psychological Characteristics". She has published research papers in the area of health Psychology.

Anupam Nath Tripathi is a reader in experimental psychology in the department of Psychology, D.D.U. Gorakhpur University. He was appointed in the department as a lecturer in 1979. He was awarded Ph.D. entitled "An experimental study of forgetting of meaningful verbal materials" in the year 1983. He has published a number of papers in the area of Experimental Psychology, Cognitive Psychology and Developmental Psychology. He has contributed chapters to different books in Hindi e.g. Adhunik Prayogik Manovigyan, Manovaigyanik Anusandhan Paddhati, Adhunik Samajik Manovigyan and Adhunik Daihik Manovigyan. Three Ph.Ds. on Reconstructive Memory for stories, Development of organizational processes in Verbal learning and Development of interpersonal cognitive system.

Vikash Chandra Tripathi is lecturer in psychology at D.A.V. college, Gorakhpur, and is working towards his Ph.D. in the department of psychology. His area of interest is "natural disaster and its management", earlier he worked in the research project on "Environmental stress and coping in victims" under the D.S.A. programme of U.G.C. being run by the department of psychology, D.D.U. Gorakhpur University. Recently he has been selected in the Provincial Police Service in U.P.

INTRODUCTION

ADESH AGARWAL & ASHOK K. SAXENA

The present book is the culmination of deliberations of two U.G.C. national seminars hosted by the Department of Psychology, D.D.U. Gorakhpur University on "Environment and Cognition" and "Current Trends in Human Development Research" under its DSA programme in 1998 and 1999. The themes of these seminars reflect the thrust areas in which work is under progress in this department. The following paragraphs express some of the concerns of the organizers and the issues taken up by the experts who attended these seminars and have contributed the chapters in this book.

Environmental cognition is recognized as a subfield within the general area of environmental psychology. Much theory concerning environmental research has links with prior theorizing in psychology but the area is definitely interdisciplinary and is also recognised as a sub-area of study in geography, economics, architecture and planning. The ability to represent, store, process and use informations about different environments defines the area of environmental cognition. Earlier research in this area was heavily influenced by positivists who subscribed to the view that scientist is a passive observer of objective reality, it also subscribed to analytical methodology. Kantians challenged this view and an "interactionalist approach" argues that we perceive and interpret our environment and the interpretation itself is influenced by our past experiences and future expectation as well as by physical, economic, and cultural factors. Due to the influence of these factors individuals perceive and interpret their environment differentially. With interactionalist view, affect just slips into the area of environmental cognition. There is, however, an alternative thinking that affect and cognition should be kept separate.

Links of culture with environmental cognition are tenuous and multiple enculturation implies active construction of meaning. There are intricate connections between cultural patterns of organising and communicating knowledge and development of this skill in individual members of cultural groups. The material and symbolic tools available in a culture provide a link to sociohistorically formulate means and operations which facilitate mental activity in members. These material (e.g., computers) and symbolic (e.g., numbers) tools do not only aid but may transform human thinking.

Socio-cultural approach to environmental cognition makes an assumption that goal directed action provides a meaningful context for thinking and behaviour. For example a taxi driver and a pilot will draw very different city maps as influenced by their daily activities. Low or zero correlations between tasks of everyday reasoning ability and formal measures of intelligence also point towards socio-cultural influence on abstract thinking. Both physical and socio-psychological environment as well as culture are, therefore, studies in the context of environmental cognition.

Researchers in the area of environmental cognition have also addressed such questions as, how do social processes influence cognition through control over network composition and available cognitive opportunities? Answer to this question may explain the relationship between environmental cognition and spatial behaviour.

Other questions which stire the imagination of environmental psychologists are like how can we make people aware and concerned about really important environmental issues. People generally worry about those issues which have short term and immediate consequences like contaminated drinking water, whereas they pay little or no attention to real environmental issues projected, e.g., scarcity of water in coming years, or deforestation fails to arouse their concern. So questions like what information is extracted from the environment and how is it stored and used? These are some of the questions which environmental psychologists try to answer. How is environmental cognition related to planning and policy making? Should we pay greater attention to eco friendly or sustainable development? Should commercial business houses be permitted to commercially exploit lunar mineral wealth? This question pertains to what is known as socio dilemma. An individual or for that matter, nation, may feel that he is in a dilemma between his personal benefits and depletion of common resources leading to endangering of the common good. Psychologists have a task to design communication to tilt the balance so that people pay heed to delayed harmful effects, rather than smaller immediate rewards. Furthermore, we psychologists have an even greater task to convince others like economists, politicians and policy makers regarding importance of environmental issues. Task is monumental but effort must be expanded. It was with these notions that a seminar on Environment and cognition was organised by the department of Psychology at DDU Gorakhpur University, under its DSA programme. Scholars from all over India participated in this seminar and the result is the present volume. A number of the questions raised above were addressed by learned psychologists.

Two chapters by R.C. Mishra and Uday Jain have argued for inclusion of social contents, culture and religion in understanding environmental cognitions. Uday Jain and Tara Singh have challenged the traditional research on environmental cognition, like study of cognitive maps. Traditionally, individual was the basis of knowledge, it is now argued that interpretation experience and knowledge are clearly functions of social and cultural values and constraints. Thus physical places and features of environment have symbolic meaning and capacity to evolve vivid and widely held social meanings among group members. There is need to study the social organization of knowledge about environment.

R.C. Mishra has focussed on the theory of psychological differentiation in the context of environmental cognition. He says that the theory maintains, that cognition processes are universal, but cognition competencies develop in different ways according to the demands of one's ecology and culture. He cites a number of cross-cultural studies carried out in various settings, but points to the difficulty in establishing a link between culture and cognition due to variations in patterning of the elements of culture, cognitions and the processes through which these are connected. He, however, is hopeful that researchers will pay attention to these in future.

Three other studies have also talked about culture and cognition, giving attention to rural and urban settings and Indian and foreign cultures. P.S.N. Tiwari in his chapter on perceived environment on aspects of social cognition among villagers presents the argument that the village life presents a case of difference rather than deficiency and village life should be understood in a psychological frame of reference which specifically pertains to village life. Pattern of beliefs and perceived environment have been investigated and such factors as land holding, physical environment and age were seen to contribute to these beliefs and perceived environment.

Dubey and Agarwal investigated the conceptualization of intelligence by lay people, in both rural and urban settings. The cultural differences and variations in settings were found to be significant contributors in conceptualization of intelligence. The four types of attributes of intelligence i.e. cognitive, social, emotional and related with task performance were mentioned by respondents. The emphasis of respondents, however, were on social and emotional attributes of intelligence. It is interesting to note that social and emotional aspects of intelligence have been found to be related with well-being. It appears that in Indian culture intelligence is not conceived only as a set of cognitive abilities, but important components of intelligence appears to be those which result in planned action, socially sensitive and emotionally controlled behaviours which promote happiness and well-being.

N. Bano and A.N. Tripathi have explored the effect of socio-cultural settings of stories and retention intervals on recall. The results point out that story schema as represented and formalized by story grammar should be a culturally determined concept challenging the concept of universality of story grammar.

The study by Shalini Srivastava and P.S.N. Tiwari explored the relationship among environmental needs and family atmosphere in Hindi and English medium schools. Main emphasis of this study is on privacy, medium of instruction and their relevance for social competence, and achievement. It revealed that environmental need (i.e., privacy) emerged as the most important and significant predictor of intelligence, achievement and social competence and family atmosphere also predicted the intelligence and social competence.

Manju Mishra and Adesh Agarwal have addressed the socio-cultural environmental issue in their chapter on "Coping and Satisfaction with Life in Working Women.' The authors have investigated the relationship between the demographic variables of socio-economic status and working status of woman, the kind of environmental changes these factors and psychological variables of future orientation and optimism bring out their joint influence on coping strategies employed by these women. Furthermore, they also examined the relationship between coping styles and well-being in women. It is interesting to note that active coping and planning are related with socio-economic and working status of women on the the one and satisfaction with life and happiness in women on other hand. It is, therefore, argued that the higher socio-economic status and working experience provide minimum basic facilities and enhance other resources. Creating an environment which is conducive for planning and active coping style leading to greater satisfaction and happiness. These environments also enhance future orientation and optimism in the respondents. Again facilitating the well-being of women living in these environments.

Two chapters deal with environmental stress. Saxena, Tiwari and Tripathi studied the natural calamity whereas Sushma Pandey worked on stress due to crowding.

Saxena, Tiwari and Tripathi have paid attention to environmental stress caused by a sudden calamity. This kind of an event is even more stress arousing because of its unpredictable nature. Various symptoms of anxiety and depression and helplessness were reported. Lack of awareness of environmental problems and dependence on the Government for support increases their anger and feelings of helplessness.

Sushma Pandey has addressed the problem of crowding and role of perceived control in coping with crowding. Inverse relation between perceived control and illness suggest the usefulness of this variable in dealing with stress resulting from crowding.

Two chapters address the issue of how to save the environment. Sheela Singh in her chapter on 'awareness of environmental degradation and perceived responsibility for its preservation' investigated the people's awareness of environmental degradation, its perceived negative consequences and perceived responsibility for its preservation. Subject age, socio-economic status and educational level were positively related with awareness level, but gravity of environmental degradation was not evaluated as very high by the respondents. Responsibility for protecting environment was viewed as the responsibility of the Government by most respondents.

Neelima Misra in her chapter addresses the fundamental inconsistency between what people think, believe and perceive about the environment and what environmental behaviour they exhibit. This investigation through interview method also revealed that although subjects were aware of the severity of the problem of environmental degradation, its causes, consequences and also of cognitions, motivations and behaviour links but they showed little indulgence in environmentally protective behaviour. It appears that awareness of causes of environmental problems is not sufficient to prompt change in behaviour. The outlook is not very rosy and we need to work to bring changes.

The second section of this book deals with life-span development research in India.

The first review of life-span development appears only two decades ago in 1980 (Baltes, Reese and Lipsitt, 1980). In this review Baltes *et al.*, (1980) expressed the view that life-span developmental psychology is not a theory but only a perspective, an orientation. According to this perspective development is a process which continues throughout life and is not confined to age period of somatic growth e.g., infancy, childhood and adolescence, assuming that development stops when growth stops in maturity.

In a review of developmental psychology in India in 1988, by T.S. Sarawathi and R. Dutta, it was pointed out by authors that the scope of developmental psychology had broadened and it had become more interdisciplinary in nature. They happily noted that psychologists had started responding to the social pressures to provide answers to some questions regarding how to tap the environmental potential to improve quality of life, and greater involvement in intervention programmes. Happily, focus on theory building and empirical studies which are the foundation stones have not been neglected. The inadequacies, however, have been felt in the areas of dissemination of knowledge, with little sharing of information available in various departments of universities. Very little work has been done on infancy, and after a lot of work has been done on influence of deprivational environment it is the need of the day to identify environmental inputs which may correct the deficits due to deprivation and optimize development. The need to reexamine the western models in the light of our traditional cultural systems has been recognised, *e.g.*, Kagiticibasi talks about economic progress in Middle East and Asian countries despite continued presence of joint families this has pointed towards need to reexamine the concept of independence and autonomy as essentials for development of need achievement. Department of Psychology at DDU Gorakhpur University organised a national seminar of Life-Span Development under its DSA programme to deliberate on some of these issues.

Professor Leela Krishnan in her inaugural address—Human Development Research in India: Some Trends and Issues, has pointed out that in the Indian tradition these are some prescriptions about child development. She has emphasized the need for studying life-span development with increase in life expectancy, role of family, because of changing family structure from joint to nuclear. Thirdly, the psychologists need to work with other disciplines and use multidisciplinary approach e.g., work with Helpage India and C.R.Y. Fourthly, specific theoretical issues need to be addressed, e.g., is human development cross-culturally universal or is it culturally specific? She goes on to cite the example of moral development, and stresses need for further research, although there is some theoretical analysis based on observations of various cultures which shows that development alone cannot account for variations in moral and social behaviour and role of cultural factors needs to be underscored. Attention is being paid to two other areas namely, pathological aspects of development and changes in methodological approaches with more emphasis on qualitative research methods, although the dilemma of too much subjectivity is yet to be resolved.

The second chapter in this section is by Professor Girishwar Misra and Ashok K. Srivastava, they have paid attention to ethno-theories of development as parental behaviours are guided by context in childhood in India: An overview of psychological research. The authors review the process of enculturation—an encompassing of the individual by one's culture and, socialization—the deliberate shaping of the individual. This chapter has three pronged strategy—it analyses the pattern of socialization of Indian child as documented by various studies, secondly in the light of political, social and economic changes the parental notions, expectations, values and beliefs have been examined and lastly parent-child discourse has been analysed. The authors have reviewed some ethnographic studies showing the paradoxical influences of mothers immediacy and responsiveness on the one hand and father's harsh disciplinarian methods on the other. Furthermore, the motherhood in India involves multiple mothering in types and forms, the larger group of caretakers prompt the loosening of child's attachment to mother and pleasure.

Some Indian studies on child rearing have been reviewed. No consistent differences could be observed due to rural-urban, lower-upper status differences, but differences due to education, age and employment of mothers, use of punishment, parents personality, socialization practices were noted.

Authors have explored the ideals and values of parents which are used in child socialization. The urban parents emphasized psychological, and rural parents emphasized the economic value of child. Children's success, becoming good citizens and care of old parents were the main expectations from children. Hardwork, honesty and obedience were the desirable, and laziness, greed and fear, disobedience and quarrelsomeness were the undesirable characteristics. The urban-rural and cross-national comparisons have been made. The individualistic *vs.* collectivistic goals, conflict *vs.* cohesion, insecurity and distrust, obligatory and exchange relationships, short-term goals were examined in the changing scenario due to western influence and industrialization. The modern parents are caught between tradition and modernity and are unable to take a consistent stance.

An interesting study of cognitive development and academic achievement in ecological perspective has been undertaken by Srivastava and Murlidharan. The authors report about cognitive development and academic achievement of children of two age groups who live in temple villages in South India. These children grow up either away from the temples or in the vicinity of the temples. Their families are religious but not related with temples or they came from families which were intimately related with temples. Curiously children associated with temples were seen cognitively more competent at both points of schooling. The role of traditional social institutions in facilitating cognitive development is underscored, and the significance of traditional social networks is also underlined.

Ira Tripathi and Adesh Agarwal have also examined the relationship between psycho-social environment created in the home due to chronic illness of the child and some cognitions of the mother's and child's behaviours. This study was carried out on 75 each chronically ill and healthy children and their mothers. Results indicated that parenting style and future expectations predicted family environment as perceived by the child.

Mother's beliefs and attitudes were related with her parental practices. Mother's beliefs about health were also found to be related with psychological symptoms in children. It is, therefore, suggested that mother's psychological characteristics and her expectation about future of the child and her health attitude influence her parenting style. These factors jointly influence perception of the family environment by the child and consequencing the psychological symptoms exhibited by the child. The psycho-socio environment, thus, influences child's coping behaviour in both healthy as well as chronically ill groups of children.

Babban Mishra has seen the impact of level of deprivation age and, different locatives, on the choice of word order, used by children in expressing spatial relationship between a pair of objects. The study tries to throw light on controversy between transformational generative grammar of chemistry and cognitive model of Bates. A possibility of separate identity of locatives, age and level of deprivation with regard to selection of word order has been suggested by the findings. Thus challenging the universal pragmatic strategy for describing locative relationship between a pair of objects.

Pushpa Mishra and Namita Srivastava have taken up the problem of feedback and the development of competence in an educational setting on VIII grade children. It is interesting to note that feedback has significant effect on efficacy judgments, as well as, on mathematical competence. Effort feedback exerted greater influence than ability feedback although ability feedback also motivates the person to persist in the activity.

In chapter 18, Srivastava and Prasad have addressed the problems of learning disabled (LD) children. LD children, having average or above average I.Q., but are educationally underachievers, whereas NLD or normal children having same I.Q. range, are educationally high achievers. The basic cognitive skills such as verbal and numerical studies are presumed to be affected by some processing deficits, hence this educational hindrance. In the present study, some of the verbal and numerical skills, as well as the attentional variables of comparable LD and NLD children were investigated. On the area of verbal learning: (a) In SR and FR, both LD and NLD performed better in written condition; LD children's SR was much poorer at the tail end of the list compared to the beginning items (within group) and NLD group (between group), (b) on recognition memory test, a signal detection analysis showed a much smaller d' for the LD group which showed more uncertainty about an item being old or new, (c) the results of category clustering showed smaller children ratios for LD group indicating their lack of subjective organization skills. On matters pertaining to numerical abilities, LD children showed extreme inability in recognizing the patterns of carefully prepared digital series for a repetition.

They also committed more omission, substitution and wrong order errors. On mental arithmetic task also the LD group displayed a poorer performance, probably because they could not hold one portion of task in memory and calculate another portion. On attentional problems, task requiring same amount of cognitive demand but varying amounts of proximal and distal distractors, showed that the presence of distractors effected both LD and NLD children, but LD children were more hampered overall and specially by external distractors.

The only chapter which addresses the problem of elderly persons is that of Pandey, Gopaljee, Diwedi and Mishra. They have chosen to study the milly demented alizhermer patients and have examined the role of socio-psychological factors in the cognitive impairment of DAT patients. It appears that the cognitive impairment in DAT patients is more if they are illiterate and belong to low SES. The study points out the psycho-social risk factor of education and socio-economic status may work as an umbrella for protecting the elderly from onset of dementia.

SECTION ONE

ENVIRONMENTAL ISSUES

1

RESEARCH IN ENVIRONMENTAL COGNITION
Relevance of Socio-Cultural Perspective

UDAY JAIN & TARA SINGH

INTRODUCTION

For centuries, the view that understanding is a process occurring in the mental world of the individual is shared and advanced by both empiricist and rationalist thinkers with their own particular emphasis. The recent cognitive revolution also regarded knowledge as individual representation of the external world where cognitive system plays a major role in the production of behaviour through which accurate cognitive representations of the world are build up and acted upon. Thus cognition was believed to be the representation of outer reality.

Since cognitive system has been traditionally regarded as having reflective relationship to the objective reality, the question arises how it becomes possible. The answer to this question contributed importantly to the cognitive revolution. The investigators, therefore, focused on the essential capacities of the individual and not the environment that determines the individual's beliefs or understandings about the environment. This understanding led to reset the traditional empiricist assumption that the internal world is a replica of the external world. However, it became problematic how cognitive structure (ideas, concepts, categories) were built up from environmental inputs. In dealing with this problem a variety of approaches have emerged. This chapter presents a review of these approaches and focuses on the possibilities of understanding environmental cognition through socio-cultural processes.

The Field of Environmental Cognition

As an interdisciplinary area of study, the environmental cognition is a well established sub-field in environmental psychology, and also an important topic of study in the fields of geography (e.g., Gulliver, 1908; Kirk, 1951; Trowbridge, 1913; White, 1945; Wright, 1947), economics (Boulding, 1956); sociology (Firey, 1945; Strauss, 1961); architecture, design, and planning (Lynch, 1960). Environmental psychology is concerned with the systematic accounting of the relationship between person and environment (Russell & Ward, 1982), or a study of the physical setting of molar behaviour (Craik, 1970). The field of environmental cognition attempts to understand a series of questions related to the ability to store and access information about different environments (Golledge, 1987). These include abstracting information from the environment, its store, and use.

Although, environmental cognition research is in its infancy (Golledge, 1987), it is full of the richness and regency of both intra- and inter-disciplinary books, reviews and research literature. Accepting the dominant science model recent research on environmental cognition has multiple connections to past research in psychology (see for example the works of Brunswik, 1944; Baird, 1979; Bartlett, 1932; Head, 1920; Piaget & Inhelder, 1967; Hart, 1978; Acredolo, 1976; Pick, 1972; Siegel & White, 1975; Shemyakin, 1962; Tolman, 1948; Ittelson, 1951; Bruner, 1957; Lewin, 1936; Mead, 1934; Kelley, 1955; Hebb, 1949; Kaplan, 1973; and Lee, 1964) providing more and more links to prior theorising (see for example Kaplan, 1983; Kaplan & Kaplan, 1982).

This approach conceives environmental cognition as involving the storage, organization, reconstruction, and recall of images of environmental features that are not immediately present. Psychological research on the ways people from mental images of the geographical environment was initiated by a series of groundbreaking studies by Kevin Lynch (Lynch, 1960). These studies led the foundation for the psychological study of environmental cognition. Lynch's investigations legitimised the scientific study of environmental images, and provided both a framework for thinking about environmental cognition and a research methodology appropriate to the scientific study of mental maps. Subsequent research on environmental cognition was conducted on 'cognitive mapping', a process that enables us to collect, organize, store, recall, and decode information about the relative location and attributes of features of the geographic environment. A cognitive map is a representation of the physical environment. The nature of cognitive representations is complex, and involves sensory and motor modalities in addition to vision. Cognitive maps are stored in the brain not as pictures, but rather as complex structures with multiple properties that may be reconstructed on demand.

One of the most important functions of environmental cognition or cognitive maps is to solve spatial problems and to provide a basis for social communication about the physical environment. Shared environmental representations provide essential symbols and collective memories for social communication. Public images of the city are also necessary for cooperative social activity. A further psychological function of environmental cognition is to provide a basis for the individual's sense of personal identity. Cognitive maps can serve as a framework in which the individual can organize memories, beliefs, feelings and fantasies as well as present and future activity. The relationship between cognitive maps and personal identity is especially apparent in the highly personalized nature of cognitive maps; mental images reflect a particular person's unique, personal, and idiosyncratic view of the world. These individual differences are reflected in variations in the completeness, distortion, and augmentation of maps. Cognitive maps are influenced by spatial activity and behaviour in the environment. Research has shown that maps differ as a function of individual differences in lifestyle, familiarity with the environment, social class, gender and social involvement.

Paradigms of Environmental Psychology

Although, the branch of environmental psychology is characterised by a plurality of paradigms (Altman, 1973; Craik, 1977; Moore, 1986, 1987; Saegert & Winkel, 1990), some of which are not very clearly distinguished (Craik, 1977; Moore, 1986). Recent work (Saegert & Winkel, 1990) has proposed a synthetic and convincing framework for it. However, co-existence of several paradigms can be traced to the two traditions of psychological research which conceptualise the physical environment in relation to psychological processes: First, the physical environment of psychology of perception, with a physicalist-molecular and individualistic paradigm; and, second, the physical environment of social psychology, characterised both in a molar and social sense, corresponding to the paradigm of the psycho-social approach. However,

Saegert and Winkel (1990) have singled out four major paradigms from two theoretical orientations. These are (a) the 'adaptation' or 'adaptive paradigm', (b) environment as opportunity structure for goal-directed action, (c) socio-cultural forces, and (d) cross-paradigm historical synthesis.

The 'adaptive' paradigm can be characterised by many areas of environmental-psychological research, with strong theoretical and methodological base, such as environmental stress, environmental perception and cognition and environmental assessment. The major theoretical constructs of such research are based on the assumption that the goal of biological and psychological survival motivates behaviour. The individual attempts to cope with threats, to meet basic biological needs, and to restore and expand capacities for coping and flourishing (Saegert & Winkel, 1990). However, this paradigm, leaves inexplicit the transactional nature of many of the processes and variables they employ (social relationships, interpretations). They also fail to place their data in the context of policy options, political influences and economic and cultural factors. The weakness of this paradigm is the tendency to treat the person as a biological and psychological individual and the environment as naturally given. Despite the constant identification of real and perceived control, as mechanisms for effective coping, the social, political, and economic processes that distribute control among people have been largely ignored (Saegert & Winkel, 1990).

The second paradigm, the environment as opportunity structure for goal-directed action, is inappropriately defined from the psychological point of view as it is close to geography, especially time geography (Parkes & Thrift, 1980; Carlstein, 1982; Hagerstrand, 1983) or to sociology in relation to time-budget studies (Andorka, 1987; Michelson, 1987). These studies pay little attention to the psychological dimension of the processes studied, which seems to be generated by the physical-geographical opportunities of the environment. Thus, this paradigm has a weak identity from the psychological point of view. The third paradigm, defined as socio-cultural forces (Saegert and Winkel, 1990) is characterised in a psycho-social sense. The major emphasis of this paradigm is on the person as a social agent rather than an autonomous individual having needs for survival or desires to carry out personal projects. The person as social agent seeks and creates meaning in the environment. As social interaction is a core feature of this paradigm, a second important process issue involves the understanding of interrelationships between the environment on the one hand, and group formation and maintenance on the other. The emphasis on individual survival in the adaptive paradigm has its social counterpart in research documenting efforts to deal with environmental threats, not as an individual concern, but as a problem for the social structure within which the individual is embedded (Saegert & Winkel, 1990). This paradigm clearly recognizes that environmental meanings and actions are not solely individual constructions. Rather, the individual both defines and is defined by the groups in which he/she participates (Saegert & Winkel, 1990). The fourth paradigm (Bonnes & Secchiaroli, 1995), the 'interparadigm historical synthesis', aims at representing the broader perspective of integration between the previous paradigms and, contrary to them, is mainly oriented towards social change. Saegert (1987) has distinguished between research having specific 'transformative intentions' and research aimed only at understanding the phenomena observed and, thus, having 'technological' or 'interpretive intentions'.

According to Bonnes and Secchiaroli (1995), these various paradigms should be considered as connected, and linked by a relationship of progressive inclusion, one within the other. The first paradigm of adaptation should be considered the most internal one, that is, included within all of the others, which should be subsequently more and more external and, thus, progressively more comprehensive, shifting from the first (adaptative paradigm) to the last (cross-paradigm historical synthesis). However, in the context of empirical research such synthesis seems not feasible and difficulty remains in operating in an integrated way between the various paradigms. In this regard, divergence is evident through the tendency towards opposition, rather than integration, between the two paradigms, represented, on the one hand, by the adaptive paradigm, characterised in both a physicalist and individualistic sense, and the socio-cultural paradigm, characterised in both a molar and social sense, primarily coinciding with the direction of social psychology. In both the paradigms it is the emphasis which is contested, leading to their groundings in positivistic and non-positivistic philosophies of sciences.

ORIENTATIONS OF ENVIRONMENTAL COGNITIVE RESEARCH

Philosophical and Theoretical Orientations

Early work on environmental cognition, and its subsequent development, was largely influenced by the philosophies of empiricism, positivism, and neopositivism. Positivism, a physicalist (or atomistic) view, regarded values and beliefs as metaphysical (non-scientific), and scientist as a passive observer of the world of objective reality. The centrality of positivistic thought was the search for 'process' theory and this search was conducted through a hypothesis-testing procedure (or methodology) that insisted on reliable and publicly verifiable results (Golledge, 1987). However, positivist research often needed to be concerned with the view which regards cognition as a significant factor mediating the dialectical relationship between man and environment. Also, in experimental work, the analytical methodology of positivism continually used the scientific method in hypothesis testing; use of logico-mathematical languages and reasoning processes; the need for public verifiability of results; and the search for generalization (Couclelis & Golledge, 1983). As cognition became a central theme of man-environment research and a new line of thinking emerged in the field, some of the assumptions of positivist tradition were selectively abandoned.

The Kantian theory of knowledge, therefore, became more influential in the early research on environmental cognition (see for example Moore & Goolledge, 1976). Kant's influence can be seen in the works of Cassirer (1944), Werner and Kaplan (1963) and Piaget (1950). This position argued that reality in general and the environment in particular are grasped through the effort of mind as the subject enters into a creative interaction with the environment. Thus mental reality became a primary object of study making the positivistic assumptions less important. This changed the positivist image from passive observer to the living interaction between researcher and human subject. Once the assumption that human beings respond to their environment as it is perceived and interpreted through previous experience and knowledge is accepted, it becomes necessary to answer the fundamental questions of environmental cognitive research related to the filtering of information through the senses, its storage, access, use and representation (See Wapner, Kaplan, & Cohen, 1973 for transactional perspective; and, Hart 1978; Moore & Golledge, 1976 for interactional/constructivist perspectives). Recently, traditional philosophies claiming the individual as the basis of knowledge and his inner mechanism is accountable through scientific methods have been questioned (Gergen & Semin 1990). It is now argued that interpretation, experience, and even knowledge are clearly a function of social and cultural values and constraints, memory, affect, emotion, fears, beliefs, prejudices, misconceptions, mental capacities, habits, expectations, and other idiosyncratic values along with all the institutional, economic, and physical factors that not only characterize the public (objective) environment but are an essential part of the flow of information from it (Bonnes & Secchiaroli, 1995).

Although psychological theories exploring environmental cognition were largely drawn from above mentioned philosophical views, a variety of concepts and embryonic theories have filtered in from other disciplines. These theories include development theory, information processing theory, theories of spatial knowledge, and principles of hierarchical ordering. Research conducted in the line of the theories of development have focused on the development of spatial representation. Although Piaget's developmental theories (role of development in environmental cognition) have provided seminal base for much of this work, many other developmentally based powerful theories do exist (Golledge, 1975; Shemyakin, 1962; Siegel & White, 1975). The essence of Piaget's theory is that knowledge progresses through different stages, and considerably research in different environments (e.g., Evans, 1980; Hazen, Lockman, & Pick, 1978) supports this theory by positing a developmental sequence consisting of an 'egocentric' stage, an 'allocentric' stage, and a 'geocentric' stage. However, some inconsistent evidence (Spencer & Darvizeh, 1981) show that there is a developmental progression in the use of different types of spatial elements (self, landmark, route, frame of reference, etc.) in addition to the developmental sequence from the use of one type to another. In addition to the Piagetian hypothesis, Siegel and White (1975) have suggested a three-phase developmental sequence for environmental cognition. On the basis of Hebb's network theory (Hebb, 1949, 1963), and Gibson's theoretical perspective on ecological perception (Gibson, 1946,1958), S. Kaplan has emphasized the spatial and the non-spatial relevance of the principles such as contiguity, proximity, sequence, and representation. S. Kaplan and R. Kaplan explored the information processing mechanisms that helped people (and animals) cope with everyday life experiences (Devlin, 1976; R. Kaplan, 1976; S. Kaplan,

1973, 1976; Peters, 1973). Their work emphasizes the metaphorical nature of the cognitive map and an overlapping network, intersecting sequencing, and non-continuous structuring process for pattern matching and representation purposes. Gibson's theories of perception (1966, 1979) also emphasized the importance of information processing. This work has been extended in the works of Evans (1980; Evans *et al.*, 1984) and Stokols (1981; Stokols & Shumaker, 1981).

During the past three decades an increasing amount of attention has focused on the development of knowledge structures and the importance of central information-processing mechanisms (CPM) as significant aspects of environmental cognition which has been accompanied by building computer process models that translate various theories of knowledge storage, acquisition, and use into symbolic terms such that specific task situations can be programmed and performed by computers (Hayes-Roth, 1979; Kuipers, 1983; Smith, Pellegrino & Golledge, 1982). Also, in cognitive science literature there has been heavy emphasis on artificial intelligence (AI) modelling and psychologists, computer scientists, electrical engineers, and others have been seeking to model knowledge acquisition and use. Thus, the concepts such as knowledge structure, declarative knowledge, procedural knowledge, spatial knowledge, semantic networks, frames (Minski, 1975; Schank & Abelson, 1977; Kuipers, 1982) and scripts (Schank & Abelson, 1977), stereotypes and schemata (Bobrow & Norman, 1975) have become very influential. Many of the above information processing concepts are being linked into 'computational process model' (CPM). Smith and colleagues (1982) have focused on the relevance of CPM in the general area of spatial cognition. It is assumed that an individual's knowledge of the environment is a function of accumulated and organized perceptual experiences representing interactions between the organism and environment. The knowledge acquisition process is thus based on episodes from which a more generalized and context-independent knowledge structure emerges that is capable of sustaining a wide range of spatial behaviours. In a review on images, Lloyd (1982) has summarized various approaches to the internal representation of spatial phenomena into classes, on the basis of how information is coded and stored, such as radical image theory (e.g., Kosslyn & Pomerantz, 1977), including various scaling studies, rotation studies, and reaction time studies), conceptual-prepositional approaches (Anderson & Bower, 1973); and the dual coding approach (Paivio, 1969, 1971).

The acquisition of spatial knowledge has been another area of theoretical concern. Empirical work on temporal aspects of the process of acquiring spatial knowledge show how cognitive maps changed over time (Golledge, 1978; Golledge, Rayner, & Rivizigno, 1982). Spector (1977) and Golledge and Spector (1978) have focused on the information sources that are used in acquiring knowledge about elements in the environment. Other researchers (Evans & Pezdek, 1980; Hintzman, O'Dell, & Arndt, 1981; Thorndyke & Stasz, 1980) have specifically examined the problem of acquiring spatial information from maps and have compared it to acquisition of spatial information by direct observation in a given environment. Acquiring spatial information by direct observation is a much more frequently used procedure (Gibson, 1966, 1979; Kozlowski & Bryant, 1977; Kuipers, 1982; Siegel & White, 1975). Building on some initial work by Miller and colleagues (1960), Leff (1978), and Russell and Ward (1982) utilize the concept of an action plan as an important co-determinant of behaviour in the everyday social and physical environment. Other research suggests that a memory representation of the spatial layout of large-scale environment may be acquired very quickly (Garling, Book, Ergezen, & Lindberg, 1981; Garling, Book, Lindberg, & Nilsson, 1981). These studies appeared to have some significant implications for the order in which different types of spatial information (landmarks, paths, and locations) are acquired.

Also, much research in environmental cognition has been based on a hierarchical model, such as developmental sequence (Hart, 1978), the path-node sequence (Siegel & White, 1975), the node-path hypothesis (Golledge, 1975), the route-to-survey progression (Shemyakin, 1963), or the spatial orientation theories embedded in different navigational system (Pike & Acredolo, 1983). The work of Smith and colleagues (1982) specifically addresses the question of hierarchical ordering and adds a further dimension by trying to develop a CPM of the way-finding activities.

Research Orientations

The area of environmental cognition research is extremely diverse. More specifically, it includes cognitive mapping, city image, route and survey knowledge, spatial cognition, spatial abilities, spatial orientation, etc. Studies in the areas of cognitive mapping and cognitive maps begin with investigating underlying processes with a model including four elements: an actor, an external situation or environment, a set of outputs from situation to actor called environmental cognition, and a set of outputs from actor to situation called environmental response behaviour. In general, it is assumed that spatial behaviour cannot be explained in terms of S-R alone, but that such behaviour requires an intervening variable, i.e., an internal mechanism that reorders, recodes, and in some sense transforms the stimuli in a way that is novel or creative. In this regard, the basic question is what kinds of information must be coded, stored, and decoded if one is to engage successfully in environmental behaviour? One possible framework is to regard the cognitive map as a set of stored propositions about the environment, each having been assigned a truth value or salience by an actor. The process of cognitive mapping consists of a set of operations designed to code environmental information and subsequently decode it to allow spatial behaviour to take place. Three of the most fundamental skills involved in this transformation process are the acquisition of shape constancy, size constancy, and a generalized pattern recognition ability related to concept formation and stimulus generalization (Gibson, 1966). Here shape constancy through rotation is homologous to the control projection; size constancy is homologous to control of scale, and pattern recognition is homologous to the symbolic reference of map sign and legend.

As the representation of spatial information in memory has been called a cognitive map, the central questions in environmental cognition concern the nature of these cognitive maps, the process of acquiring and forming such maps, and the use of cognitive maps in processes such as way-finding or other spatial behaviour. In general, the process of acquiring spatial knowledge is denoted as the cognitive mapping process and the product or the sum total of environmental information stored in memory, is called a cognitive map. The process of cognitive mapping is a means of structuring, making sense of, and coping with the complexities of environments external to mind. These include both observable physical environment as well as the many and varied social and cultural environments that impinge on our lives and behaviours (Stokols & Shumaker, 1981). Cognitive mapping basically is concerned with describing and understanding people's awareness of the physical phenomena surrounding them. It is a comment on the completeness, degree of schematisation, and types of augmentation found in the information sets that people collect about their environments (Stokols & Altman, 1987).

Although, researchers have made serious efforts to develop methodologies to understand cognitions people hold about a given environment, the data obtained through these procedures indicate that spatial knowledge is incomplete, partial, and disconnected (Golledge & Hubert, 1982; Kosslyn, Pick, & Fariello, 1974). Siegel and Cousins (1983) present a number of basic assumptions that appear to underlie the cognitive mapping processes and further stress the need for researchers to be extremely sensitive to the characteristic of the settings in which behaviours are studied and from which environmental cognitions are derived. Other fundamental questions that appear to be the focus of architectural, planning, and design speculations about cognitive maps concentrate on finding whether some particular environments are more imageable and more easily and accurately represented than others. In this regard many questions relating to the selection and use of environmental information as well as to the appropriateness of externally representing it require much more research activity.

The process of cognitive mapping includes not only the learning of locational and connective properties of landmarks and paths but also information about their relative locations and connectivities. A critical component of relative location is spatial separation which has generally become known by the term cognitive distance or subject distance. Early studies on cognitive distance produced some apparently contradictory results (e.g., see studies of Lee, 1962; Bridges, 1972; Erickson, 1975; & Golledge *et al.*, 1969 for this contradiction). Reasons for the apparent differences were related to the size and functional complexity of the cities in question, i.e., they varied with qualities of the build environment. Other research has focused on sex differences in the cognition of distance (Lee, 1970), the effect of intervening barriers (Lowrey, 1973), the influence of curves or bends (Briggs, 1972), and asymmetries in distance estimates (Burroughs & Sadalla, 1979; Sadalla & Staplin, 1980).

Another important area of environmental cognition is related to orientation and frames of reference, i.e., an ability to recognise self in relation to sets of points or reference systems existing in the general cognitive map of an area (Howard & Templeton, 1966). Human spatial orientation characterised as the perception of one's position relative to the environment (Garling, Book, & Lindberg, 1984). There is a fundamental dispute in the literature on environmental knowing and cognitive representations as to whether mental representations of space are propositional or analog in nature (see Norman & Rummelhart, 1975; Pylyshyn, 1981). Also, a critical aspect of environmental cognition is the problem of how we keep track of the location of things when our body coordinates continually undergo change. Some research in cognitive theory suggests that locations of objects with respect to one's body coordinates are represented directly in propositional form. In regard to orientation, Hintzman and colleagues (1981) offer a hypothesis that subjects directly locate the origin and the target in memory, activate the shortest route between them, and then sequentially span this potential route to determine a correct response. They also point to the unsatisfactory nature of some theories in that they do not account for mechanisms whereby spatial relations not already directly represented by memory can be inferred from other relations. Book and Garling (1980) pointed out that an important function of a cognitive map is simply to make it possible to infer the location of reference points not in sight. They argued that one way of studying the acquisition of such information would be to investigate to what extent maintenance of orientation relative to such points improves with repeated exposure to an initially unfamiliar path environment. In general, they emphasised that acquisition of a cognitive map of any particular environment through which one moves repeatedly can be defined as the increase in long-term stored information that improves the ability of a subject to recognise reference points in sight and allows him or her to implement direction changes associated with locomoting through the environment even though new destination points or reference points are not in sight.

While summarising the status of the field of environmental cognition, Golledge (1987) has pointed out that environmental cognition research is still in its infancy. Although researchers have examined many of the cognitive variables which have been developed, defined and measured their verification, validation, and measurement at large scale has not been achieved. Golledge (1987) suggests that researchers should start by examining cognitive concepts to see whether they had spatial relevance; examining existing behavioural theory to see whether it contributed to the understanding of environmental knowing; attempting to see whether information about complex large-scale environments could possibly be recovered from individuals, developing appropriate experimental designs for the collection of meaningful data concerning environmental cognitions, and developing or adapting existing methodologies for the external representation of subjective information and for analysing its properties. While all these problems have not been effectively solved, many of them have been given substantial attention.

Although it is possible to access and represent cognitive information externally, it appears that we may not have reached the stage of being able to recover the full meaning of such cognitive representation.

Obviously, the question of how best to represent cognitive information has not been solved. Recent experiments in cognitive science and artificial intelligence are even now suggesting alternate ways for representing such information (Hayes-Roth, 1979; Smith *et al.*, 1982). There are many other unsolved problems related to the cognitive representation which can provide exciting prospects for future work. For example, the nature of the relationship between cognitive images and actual spatial behaviour still remains a vastly under-researched area whereas some evidence indicated that the two appear to be strongly connected. But more evidence needs to be collected before we have sufficient faith that this type of premise is suitable as a base for explanations and understandings of spatial phenomena. A second problem, which again details an existing area for future research, concerns the process of acquiring spatial knowledge because there is considerably speculation concerning how information is selected, attended to, coded, structured, stored, and represented in the mind. In this regard, questions concerning the role of experience, familiarity and environmental interaction in the construction and maintenance of this basic knowledge structure seem crucial.

Finally, the basic question is, how do variations in the environment itself influence the nature of cue selection and the storage of environmental information (see Evans *et al.*, 1981; Wohlwill, 1973)? Are some environments more imageable that others? How complex need the environment be before it becomes overwhelming? And how do variations in the physical landscape or changing land-use patterns affect cognitive images? Also, we have not adequately researched the problem of how variations of personal, social and cultural characteristics of individuals affect cognitive images. We have had some evidence on the nature and role of historical, social and cultural features on the selection of environmental information, but the general problem of determining the role of values and beliefs in forming environmental images has not been examined in great detail. Given the discussion of problems and prospects, one can see that there is much work still to be done on many aspects of environmental cognition. This should make it one of the more exciting areas of future interdisciplinary research.

Methodological Concerns

Investigators of environmental cognition have used a variety of tasks and methods to collect information on environmental cognition. These include introspection (Binet, 1894), maze leaning (Brown, 1932; Tolman, 1932, 1948), sketch map technique (Lynch, 1960), topological clustering and mapping categorization (Appleyard, 1969), imaging scenes from different perspectives (Piaget & Inhelder, 1967), recognizing city scenes (Milgram & colleagues, 1972), multidimensional scaling of paired interpoint distance judgements (Golledge & colleagues, 1969), use of linear scaling of interpoint distance judgements (Briggs, 1972), judging locations and orientation of objects placed behind the head (Attneave & Pierce, 1978), imaging unseen objects (Kozlowski and Bryant, 1977), and estimating lengths of streets and the angles for intersections (Byrne, 1979). Golledge and Spector (1978) combined scaling and category grouping methods to obtain judgements of interpoint proximities. Baird (1979) required subjects to interact with a computer in order to develop configurations of places. Blaut and colleagues (1970) used toy play with children. Golledge, Parnicky, and Rayner (1980) used photos of places located on a map board by both borderline retarded and normal subjects, and so on.

Suitable methods have also been developed by investigators which can represent stored spatial information externally. Alongwith the sketch maps and verbal protocols of spatial experience used by early researchers (Appleyard, 1970; Lynch, 1960; Piaget, Inhelder, & Czeminska, 1960), investigators have tested with many other representational forms as they realized that developmental differences in spatial abilities and differences in verbal and drawing skills were confounding such tasks. Other methods include the constructive use of models and toy-play with children (Blaut & Stea, 1971; Siegel & Schadler, 1977) and the use of two- and three-dimensional models with normal and borderline retarded adults (Golledge, Parnicky & Rayer, 1980; Richardson, 1982). The initial problems associated with sketch mapping procedures, which later attempts were designed to overcome, were (i) the assumption that the subject understood the abstract notion of a model and its relation to the real world; and (ii) the initial difficulty of translating cognised spatial information from large to small scales. Geographers and psychologists have used a variety of sophisticated methodologies to analyse spatial data recovered from the knowledge structure of individual (Baird, 1979; Golledge, 1977; Tobler, 1976). Such methodologies have supported the fact that strong inferences can be made about the spatial properties of cognitive maps. Evidence also indicate that at least some parts of cognitive maps are usually spatially distorted depending on the task situation, familiarity of the subject with the task environment, and the degree of interaction between the individual and environment, and so on. There is need of the use of converging methods that help understand environmental cognition processes as well as help overcome some of the limitations inherent in each separate methodologies (e.g., see Evans, 1980; Golledge & Rushton, 1976).

In order to externalise configuration that can represent the internal representation of the location of certain phenomena in the environment, it is necessary to take several approaches and use a variety of analytical techniques. The selection of method in any given problem situation depends on how the task is defined by the researchers and what output is expected. There is abundant evidence that carefully controlled experiments will provide valid and reliable data and will allow the researcher to choose the most appropriate analytical tools for obtaining and interpreting results. Scientific experimentation and statistical techniques can provide useful information by which properties of mappings, judgements, toy play, recall, or other methods are commonly interpretable. The use of parallel experiments and converging methodologies have provided hard scientific evidence of cognitive map properties and have laid the foundations for many of the commonly accepted generalization about the environmental cognition process. Future researchers should be aware about the controversy that still exists over the relative merits of different methods for representing and interpreting cognitive information. Also, in addition to the above, there is need to select, devise and adopt methods for studying naturalistic and field situations rather than experimental and laboratory research. This methodological diversity is seen as more suitable for examining the spatio-physical aspects of the environment, that is, naturalistic rather than artificial laboratory situations, such as those taught by the ethological (Lorenz, 1965; Eibel-Eibesfeldt, 1970) and anthropological traditions (Hall, 1966).

Recent Trends in Environmental Cognitive Research

Perceptual processes occupy central place in the field of environmental psychology for explaining person-environment relationships as well as for gaining adequate understanding about environmental knowledge. The psychological process involved in environmental knowledge regards ways individuals perceive the surrounding environment. The relations between properties of the physical environment and ways individuals respond to them through perception has also been the major concern of environmental psychology as well as other areas of environmental research such as geography (Kates & Wohlwill, 1966), planning (Lynch, 1960), anthropology (Romney & D'Andrade, 1964), and sociology (Strauss, 1961; Orleans, 1973). However, there has been much confusion, conceptual imprecision and misunderstanding, as the terms 'perception' and 'cognition' have been used in a variety of extremely confused contexts (Downs & Stea, 1973). The main differences include the role and the functions assigned to perceptual processes in knowledge of the environment, the ways these processes are conceptualised with respect to behaviour, and the types of indications to be expected from the study of the output of the same processes. Psychological theories have focused on the perceptual responses people give to the environment and to its spatio-physical characteristics. Thus, environmental perception has been basically approached in terms of the information provided by the formal organization of physical space as a function of the cognitive maps. There has been much emphasis on questions dealing with the functioning of processes of acquisition, organization and the use of spatial information, apart from the evaluative affective component involved in these processes. Only more recently has this schema of analysis been enlarged to consider the relationships between knowledge and action.

Also, distinctions between objective and subjective environment is crucial in the field of environmental cognition where emphasis is centered exclusively on the evaluative dimension and on the personal meanings attributed by individuals to the environment. There appears a shift of interest from the solely formal aspects of organized physical space to the content components through which space is defined; and to a more integrated consideration of the cognitive, evaluative and behavioural components in the structuring of environmental knowledge in terms of meanings actively made by individuals. This approach assumes the socio-physical environment as object of knowledge and defines the processes involved in it as processes of cognitive representation. Ittelson *et al.*, (1974) emphasizes the multidimensionality of the environment within which he distinguishes physical and social dimensions as symbolic meanings and motivational messages as properties of environment are crucial. He also considers environment as part of a social activity. Thus, persons are always part of the situation, and environmental perception is mainly a social phenomenon (Ittelson, *et al.*, 1974). Ittelson (1973a) considers stimulus as the 'source of information' which has been a general framework for research on environmental perception. In the line of Brunswik (1957), he specifies that information refers to a wider context. For a long time psychology operated with the wrong assumption that two distinct and separate systems, perceptual processes and cognitive processes, are linked by fixed and unidirectional bonds, and that the most recent research shows the importance of considering the entire perceptual-cognitive system as part of a larger system, whose basic function is the elaboration of information. Thus, the term cognitive map implies a modality of study which does not treat the perceptual and cognitive processes separately and distinctly.

Another significant emerging tendency in the field of spatial cognition is the decreased emphasis on the formal characteristics of physical space and a more attentive consideration of the contents composing that space. According to Garling and Golledge (1989), in order to understand how persons mentally form cognitive maps, the travel plans they propose and carry out in their environment must be considered. In this context an already acquired degree of familiarity with environments which constitute the socio-physical context of the individual's daily life are crucial. Also, the spatial dimension figures as a component within which units or environmental elements are placed and their specificity is marked by functional and symbolic-representative attributes as well as perceptual ones. In its role as synthetic but effective guide to action, the cognitive map is meant to represent at least three interrelated components: information regarding units or elements constituting environmental space; the spatial relations which can be established between them in terms of inclusion, direction-distance and proximity, but with respect to references which have a particular perceptual and/or symbolic saliency for persons; and travel plans, which include indications about the ways they can reach others, starting from a determined point in environmental space (Garling *et al.*, 1984). Recently, spatial cognition studies can be regarded as representative of the more general tendency to analyse the processes of environmental knowledge in connection with goals and plans of action people propose to accomplish in the respective environments; that is, to recognize these goals as general references which, analogously with what Neisser (1976) indicated with the concept of schema, direct both processes of perception and processes regarding the elaboration of environmental information, represented at the cognitive level (Garling and Golledge, 1989). Recent research on spatial cognition attempts to facilitate a more integrated analysis of the formal aspects and content of the environmental space represented in a cognitive map by considering the strict correlation between knowledge and action.

Research findings have shown consistent correlations between the spatial characteristics of the environment represented graphically and the symbolic and functional meanings attributed by subjects to them. This indicates that the study of environmental knowledge overflows the boundaries traced by the cognitive map construct around the formal aspects of spatio-physical dimension. It also reflects a more general perspective which emphasizes a molar approach to the environment (Craik, 1970) and to the processes that control its perception or cognition (Ittelson, 1973b). This approach becomes more necessary, the more complex the nature of the environmental settings people interact with, that is, the more environments figure as socio-physical contexts which specify the organization of people's figure as socio-physical contexts which specify the organization of people's daily lives. Bonnes and Sechiaroli (1995) have proposed a model of analysis which identifies knowledge with the representation of the external world to the mind and describes this representation as the outcome of constructive activity carried out by cognitive processes. Therefore, an active role is recognised for individuals with respect to these processes, primarily in the sense that the approach they have with information coming from the environment is considered to be guided by pre-existing structures of knowledge or schemata (Neisser, 1976). This model seems to preclude the possibility of an integrated analysis of cognitive and affective dimensions. As Saegert and Winkel (1990) point out, since this model refers to the environment exclusively in terms of source of information, it tends to reduce the multiform nature of person-environment interaction to outcomes of the functioning of the person's internal processes. These aspects constitute major issues for environmental psychological research, considering, on the one hand, the role played by the evaluative component of processes leading individuals to trace differences between generic environments and more specific places; and, on the other hand, the importance the social component can assume in outlining shared reference points concerning attributions of meaning to environments, especially through exchange and social interaction. In effect, environmental psychology has dedicated more and more attention to these issues in studying environmental cognition. Also, the increasing emphasis on the construct of 'place' (Canter, 1977; Stokols, 1981) and of 'social imageability (Stokols, 1981) has emerged as the most significant sign in this direction which outline a theoretical framework consistent with the more general perspective of contemporary social psychology. In fact, contrasting the images of individuals as pure 'active thinking organisms' and/or 'information processors', the European approach to social cognition is based on the hypothesis of a strict relationship between cognitive (individual) and social processes.

For many researchers (Doise, 1976, 1982; Farr and Moscovici, 1984; Tajfel, 1984; Palmonari, 1989), the articulation of this general hypothesis lies in the following premises: (a) cognitive processes are considered as properties of individuals-in-context and not as autonomous peculiarities of mental functioning. The cognitive man/woman is conceived as someone who looks for information (and does not only receive it from the environment) in connection with his/her own goals; (b) 'implicit theories' or 'images of reality' which guide information processing are considered as representational and symbolic frames of reference whose structure and/or change are established during the many and various interactions individuals engage in and with the physical and social contexts they live in. In view of these it can be said that environmental cognitive research is not so much interested in the outputs of perception/cognition as in the processes and conditions generating the collectively shared 'representations' which allow individuals to master the complex world they are part of. This dynamic approach to the study of the symbolic dimension of human behaviour has its major focus in the complex interactions involving individual, inter-individual and collective processes. The most significant suggestions in this direction have certainly been proposed by Moscovici (1961-76, 1981, 1982, 1984a, 1984b) in his 'theory of social representations'.

SOCIO-CULTURAL PERSPECTIVE ON ENVIRONMENTAL COGNITION

Recent advances in arcas such as environmental, social, personality, cognitive, and developmental psychology reflect an increasing emphasis on the importance and complexity of the molar environment. The traditional focus of psychology on the experience and behaviour of the person is shifting toward a broader, contextual orientation in which the transactions between people and their socio-physical settings are emphasized. Also, importance of developing a "cross-paradigm" approach to the study of environment and behaviour (Craik, 1977; Stokols, 1978) becomes increasingly apparent as we move from microlevel analyses of stimuli and events to the conceptualisation of molar, socio-physical settings. For this, theories must begin to integrate geographical, social-structural, and psychological properties of settings. Although architects, sociologists, and planners have focused primarily on the first two facets of the environment, psychologists have paid most attention to the third and (only recently) have begun to consider the nature of the interface among physical, social, and psychological dimensions of settings (Magnusson, 1981).

One of the most essential aspect of environmental cognition is knowledge of place which is generally and explicitly spatial (i.e., locational, relational, and configurational), but it may be non-spatial and be culturally coded in terms of symbolism, values, beliefs, and so on (Appleyard, 1979; Stokols & Shumaker, 1981). For Tuan (1977), part of the environmental meaning is symbolic and a particular place can stand for an idea. From a cross-cultural perspective this characteristic of environmental meaning has been emphasized by Rapoport (1976), particularly with respect to the religious significance of place. The Navajo, for example, attribute religious significance to both the location and the orientation of a house. Similarly, Saegert and Winkel (1990) point to a symbolization of home by many women in terms of the importance of self, family, and social relationships; home for men may in turn symbolize ownership of childhood memories. Blaut and Stea (1971) have defined the functions of cognitive mapping in terms of a simple communication model and tested their model in cross cultural context.

Cross-cultural implications of environmental cognition focuses on way-finding activities-particularly on the use of navigational systems that are not conveniently cartographic in nature (Gladwin, 1970). In such a system, orientation occurs with respect to a fixed reference system such as an island or star position, direction of currents, or wave formations that is claimed to be non-cartographic. Also, evidence show a hierarchical ordering of information with critical elements of the real environment triggering meaningful associations and initiating decisions that may involve repetition of behaviour of change of behaviour (Pick & Aacredolo, 1983). In a cross-cultural comparison paper, Kearins (1981) investigated visual spatial memory in Australian aboriginal children of desert origin. Aboriginal children from 6 to 17 years were found to perform at significantly higher levels than white Australian children on particular skills related to survival habitats. This work is again typical of a growing concern with cross-cultural characteristics of environmental cognition.

Social Representation of Place

For Bonnes and Sechiaroli (1995), the most appropriate definition for the field of environmental psychology is the area of psychology which is concerned with the relationships between psychological processes and processes of the socio-physical environment. Thus, in view of the diversity and heterogeneity of theoretical perspectives in psychology dealing with the relationship of the individual with the spatio-physical characteristics of the environment, the initial proposals of the principal founders of environmental psychology (Craik, 1970; Proshansky *et al.*, 1970; Altman, 1973; Ittelson, 1973a, 1973b; Stokols, 1978) leave no doubt about the choice of the psycho-social paradigm rather than the physico-perceptual one which emerges clearly in their various theoretical works.

The increasing interest of environmental psychology in cognitive, affective and motivational factor has revealed the complex nature of the relationships between individuals and their socio-physical environment. This emphasis focuses on person-environment relations in terms of interdependence rather than of linear determinations. As it is concerned with the relation between cognition and action, the theoretical construct of place proposed by Canter is particularly important. Among other Proshansky's (1978; Proshansky *et al.*, 1979, 1983; Proshansky and Kaminoff, 1982) construct of place identity offers a very promising perspective for research. According to Proshansky *et al.*, (1983) the processes through which a person defines him/herself in a society are not restricted to making distinctions between oneself and significant others, but extend with no less importance to objects and things, and the very spaces and places in which they are found. Since places carry out a relevant role in the satisfaction of biological, psychological, social and cultural needs of the person in the many situations faced in his/her lifetime, they assume the function of meaningful reference points in the processes of identity definition. More recently, Neisser (1988) has defined this component as the ecological self. However, while carrying out relationships with the places in his/her own life context, the individual is not limited to experience and to record the physical environment and its objective characteristics. As people act to satisfy his/her needs, values, attitudes and beliefs about the physical world enter in the field. According to Proshansky *et al.* (1983), this is the way the physical environment and its characteristics become effective reference points for defining and integrating place identity in the individual.

In this context, the construct of place as developed by Daniel Stokols (1981; Stokols and Shumaker, 1981) appears to move in the same direction as Canter's. Stokols also considers the construct of place as enrichment of the primitive construct of behaviour setting which has symbolic implications. The places are seen as the "physical and symbolic context of human action" (Stokols and Shumaker, 1981, p. 443). Places are viewed not only as composite of behaviour-shaping forces, but also as the material and symbolic product of human action (Stokols and Shumaker, 1981, p. 443). Also, there has been insufficient specification to the physical-structural characteristics of the setting by the theory of behaviour setting and ecological psychology. Previous analyses of settings have emphasized the social and behavioural aspects of setting, while disregarding the relationships between these dimensions and the architectural-geographical milieu. Thus, Stokols defines place a relational entity between physical properties, aspects of meaning and relative activity. However, Stokols's analysis tends to touch on some aspects relative to the construct, proposing further investigation of the dimension of 'shared meanings'.

This perspective aims mainly at recomposing the fundamental dualism between the objectivist and subjectivist perspective which environmental psychological research has traditionally confronted. Also, it overcomes the tendency towards an individualistic view which environmental psychological research has generally assumed in studying the phenomena of representation of the environment, dealing with them in terms of cognitive or mental maps, cognitive representations, cognitions and environmental knowledge. According to Stokols and Shumaker (1981), whereas most research on environmental cognition has emphasized the individual's perception of the environment (*cf.* Moore & Golledge, 1976), the present analysis encompasses the phenomena of social perception, that is, the process by which setting members collectively perceive and ascribe meaning to their socio-physical milieu. By focusing on the common or widely recognized meanings that become associated with the molar environment, this analysis offers a middle ground between subjectivist perspectives, which construe environmental perception as essentially a personal, idiosyncratic phenomenon, and objectivist views of the environment, which avoid reference to perceptual processes altogether.

Stokols (1981) suggests that investigations of the shared meanings of places should be based on the construct of social imageability to understand the perceived social field of the physical environment. Like imageability or memorability of their physical elements, environments can also be characterized in terms of their social imageability, i.e., their capacity to evoke vivid and collectively held social meanings among the occupants and users of a place (Stokols & Shumaker, 1981). This imageability of places can also be supported by a perceptual salience connected to the number and intensity of highly noticeable features within an environment; these elements include those also indicated by the tradition of experimental and cognitive aesthetics (Berlyne, 1960; Wohlwill, 1976; Kaplan & Kaplan, 1982) such as stimulus contrast, novelty and complexity (Stokols, 1981). Alongwith perceptual salience, a salience of significance or of sociocultural meanings can also be identified which encompasses collectively shared images. The widely recognized images or meanings conveyed by places constitute the non-material properties of the physical milieu, the sociocultural residue or residual meaning that becomes attached to places. Stokols (1981) also suggests possible strategies for examining the images of places in terms of their social imageability or perceived social field, to determine their degrees of complexity, clarity, heterogeneity, distortions and contradictions. He also examines the characteristics of settings which he believes most contribute towards orienting the social imageability of places, singling out three main dimensions, i.e., functions, goals, and evaluations. He proposes a direct link between the social imageability of places and what he defines place dependence of the occupants. As a place becomes increasingly layered with social meanings, the interdependence among social and physical components of the setting increases. Thus the sociocultural meanings associated with a setting are viewed as the glue that binds groups to particular places.

The place dependent construct (Stokols & Shumaker, 1981) emphasizes the shared components of the bond between people and places and the shared origin of that bond. The person is considered as part of social groups or categories, and places as sociocultural significant objects. This construct can be more directly linked with that of place identity, and in the same way with the entire psycho-social tradition of research on the topic of identity and/or self and social identity (Doise, 1976; Palmonari *et al.*, 1979; Tajfel, 1981; Bonnes, 1988). As this theory focuses primarily on the processes of cognitive construction and symbolic representation of social reality, it may be crucial for understanding the person-socio-physical environment relationship. According to Tuan (1979; Potter and Wetherell, 1987) places are also created, recreated and undone by speaking of them and, thus, by means of language and discourse. Thus, social representation of place paradigm tends to shift from the visual-perceptual to the psycho-social and socio-cultural. There is close connection between shared and individual aspects of place representation and its tendency to integrate cognitive, affective and behavioural aspects concerning the place experience.

Social Dimensions of Place Identity

Place identity is a cognitive sub-structure of self-identity which consists of an endless variety of cognitions (structures and functions) related to the past, present, and anticipated physical settings that define and circumscribe the day-to-day existence of the person (Proshansky *et al.*, 1983). These cognitions develop by means of a selective involvement of the person with his environment and possess the typical characteristics of every other cognitive structure, organized in an interconnected way. The structure of place identity is described as a grouping of cognitions regarding a complex of physical setting related clusters of cognitions in which component cognitions of a given cluster are related to each other and also, to a greater or lesser degree, to the component cognitions of other clusers (Proshansky *et al.*, 1983). Place identity is not only the way individual habitually experiences different places, but also the relations he/she establishes through the daily actions carried out in these places. Like every other cognitive system, place identity is meant to accomplish the cognitive backdrop function which enables people to recognise what they see, think, and feel in their situation to situation transactions with the physical world (Proshansky *et al.*, 1983). It discriminates between familiar and unfamiliar; serves as cognitive reference points for comparisons between old and new as well as between known and perceived. Individuals living in an environment do not structure experiences only with respect to its physical reality. The meanings and social beliefs are always attributed to the physical environment both by those living in it and by those external to it. Proshansky *et al.*, emphasize that there is no physical environment that is not also a social environment and vice versa, and point out the two connected indicators that confirm the role played by the social dimension in specifying the physical components of place identity. The first one consists in some basic uniformities which result from belonging to a certain culture; the other concerns some differentiations manifesting themselves within the same culture and linked to the specificity of different social groups.

Cognitive clusters also include a system of memories, feelings and personal interpretations about single physical settings and in the organization of these clusters, an important role is assigned to the social definitions of settings that consist of the norms, behaviours, rules and regulations that are inherent in the use of these places and spaces. Although, physical or objectively real, these settings are inextricably tied to the social and cultural existence of a group, as expressed by its valued activities, interpersonal relationships and individual and group role functions (Proshansky *et al.*, 1983). In other words, place identity of different groups in a certain society and culture is not to be taken only as differentiated with respect to the uses and experiences of space and place, but also with respect to the corresponding variations in the social values, meanings and ideas which underlie the use of those spaces (Proshansky *et al.*, 1983). Thus, the cognitions on which place identity is structured are, in turn, seen as the expression and reflection of physical settings and their properties that support, and are directly relevant to the social roles and attributes that define who the person is, how he or she is to behave, and what he or she is worth (Proshansky *et al.*, 1983).

CULTURAL FOUNDATION OF ENVIRONMENTAL COGNITION

The socio-cultural bases of human psychological functions have an impressive history within the discipline of psychology (see Jahoda, 1990 for details) and they were recognized quite early. For instance, Woundt's early writings on folk psychology clearly recognized the significance of collective level psychological processes in their own terms. Bartlett (1932) described the role of social factors in the cognitive processes of remembering. However, later psychology became thoroughly individual centered. The culture was replaced by the individual and all the processes were to be discovered in him or her. Everything was analysed at the level of the individual and higher level processes were treated as products of mental structures and functions. This situation was reinforced by the western construction of individual and related ideology (Sampson, 1988) which underlay all the assumptions of western psychology. The individual, which became the unit and container of social and psychological functions, represented "merely that which lies within the organism i.e., within the skin" (Allport, 1937, p. 30).

While cognition, in general, refers to all types of knowing, the psychological analysis practically confined it to the intra-individual or intra-psychic processes and products. Being context-free, the information processing approach treats cognition as a generic label encompassing the social as well as non social domains (Schneider, 1991). More recently, a growing interest in cultural psychology recognises the constitutive role of culture in a significant manner. Cultural psychology studies "the ways subject and object, self and other, psyche and culture, person and context live together, require each other, and dynamically, dialectically and jointly make each other up" (Shweder, 1990, p. 4). Culturc consists of learned and shared systems of meaning and understanding, communicated primarily by means of natural language. These meanings and understandings are not just representations about what is in the world; they are also directive, evocative, and reality constructing in character. Through these systems of meanings and understandings individuals adapt to their physical environment, structure interpersonal relationships, and adjust psychologically to problems and conflicts (D'Andrade, 1981, 1984). These systems of meanings and understandings are only one set of variables that influence human behaviour; social and environmental conditions, the distribution of power, economic opportunity, personality characteristics, genetic constitution, and other classes of variables also influence what people do and think.

Experimental studies of symbolic representation among animals (Savage-Rumbaugh and her associates, 1985) show that symbolic representation is involved in animals' ability to generalize a sign from a small class of specific objects to a larger abstract class of tools or foods, and further to generalize a sign from a small class of signs to a larger class of signs. Thus, it appears that it is not just a link between a specific object and a physical sign, but rather a complex linkage between physical signs, physical objects, and abstract concepts. However, there seems to be a great difference between humans and animals. In experimental anthropology, one is never content simply to measure performance rather experimental procedures are usually modified to allow subjects to display their real cognitive competence. In everyday cognitive studies, cognitive behaviours are studied in a natural situation, usually through a combination of observational and more experimental methods. These behaviours are sometimes so banal that until very recently, they hardly attracted the attention of researchers. Everyday cognition research is concerned with the informal, oral, traditional, or popular knowledge, meaning the knowledge of ordinary people, in contrast with school- or book-based, expert or scientific, knowledge.

Research on everyday cognition is a field that has emerged in the last two decades and illustrates well the interdisciplinary nature of cross-cultural psychology. It is an attempt to study cognition in its socio-cultural context, that is, culturally relevant cognition. Through the emphasis on specific contexts, the particularities of knowledge in action may have been overemphasized, as well as the lack of transfer to new problems. Lave (1988) recently called into question the whole paradigm of transfer research, pointing out how its basic assumptions are linked to laboratory procedures. One goal of everyday-cognition studies is to maximize cultural validity; to achieve this, some experimental control may be lost. Also, experimental methods must be combined with natural observation in particular cultural milieus. Many everyday cognition studies employ situations that are rare in Western society. Informal learning is a common phenomenon, even in complex and highly institutionalised societies. Recent research in this domain has been conducted in North American supermarkets, in factories, and in cocktail lounges (Rogoff & Lave, 1984). These studies have in common the researcher's departure from the laboratory in order to become involved in daily-life settings.

Also, in the field of ethnology, the science of everyday, researchers use cognitive anthropological approaches more frequently for study of daily life in the context of its surrounding environments. Such approaches, have been found extremely fruitful in any society. For example, we find work in France on the invention of the everyday (deCerteau, 1980), which describes and analyses popular culture activities and the rituals of daily life in urban space. A finely detailed description of everything involved in cooking in contemporary French society (Giard, 1980) includes, of course, customs and mores, but also individual knowledge and know-how and the cognitive processes that support them. It is expected that ethnology will do more than describe and transcribe, and reveal the hidden meaning of the activities. It is a form of analysis, then, in which the role of the anthropologist is substantial. Thus, the cognitive anthropology or ethno science approach seeks to build a model of an underlying cognitive structure from systematically gathered empirical facts (Tyler, 1969; Gardner, 1985; Jahoda; 1982). Ethnoscience tries to work emically (i.e., using a society's own category system) to ascertain the cognitive principles by which the society's members apprehend their world. In epic research, we try to study a culture so as to see it as its own members do. Therefore, it attempts to determine which aspects of the environment are considered important, what they are called, and how the local populace related them to one another. In this manner, cognitive anthropology tries to discover how each culture creates order out of chaos. Ethnoscience is, in many ways, related to everyday cognition as it tries simultaneously to determine modes of popular thought and to derive the cognitive principles that underline them.

Thus, research designed to show how a particular people classifies experience, yielding the classification system they habitually employ, is a form of epic research known as ethnoscience (Tyler, 1969; Gardner, 1985; Dougherty, 1985). Ethnoscience is usually ideographic, i.e., it describes, for a particular group of people, how they understand the world, what the elements are that are considered important, what they are called, and what relations exist among them, without attempting to compare this scheme with others. It is of course also perfectly legitimate to ask how different cultures classify their world and to produce some comparison among the different schemes. What needs emphasizing, however, is that any single culture's classification system should first be expressed in the terms employed indigenously. It is that system, after all, that makes up the cognitive map of persons in that culture, and it is that system, expressed in its own terms, that is of paramount interest to the psychologist who would seek reasons, embedded in other facts about the behavioural setting, for the presence of such a system. To understand why people think the way they do, we must first appreciate how they think. And for that we must discover each people's own system.

Environmental Cognition in Ancient Indian People

The concept and cognition about environment changes with social change. As man's ideas and attitudes towards its own habits find a crystal clear place in his language and literature, the *Vedic* literature clearly shows the environmental cognition and attitudes that existed in ancient India. Kulkarni (1991) has shown that the ancient Indian people belonging to various cultures were much concerned to the environment in which they breathe in. Attitude of these people was based on the stated relationship between man and nature. *Vedic* people interacted with nature by treating them as its part, and wishing well-being of other creatures and plants alongwith himself. They were treating environmental factors at par and therefore caring them and wishing well-being of them.

In *Sukla Yajurveda*, it is suggested that needs are fulfilled by the grace of Nature-God, therefore, the man is always indebted to nature. He seeks familiar relations in environment. For example, he calls both earth and water as *mata* (the mother) and keeps friendly feelings towards water and trees. Many creatures and plants are regarded as mothers and goddesses. In *Atharvaveda*, the terms like *tridhatu, triprakaraka, tribhumika, trikhanda, trisala* (i.e., three-fold or three-storeys nature of house) show that the house must be comfortable to the dwellers in all seasons, the peculiar floor being comfortable in a particular season. This house cannot disturb balance with nature and also there would not be problems like over crowding in some places and isolation in others; congestion in some and extra air in others. Such an imbalance between man and his environment may cause many other calamities, such as the air pollution, scarcity of water, dirt, and in cleanliness etc. (Mande, 1991). The selection of the plot for building the house also shows the understanding of *vedic* people for restoring a balance between man, his residence and the surrounding environment. For house construction airy surroundings were suggested. The fire (*agni*) was used as purifier to purify the air and protect them from the black magicians, the blood eating animals and the poisonous insects. The importance of *agni*, in the thinking of *vedic* people, for many other purposes is emphasised since the time of *Rigveda.*

Vedic people's knowledge and cognition about the importance of pure air and ventilation was great. *Vedic risis* approach toward air clearly shows their understanding about the most important aspect of the environment. They recognized air (*vayu*) as a vital cosmic constituent as it is referred to as a deity presiding over the mind-region. In *Pravargya, vayu* is referred to as the soul of sacrifice. In the formulas for *vata* offerings in *Agni-citti, vata* is addressed as *Sambhu* and *Mayobhu* i.e., bringing welfare and happiness. The formulas and *Brahmana* for *vata* offerings in *kariri*, reveal the rain bringing character of *Vayu.* It was also observed that the pure, unpolluted air is a source of health, happiness and consequently of long life. In *Rigveda, vata* is referred to as causing welfare and happiness. The *risi* is so emotional to this element that he addresses *vata* as his father, brother and friend. V*ata* is a store house of ambrosia for him. He prays to give him of it and requests it, to blow with its medicinal qualities. *Rigveda* divides the wind into two categories, the one bringing vigour and other blowing away the evil. Thus, in *Veda, vayu* is regarded as universal medicine and purifier. According to *vedic risis*, air inherits the intrinsic quality of neutralising pollution.

In *Rigveda*, the word water has many synonyms like *apah, jala, udaka* etc. which have different connotations. The water is also called as *jivana* (life), *amrta* or 'ambrosia' (immortal) as it does not dry or die. Water is life (*jevana*) because all foodgrains, plants, herbs are dependant on it without which man cannot be alive. *Aitareya Kausitaki Brahmanas* also describe vedic people's thinking about water and rain. Rain is said to be fulfilling all desires. Waters are considered to be peace bringing factors. In *vedic* texts, water is considered to be a powerful curing substance, a great healer and remedy (Mishra, 1991). *Rigveda* declares water to be the abode of all medicines. The *Vajasaneyi Samhita* establishes the medicinal utility of water. Wherever water flows medicines are invariably found there and it is a peace giver through its capacity of being a medicine. According to *Maitrayani Samhita*, water is the pacifier of a mentally disturbed person. *Satapatha Brahmana* declares *apah* (water) as a great peace giver. As it is used as therapeutic substance, it cures human beings for *ksetriya* disease. Also, *Taittiriya Aranyaka, Gopatha Brahmana, Aitareya Brahmana* treat water with high esteem for its being of medicinal utility. Thus, there was an intimate relation and positive approach of *vedic* people with and towards this vital natural resource, i.e., water. They extol water with high reverence.

Vedic people did not regard rivers merely as a flowing mass of waters. They regarded the rivers as life-bestowing and themselves pulsating with life (Lal, 1991). They have classified rivers in different groups: *Pravatah* (which flow over slopes), *Nivatah* (which flow in low places), and *Udvatah* (which flow over high places). The rivers are further classified as *Udanvatih* (perennial river), *anudakah* (those which dry in summer or monsoon rivers). Further, the *Rigvedic* poets have classified their water resources in different physical groups: *divyah* (rain water), *Sravanti* (natural springs), *Khanitrimah* (wells and canals), *Svayamjah* (lakes), and *Samudrarhah* (rivers). Also, rivers played important roles in *vedic* sacrifices. Many personages have also been associated with the rivers. The *vedic* man looked at the rivers as mothers par excellence. They were regarded as removers of sins and defilements. They are granters of boons and givers of protection, fame and renown. Right from the *Rigveda* down to the *Puranic* literature, divine aspects of rivers have been maintained which clearly indicates the mental attitude, i.e., how one looks around him and around the nature. For a pious Hindu, the earth is not simply a natural object. The earth is a loving mother who sustains all beings.

Thus, the idea of the three-storeyed house may be the solution for the problem of population. Fire is helpful for the air purification. Wind is the life-force of living beings. The pure wind is an essential thing. Also, there cannot be any substitution for water. Herbs and plants are the friends of mankind. All this shows that our ancestors had very clear cognition and understanding of environmental aspects.

A very rich and clear thinking, and cognition about various aspects of environment can be found in *Grhyasutras* which contain the rules considered as guidelines for the priests and the performers to pass through various stages of the rituals satisfactorily. It is in the form of prescriptions for worship of nature, appreciation of better surroundings, cleanliness as necessity for rituals, close observation of specific aspects of nature for enriching the rituals, observance of silence, general attitude toward domestic animals, and benefits of non-domestic animals for ritual practices. Tranquillity of nature was a necessity for study and meditation. In adverse climatic conditions like thunders, lightning and storm, the study of *vedas* was not undertaken. Cleanliness pervaded the entire duration of ritual activity from beginning to end. Specific care was taken not to pollute the surrounding as well as place of rituals. There were also motivations for performing specific ritual activities. The phenomenon of rain from the sky and the vegetation of the earth is cited in connection with the *garbhadhana* ceremony. The attitude of the *Grhyasutras* towards the pet and domestic animals was one of the care and attention. In the marriage and *simantonnayana*, the bulls and cows were generally given as *daksina.* Horses and sheep were also given by the *ksatriyas* and *vaisyas. Vedas* were not undertaken when the cows were hungry. The *vrsotsarga*, a rite performed on the full moon day of *Kartika*, to let loose a bull along with four cows did help to preserve better species of cows. The *Dharmasutra* and the S*mrtis* say that the flesh of a number of birds like cock, heron, sparrow, crow, cuckoo, pigeon, dove, *cakravaka*, vulture, crane, peacock, swan, *maina, tittbha* were prohibited for food.

In *Manusmrti*, Manu has made it very clear about the thinking that although the laws in his code are meant for man, he must remember that he is a part and parcel of a huge independent as well as interdependent system of the universe. He clearly points out the existence of rivers, oceans, mountains, plains and uneven lands (valleys). Manu suggests that no human being has any right to interfere with these other constituents of nature. Manu asserts that trees and plants not only have life but also consciousness. The *Agnipuran* prescribes a garden near the residence and various directions for various trees. For example, the plaksa tree is auspicious when planted to the north, banian tree should be to the east and so on. This might be having the connection with removal of air pollution from different directions. The *Sivapuran* takes a great lead in popularising the plantation of trees by giving tree the status of son. It also tries to frighten the person who cuts the trees unnecessarily.

Kautilya in his *Arthasastra*, says that to provide ample facilities to carry on mining operation, exploit timber and elephant forests, cattle breeding, construction of roads and set up *pnyasthanas*, viz. taking care of the environment as a whole is the first duty of the king. *Arthasastra* describes three kinds of forests: forests used for the purpose of hunting (*mrgaya*) by the king; forests developed for best kind of timbers and other forest products; forests being prepared for the elephants. Different kinds of punishments were being given for cutting trees from restricted lands and forests. In *Arthasastra* there are methods of dealing with the care, training and harnessing of animals. The treatment with different animals and punishment for torturing them show the feeling of man towards animals. Apart from the relation between man with flora and fauna there are references to agriculture, weather phenomenon, forecast of rainfalls, measurement of rainfall, etc.

Mahabharata condemns in unequivocal terms any decisive and disruptive activity of man that tends to promote environmental imbalance and advocate holistic approach to life. Man, animals, plants, the forces of nature, Gods, stars, earth and other planets all together constitute one vibrant system every part of which is alive and responsive. Man is called upon to develop the *daivi sampat* which respects all existent beings alike and which advocates the utilization of resources of nature with a sense of gratitude and humility. According to Vyas, control over one's senses and a good and healthy management of one's life is at the root of a good society and a good physical environment. In response to what extent and how should we exploit national resources, Bhishma advices Yudhishthira that one has to be like a flower growing gardener and like a charcoal trader. The plants and trees possess the faculty of feeling like hearing, seeing, smelling, tasting and touching. They have their facilities of sensing, sorrow and joy. Hurting plants and killing them indiscriminately is a sin. In *Mahabharata*, a king is advised to follow the ways of a tree, and a bee collecting honey is set as a model for a king to collect the taxes. The cuckoo, the cow, the pig, the owl, the lion, the serpent, the crane and the mountains each has a valuable lesson to offer.

Ancient Indian *Dharmasastra* authors or law givers, understood the importance of gardens, lakes, wells etc. and have given an important place to them in the scheme of human life. *Dharmagranthas*, the books of laws of conduct, reflect many aspects of human life. To prevent pollution, *Visnusmrti* says, one should leave his excreta getting up early in the morning. He should not leave it on an uncovered land, not in the field, not on the unploughed ground, not on the lawn, not in the street, not on a small road, not in the garden, not near the garden or water-reservoir, not in the cowpen, not in the air or space, and not in water-reservoir. *Dharmasastra* texts have prescribed worship of various animals on various days of a year. The reason is that once you treat something as a deity, you will simply worship it lest harm or destroy it. *Dharmasindhu* has prescribed proper time for the plantation of trees. *Panchatantra* and *Hitopadesa* stories visualise a live picture of the nature and the behaviour of animals and their relations with one another. For example the story of 'a lion and an old rabbit' indicates that how one can live without efforts and our total destruction will also be stopped. Another story in *Panchatantra* describes the consequences of killing animals or insects for food. These references show the types of cognitions present in fable literature.

The above description brings out the traditional features related to the environment. Unlike the present emphasis on scientific investigations of the environment and its ill-effects on the individual's well-being, the *risis* translated the environmental issues into an ethical code which if observed will lead to protection of the holistic universe. It appears that a rational outlook to the environment has to be replaced by an ethical outlook.

CONCLUSION

It is a widely shared view by both empiricist and rationalist thinkers, at least since enlightenment, that understanding is a process occurring in the mental world of the individual. While psychology has been largely committed to logical empiricist view of science, theories of knowledge as mental representation were not readily forthcoming (Gergen & Semin, 1990), as behavioural scientists believed in their own power of reason and observation. There has also been diversity of assumptions and propositions about cognitive representation. For Gergen and Semin (1990), recent cognitive revolution has been directed at reinstating the traditional commitment to knowledge as individual representation of external world. Traditional language of ideas, thoughts, categories, attributions, and representations are converted to and homogenized by the pervasive metaphor of the mind as a form of computer or computational device.

In this regard Gergen and Semin (1990) has outlined three major assumptions that characterize the majority view. First there is a shared commitment to the view that the cognitive world is in some way sensitive to, correspondent with or reflective of events within the objective world. In this sense, knowledge or understanding of the real world is carried within the cognitive system, and it is in the degree that this system is correspondent with the world that one can speak of correct understanding or accurate knowledge. Second, cognitive system plays a major role in the production of behaviour. Behaviour should be guided by accurate representation on the cognitive level. One should build up knowledge of the world, and act on the basis of this knowledge. To the degree that cognition is correspondent with reality and behaviour is dictated by cognition, we may speak of behaviour as adaptive. Third, language as a form of behaviour is guided by cognition. If the categories in language reflect or are systematically linked to the features of the cognitive system, and this system is tied to the real world, we may speak of the communication of knowledge or understanding. In any case, language itself represents a secondary or derivative process. It is useful as a conveyance of knowledge, but does not constitute knowledge itself. Such assumptions pervade much of the literature on social cognition. In this context, Gergen and Semin (1990) have described four major problems which have emerged within recent debates in psychology. These are the problems of (i) the generation of the representational system, (ii) the internal determination of the real, (iii) the identification of internal structure, and (iv) the influence of understanding an action. On the basis of these and other problems in the cognitive representationist position, some investigators have begun to explore alternative conceptions of understanding especially in terms of socially based cognition and discursive construction of cognition (see Gergen and Semin, 1990; Semin & Gergen, 1990 for detailed discussion).

Although it is legitimate and inevitable to study environmental cognition from a psychological point of view, a strictly individual-centered psychology would miss or cut off the basic person-environment interaction and provide a partial or incomplete picture of the environmental cognition of individuals and its behavioural outcomes. Environmental psychology has, from the beginning, been interdisciplinary. Each individual ecological problem is causally connected with the political, economic and other cultural subsystems of a given society. Hence, a system, rather than individual oriented approach is required to gain an understanding of environmental cognition. This system must be based on psycho-social rather than physico-perceptual paradigm. There is no physical environment that is not embedded in and inextricably related to a social or cultural system. We cannot respond to an environment independently of our role as socio-cultural being. Proshansky and O'Hanlon (1977) reject the conceptions of physical environment like stimuli or patterns of stimuli because they represent analytical abstractions of the environment rather than a realistic description of it as it relates to the actual behaviour and experience of the individual. The physical environments to be observed and studied are all those places and spaces that provide the locus and definition of the varied multiple of human activities that characterize day-to-day existence (Jain & Singh, 1996). These spaces and places are in turn defined by the social realities. According to Stokols (1978), environment is construed in multidimensional, molar terms, and the focus of analysis generally is on the interrelations among people and their sociophysical milieu rather than on the linkages between discrete stimuli and behaviour responses.

While describing individual's relationship with his/her environment, transactional view assigns central role to cognitive processes, which are considered as typical transactive processes at the individual level for constructing and orienting the individual's relationship with his/her environment. However, according to Ittelson *et al.* (1974), "man is a cognitive animal. He does far more than see, hear, feel, touch, smell, in the simple sense of 'recording' his environment. He interprets it, makes inferences about it, dreams of it, judges it, imagines it, and engages in still other human forms of knowing. It is all of these forms of knowing that permit the individual to accumulate a past, think on the present, and anticipate the future" (p. 85). They further emphasize that the environment primarily consists in a setting, that is, an organized whole in space and time of physical aspects, social activities and symbolic aspects of meanings. The demand characteristic of the environment is more than the sum of its ongoing activities. Individuals as members of broad social groups, are socialized not just to behave, but to behave appropriately in relation to relevant physical settings; and not simply to the immediate sensory stimuli of the setting, but to its symbolic qualities as well. In every environmental setting physical aspects are closely linked to socio-cultural ones, giving spatial and temporal regularity to their occurrence in the setting. Settings are closely and tightly interwoven with the fabric of social organisations, and cultural systems that circumscribe the day-to-day life of any group of individuals. In effect, any given physical environment is not only a behaviour environment but also a social, organisational, and cultural environment (Singh & Pathak, 1986).

Culture and religion play a crucial role in shaping the cognition of people about the environment in which they live. In the preceding section we have presented exclusive description of the relationship of nature and religion and the environmental understanding and behaviour of ancient Indian people. Although, historically it has been quite common to link environmental problems with religion and culture, but it is a recent idea to link environmental problems to religion in the sense that human environmental cognition and behaviour is conceived as determined by religious beliefs and values. In fact, our vision of the environment is global (Pedersen, 1995). It involves a strong sense of the interconnectedness of all things in nature, of local events with global consequences. Our knowledge and understanding (i.e., our representations) of nature are interpretations, that is, social and cultural constructions (Bird, 1987). Many of our beliefs, ideas and practices are part of the common-sense and taken-for-granted aspects of routine daily action which we do not consciously reflect upon. Therefore, it is essential to study the social organisation of knowledge about the environment or nature in its widest sense, in order to trace how particular ideas, values, beliefs and practices become salient features in relation to environment which in turn shape the environmental cognition of people.

References

Acredolo, L.P. (1976). Frames of reference used by children for orientation in unfamiliar spaces. In G.T. Moore and R.G. Golledge (Eds.), *Environmental Knowing*. Stroudsburg, PA: Dowden, Hutchinson, & Ross.

Allport, G.W. (1937). *Personality, Character and Temperament*. New York: Holt.

Altman, I. (1973). Some perspectives on the study of man-environment phenomena. In W. Preiser (Ed.), *Environment and Design Research Association Fourth International Conference*, (Vol. 1): Selected papers. Dowden, Hutchinson & Ross, Stroudsburg, PA, (pp. 99-113).

Anderson, J.R., & Bower, G.H. (1973). Human associative memory. Washington, DC: Winston & Sons.

Andorka, R. (1987). Time budgets and their uses. *Annual Review of Sociology*, 13, 149-164.

Appleyard, D. (1969). Why buildings are known. *Environment and Behaviour*, 1, 131.

Appleyard, D. (1970). Styles and methods of structuring a city. *Environment and Behaviour*, 2, 100-118.

Appleyard, D. (1979). The environment as a social symbol. *Journal of the American Planning Association*, 45, 143-153.

Attneave, F., & Pierce, C.R. (1978). Accuracy of extrapolating a pointer into perceived and imaged space. *American Journal of Psychology*, 91, 371-387.

Baird, J.C. (1979). Studies of the cognitive representation of spatial relations: An overview. *Journal of Experimental Psychology General, 108*, 90-91.

Bartlett, F. (1932). *Remembering*. Cambridge, England: Cambridge University Press.

Bartlett, F.C. (1932). *Remembering: A Study in Experimental and Social Psychology*. New York: Doubleday.

Berlyne, D.F. (1960). *Conflict, Arousal, Curiosity*. New York: McGraw-Hill.

Binet, M.A. (1894). Reverse illusions of orientation. *Psychology Review, 1*, 337-350.

Bird, E.A.R. (1987). The social construction of nature: Theoretical approaches to the history of environmental problems. *Environmental Review, 11(4)*, 255-264.

Blaut, J.M., McCleary, G., & Blaut, A. (1970). Environmental mapping in young children. *Environment and Behaviour, 2,* 335, 349.

Blaut, J.M., & Stea, D. (1971). Studies of geographic learning. A*nnals of the Association of American Geographers, 61 (2)*, 387-393.

Bobrow, D.A., & Norman, D.A. (1975). Some principles of memory schemata. In D.A. Bobrow and A. Collins (Eds.), *Representation and Understanding*. New York: Academic.

Bonnes, M. (1988). Mascolinita e femminilita. In G.V. Caprara (Ed.), *Personalita e rappresentazioni sociale* (pp. 190-209). Rome: La Nuova Italia Scientifica.

Book, A., & Garling, T. (1980). Processing of information about location during locomotion: Effects of concurrent task and locomotion patterns. *Scandinavian Journal of Psychology, 21*, 185-192.

Bonnes, M., & Secchiaroli, G. (1995). *Environment Psychology: A Psycho-Social Introduction*. London: Sage.

Bowers, D.S. (1973). Situationism in psychology: An analysis and a critique. *Psychological Review, 5*, 307-337.

Briggs, R. (1972). *Cognitive Distance in Urban Space*. Unpublished doctoral dissertation. Ohio State University, Columbus.

Brown, W. (1932). Spatial integrations in a human maze. *University of California Publications in Psychology, 5*, 123-134.

Bruner, J.S. (1957). Ongoing beyond the information given in. In J.S. Bruner (Ed.), *Contemporary Approaches to Cognition: A Symposium* (pp. 41-69). Cambridge, MA: Harvard University Press.

Brunswik, E. (1944). Distal focusing of perception. *Psychological Monographs, 56*, 1-48.

Brunswik, E. (1957). Scope and aspects of cognitive problems. In J. Bruner *et al.* (Eds.), *Contemporary Approaches to Cognition* (pp. 5-31). Cambridge, MA: Harvard University Press.

Burroughs, W.J., & Sadall, E.K. (1979). Asymmetries in distance cognition. *Geographical Analysis, 11(14)*, 414-421.

Byrne, R. (1979). Memory for urban geography. *Quarterly Journal of Experimental Psychology, 31*, 147-154.

Canter, D. (1977). *The Psychology of Place*. London: Architectural Press.

Carlstein, T. (1982). *Time, Resources, Society and Ecology: On the Capacity of Human Interaction in Space and Time, Preindustrial Societies*. London: Allen & Unwin.

Cassirer, E. (1944). *An Essay on Man: An Introduction to the Philosophy of Human Culture*. New Haven, CT: Yale University Press.

Couclelis, H., & Golledge, R.G. (1983). Analytic research, positivism, and behavioural geography. *Annals of the Association of American Geographers, 73(3)*, 331-339.

Craik, K.H (1970). Environmental psychology. In K.H. Craik, R. Kleinmuntz, R. Rosnow, R. Rosenthal, J.A. Cheyne and R.H. Walters (Eds.), *New Directions in Psychology* (Vol. 4, pp. 1-20). New York: Holt Rinehart & Winston.

Craik, K.H. (1977). Multiple scientific paradigms in environmental psychology. *International Journal of Psychology, 12*, 147-157.

D'Andrade, R.G. (1981). The cultural part of cognition. *Cognitive Science, 5*, 179-196.

D'Andrade, R.G. (1984). Cultural meaning systems. In R.A. Shweder and R.A. Levine (Eds.), *Culture Theory: Essays on Mind, Self, and Emotion*. New York: Cambridge University Press.

DeCarteau, M. (1980). L'invention du quotidien. Tome 1. Arts de faire. [The invention of daily life. (Vol. 1). The art of doing]. Paris: Union Generale d'Editions (Collection 10/18).

Devlin, A. (1976). The small town cognitive maps: Adjusting to a new environment. In G.T. Moore and R.G. Golledge (Eds.), *Environmental Knowing* (pp. 58-66). Stroudsburg, PA: Dowden, Hutchinson, & Ross.

Doise, W. (1976). *L'articulation psycho-sociologique et les relations entre groupes*. Brussels: De Boeck.

Doise, W. (1982). *L'esplication en psychologie sociale*. Paris: Presses Universitaries de France.

Dougherty, J.W.D. (Ed.) (1985). *Directions in Cognitive Anthropology*. Urbana, IL: University of Chicago Press.

Downs, R.M., & Stea, D. (Eds.) (1973). *Image and Environment: Cognitive Mapping and Spatial Behaviour*. Chicago: Aldine.

Eibel-Eibesfeldt. I.(1970). *Ethology, The Biology of Behaviour*. New York: Holt, Rinehart & Winston.

Erickson, R.H. (1975). *The Effects of Perceived Place Attributes on Cognition of Urban Residents*. (Discussion Paper No. 23). University of Iowa, Department of Geography.

Evans, G.W. (1980), Environmental cognition, *Psychological Bulletin, 88*, 259-287.

Evans, G.W., Marrero, D.G., & Butler, P.A. (1981). Environmental learning and cognitive mapping. *Environment and Behaviour, 13*, 83-104.

Evans, G.W., & Pezdek, K. (1980). Cognitive mapping: Knowledge of real world distance and location information. *Journal of Experimental Psychology: Human Learning and Memory, 6*, 13-24.

Evans, G.W., Brennan, P., Skorpanich, M.A., & Held, D. (1984). Cognitive mapping and elderly adults: Verbal and location memory for urban landmarks. *Journal of Gerontology, 39*, 452-457.

Farr, R., & Moscovici, S. (Eds.) (1984). *Social Representations.* Cambridge: Cambridge University Press.

Firey, W. (1945). Sentiment and symbolism as ecological variables. *American Sociological Review, 10*, 140-148.

Gardner, H. (1985). *The Mind's New Science: A History of the Cognitive Revolution.* New York: Basic Books.

Garling, T., & Golledge, R.G. (1989). Environmental perception and cognition. In H. Zube and G.T. Moore (Eds.), *Advances in Environmental Behaviour and Design* (Vol. 2, pp. 203-236). New York: Plenum.

Garling, T., Book, A., Ergezen, N., & Lindberg, E. (1981). Memory for the spatial layout of the everyday physical environment: Empirical findings and their theoretical implications. In A.E. Osterberg, C.P. Teirman, and R.A. Findlay (Eds.), *Design Research Interactions. Proceedings of the Environmental Design Research Association 12 Conference*. Ames, IA.

Garling T., Book, A., & Lindberg, E. (1984). Cognitive mapping of large-scale environments, action plans, orientation and their interrelationships. *Environment and Behaviour, 16*, 3-34.

Garling, T., Book, A., Lindberg, E., & Nilsson, T. (1981). Memory for the spatial layout of the everyday physical environment: Factors affecting the rate of acquisition. *Journal of Experimental Psychology, 1*, 263-277.

Gergen, K.J., & Semin, G.R. (1990). Everyday understanding in science and daily life. In G.R. Semin and K.J. Gergen (Eds.), *Everyday Understanding: Social and Scientific Implications* (pp. 1-18). London: Sage.

Giard, L. (1980). Faire la cuisine. [Cooking.]. In L. Giard and P. Mayol, *L'invention du quotidien: Tome 2. Habiter, cuisiner*. [The invention of daily life: Vol. 2 Housing, cooking.]. Paris: Union Generale d'Editions (Collection 10/18).

Gibson, J.J. (1958). Perception of distance and space in the open air. In D.C. Beardslee and M. Wertheimer (Eds.), *Readings in Perception* (pp. 415-431). New York: Van Nostrand Reinhold. (Reprinted from *Motion Picture Testing and Research*, 1946, AAF Program Report No. 7, 181-195.

Gibson, J.J. (1966). *The Senses Considered as Perceptual Systems.* Boston: Houghton Mifflin.

Gibson, J.J. (1979). *The Ecological Approach to Visual Perception.* Boston: Houghton Mifflin.

Golledge, R.G. (1975). *On Determining Cognitive Configurations of a City.* Columbus: Ohio State University Research Foundation, Department of Geography. National Science Foundation Report #6S-37969.

Golledge, R. G. (1977). Multidimensional analysis in the study of environmental behaviour and environmental design. In I. Altman and J.F. Wohlwill (Eds.),

Human Behaviour and Environment: Advances in Theory and Research (Vol. 2, pp. 1-42). New York: Plenum.

Golledge, R.G. (1978). Learning about urban environments. In T. Carlstein, D. Parkes, and N. Thrift (Eds.), T*iming space and spacing time* (Vol. 1). London:Edward Arnold.

Golledge, R.G. (1987). Environmental cognition. In D. Stokols and I. Altman (Eds.), *Handbook of environmental psychology* (Vol. 1, pp. 131-174). New York: Wiley.

Golledge, R.G., Briggs, R., & Demko, D. (1969). The configuration of distances in intra-urban space. *Proceedings of the Association of American Geographers, 1*, 60-65.

Golledge, R.G., & Hubert, L.J. (1982). Some comments on non-Euclidean mental maps. *Environment and Planning A, 14,* 107-118.

Golledge, R.G., Parnicky, J.J., & Rayner, J.N. (1980). *The spatial competence of selected populations.* Columbus: Ohio State University Research Foundation.

Golledge, R.G., Rayner, J.N., & Rivizzigno, V.L. (1982). Comparing objective and cognitive representations of environmental cues. In R.G. Golledge and J.N. Rayner (Eds.), *Proximity and preference: Problems in the multidimensional analysis of large data sets* (pp. 233-266). Minneapolis: University of Minnesota Press.

Golledge, R.G., & Rushton, G. (Eds.) (1976). *Spatial Choice and Spatial Behaviour.* Columbus: Ohio State University Press.

Golledge, R.G., & Spector, A.N. (1978). Comprehending the urban environment: Theory and practice. *Geographical Analysis, 10,* 403-426.

Gulliver, E.P. (1908). Orientation of maps. *Journal of Geography, 7*, 55-58.

Hagerstrand, T. (1983). In search for the sources of concepts. In A. Buttimer (Ed.), *The Practice of Geography (238-256).* London: Longman.

Hall, E.T. (1966). *The Hidden Dimension.* New York: Doubleday.

Hart, R.A. (1978). *Children's Experience of Place: A Developmental Study.* New York: Halsted.

Hayes-Roth, F. (1979). Distinguishing theories of representation: A critique of Anderson's "arguments concerning mental imagery." *Psychological Review, 86,* 376-382.

Hazen, N.L., Lockman, J.J., & Pick, H.L., Jr. (1978). The development of children's representations of large-scale environments. *Child Development, 4*, 71-115.

Head, H. (1920). *Studies in Neurology.* Oxford, England: Oxford University Press.

Hebb, D.O. (1949). *The Organization of Behaviour.* New York: Wiley.

Hebb. D.O. (1963). The semi-autonomous process: Its nature and nurture. *American Psychologist, 18*, 16-27.

Hintzman, D.L., O'Dell, C.S., & Arndt., D.R. (1981). Orientation in cognitive maps. *Cognitive Psychology, 13*, 149-206.

Howard, I.P., & Templeton, W.B. (1966). *Human Spatial Orientation.* Chichester: Wiley

Ittelson, W.H. (1951). The constancies in perceptual theory. *Psychological Review, 58*, 285-294.

Ittelson, W.H. (Ed.) (1973a). *Environment and Cognition*. New York: Academic Press.

Ittelson, W.H., (1973b). Environment perception and contemporary perceptual theory. In W.H. Ittelson (Ed.), *Environment and Cognition* (pp. 1-19). New York: Academic Press.

Ittelson, W.H., Proshansky, H.M., & Rivlin, A., & Winkel, G. (1974). *An Introduction to Environmental Psychology*. New York: Holt, Rinehart & Winston.

Jahoda, G. (1982). *Psychology and Anthropology: A Psychological Perspective*. London: Academic Press.

Jahoda, G. (1990). Our forgotten ancestors. In J.J. Berman (Ed.), Nebraska symposium on motivation 1989: Cross-cultural perspectives (Vol. 17, pp. 1-40). Lincoln and London: University of Nebraska Press.

Jain, U., & Singh, T. (1996). *Quality of Life as Reflected in Human-Environment Relationships*. Proceedings of the Seminar on the quality of life. Department of Applied Psychology, Delhi University, Delhi.

Kaplan, R. (1976). Way-finding in the natural environment. In G.T. Moore and R.G. Golledge (Eds.), *Environmental Knowing* (pp. 46-57) Stroudsburg, PA: Dowden, Hutchinson, & Ross.

Kaplan, S. (1973). Cognitive maps in perception and thought. In R. Downs and D. Stea (Eds.), *Image and Environment: Cognitive Mappings and Spatial Behaviour*. Chicago: Aldine.

Kaplan, S. (1976). Adaptation, structure, and knowledge. In G.T. Moore and R.G. Golledge (Eds.), *Environmental Knowing* (pp. 32-45). Stroudsburg, PA:Dowden, Hutchinson, & Ross.

Kaplan, S. (1983). A model of human/environment compatibility. *Environment and Behaviour, 15*, 311-322.

Kaplan, S., & Kaplan, R. (1982). *Cognition and Environment*. New York: Praeger.

Kates, R.W., & Wholwill, J.F. (Eds.) (1966). Man's response to the physical environment. *Journal of Social Issues, 22*, 1-140 (Special issue).

Kearins, J.M. (1981). Visual spatial memory in Australian aboriginal children of desert regions. *Cognitive Psychology, 13*, 434-460.

Kelley, G.A. (1955). *The Psychology of Personal Constructs* (Vol. 1 & 2). New York:Norton.

Kirk, W. (1951). Historical geography and the concept of the behavioural environment. In G. Kuriyan (Ed.). *Indian Geographical Journal* (Silver Jubilee ed.) (pp. 152-160). Madras, India: Indian Geographical Society.

Kosslyn, S. M., Pick, H. L., Jr., Farielo, G. R. (1974). Cognitive maps in children and men. *Child Development*, 45, 707-716.

Kosslyn, S.M., & Pomerantz, J.R. (1977). Imagery, propositions and the form of internal representations. *Cognitive Psychology, 9*, 52-76.

Kozlowski, L.T., & Bryant, K.J. (1977). Sense of direction, spatial orientation and cognitive maps. *Journal of Experimental Psychology: Human Perception and Performance*, 3, 590-598.

Kuipers, B. (1982). The "map in the head" metaphor. *Environment and Behaviour, 4*, 202-220.

Kuipers, B. (1983). The cognitive map: Could it have been any other way? In H.L. Pick, Jr. and L.P. Acredolo (Eds.), *Spatial Orientation, Theory, Research and Application* (pp. 345-360). New York: Plenum.

Kulkarni, N. (1991). Man and nature relationship reflected in the *Sukla Yajurveda*. In V.N. Jha (Ed.), *Proceedings of the National Seminar on Environmental Awareness Reflected in Sanskrit Literature* (pp. 1-6). University of Poona, Pune.

Lal, S.K. (1991). Drainage system in vedic India. In V.N. Jha (Ed.), *Proceedings of the National Seminar on Environmental Awareness Reflected in Sanskrit Literature* (pp. 41-46). University of Poona, Pune.

Lave, J. (1988). *Cognition in Practice: Mind, Mathematics and Culture in Everyday Life.* Cambridge: Cambridge University Press.

Lee, T. (1962). Brennan's law of shopping behaviour. *Psychological Reports, 2*, 662.

Lee, T. (1964). Psychology and living space. *Transactions of the Bartlett Society, 2*, 11-36.

Lee, T. (1970). Perceived distance as a function of direction in the city. *Environment and Behaviour, 2,* 40-51.

Leff, H. (1978). *Experience, Environment and Human Potentials.* New York: Oxford University Press.

Lewin, K. (1936). *Principles of Topological Psychology.* New York: McGraw-Hill.

Lloyd, R.E. (1982). A look at images. *Annals of the Association of American Geographers, 27(4)*, 532-548.

Lorenz, K. (1965). *Evolution and Modification of Behaviour.* Chicago: University of Chicago Press.

Lowrey, R.A. (1973). A method for analysing distance concepts of urban residents. In R.M. Downs and D. Stea (Eds.), *Image and Environment: Cognitive Mapping and Spatial Behaviour* (pp. 338-360). Chicago: Aldine.

Lynch, K. (1960). *The Image of the City.* Cambridge, MA: MIT Press, Cambridge.

Mande, K.V. (1991). Environmental awareness according to *Atharvaveda.* In V.N. Jha (Ed.), *Proceedings of the National Seminar on Environmental Awareness Reflected in Sanskrit Literature* (pp. 7-13). University of Poona, Pune.

Mead, G.H. (1934). *Mind, Self, and Society.* Chicago: University of Chicago Press.

Magnusson, D. (Ed.) (1981). *Toward a Psychology of Situations.* Hillsdale, NJ: Lawrence Erlbaum.

Michelson, W. (1987). Measuring macroenvironment and behaviour: The time budget and time geography. In R. Bechtel, R. Marans and W. Michelson

(Eds.), *Methods in Environment and Behaviour Research* (pp. 216-246). New York: Van Nostrand Reinhold.

Milgram, S. Greenwald, J., Kessler, S., McKenna, W., & Waters, J. (1972). A psychological map of New York city, *American Scientist, 60,* 194-200.

Miller, G.A., Galanter, E., & Pribram, K.H. (1960). *Plans and the Structure of Behaviour:* New York: Holt, Rinehart & Winston, Inc.

Minsky, M.A. (1975). A framework for representing knowledge. In P.H. Winston (Ed.), *The Psychology of Computer Vision.* New York: McGraw-Hill.

Mishra, M. (1991). Apah in vedic literature: An environmental approach. In V.N. Jha (Ed.), *Proceedings of the National Seminar on Environmental Awareness Reflected in Sanskrit Literature* (pp. 35-40). University of Poona, Pune.

Misra, G., Jain, U., & Singh, T. (1995). On the cultural frame of social cognition. *Indian Psychological Abstracts and Reviews, 2,* 3-36.

Moore, G.T. (1986). A framework for theories of environment and behaviour: Unit of analysis and the locus of control of behaviour. *Paper presented to the 21st International Congress of Applied Psychology.* Jerusalem.

Moore, G.T. (1987). Environment and behaviour research in North America: History, developments, and unresolved issues. In D. Stokols and I. Altman (Eds.), *Handbook of Environmental Psychology* (Vol. 2, pp. 1371-1410). New York: Wiley.

Moore G.T., & Golledge, R.G. (1976). Environmental knowing: Concepts and theories. In G. Moore and R.G. Golledge (Eds.), *Environmental Knowing* (pp. 3-24). Stroudsburg, PA: Dowden, Hutchinson & Ross.

Moscovici, S. (1961-76). *La Psychanalyse: Son Image et Son Public.* Paris: Presses Universitaires de France.

Moscovici, S. (1981). On social representations. In J.P. Forgas (Ed.), *Social Cognition: Perspectives in Everyday Understanding* (pp. 181-209). London: Academic Press.

Moscovici, S. (1982). The coming era of representations. In J.P. Codol and J.P. Leyens (Eds.), *Cognitive Approaches to Social Behaviour* (pp. 115-150). The Hague: Nijoff.

Moscovici, S. (1984a). The phenomenon of social representations. In R. Farr and S. Moscovici (Eds.), *Social Representations* (pp. 3-69). Cambridge: Cambridge University Press.

Moscovici, S. (1984b). *Psychologie Sociale.* Paris: Presses Universitaires de France.

Neisser, U. (1976) *Cognition and Reality.* San Francisco: Freeman.

Neisser, U. (1988). Five kinds of self knowledge. *Philosophical Psychology, I,* 35-59.

Norman, D.A., & Rummelhar, D.E. (1975). *Explorations in Cognition.* San Francisco: Freeman.

Orleans, P. (1973). Differential cognition of urban residents: Effects of social scale on mapping. In R.M. Downs and D. Stea (Eds.), *Image and Environment: Cognitive Mapping and Spatial Behaviour* (pp. 78-96). Chicago: Aldine.

Palmonari, A. (1989). *Processi simbolici e dinamiche sociali*, II Mulino, Bologna.

Palmonari, A., Carugati, F., Ricci-Bitti, P.E., & Sarchielli, G. (1979). *Identita imperfette*, II Mulino, Bologna.

Parkes, D.N., & Thrift, N.J. (1980). *Time, Space, and Place.* New York: Wiley.

Paivio, A. (1969). Mental imagery in associative learning and memory. *Psychological Review, 76*, 241-263.

Paivio, A. (1971). *Imagery and Verbal Processes.* New York: Holt, Rinehart, & Winston.

Pedersen, P. (1995). Nature, religion and cultural identity: The religious environmentalist paradigm. In O. Bruun and A. Kalland (Eds.), *Asian Perceptions of Nature: A Critical Approach* (pp. 258-276). Richmond, Surrey: Curzon Press.

Peters, R.P. (1973). Cognitive maps in wolves and men. In W.F.E. Preiser (Ed.), *Environmental Design Research* (Vol. 2, pp. 247-253). Stroudsburg, PA: Dowden, Hutchinson, & Ross.

Piaget, J. (1950). *The Psychology of Intelligence*. (M. Piercy & D. Berlyne, Trans) (orig. French ed. 1947). London: Routledge and Kegan Paul; New York: Harcourt Brace; Totowa. NJ: Littlefield Adams, 1963.

Piaget, J., & Inhelder, B. (1967). *The Child's Conception of Space*. New York: Norton.

Piaget, J., Inhelder, B., & Czeminska, A. (1960). *The Child's Conception of Geometry*. New York: Basic.

Pick, H.L., Jr. (1972). Mapping children-mapping space. *Paper Presented at the Meeting of the American Psychological Association*, Honolulu, HI.

Pick, H.L., Jr., & Acredolo, L. (1983). *Spatial Orientation: Theory, Research and Application*. New York: Plenum.

Potter, J., & Wetherell, M. (1987). *Discourse and Social Psychology*. London: Sage.

Proshansky, H.M. (1978). The city and self identity. *Environment and Behaviour, 10*, 147-169.

Proshansky, H.M., & Kaminoff, R.D. (1982). The built environment of the young adult. In S. Messick (Ed.), *Development in Young Adulthood: Characteristics and Competences in Education, Work and Social life*. San Francisco: Jossey Bass.

Proshansky, H.M., & O'Hanlon, T. (1977). Environmental psychology: Origins and development. In D. Stokols (Ed.), Perspectives on environment and behaviour (pp. 101-127). New York: Plenum.

Proshansky, H.M., Fabian, A.K., & Kaminoff, R. (1983). Place-identity: Physical world socialization of the self. *Journal of Environmental Psychology, 3*, 57-83.

Proshansky, H.M., Ittelson, W., & Rivlin, L.G. (Eds.) (1970). *Environmental Psychology: Man and his Physical Settings* (1st Edition). New York: Holt, Rinehart & Winston.

Proshansky, H.M., Nelson-Schulman, Y., & Kaminoff, R.D. (1979). The role of physical setting in life crisis experiences. In I. Sharon and C. Spielberger

(Eds.), *Stress and Anxiety* (Vol. 6, pp. 3-26). Washington DC: Hemisphere.

Pylyshyn, Z.W. (1981). The imagery debate: Analogue media *vs*. Tacit knowledge. *Psychological Review, 88*, 16-45.

Rapoport, A. (1976). Environmental cognition in cross-cultural perspective. In G.T. Moore & R.G. Golledge (Eds.), *Environmental Knowing* (pp. 220-234). Stroudsburg, PA: Dowden, Hutchinson, & Ross.

Rogoff, B., & Lave, J. (1984). *Everyday Cognition: Its Development in Social Context*. Cambridge: Harvard University Press.

Richardson, G. D. (1982). *Spatial Cognition.* Doctoral Dissertation, University of California, Santa Barbara.

Romney, A.K., & D'Andrade, R.G. (1964). Transcultural studies in cognition. *American Anthropologist, 66*, 140-170.

Russell, J.A., & Ward, L.M. (1982). Environmental psychology. *Annual Review of Psychology, 33*, 651-688.

Sadalla, E.K., & Staplin, L.J. (1980). The perception of traversed distance: Intersections. *Environment and Behaviour, 12*, 183-193.

Saegert, S. (1987). Environmental psychology and social change. In D. Stokols and I. Altman (Eds.), *Handbook of Environmental Psychology* (Vol. 1, pp. 99-128). New York: Wiley.

Saegert, S., & Winkel, G. (1990). Environment psychology. *Annual Review of Psychology, 41*, 441-477.

Sampson, E.E. (1988). The debate on individualism: Indigenous psychologies of the individual and their role in personal and societal functioning. *American Psychologist, 44*, 914-921.

Savage-Rumbaugh, E.S., Sevcik, R.A., Rumbaugh, D.M., & Rupet, E. (1985). The capacity of animals to acquire language: Do species differences have anything to say to us? *Philosophical Transactions.* Royal Society of London, B308, 177-185.

Schank, R., & Abelson, R. (1977). *Scripts, Plans, Goals, and Understanding.* Hillsdale, NJ: Erlbaum.

Schneider, D.J. (1991). Social cognition. *Annual Review of Psychology, 42*, 527-561.

Semin, G.R., & Gergen, K.J. (Eds.)(1990). *Everyday Understanding: Social and Scientific Implications*. London: Sage.

Shemyakin, F.N. (1962). General problems of orientation in space and space representations. In B.G. Ananyev (Ed.), *Psychological Science in the USSRS* (Vol. 1) (NTIS No. TT62-11083). Washington, DC: Office of Technical Reports.

Shweder, R.A. (1990). Cultural psychology—What is it? In J.W. Stigler, R.A. Shweder, and G. Herdt (Eds.), *Cultural Psychology: Essays on Comparative Development* (pp. 1-43). Cambridge: Cambridge University Press.

Siegel, A.W., & Cousins, J.H. (1983). The symbolizing and symbolized child in the enterprise of cognitive mapping. In R. Cohen (Ed.), *The Development of Spatial Cognition.* Hillsdale, NJ: Erlbaum.

Siegel, A.W., & Schadler, M. (1977). Young children's cognitive maps of their classrooms. *Child Development, 48*, 388-394.

Siegel, A.W., & White, S.H. (1975). The development of spatial representations of large-scale environments. In H.W. Reese (Ed.), *Advances in child Development and Behaviour* (Vol. 10). New York:Academic.

Singh, T., & Pathak, S. (1986). Human environment relationships: An empirical study of attitudes, values and perceptions, *Trends in Social Science Research, 3(1)*, 25-33.

Smith, T.R., Pellegrino, J.Q., & Golledge, R.G. (1982). Computational process modelling of spatial cognition and behaviour. *Geographical Analysis, 14*, 305-325.

Spector, A.N. (1978). *An Analysis of Urban Spatial Imagery.* Columbus, Ohio State University, Unpublished doctoral dissertation.

Spencer, C., & Darvizeh, C. (1981). The case for developing a cognitive psychology that does not underestimate the abilities of young children. *Journal of Environmental Psychology, I*, 21-31.

Stokols, D. (1978). Environmental psychology. *Annual Review of Psychology, 29*, 253-295.

Stokols, D. (1979). A congruence analysis of stress. In I. Saranson and C. Spielberger (Eds.), *Stress and Anxiety* (Vol. 6, pp. 27-53). New York: Hemisphere.

Stokols, D. (1981). Group X place transactions: Some neglected issues in psychological research on settings. In D. Magnusson (Ed.), *Towards a Psychology of Situations: An International Perspective* (pp. 393-415). Hillsdale, NJ: Lawrence Erlbaum.

Stokols, D., & Shumaker, S. (1981). People in place: A transactional view of settings. In J. Harvey (Ed.), *Cognition, Social Behaviour, and the Environment* (pp. 441-488). Hillsdale, NJ: Lawrence Erlbaum.

Strauss, A.L. (1961). *Images of the American City*. New York: Free Press.

Tajfel, H. (1969). *Human Groups and Social Categories*. Cambridge: Cambridge University Press.

Tajfel, H. (1981). *Human Groups and Social Categories*. Cambridge: Cambridge University Press.

Tajfel, H. (Ed.)(1984). *The Social Dimensions* (Vols. 1-2). Cambridge: Cambridge University Press.

Thorndyke, P.W., & Stasz, C. (1980). Individual differences in knowledge acquisition from maps. *Cognitive Psychology, 12*, 137-175.

Tobler, W.R. (1976). The geometry of mental maps. In G. Rushton and R.G Golledge (Eds.), *Spatial Choice and Spatial Behaviour*. Columbus: Ohio State University Press.

Tolman, E.C. (1932). *Purposive Behaviour in Animals and Men.* New York Appleton-Century-Crofts.

Tolman, E.C. (1948). Cognitive maps in rats and men. *Psychological Review 55*, 189-208.

Trowbridge, C.C. (1948). *Comparative Psychology of Mental Development* New York: International University Press.

Tuan, Y. F. (1977). *Space and Place: The Perspective of Experience.* Minneapolis: University of Minnesota Press.

Tuan, Y. F. (1979). *Landscapes of Fear.* New York: Pantheon.

Tversky, B. (1981). Distortions in memory for maps. *Cognitive Psychology, 13*, 407-433.

Tyler, S.A. (Ed.) (1969). *Cognitive Anthropology.* New York: Holt, Rinehart & Winston.

Wapner, S., Kaplan, B., & Cohen, S.B. (1973). An organismic-developmental perspective for understanding transactions of men in environment. *Environment and Behaviour, 5*, 255-289.

Werner, H., & Kaplan, B. (1963). *Symbolic Information: An Organismic-Developmental Approach to Language and the Expression of Thought.* New York: Wiley.

White, G. (1945). *Human Adjustments to Floods* (Research Paper No. 29). Chicago: University of Chicago, Department of Geography.

Wohlwill, J. F. (1973). The environment is not in the head. In W. Preiser (Ed.), *Environmental Design Research* (Vol. 2). Stroudsburg, PA: Dowden, Hurtchinson, & Ross.

Wohlwill, J.F. (1976). Environmental aesthetics: The environment as a source of affect. In I. Altman and J. Wohlwill (Eds.), *Human Behaviour and Environment: Advances in Theory and Research* (Vol. 1, pp. 37-86). New York: Plenum Press.

Wohlwill, J.F. (1979). Environmental aesthetics: The environment as a source of affect. In I. Altman and J. Wohlwill (Eds.), *Human Behaviour and Environment: Advances in Theory and Research* (Vol. 1, pp. 37-86). New York: Plenum Press.

Wright, G. (1947). Terrae Incognitae: The place of imagination in geography. *Annals of the Association of American Geographers, 37*, 1-15.

2

CROSS-CULTURAL PERSPECTIVES ON COGNITION

RAMESH CHANDRA MISHRA

INTRODUCTION

This chapter is dedicated to the memory of Professor Durganand Sinha. The theme chosen for discussion here represents one of his major research concerns during the last two decades. He carried out several studies by himself, and guided many students to work in this important area of research. The focus is on the theory of psychological differentiation. We will see how this theory has been developed further by the innovative research, mostly carried out in the Indian cultural context during the last twenty years. The relationship between culture and cognition has drawn considerable attention in psychological theory and research during the last two decades. In research the question pertains to the role of physical, social and cultural experiences obtained by individuals while negotiating day-to-day life in their respective environments. In theory the question pertains to (1) the patterning of eco-cultural experiences in different environmental settings, (2) the patterning of individual's performance on a variety of cognitive tasks, and (3) the relationship between eco-cultural experiences and cognitive performances. All theories of cognitive development (e.g., general intelligence, genetic epistemology, specific skills, psychological differentiation) seem to deal with these issues in their own peculiar ways.

Among the various theories of cognitive development, the theory of psychological differentiation (Witkin, Dyk, Faterson, Goodenough, & Karp, 1962) has generated great interest among researchers during the brief 30 years of the cross-cultural enterprise. The theory postulates that an individual's cognitive development proceeds from a less differentiated to a more differentiated pattern of functioning, which is manifested in the segregation of psychological activities. One of the indicators of greater segregation is the "articulated cognitive functioning". The process involves "perceptual analysis and disembedding" of certain items from a complex field. Because it refers to the extent of an individual's reliance on the self or external field, the process is referred to as "field independent (FI)-field dependent (FD) cognitive functioning. In perception, the FI refers to the ability to disembed a part from the total field. In cognition, it refers to the ability to analyse, restructure, reorganize or break up certain cognitive materials or problems in order to achieve solutions. People differ in the extent to which they rely on internal or external referents. Because the ability is consistently reflected in a variety of cognitive, interpersonal and neurophysiological domains, it has been referred to an "cognitive style". In understanding the relationship between culture and cognition, the cognitive style approach begins with an analysis of what people do cognitively in their particular ecological and cultural contexts. There is an interest in the analysis of the demands of one's ecological context whose elements are so textured (Berry, 1983) that they cannot be taken apart. The elements may be structured differently in different ecological settings. The approach looks for interrelationships (patterns) in cognitive performances, and postulates that different patterns of abilities may develop in different eco-cultural settings depending on the nature on demands placed on the individual's life.

The FD-FI cognitive style has received substantial recognition in cross-cultural research on cognition, but more so in the Indian cultural context. Several components of cognitive style have been identified and refined during the course of research (Gruenfeld & Lin, 1984; Goodenough, 1986). Witkin and Goodenough (1981) have traced the general state of affairs in this field, and Berry (1981, 1991) has discussed the cross-cultural issues in comparative study of the development of cognitive style. As mentioned above, the construct refers to the extent to which an individual typically relies upon or accepts the physical or social context as given (FD) in contrast to working on (analysing or restructuring) it (FI). The construct is a bipolar dimension. There is no absolute value attached to anyone of the poles, and the individuals are not considered as "fixed" into their usual places on the dimension. It represents individual differences in the "how" rather than the "what" of behaviour (Witkin & Goodenough, 1981, p. 57).

Cross-cultural research using cognitive style approach has largely been pursued in an eco-cultural framework proposed by Berry (1966, 1976), which has undergone some revision to accommodate new data (Berry, 1987). In this framework, ecology and acculturation are proposed as two major sets of "input" variables, and the culture of groups and behaviour of individuals are considered as adaptive to the demands placed on individuals and groups in their respective ecological settings. Comprehensive reviews of the concerned literature are available in Witkin and Berry (1975), Berry (1981, 1991) and Mishra (1997). The role of ecological, cultural and acculturation variables in the development of FD-FI cognitive style has been clearly delineated.

Major Issues in Research

A number of issues relating to cognitive style have been raised in research. These issues have emerged from the patterns of performance obtained on different tests used for the assessment of FD-FI cognitive style. In early research, Body Adjustment Test (BAT), Rod and Frame Test (RFT), and Embedded Figures Test (EFT) were widely used. In later research, a portable version of RFT, called Portable Rod and Frame Test (PRFT), has been employed. Similarly, several forms of EFT have been developed and used in research with children and adults in various cultural groups. The Children's Embedded Figures Test (CEFT), African Embedded Figures Test (AEFT), Indo-African Embedded Figures Test (IAEFT) and Story-Pictorial Embedded Figures Test (SPEFT) have been widely used by researchers. Tests measuring FD-FI style in tactual and auditory domains have also been given to samples in recent research. A central issue relates to the consistency in scores obtained on tests tapping different cognitive domains. Gender difference in the level of field dependence-independence is another important issue. Individual and group difference in the level of field dependence-independence is a third major issue. The adaptability of cognitive style to ecological pressures and acculturative influences (e.g., urbanization, wage employment, education) constitutes the fourth major issue in research.

With respect to *self-consistency*, earlier studies generally explored into the perceptual domain, and found favourable evidence, except for the PRFT in Africa. Evidence for less consistency appeared between perceptual and other domains. Studies seeking *sex difference* revealed the same to be in evidence in agricultural samples, but not in hunting and gathering populations (Berry, 1966; Mac Arthur, 1967). Studies of development revealed a shift from FD to FI in the period from childhood to adulthood, and there was general evidence for stability of the styles over time.

The search of *individual and group differences* in cognitive style has led to the study of the characteristics of family and child-rearing practices, including socialization pressure on "conformity", ecological engagements of people (hunting-gathering or agriculture), and acculturative experiences. Findings suggest that it is possible to predict with a reliable degree of confidence the cognitive style of individuals and groups from the knowledge of these eco-cultural features.

Empirical Tests

Cross-cultural research on FD-FI cognitive styles during the last decades has continued along these lines. There is evidence for both the sporadic and programmatic kind of research. The large-scale research programmes have been pursued in northern India and Central Africa. Durganand Sinha and his students have undertaken the largest programme of research on these styles. Generally, the eco-cultural framework proposed by Berry (1976, 1987) has been adopted in these studies.

In an early study, Sinha (1979) worked with two subgroups of the Birhor Tribal culture. One of these led a nomadic hunting-gathering life, whereas the other one Haas made transition to a sedentary agricultural life. A long-standing agricultural group of the Oraon Tribal culture was also included. Boys and girls of 8-10 years, sampled from each of these groups, were administered the SPEFT (Sinha, 1978). This test was modelled on the CEFT by embedding local natural stimuli (e.g., squirrels, snakes, butterflies) in larger organised natural scenes (e.g., forests, gardens). Findings revealed that compared to the agricultural group, children of the hunting-gathering group showed greater disembedding of stimuli. In another study, Sinha (1980) attempted a comparison between the Tribal and non-Tribal samples, with a view to analysing sex difference in performance of the SPEFT. While there was no difference between boys and girls in the tribal sample, a clear-cut gender difference (favouring boys) in the non-tribal sample was noted in the 4-5, 7-8 and 9-10 year groups.

These results were interpreted as supporting Berry's (1976) prediction that hunters and gatherers would be psychologically more differentiated than agriculturists, and that in more complex and stratified societies, distinct sex roles are culturally prescribed, leading to differing psychological outcomes. In a review of Indian studies on perceptual and cognitive skills, Sinha (1982) offered interpretations that were distinctly in favour of eco-cultural model. However, in none of these studies were the socialisation practices and social structure of the groups directly assessed.

Predictions pertaining to the role of social structure and socialisation practices attendant on them were tested in a study conducted with children reared in monogamous, polyandrous, polygynandrous families found in the cis-Himalayan region of India (Sinha & Bharat, 1985). The monogamous families comprise one husband, one wife, and their children. The polyandrous families comprise one wife with two or more husbands (often brothers) and their joint children. In polygynandrous families, there are two or more husbands (again often brothers) sharing two or more wives, and their common children. Children of 7-9 and 13-15 years were administered the SPEFT and Block Designs. Family experiences (e.g., mother and father involvement), disciplinary practices used with children and mother-father dominance were observed, enquired about through interviews and rated. While some of these variables showed variations across family types, these were not potent enough to influence the level of psychological differentiation of children of the concerned groups to a significant extent.

The direct role of the hill and plains ecology in cognitive style (on the SPEFT) has been studied with schooled and unschooled children of Brahmin and Gurung cultural groups of Nepal (Sinha & Shrestha, 1992). Schooled children (7-10 years) scored higher than unschooled children did. This finding was consistent with those reported in other studies. On the other hand, hill Brahmin children scored higher than hill Gurung, but plains Brahmin scored lower than plains Gurung. This indicated that ecology reinforced the process of differentiation by being associated with certain cultural practices of the groups. Shrestha and Mishra (1996) worked with the same cultural groups in Nepal, and reported a significant gender difference in the level of psychological differentiation in the Brahmin sample, but not in the Gurung sample. On the other hand, Brahmin children appeared to be psychologically more differentiated than Gurung children in hill ecology than in the plains.

The role of acculturation context (another component of Berry's model) in the emergence of cognitive style was addressed in a study of children of Santhal tribal culture (G. Sinha, 1988) by unpackaging the experience of schooling, urbanization and industrialization. The effects of all variables on SPEFT scores were found to be in the predicted direction. However, a stronger influence of industrialization than that of schooling or urbanization was clearly in evidence. Some qualitative features of schools found in the Santhal region were held responsible for less pervasive effect of schooling as reported in other studies. An extensive test of both Witkin's theory and eco-cultural model has been attempted in Central Africa (Berry, van de Koppel, Senechal, Annis, Bahuchet, Cavalli-Sforza & Witkin, 1986). This research has attempted to take care of various criticisms raised against cross-cultural studies of cognitive style. It has also carried out a more sophisticated assessment of ecological, cultural and acculturation contexts, as well as of behaviours indicative of FD-FI cognitive style. A sample of 374 participants, including male and female children and adults of the Beak (Pygmy hunters and gatherers), the Bangandu (agriculturists with some hunting and gathering), and the Gbanu (full-fledged agriculturist) cultural groups was studied. The participants were administered the African Embedded Figures Test (AEFT), Portable Rod and Frame Test (PRFT), Body Adjustment Test (BAT), Sophistication of Body Proportioning Scale (SBPS), Block Designs Training Test (BDTT), Auditory Sequential Tones Test (ASTT), Auditory Embedded Tones Test (AETT), and Tactile Embedded Figures Test (TEFT). These tests intended to measure cognitive differentiation in visual, auditory and tactual domains. Looking, telling and sitting behaviours were assessed in order to collect evidence of differentiation in the social domain. Socialization aspects of the groups were studied through parent and neighbour interviews, child ratings, and observation of parent-child interaction on a specially designed task. For the study of acculturation, measures were developed to assess it at both the subjective and objective levels.

Factor analysis of the cognitive test data generally revealed a "single factor" solution to be the most appropriate outcome. The systematic relationships among test scores (with exception of PRFT and Telling) broadly supported the notion of cognitive style. Evidence for socialization for independence and self-reliance in the Gbanu also appeared to correspond to the general predictions of the eco-cultural model. Prediction of test-performance from socialization measures appeared to be very weak. In spite of considerably group differences in various measures of socialization (aggregated at the group level), their predictive validity for the development of cognitive style appeared to be doubtful.

The difference among groups with respect to their experience of acculturation was substantiated by ethnographic accounts of the groups, standardized test-related and contact-acculturation measures. There was clear evidence for their influences on test performance. The overall findings revealed significant evidence of cultural group differences in performance even when the covarying effect of acculturation was disregarded.

Mishra, Sinha, and Berry (1996) carried out a large-scale study in the State of Bihar in India. Children and adults of the Birhor (nomadic hunters-gatherers group), Asur (recent settlers pursuing a mixed economy of hunting gathering and agriculture), and Oraon (long-standing agriculturists) tribal cultural groups served as samples. In each group, sampling variations were obtained with respect to a number of objective and subjective measures of contact-acculturation. The test-acculturation of individual's was also measured. Socialization emphases (pressure towards compliance or assertion) in these groups were assessed through a combination of observation, interview and testing. SPEFT, TEFT, and Block Designs Test were used as the measures of cognitive style. The significant effects of eco-cultural and acculturation features of groups were found to be in the predicted direction. The interaction between eco-cultural background and acculturation revealed the effect of the latter largely for the Oraon with a nonexistent or negligible effect for Birhor and Asur groups. A "threshold hypothesis" was used to explain the culture-bound effect of acculturation. It was argued that acculturation could change the psychological characteristics of individuals only when it has been successful in making way into their life beyond a threshold point. Failing to achieve that, the effects could be superficial and incapable of changing the psychological make-up of individuals. Although test acculturation also appeared to be an important predictor of people's test-performance, it could not displace the effect of the long-standing eco-cultural adaptation of groups. The findings revealed that parent- or child-reported socialization emphases were weak predictors of children's cognitive style. On the other hand, variables like helping and feedback (extracted from factor analysis) could reliably predict children's cognitive style in the expected direction. Similar results were obtained in another study with children of hunting-gathering, agricultural and wage-earning samples of the Tharu culture in the Himalayan *terai* region of India (K. Mishra, 1998).

Mishra (1996) studied unschooled children of the Birjia cultural group in Bihar, using SPEFT and Indo-African EFT as measures of cognitive style. Distances travelled away from home either in the forest or within the village and their self-directed activities were assessed.

The findings revealed that, in general, children moving into the forests travelled longer distances and engaged in more self-directed activities than those moving in the village surroundings. The forest moving children scored significantly higher on both the measures of cognitive style than village children, which was attributed to greater self-exploration opportunities and high differentiation demands placed on children in the forest settings.

The role of specific socialization variables in the level of field dependence-independence was examined in a study with boys and girls in rural and urban settings of Varanasi (Mishra & Singh, 1999). The socialization variables were extracted from a parent-child interaction task (Mishra *et al.*, 1996). These included: parental utterances (positive, negative, task-specific), parental help, and looking to parents and researcher (indicators of help-seeking behaviour of children). Level of field dependence-independence was assessed with the help of the SPEFT. The findings revealed no evidence of difference in the interaction patterns of parents with boys and girls. On the other hand, variables such as less parental utterances, less positive utterances, more specific utterances, less parental help, and less help seeking behaviour of children were associated with higher scores on the SPEFT.

The predictions of cognitive style from the knowledge of cultural features have not been borne out in some studies carried out in other cultures; instead results counter to the prediction have been demonstrated. Bagley, Iwawaki and Young (1983) compared Japanese children (in Japan and London) with English children with respect to CEFT performance. The hypothesis that Japanese children, having grown up in a group-oriented culture, would have lower self-nonself segregation and score lower on the CEFT, was not supported by the findings. "... the prolonged training which Japanese children undergo in acquiring knowledge of written Japanese" (p. 33) was held responsible for highly developed perceptual skills among them.

Bagley (1984, 1988) has reviewed these studies and supplemented them with empirical data obtained from some native (Blackfoot) and immigrant groups in Canada (Japanese-, Jamaican-, Italian-, and Angloceltic-Canadians) on the CEFT. Cognitive style of Japanese-Canadians has been found to resemble that of the Japanese elsewhere (more FI) and higher than all other groups. With acculturation, a shift towards greater FI style was noted for the Italian and Jamaican samples, which was interpreted in terms of learning to survive in a fast moving and multiple stimulating environment.

Recent Developments

These studies indicate that cross-cultural study of cognitive style has followed a common path in the evolution of research during the last three decades. While earlier studies provide clear results, findings appear to be more complex and variable as more data have set in. Consequently, a number of theoretical developments have surfaced in respect of psychological differentiation. These developments involve both cultural level variables and psychological level phenomena, including the relationship between them. At the cultural level, the main concern has been with respect to specifying cultural experiences that are conceptually important for understanding psychological differentiation. In much of the work, the eco-cultural framework (Berry, 1976) has been used as a guide to look for variables that are psychologically important in a given culture. In this framework, ecological (economic activity, settlement pattern and societal size) and cultural (role diversity, socio-cultural stratification and socialization) variables have been combined into a single index. The dimensions involved in this index are those of "societal size" and "social conformity" (Berry, 1987). A distinction has been made between "role diversity" and "role obligations" (Gamble & Ginsberg, 1981). A similar proposal has been made by Denny (1988), based upon the linguistic data. He has referred to the two dimensions as "differentiation" and "contextualisation". Boldt (1989) has argued that these dimensions should be treated independently because they vary considerably as a function of the subsistence strategies of the groups. Societal size and role diversity increase linearly as we move from hunter-gatherer (low), through agriculturist (medium) to urban-industrial samples (high). On the other hand, social conformity and role obligations tend to be low in hunting-gathering and urban-industrial samples, but high in agricultural samples (Boldt, 1989; Gamble & Ginsberg, 1981). Relatively high field-independence in both Western and Japanese samples found in studies can be accounted for in terms of the importance of "role obligation" for samples during acculturation. It may be argued that the decrease in role obligation and norm imposition within the intimate in-group would increase the probability of "self-nonself segregation" and produce cultural group differences in cognitive style.

This new proposition has been tested in two recent studies. In one, carried out within India, Mishra (1996), tested samples from four subsistence level strategy groups (hunting-gathering, dry agriculture, irrigation agriculture, wage earning). Measures of societal size, social conformity, social connectedness, individual connectedness and socialization patterns were used for the assessment of cultural dimensions. SPEFT, Hidden Words Test, Locating Objects Test, Syllogistic Reasoning Test, Unknown Words Test, Visual Closure Test and Object Enumeration Test were used for the assessment of cognitive dimensions of "intraunit distinctiveness" (differentiation) and "extraunit connectedness" (contextualisation). An attempt was to examine the relationship between the two cultural and cognitive dimensions. Children's achievement in language, mathematics and science in relation to cultural and cognitive dimensions were also explored.

A number of interesting findings emerged with respect to the understanding of cultural dimensions. While societal size showed a progressive increase from the hunting-gathering to wage earning through agricultural samples, social conformity was low in the hunting-gathering and wage earning samples, but high in the agricultural samples. Both social and individual connectedness were found to be relatively higher in agricultural than the hunting-gathering and wage earning samples. It was also evident that cultural variables (societal size, social conformity, social and individual connectedness) formed a cohesive cluster indicating that there was a definite patterning among these variables and that they were inseparable from each other.

With respect to cognitive dimensions, the analyses revealed that the level of intraunit distinctiveness (differentiation) of hunting-gathering and wage earning samples was higher than that of the agricultural samples. On the other hand, the level of extraunit connectedness (contextualisation) of the hunting-gathering sample was lower than that of the agricultural and wage earning samples respectively. In general, the agricultural and wage earning samples presented evidence of greater achievement in the domains of language, mathematics and science than the hunting-gathering sample. However, differences between boys and girls in all test performances were less evident in the hunting-gathering than other samples. There was also evidence for "task specificity" with respect to gender effect on performance across different subsistence level groups. Multiple Regression Analyses revealed that "years of school education" was the strongest predictor of children's performance on both cognitive as well as achievement measures. Subsistence economy and urban contact also made significant contribution to a number of measures.

In the second study Berry, Bennett, Denny, Mishra & Turner (1999) examined variations along two cognitive dimensions (contextualisationdecontextualisation and differentiation-integration) using six measures: problem solving, perceptual judgement, disembedding, linguistic, visual and reasoning. Seven samples were drawn that varied in ecological adaptation, representing gathering (India), hunting (Canada, Ghana), agricultural (China, Ghana, India) and industrial-based (Canada) populations. Results provide moderate support for the hypothesized linear decrease in contextualisation and the curvilinear variation in differentiation, across this ecological range.

At the level of cultural experiences, attempts made in respect of unpackaging acculturation show a considerable promise for the development of theory. Distinction between "test" and "contact" acculturation (Berry *et al.*, 1986; Mishra *et al.*, 1996) is quite useful. Despite being highly interrelated, they are not potent enough to displace the effects of long-lasting cultural and psychological adaptations of groups to their ecology, unless they are rooted deeply into the life of people.

On the contrary, there appears to be little consistent evidence within cultures for the postulated role of socialization in cognitive style. From a methodological viewpoint, the "operative" role of socialization can be claimed only when evidence for its importance is demonstrated both across and within cultures. While evidence for the former appears to be consistently present for socialization, within-culture studies are seriously required to make theoretically strong assertions about the postulated role of socialization in the development of psychological differentiation. There is also need to incorporate other dimensions of socialization besides focusing on the "compliance-assertion" dimension. Cross-cultural application of this theory has provided ample evidence for differences in the level of differentiation among individuals and groups at various age levels. One may choose to interpret these differences as indicating different levels (high or low) of development of individual or groups. If this interpretation is used, then the notion of "developmental deficit" or "developmental lag" is highly likely to be imposed on individuals or groups who obtain lower scores on the tests of perceptual or cognitive differentiation. Data accumulated over the last three decades from diverse cultural settings do not lead to this interpretation. On the other hand, the proposition that FD people would have highly developed interpersonal skills has not been thoroughly tested. Hence, the bipolarity of the dimension (that FI are high on cognitive restructuring and FD on interpersonal competencies) is less strongly established. This domain needs to be addressed seriously in research, particularly in the Indian society, which is generally characterized by enduring relationships of individuals and groups.

CONCLUSION

The theory of psychological differentiation makes a great promise to the study of cognition and cognitive development across cultures. It demonstrates different patterning of cultural elements, cognitive performances as well as the central processes that connect them. It reveals that the effect of culture on cognition cannot be explored simply by observing the performance of certain cultural groups on some cognitive tasks. What we need to do is to analyse the cultural life of groups, behavioural competencies that are valued in a given culture, and the manner in which these are nurtured among individuals in a given culture. A distinction of cognitive process, ability, competence and performance has also to be maintained in order to reveal the complexity of their relationships.

As we have mentioned in the beginning, theories differ enormously with respect to the patterning of the elements of culture, cognition and the processes through which these are connected. This diversity does not permit an easy conclusion with respect to the relationship between culture and cognition. Psychological differentiation theory maintains that cognitive processes are universal, but cognitive competencies develop in different ways according to the demands of one's ecology and culture. A valid inference about these competencies cannot be drawn without situating assessment into the broader cultural life of individuals or groups. Recent developments with respect to the conceptualisation of cultural and cognitive dimensions are quite encouraging. We may hope that researchers would pay more attention to these elements in future studies in this field particularly in the context of social and cultural changes taking place globally.

References

Bagley, C. (1984) Cultural diversity, migration and cognitive styles in R. Samuda, J.W. Berry, & M. Lafferriere (Eds.), *Multiculturalism in Canada: Social and Educational Perspectives* (pp. 368-381). Toronto Allyn & Bacon.

Bagley, C. (1988) Cognitive style and cultural adaptation in Blackfoot, Japanese Jamaican, Italian and Angloceitic children in Canada in G. Verma & C.

Bagley (Eds.), *Cross-cultural Studies of Personality, Attitudes and Cognition*. London: Macmillan.

Bagley, C. Iwawaki, S. & Young, I. (1983) Japanese children: Group-oriented but not field dependent in C. Bagley & G. Verma (Eds.), *Multicultural Childhood.* Aldershot Gower.

Berry, J.W. (1966). Temne and Eskimo perceptual skills. *International Journal of Psychology, I,* 207-229.

Berry, J.W. (1976) Human ecology and cognitive style: Comparative studies in cultural and psychological adaptation. New York: Sage/Haisted

Berry, J.W. (1981). Developmental issues in the comparative study of psychological differentiation in R.H. Munroe, R.I., Munroe, & B.B. Whiting (Eds.), *Handbook of Cross-Cultural Human Development* (pp. 475-498). New York: Garland.

Berry, J.W. (1983). Textured contexts: Systems and situations in cross-cultural psychology. In S.H. Irvine & J.W. Berry (Eds.), *Human Assessment and Cultural Factors* (117-126) New York: Plenum.

Berry, J.W. (1987). The comparative study of cognitive abilities. In S.H. Irvine & S. Newstead (Eds.), *Intelligence and Cognition: Contemporary Frames of Reference* (pp. 393-420). Dordrecht: Nijhoff.

Berry, J.W. (1991) Cultural variation in field dependence-independence in S. Wapner & J. Demick (Eds.), *Field Dependence-Independence: Cognitive Style Across the Life Span* (pp. 289-308) Hillsdale, N.J. Lawrence Eribaum.

Berry, J.W., Bennet, J.A., Denny, J.P., Mishra, R.C., & Turner, N. (1999). *Ecology, Culture and Cognitive Processing.* Unpublished manuscript.

Berry, J.W., van de Koppel, J.M.H., Senechal, C., Annis, R.C., Bahuchet, S., Cavalli-Sforza, D.D., & Witkin, H.A. (1986). *On the Edge of the Forest: Cultural Adaptation and Cognitive Development in Central Africa.* Lisse: Swets & Zeitlinger.

Boldt, E. (1989). Social conformity and structural tightness. Unpublished manuscript.

Gamble, T., & Ginsberg, P. (1981) Differentiation: Cognitive and social evolution *Journal of Cross-cultural Psychology, 12*, 445-459.

Goodenough, D.R. (1986). History of field dependence construct. In M. Bertini, C. Pizzamigho, & S. Wapner (Eds.), *Field Dependence in Psychological Theory Research and Application* (pp. 5-14) Hillsdale, N.J. Eribaum.

Gruenfeld, I.W., & Lin. T (1984) Social behaviour in field independents and dependents in an organic group. *Human Relations, 37*, 721-741.

Mishra, K. (1998) Cognitive style of Tharu children in relation to daily life activities and experience of schooling. Unpublished doctoral thesis, Banaras Hindu University, India.

Mishra, R.C. (1996a) Perceptual differentiation in relation to children's daily life activities. *Social Science International, 12*, 1-11.

Mishra, R.C. (1996b) Cognitive processes, cultural adaptations, and education of children of some tribal groups. New Delhi: NCERT.

Mishra, R.C. (1997) Cognition and cognitive development. In J.W. Berry, P.R.

Dasen, & T.S. Saraswathi (Eds.), *Handbook of Cross-cultural Psychology, Vol. 2* (pp. 143-175) Boston Allyn & Bacon.

Mishra, R.C. (2000). Perceptual, learning, and memory processes. In J. Pandey (Ed.), *Psychology in India Revisited: Developments in the Discipline, Vol. 1* (94-150). New Delhi: Sage.

Mishra, R.C., & Singh, D.V. (1999). *Socialization Variables in Cognitive Development of Rural Indian Children.* Presented at the symposium on "Ethnotheories of child development and value of children in cultural context", University of Konstanz, July 11-13.

Mishra, R.C., Sinha, D. & Berry, J.W. (1996). Ecology, acculturation and psychological adaptation: A study of Adivasis in Bihar. New Delhi: Sage.

Sinha, D. (1978) Story-pictorial F.F.T.: A culturally appropriate test of perceptual disembedding *Indian Journal of Psychology, 53*, 160-71.

Sinha, D (1979) Perceptual style among nomadic and transitional agriculturalist Birhors. In L. Eckensberger, W.J. Lonner, & Y.H. Poortinga (Eds.), *Cross-cultural Contributions to Psychology* (pp. 83-93). Lisse: Swets & Zeitlinger.

Sinha, D. (1980). Sex differences in psychological differentiation among different cultural groups *International Journal of Behavioural Development, 3*, 455-466.

Sinha, D. (1982). Socio-cultural factors and the development of perceptual and cognitive skills. *Review of Child Development Research, 6*, 441-472.

Sinha, D. (1997). Indigenising psychology in J.W. Berry, Y.H. Poortinga, & J. Pandey (Eds.), *Handbook of Cross-cultural Psychology,* Vol. 1 (pp. 129-169) Boston Allyn & Bacon.

Sinha, D., & Shrestha, A.B. (1992). Eco-cultural factors in cognitive style among children from hills and plains of Nepal *International Journal of Psychology, 27*, 49-59.

Sinha, G. (1988). Exposure to industrial and urban environments and formal schooling as factors in psychological differentiation. *International Journal of Psychology, 23*, 707-719.

Witkin, H.A. Dyk, R.B., Faterson, H.F., Goodenough, D.R., & Karp, S. (1962) *Psychological Differentiation.* New York Wiley.

Witkin, H.A., & Goodenough, D.R. (1981). *Cognitive Style: Essence and Origins.* New York: International University Press.

3

PERCEIVED ENVIRONMENT AND ASPECTS OF SOCIAL COGNITION AMONG VILLAGERS

PREM SAGAR NATH TIWARI

INTRODUCTION

India is a country of villages and agriculture is a central vocation. However, the unavoidable effects of modernization, westernization, urbanization, and industrialization have been instrumental in changing the traditional life style of the villagers. The gap between city and village, in many areas, has decreased. At the same time, village population is suffering from poverty, lack of resources and large masses are compelled to live under impoverished conditions. These problems have been recognized by the national leaders and as well as planners and attempts have been made to change the situation. Such effort, have been directed towards mainly generating resources. The various development agencies have been engaged in this endeavour. As a matter of fact, a lot of input is being given to villages for their progress. The outcome of such efforts are visible in terms of infrastructure development and related activities. The changes, thus introduced through injecting the resources are expected to change the mental make-up of the rural people, which in turn may sustain the process of development. Unfortunately, rural development does not follow a mechanical model and the responses of the villagers to various developmental programmers have been quite different. This raises a pertinent question about the development plans and corresponding changes in the psychological make-up of rural people.

It was realized that in a predominantly agrarian economy like that of India where majority of the population lives in the villages, solution of the massive problems of poverty and employment lay in the iterated development of rural areas. Hence the Government decided to focus on bringing about all-round development of the villages.

In the pre-independence era many sporadic attempts were made to certain projects like Shri Niketan Project (1920), Gorgon Project (1920), Marathon Project (1926), Baroda Rural Reconstruction Scheme (1929-30) and Firka Development Scheme (1946). At this stage a specific mention may be made of "the Grow More Food Campaign" (19 GMFC, 1943), as the first main landmark in the direct efforts of the Government to increase food production rapidly. However all policies and schemes proved futile. All the benefits were availed by landlords and zamindars. It could not improve the lot of the common villager. In the post-independent era, some such efforts like 'Nilokheri Experiment' and 'Etawah Pilot Project" were significant. All these attempts had their own strengths weaknesses and limitations. Though all these projects could not create expected impact but their successes and failures stood the planners in good stead in designing rural development strategy in the independent India.

In 1950-51 when the Planning Commission formulated First Five Year Plan, the working of GMFC was reviewed by the Ministry of Food and Agriculture and certain important policy changes were made and a variety of programmes like Land Reform, Cooperative Farming, Intensive Agricultural Programme (IAP), Intensive Agricultural District Programme (IADP), Small Farmers Development Agency (SFDA), Marginal Farmers and Agricultural Labourers Development Agency (MFAL), Drought Prone Area Programme (DPAP), Command Area Development Agency (CADA), Special Livestock Production Programme (SLPP), Rural Industrialization and District Industries Centre (DIC), Antyodaya Programme, Training of Rural Youth for Self Employment (TRYSEM) and Integrated Rural Development Programme (IRDP) were started.

The world has witnessed a phenomenal progress in the field of science and technology which holds in credible promises to the well-being of the mankind. But at the same time it is also a fact that the benefits of this grandeur has not permeated in all the parts of the world and all the sections of society uniformly, with the result, a large section of mankind has been staggering in inertia and inadequacy while the few psycho-socio economic elite has been successful in manipulating the technology for exploring new heights of their aspiration. Majority of Indian villages still live in poverty.

Because of so many impediments, like inadequate emphasis on rural development, inadequate agricultural technology and inadequate land distribution, the proper and adequate development of Indian villages could not take place. Another handicap which delimits the prospects of agrarian transformation is related to socio-cultural and psychological barriers. It has been observed by the students of village-India, that the rural people are ignorant, conservative and uneducated. This makes them nonadaptive and reluctant. The susceptibility to modern influences is low.

It must be clearly understood that rural development in any democratic society cannot be brought about only by plans, targets, budgets, technology and functional gadgets but by effective use of these elements for changing the mind and consequent action of the people in such ways that they use these resources for their socio-economic betterment. The process of all-round rural development is a complex phenomenon, wherein, various factors are interwoven and often interchangeably interrelated. Broadly, the factors may be categorized as (a) environmental factors and (b) human factors. The environmental factors will encompass the village problems which need to be attended to. Development, essentially is a change in a desirable direction. It is here that the human factors play an important role as they hold the key to retard or accelerate the process of change.

According to Singh (1986) the importance of human factor in development was greatly undermined because of obsession with economic development. Development was considered a synonyms of economic growth and prosperity. The experiences of economic development in the third world countries after the Second World War and also the emergence of West Germany and Japan from ashes to world economic powers have demonstrated the role of non-economic and human factors in economic development. Three important points have emerged from the developmental studies of the last few decades. The human factor is an important correlate of economic development. It has been realised that economic development *per se* is not goal of a society. It is only a means to obtain necessary conditions for the development of the potentialities of human individuals. It is becoming increasingly obvious that the present socio-political and economic structure in India entrenched in social inequality, is a deterrent to the human resource mobilization on a mass scale.

In fact the situation demands creation of new outlook among the village people towards the way they feel and react to their present surroundings, the way they think and feel about the forces of change which confront them from within and outside. The village people must first become conscious of the deficiencies of the way they live before they may be expectant to desire to live differently. But the desire will be realised only when they take positive approach towards building new values, new ways of living and the improved ways of making a good living. This ultimately needs concerted efforts for creating the social climate charged with favourable attitude towards change, faith in science and technology, higher aspirations, extensive information seeking thirst etc. which should be the business of all those who are entrusted with the responsibilities of helping rural people, developing socially, psychologically and economically.

It is surprising that the study of rural masses has been subjected to a gross negligence on the part of Indian social scientists in general and psychologists in particular. We still have only meagre empirical data concerning the psycho-dynamics of the rural people, which can be utilised in planning for transformation of rural folk. With increasing realization of these problems, we note a gradual shift towards socially relevant research. In the last three decades, a number of studies have been sponsored by Government and Semi-government agencies like Institute of Community Development, Indian Council of Agricultural Research, Agricultural Universities, Indian Council of Social Science Research. Besides this individual research have also contributed. In these studies some critical variables involved in rural growth and development have been identified.

Social scientists generally agree that attitudes, motives and other psychological characteristics of farmers are associated with level of rural development. Several studies have explored the role of these factors in behaviours of farmers. Sinha (1969) has extended the scope of these studies by including attitudes aspirations, risk taking and opinion in his investigations. For Sinha, the main reason for reluctance to change lies in the realm of Human Motivation. In one of his studies Muthayya (1971) revealed that the people of villages still clamouring for satisfaction of the basic needs and the expectations that were raised by variety of programmes could not be fulfilled as the people did not have the basic resources to alleviate their existing conditions. Jaiswal & Deva (1974) observed that progressiveness of farmers was related to a number of social, personal and psychological characteristics. Deokar, Thorat and Sawant (1978) studied the influence of certain psychological characteristics i.e., knowledge, attitude, aspiration, incentive, perception, business-outlook and planning orientation on the productivity level of farmers. Tiwari (1986, 88) on the basis of his studies conducted in villages of Eastern Uttar Pradesh presented a working model of process of rural development. This model contends that development involves individual as well as societal (structural) level variables. It is argued that the individual exists and operate within a social structure, which is responsible for the provision of necessary input of developmental process. However structure itself is not sufficient. Individual's behaviours are the proximal and the necessary operations involved in the process which like other behaviours have some motivational and attitudinal pre-requisitions. Also the developmental outcomes constantly influence the social structure as well as individual motivation by providing feedback. In the case of Indian villagers the social system is largely incompatible with the demands of development. This mismatch can be resolved by transforming the motivational orientation of the individual as well as introducing changes at the structural level. This model assumes that individual's motivational orientation leads to attitudinal change (readiness to accept change) which in turn leads to behaviours (e.g. risk taking) and consequently to rural development. Singh (1984) has also identified the socio-psychological pre-requisites of rural development and argued for multi-level strategies for development.

In psychological literature studies on various aspects of social cognition have been reported in relation to certain psychological and background variables. Muthayya (1972) reports that the belief system of the villagers is strong in matters relating to God and religion but not so in other areas. Pandey (1973) in his study found that religious knowledge was a source for development of beliefs and practices but the process of translating knowledge into beliefs and practices are influenced by many socio-psychological and other external factors. Religion is critical factor for economic life in India. Vyas *et al.* (1975) found that one of the poorest tribal groups of India, the Warlis, were found to have strong religious belief that God created them last as the lowest tribe. Singh (1984) found that stereotypes of the low caste and tribal subjects about themselves were unfavourable, while they held favourable stereotypes for upper caste. He has also reported that socially disadvantaged groups have more negative and less positive personality-cum-attitudinal traits. Shand (1978) analysed the policy of developing agriculture mainly with government help, and observed that most countries, including India, are faced with the problem of modernising traditional agriculture.

Thus the past developmental activities have a history of several decades. There have been many attempts to study the impact of developmental activities on production and psychological changes among villagers. But little attempt have been made to see the way these changes lead to formulation and modification of value, attitude, beliefs, etc. which constitute social cognition in important ways. The study of these aspects of social cognition is important not only to see the impact of developmental activities but also to look into the dynamics involved in sustaining those changes. Very little attempts have been made from this perspective.

It is a truism that rural people are treated within a defined category which is prefixed and accepted stereotypically without any empirical evidence. The implications of these notions are decisive in our planning efforts proposed for the upliftment of these people in important ways. The empirical studies of the rural masses undertaken by sociologists, anthropologists and psychologists have generally treated village life as secondary to urban life and considered it as a form of deviation from the majority or the proper urban culture. Their analysis begins with acceptance of the urban life as desirable goal for villages or for any other group. Villagers are treated as deficient. The present study is an attempt to put village life in its own perspective and treating it as a case of difference rather than deficiency. It is argued that villagers life should be understood in its own right since imposition of external criteria is bound to distort the nature of reality. Thus the study emphasises the psychological frame of reference within which rural people operate and function. More specifically beliefs are among various aspects of social cognition, which enables an individual to deal effectively with the society. Now human race seems to realize with some panic, that the environmental dimensions of human existence cannot be ignored anymore. Environment plays an important role in development. Physical and psychological aspects of environments constitutes a large part of an individual experience and should therefore effect his/her attitudes and beliefs not only directly but also indirectly through their impact on the social and economic organisations of society in which the individual lives. Therefore an attempt has been made to identify the pattern of beliefs and perceived environment of rural people, who have experienced various developmental programme and have responded well. A set of similar villages lacking developmental activities is used for comparison purposes.

METHOD

Sample

A sample of 150 villagers were drawn from three developed and three undeveloped villages of eastern Uttar Pradesh. Subjects were further divided into three age groups (18-25 years), (26-40 years) and above 40 years. They represented several caste groups and socio-economic levels prevailing in the region.

Measures

In order to study various aspects of beliefs and perceived environment among villagers, two different measures were employed.

(I) Beliefs

This measure dealt with different types of beliefs which are prevalent in villages. The items were related with rural rituals, ceremonies, customs, religious rituals, social harmony, moral behaviour, entertainment activities family life, relationship with other members of villages, friendship, etc. For each item three alternative responses were provided (i.e. agree, uncertain and disagree). The brief description of the measure is given in Table 3.1.

Table 3.1: Psychomatric Characteristics of Various Measures

	Measures	*No. of Items*	*Range*	*Split-half Reliability*
1.	Beliefs:			
(a)	Religious	20	20-36	.81
(b)	Social	10	10-30	.72
(c)	Moral	19	19-57	.74
(d)	Aesthetic	2	2-6	.68
2.	Perceived Environment			
(a)	Physical	13	13-39	.71
(b)	Psycho-social	21	21-63	.74

(II) Perceived Environment

On the basis of interviews of villagers some important environmental characteristics were identified and a set of items related to these characteristics was prepared. For each of these items three alternatives were provided. Scores 3, 2, and 1 were assigned to the responses reflecting the richest moderate and the poorest perception of the environment respectively. The items were related with physical features, mass media, family atmosphere, community atmosphere, etc. They dealt with two major aspects of environment i.e., physical and psychosocial. The final version of the measure consisted of 34 items. A brief description of this measure is also presented in Table 3.1

(III) Personal Observation

Apart from obtaining pertinent empirical data by employing a set of measures in a quantitative approach, a qualitative approach was also used together the patterns of beliefs. In this approach interviews of informants, observations and field notes were used. Villagers were interviewed about awareness of their rights, national and provincial leaders, political parties, etc. Informants were asked about rural rituals, ceremonies, religious rituals, conflicts, relation with neighbour, village atmosphere, attitude towards ruling party, liquor consumption, effect of religion on their life style, role of education in development, etc. The answer recorded by the researcher. A subjective observational method was also used and field notes were taken of the life style of rural people.

RESULTS AND DISCUSSION

The data obtained in the present study has been subjected to a variety of analysis. For the purpose in this chapter only findings based on 2 × 3 ANOVA, multiple regression analysis and observations shall be discussed.

The scores obtained on various types of beliefs were subjected to separated 2 × 3 ANOVA with two levels of development (i.e., developed and undeveloped) and three levels of age (Younger, Middle and Older). Results are presented in Table 3.1 suggests that villagers belonging to developed categories scored higher on each and every belief except for religious belief where subjects from undeveloped villages scored higher than their counterpart subjects from developed villagers. Similarly the main effects of age also reached the significance levels suggested that relatively older villagers scored higher on various beliefs except for aesthetic beliefs. Development and age interaction also reach the significance level for religious beliefs that villagers belonging to different categories of villages and different age level differ significantly on religious beliefs. However interaction effects for other beliefs could not reach the significance level. Even in a better way then counterpart subjects belonging to older age levels.

Similarly main effects of development was found to be significant for perceived physical as well as psycho-social environment suggests that villagers belonging to developed categories perceived their environment better in comparison to villagers of undeveloped categories. Main effects of age as well as the interaction effects could not reach the significance level. Except for main effect of psycho-social event which suggests that relatively younger villagers perceived their psycho-social environment better than their counterpart subjects.

Table 3.2: Mean Scores on Measures of Beliefs and Perceived Environment as a Function of Main Effect

	Dev.	*Undev*	*F (1, 144)*	*Younger*	*Middle*	*Older*	*F (2, 144)*
Beliefs							
(a) Religious	40.96	49.08	88.90	42.02	45.17	47.17	12.89
(b) Social	25.75	22.43	58.16	23.12	24.19	24.75	6.00
(c) Moral	51.30	47.43	26.13	47.05	49.28	51.76	12.92
(d) Aesthetic	4.71	4.05	11.74	4.89	4.16	4.09	7.15
Perceived Environment							
(a) Physical	27.45	21.72	92.37	25.21	24.10	24.41	1.25
(b) Psycho-Social	46.82	42.60	18.80	45.82	45.15	42.61	4.54
P<01							
P<05							

In order to explore the contributions of certain background variables (Age, Education and land holding) as well as physical and psycho-social aspects of perceived environment for different type of beliefs, multiple regression analysis was performed. (See Table 3.3). Results indicate that for the religious belief the total variance contributed by significant predictors (age, land holding and physical environment) was 25%. However land holding and physical environment were negatively correlated with religious beliefs.

As it is evident from the total that age and physical environment

Table 3.3: Summary of Multiple Regression Analysis

Predictors	*Beliefs*											
	Religious			Social			Moral			Aesthetic		
	r	Reg coef	t	r coef	reg	t	r coef	reg	t	r coef	reg	t
Age	.23	.14	3.29*	.27	06	3.24*	33	.13	4.18*	–.18	–.02	–2.12*
Education	.18	.08	.59	.05	.05	.79	.04	.17	1.46	.04	–.01	–.47
Land Holdings	–.20	–.09	–2.04*	.23	.03	1.30	.20	.04	1.03	–.04	–.01	–.36
Physical Env.	–.41	–.53	–4.31	.33	.21	3.69*	.21	.22	2.31*	–.16	–.05	2.03*
Psycho-Social Env.	–.28	–.08	–.83	.10	–.02	–.49	.02	–.06	–.86	0.6	–.05	–.35

R = .50 R2=	R = .44 R2 = .19	R = 024 R2 = .05
F (5, 144) = 9.63	F (5, 144) – 7.10	F (5, 144) = 15.8
p<.01	p<.01	P<.01

contributed significantly for social and moral beliefs explained 19 per cent, 18 per cent of the total variance respectively.

Observational Findings

In addition to self-report data collected with the help of questionnaires and other verbal measures, an attempt was also made to understand the aspects of social cognition in terms of categories and experiences of villagers. To this end, observations and field notes of the researchers were used. A qualitative analysis of the data available through these techniques was undertaken to furnish an account of social cognition pertaining to some of the relevant aspects of village life. This analysis was used to supplement the findings from a different methodological perspective. It may be noted that the present qualitative analysis did not cover the entire range of social cognition included in the preceding analysis and was a preliminary attempt rather than exhaustive venture.

Religion still occupies the central position in the life of villagers. Villagers shared a broader notion of religion in terms of "*dharma-karma*". In fact, a number of villagers expressed the view that everything is organised around "*dharma*". Individual, interpersonal and community level activities manifested on intimate relationship with principles of "*dharma* and *karma*". At an abstract level they displayed the notion that whatever exists, exists in certain relationships which is guided and coordinated by the principles of "*dharma* and *karma*". This was also reflected in the various practices of daily life including performance of individual duty, meeting of social obligations and conduct of secret religious ceremonies. It was observed that villagers participated in religious (*dharmik*) activities with joy and commitment. Another remarkable feature of religious activity was that it constituted individual as well as social phenomenon simultaneously. In all such activities individual responsibility is crucial but social orientation is found to be of equal significance. All life rituals (*sanskaras*) provided a clear evidence to this effect. None, of them was complete unless the whole community participated. On several occasions, it was observed that participation of a member of not only one's own family or community but of other communities was an essential ingredient. Illustrations of this type of socio-religious transactions were observed on occasions of *barhi*, *mundan*, *janeu*, marriage, *katha*, Holi, etc. The villagers could not distinguish between "the social" and "the religious" as distinct and separate compartments. The interrelatedness, however, was often shaped by the dominance of social and religious on different occasions.

The pattern of religious, social beliefs observed in the villagers displayed noticeable impact of prosperity and affluence of the people. In terms of developed and undeveloped villages it was found that while basic structure of socio-religious beliefs was similar, the sophistication and details shared variations. This was largely a function of resource availability and social prestige attached with the people. It was observed that rituals were relatively more elaborate and complex in high socio-economic level villagers from developed villages. It is also important to note that the level of sophistication in rituals and ceremonies was also related to the position of caste group along the caste hierarchy.

The religio-social beliefs and related behaviours were also related to the level of education and modernisation. In this context, it may be noted that the elaborate and sophisticated performance of rituals in developed villages does not necessarily mean that the people are more religious. On the contrary, high education and high socio-economic status were more pertinent to the social aspects of religious activity rather than religious activity as such. The villagers from less developed villages were relatively more religious and less social. The prosperous villagers used religious occasions, as occasions for the display of their prosperity and social status rather than real religious values and beliefs. Thus it seems that the religious component in itself has become secondary in developed villages.

In terms of patterns of social interaction and community life, it was noted that there was greater awareness of social purposes and community goals in developed villages. Interestingly, the network of social organisation in developed villages was stronger and more functional. They were taking more interest in group level activity and pursuit of social goals. This pattern corresponded with the increased needs of these people and was also reflected in the structure of socio-political configuration of the respective villages. Thus, social orientations, political activity and participations went together.

Observations also indicated that villagers in general subscribed to a pervasive moral belief. Closely related to the belief in "*dharma* and *karma*", it was observed that villagers considered *Ahimsa* (non-violence), duty obedience, forgiveness and harmony as core moral beliefs. This was common to both groups of villagers : developed as well as undeveloped. Although, the villagers of undeveloped area were less exquisite and elaborate in their experiences. It appeared that morality is not a matter of mutual contract rather it covers the entire range of human and nonhuman existence. Whatever exists, has a place and obligation to everything else. Also, human actions were believed to be continuous rather than discrete. The continuity in human behaviour and characteristics integrates individual across time and space. Thus the kind of natural moral order is believed to exist. In this moral principle related behavioural exchange across individuals and across transactions within the individual, the actions and consequences form a continuous stream and individual cannot absolve himself from responsibility. Their actions are good or bad, positive or negative. Many villagers pointed out that the intention and quality of effort are important rather than consequences. However, the younger and cognitively modern people favoured the view of behaviour in which the consequence of action was more crucial than the factors responsible for the outcome. Usually the villagers cited stories from Hindu mythology in support of their arguments and convictions. These narratives were handed over from generation to generation through oral discourse.

In this way a cluster of social moral, religious beliefs is operative in villagers. These beliefs are largely similar across developed and undeveloped villages but their manifestations are moderated by the availability of resources.

Village life is exposed to many new changes in the language, style of life and vocation. Due to various reasons, agriculture is becoming a less and less interesting and useful. The responses of villagers indicated that the practice of agriculture is becoming more complex and challenging. The traditional ways and means of agriculture are not cost effective. It was found that a number of villagers from developed villages favoured new technology including from developed villages favoured new technology including pesticides and other materials for greater agricultural production. Also they were more open minded and experimented with agricultural practices. On the other hand, majority of villagers from undeveloped villages were rigid in their approach and hesitant so far as innovative and modern agricultural practices are concerned. It seemed that the difference between two groups of villagers is not due to differences between the resource availability rather it indicated differential in approach to issues.

In conclusion it can be said that the present study has generated a linkage between various beliefs as well as the perceptions about their environment with rural development. In recent years a high priority has been attached to develop to rural areas in most of the developing countries including India. Rural Development is viewed as the progressive transformation of rural areas. This is a part of larger process of social development, which refers to the process of planned institutional change to bring about a better fit between human needs and aspirations on the one hand and social policies and programmes on the other. Sunthanam (1989) suggests that the whole planning process should be of bottom-up approach, viz. start where the people are. The user of the programme should also be the decision maker. Hence the present approach of top-down where the programmes/schemes are formulated at a higher levels for the people in the rural areas need to be reviewed and modified so as to give importance to the person to involve him right from the stage of need identification and also in fixing priorities. May be the existing set-up does not permit such sudden change from top-down bottom-up approach. Hence an attempt need be made to merge the top-down and bottom-up approaches, where both the givers and the receivers of the programme play a mutually supportive role in evolving a programme.

References

Abram, D. (1997) *The Spell of the Sensuous*. New York, Vintage

Deokar, S.D., Thorat, S. and Samant, G.K. Farm productivity level of farmers in relation to their psychological characteristic. *Indian Journal of Applied Psychology*, 1978, 15, 93-99.

Derrida, J. (1987) *Writing and Difference*. (Trans.) University of Chicago Press.

Eggert, J. (1999) *Song of the Meadowlark: Exploring Values for Sustainable Future*. Berkeley, Calif., Ten Sped Press

Jaensch, E.R. (1920) Einege allgeminnere Frageb der Psychologie undo Biologie de Denkens. Arb. *Psychol. Phil.*, 1.

Jaensch, E.R. (?) Eidetic Image (Trans.)

Jaiswal, N.K. and Deva A.K. Relative Importance of factors associated with progressiveness of farmers. *Behavioural Science and Community Development*, 1974, 8, 12-25.

Kurukkal, S. (1997) The "Other" in Anthropology and Philosophy, *Economic & Political Weekly*, 1406-09.

Levinas, E. (1981) *Otherwise than Being or Beyond Essence*. (Trans.) Martinus Nijhoff.

Muthayya, B.C. Superstitious beliefs of villagers. *Community Development and Panchayati Raj Digest*, 1972 3(4) 267-272.

Muthayya, B.C., *Farmers and Their Aspiration*. Hyderabad. National Institute of Community Development, 1971.

Pandey, Uma Dutta, Religiosity, Religious Tactics and Adoption of Innovation. Doctoral thesis in Psy., Patna. Univ. 1973, pp. 207.

Piaget, J. (1923) *Language and Thought of the Child.* (Trans.)

Shand, R.T. (Ed.) *Agricultural Development in Asia*, London: Allen & Unwin, 1972.

Singh, A.K. Poverty and Prejudice in India, Psychological Studies in Dehumanisation, UGG National Lecture, Psy. Deptt. Ranchi Univ. 1984.

Sinha, D. *Indian Villages in Transition: A Motivational analysis.* New Delhi : Associated Publishing House, 1969.

Tiwari, P.S.N. Motivational Correlates of Changes Proneness Among Farmers. *Indian Journal of Community Guidance Service*, Vol. 3, No. 3, Sept. 1986.

Tiwari, P.S.N. Change Progeness and Agro-Economic Development, *Personality Study and Group Behaviour* Vol. 8, No. 1 January, 1988.

Vyas, V.S., Moulik, T.K., Desai, B.M. and Gupta, Ranjit, Rural Development for Rural Poor, Dharampur Project Part I. The Setting Ahmedabad : Indian Institute of Management, 1975.

Vygotsky, *Language and Thought.* (Trans.) Cambridge, Mass. Instt. Technol. Press.

Werner, H. (1961) *Comparative Psychology of Mental Development.* New York, Science Edition Inc.

4

CONCEPTUALIZATION OF INTELLIGENCE IN RURAL AND URBAN GROUPS

ANUBHUTI DUBEY & ADESH AGARWAL

INTRODUCTION

The role of context in organising and directing human growth has been underscored in the last two decades. Besides the genetic factors content and process of development of cognition is strongly influenced by sociocultural factors. These sociocultural factors determine the manner in which intellectual processes and skills develop and grow. Culture is fundamentally associated with cognition. Various attempts have been made to study socially embedded and socially shared cognitions (Resnick, Levine and Teasloy, 1991). Some psychologists take the view that knowledge is socially constructed and interpretive (Gergan, 1985). We human beings both create the culture, as well as, are inevitable parts of it and, learn culturally coded activities from generation to generation. Our assumptions about knowledge itself thus influence social cognition. Psychologists are realising that there is a need to consider cultural perspectives in order to deal with diverse social phenomena in different cultures (Moscovici, 1972; Schweder, 1991).

Western psychological theories and concept of intelligence is taken as universal but is influenced by the cultural experiences of people who have defined intelligence. Intelligence means different things to different people as—cleverness, understanding, abstract thinking, acquiring knowledge, wisdom, prudence and many others, thus underlying intellectual processes may be similar but the resultant intelligent behaviour will have to take into account the contextual factors and may, therefore, vary according to cultural factors (Sternberg, 1997).

The western concept of intelligence is totally different from that of eastern. Weschler defined intelligence as "the aggregate capacity of the individual to act purposefully, to think rationally and to deal effectively with his environment". While our Indian philosophical literature termed intelligence as "*Buddhi*". *Buddhi* must be situated in context (*Bhagwat Gita*). Buddhi includes such abilities as determination, mental effort and feelings and opinion in addition to such intellectual processes, as knowledge, discrimination and decision making (Srivastava, Tripathi and Misra, 1995b). In the Indian view, it is conceived that the mind is too closed to the source of knowledge and there is a possibility of its being influenced by the perception and activities, therefore, it is envisaged that discriminating intelligence must be developed which can observe the activities of mind yet, distance itself and from it and attain pure knowledge. In *Shankhya Yoga* the five sense organs and five motor organs are for perception and action. The mind collects the experiences and presents them to the ego which discerns and discriminates them through intelligence. *Buddhi* is said to be the driver and, mind has reins of the chariot which is owned by the self and, senses are only horses, without gaining understanding the senses are totally out of control (Das and Thapa, 2000). Japanese concept of intelligence is different from both of these. It is, therefore, clear that one cannot apply an intelligence test developed in one culture to members of another culture. It is contended that the available intelligence tests are not sensitive to sociocultural demands. It is curious to note that number of Chinese Americans employed in managerial, professional and technical occupations was approximately 55%. Flynn (1991) calculated the mean hypothetical IQ of White Americans in similar occupations would have to be 120. Whereas, in these Chinese Americans the mean IQ was only slightly below 100. This shows the limitation of IQ based predictions and limitations of accepting Western definition of intelligence as universal (Neisser *et al.*, 1996).

Several methods have been used by psychologists and educationists to find people's concepts of intelligence. These vary from direct interviews of the people, to rating of intelligent behaviours. The scales generally used to assess intelligence in India are not indigenous but, replication of western ones. When our culture, philosophy, life styles differ then it is logical to expect that the conceptualization of intelligence will also be different. It does not mean that different groups of human beings possess different intellectual abilities and processes, nevertheless, social and cultural experiences help determine the form or shape that these processes take (Neisser *et al.*,, 1996). It is with this assumption that the present investigation was undertaken. Most studies in India comparing life in urban and rural areas have focused primarily on the intensity of aversive environmental conditions across the two settings. A stimulating social setting invites and encourages the person to explore his or her surroundings which contain an abundance of opportunity for the discovery of objects, attributes and cause and effect relationships. Both social atmosphere and genetic factors contributes to the availability and utilisation of environmental information Environmental settings bearing multifarious activities, features and stimuli will produce more elaborated and more finely differentiated cognitive structures and schemata than an environment lacking stimulus variability. It also follows that, more highly differentiated society or social structures (due to its specialised institutions, settings, rules of conducts, rules of individuals and its status etc.) can lead to development of a larger number of concepts.

Living in a rural environment provides different type of stimulation and information complexity than, an urban environment, although they may have similar institutions like, schools. The specialised contribution of the educational system is directed to the acquisition of symbolic knowledge represented by language, numerical operations, vocabulary or comprehension etc.

This study is particularly designed to study the notion of intelligence as socially defined. The socially defined notion of intelligence envisages that people construe intelligent behaviour on the basis of their efforts to solve problems of daily life (Cantor and Harlow, 1994). An individual's view of what represents intelligent behaviour may well not be the same as another's. The objective of this study is to understand 'Intelligence' as conceptualized by Indian people. Differences between rural and urban, schooled and unschooled, and male and female participants concerning concept of intelligent behaviour were investigated.

METHOD

Sample: In this study a total of 160 respondents participated. They were categorised as:

Age groups	*Rural*				*Urban*			
	Schooled		*Unschooled*		*Schooled*		*Unschooled*	
	Male	*Female*	*Male*	*Female*	*Male*	*Female*	*Male*	*Female*
12-14 Years	10	10	10	10	10	10	10	10
16-18 Years	10	10	10	10	10	10	10	10

The rural respondents belongs to one of the three villages of Kushinagar district, namely Zhokawa Bazar, Pandey Patti and Dhawarahara. The unschooled rural males respondents were either working in the fields as labour or working at local tea shops. The unschooled female respondents were also doing either household works or working in the fields as labour. The schooled respondents were studying in the co-education intermediate school situated in Dhawarahara. The urban respondents were resident of Gorakhpur district headquarters. The schooled urban respondents were studying in public and government schools of Gorakhpur. The unschooled respondents were mainly working at tea shops or domestic servants or children of such people.

Materials

The tool used in this study was originally developed at NCERT and Delhi University by A.K. Srivastava and G. Misra. It consisted of an interview schedule with both free listing and closed-ended type of questions. There were a total of 14 questions. The free listing questions included the characteristics of very intelligent, less intelligent and foolish persons, the factors facilitating and restraining the development of intelligence, description of any event or story showing intelligence, the criterion for choosing characteristics of very intelligent, less intelligent and foolish people.

In closed ended type of questions there were two options, yes/no. The questions included – Whether intelligence is God-gifted? Have you ever used intelligence test? Does intelligence increases with age or decrease with age or remain stable? Whether intelligent persons are more impulsive? Do they have self control on emotions? Whether intelligent person understands the feelings of other easily? etc.

Procedure

Rapport was established with respondents and then investigator requested them to answer the questions as given in the questionnaire. They were informed that the investigator wished to find out about the qualities of intelligent and foolish people as perceived by them. For each question there were separate instructions given in the booklet which were read to respondents. The schooled respondents also read them alongwith the investigator. Both in rural and urban groups a sufficient amount of probing was done. The responses of unschooled respondents were recorded by the investigator. After data collection was completed, it was analysed.

RESULTS

The characteristics of very intelligent, less intelligent and foolish persons as stated by rural and urban, and schooled and unschooled participants were analysed on the basis of the common characteristics (given by all groups) and unique characteristics (given only by either groups).

The common characteristics of **very intelligent** people stated by both rural and urban and schooled and unschooled group of respondents have been presented in Table 4.1

The Z-values were computed which reveal differences in emphasis between subgroups of subjects. The common characteristics of very intelligent persons include characteristics reflecting social intelligence, emotional intelligence and characteristics related with task performance (Table 4.1).

The differences between groups on these characteristics were observed. In all the Z-values reported here, the group which gave significantly greater frequency of responses is mentioned first. On the following dimensions there were significant differences found in both rural *Vs.* Urban and Schooled *Vs.* Unschooled groups of respondents, i.e., "Good nature" [Rural *Vs.* Urban Z (1df)=5.32 P>.01] and (Unschooled *Vs.* Schooled [Z (1df)=5.32 P>.01], "Helping Others" [Rural *Vs.* Urban [Z (1df)=6.34 P> .01 and Schooled *Vs.* Unschooled [Z (1df) = 1.948 P> .05]. "Patience/Tolerance" [Rural *Vs.* Urban Z (1df)=5.11 P> .01] and [Schooled *Vs.* Unschooled Z (1df)=2.28 P> .05], "Respect for elders" [Rural *Vs.* Urban Z (1df) = 4.54 P> 0.1] and [Schooled *Vs.* Unschooled Z (1df) = 2.44 P> .05].

There were some characteristics on which significant differences were found between rural and urban groups of respondents but no significant differences were found in schooled and unschooled groups of respondents. These characteristics are "Active Worker" [Urban *Vs* Rural Z(1df)=2.027 P>.05] and "Do not Quarrel" [Urban *Vs.* Rural Z (1df)=2.40 P>.05].

Some unique characteristics of very intelligent people were stated only by schooled participants (regardless of rural and urban background), there were both cognitive characteristics e.g., "good decision making" and "good in studies" and emotional characteristics e.g. "loving" and

Table 4.1: Free Listing of Characteristics of Very Intelligent, Less Intelligent and Foolish Persons, Frequencies and Z values

	Rural	*Urban*	*Schooled*	*Unschooled*	Z
Very Intelligent Good Nature	45	19	26	38	a=5.32** b=5.32**
Helping Others	34	1	25	10	a=6.34** b=1.948**
Active Worker	20	32	26	26	a=2.027* b=N.S.
Patience/Tolerance	38	9	30	17	a=5.11** b=2.28*
Less Talkative	21	23	31	13	a=N.S. b=3.14**
Does not Quarrel	13	26	19	20	a=2.40* a=N.S.
Respect for elders	36	10	30	1¾	a=4.545** b=2.44*
Less Intelligent					
Quarrelling and Abusing	38	12	26	24	a=4.452** b=N.S.
Poor Work Quality	16	30	25	21	a=2.46* b=N.S.
Very Talkative	24	23	31	16	a=N.S. b=2.57*
Weak in Studies	10	24	20	14	a=2.73** b=25**
Foolish					
Lazy	27	7	18	7	a=3.906** b=2.41*
Work without prior thinking	33	13	34	12	a=3.35* b=3.84**
Show off as smart	27	2	12	17	a=5.058** b=N.S.
Do not obey elders	9	4	7	6	a=N.S. b=N.S.
Quarrelling/Abusing	51	32	28	55	a=2.948** b=4.23*
Less educated	21	11	26	6	a=2.136* b=3.96**

a=Rural *Vs.* Urban, b=Schooled *Vs.* Unschooled
p>.01**, p>.05*

task performance related characteristics e.g. "disciplined behaviour". The unique characteristics stated only by unschooled participants included cognitive characteristics as "educated" and "gives advice", as well as, characteristics of social intelligence as "has good friends", "making family happy", "pay attention to others". It also includes reference to practical intelligence, i.e., "earns money and becomes rich". Two unique characteristics stated only by urban schooled participants were "curious" and "competitive" and "understands feelings of others", which refer to aspects of social, cognitive and emotional intelligence.

The respondents were asked to point out the characteristics of "less intelligent" people also. The common characteristics of less intelligent persons included emotional, task performance and cognitive aspects of intelligence. These were – "quarrelsome and abusive", "very talkative", "poor work quality" and "weak in studies". The characteristics of "less intelligent" persons have been presented in Table 4.1. In order to find out the significance of difference between frequency of responses of various groups the Z-values were computed. There was no significant difference between schooled and unschooled groups of respondents on characteristics related to task performance i.e., "poor work quality" and characteristic of emotional intelligence, i.e., "quarrelling and abusing". There were significant difference found on emotional characteristics of "very talkative" [Z (1df)=2.57 P>.05] but there was no significant difference found between rural and urban groups. In rural and urban groups, however, there were significant differences on such characteristics as "Quarrelsome and abusive" [Rural *Vs.* Urban Z (1df)=4.452 P >. 01], "Poor work quality" (Urban *Vs.* Rural Z (1df)=2.46 P>.05) and "Work in studies" (Urban *Vs.* Rural Z (1df)=2.73 P>.01).

A significant number of rural respondents (regardless of schooling) stated three characteristics of less intelligent persons viz., "disobeying elders" (f=15) and "proud" (f=15) and "poor decision making" (f=15).

The respondents also had to free list the characteristics of "foolish" persons. The characteristics of foolish person as stated by all the groups of respondents included cognitive, social, emotional and task performance related characteristics respectively as "less educated", "show off as smart", "laziness", "do not obey elders", "quarrelling and abusing" and "work without prior thinking". The frequency and Z values, as computed for the significance of difference between groups were presented in Table 4.1 except the emotional characteristics i.e. "Do not obey elders". On all the above mentioned characteristics of foolish persons, there were significant differences found in rural and urban groups viz., "less educated" [Rural *Vs.* Urban Z (1df)=2.136 P>.05], "Show off as smart" (Rural *Vs.* Urban Z (1df)=5.058 P>.01), "Lazy" [Rural *Vs.* Urban Z (1df)=3.906 P >.01], "Quarrelling and abusing" (Rural *Vs.* Urban Z (1df)=2.948 P>.01) and "Work without prior thinking" (Rural *Vs.* Urban Z (1df)=3.35 P >.01). The rural group had mentioned all these characteristics significantly more than urban respondents. There were significant differences found between schooled and unschooled participants on the characteristics like "less educated" (Schooled *Vs* Unschooled Z (1df)=3.96 P >.01), "laziness" [Schooled *Vs.* Unschooled Z (1df)=2.41 P>.05), "Quarrelling and abusing [Unschooled *Vs.* schooled Z (1df)=4.23 P>.01], "Work without prior thinking" [Schooled *Vs.* Unschooled Z (1df)=3.84 P>.01]. The unschooled participants have reported the emotional characteristics "Quarrelling and abusing" significantly more than schooled respondents.

The unique characteristics of "foolish" persons stated only by urban schooled participants included characteristics related with cognitive, social and performance of task as "weak in studies", "unmannered" and "waste time". The unique characteristics stated only by rural participants was "intoxication" which is related with emotional and social aspect of intelligence.

Besides emphasizing the characteristics of very intelligent, less intelligent and foolish persons, the participants were requested to list freely the factors which help the development of intelligence and factors which restrain the development of intelligence. A number of factors were mentioned which are shown in Table 4.2 The respondents agreed that factors like – education, healthy atmosphere of family, good school, level of education of parents and good friends are significant contributor in facilitating the development of intelligence. Although all of the above mentioned factors were emphasized by all groups but there were significant differences in emphasis laid by different groups. The Z-value was computed which revealed the difference in rural and urban and schooled and unschooled groups for factors like – "Education" [Rural *Vs.* Urban Z(1df)=3.57p>.01] and Schooled *Vs.* Unschooled Z(1df)=1.60P>.05] and "Good" schools [Rural *Vs.* Urban Z(1df)=3.94 P>.01 and Schooled *Vs.* Unschooled Z(1df=3.94P>.01]. There was no significant difference found between both groups for the factor "level of education of parents". All the groups equally agreed about importance of this factor.

The participants were also asked to provide free listing of the factors which restrain the development of intelligence. Four such factors were

Table 4.2: Free Listing of Factors Helping and Restraining Development of Intelligence, Frequencies and Z Values

Factors which help in the development of intelligence	*Rural* *f*	*Urban* *f*	*Schooled* *f*	*Unschooled* *f*	*Z*
Education	58	36	52	42	a=3.571** b=1.608*
Healthy atmosphere of family	14	26	22	18	a=2.45* b=N.S.
Good School	20	3	20	3	a=3.944** b=3.944**
Level of education of parents	13	8	12	9	a=N.S. b=N.S.
Good Friends	11	16	21	6	a=N.S. b=3.135**
Factors which restraining the Development of Intelligence					
Bad Company	35	19	18	36	a=2.85** b=3.285**
Intoxication	16	27	27	16	a=1.99* b=1.99**
Poverty	19	6	9	16	a=2.719** b=1.54*
Illiteracy	9	35	28	16	a=4.642** b=2.14*
Criteria for choosing characteristics of intelligent behaviour					
On the basis of experience	56	11	43	24	a=7.402** b=2.987**
Watching Television	45	5	32	18	a=6.82* b=2.39*
Watching people around	65	31	50	46	a=5.584** b=N.S.
On the basis of own knowledge	0	29	15	14	a=6.04** b=N.S.
Watching Family Members	9	0	5	4	a=2.29* b=N.S.

stated by all group of respondents viz. – bad company, intoxication, poverty and illiteracy has been shown in Table 4.2. The Z values were computed which revealed the differences in groups. The difference between rural and urban, schooled and unschooled groups were – "Bad company" [Rural *Vs.* Urban Z(1df)=2.05p>.01 and Unschooled *Vs.* Schooled Z[(1df)=3.285P>.01] "Intoxication" [Urban *Vs.* Rural

Z(1df)=1.99 P>.05 and Schooled *Vs.* Unschooled Z(1df)=1.99 P>.05], "Poverty" [Rural *Vs.* Urban Z(1df)=2.71P>.01 and Unschooled *Vs.* Schooled Z(1df)=1.54P>.05], "Illiteracy" [Urban *Vs.* Rural Z(1df)=4.642 p>.01 and Schooled *Vs.* Unschooled Z(1df)=2.14P>.05]. There were two other factors which were stated only by rural participants were "unhealthy atmosphere of family" and "any chronic disease".

The respondents were asked to list freely the criterion about "how did they decide upon the characteristics of very intelligent, less intelligent and foolish person?". There were five such criterion found as "on the basis of experience", "watching television", "watching people around", "on the basis of own knowledge" and "watching family members", which have been presented in Table 4.3. This table also revealed the Z values computed for significance of difference in four groups namely – rural, urban, schooled and unschooled.

There were significant differences found between rural and urban group of respondents on all the above mentioned criterion viz., "On the basis of experience" (Rural *Vs.* Urban Z (1df)=7.402 P>.01), "Watching television" (Rural *Vs.* Urban Z (1df)=6.82 P>.01), "Watching people around" (Rural *Vs.* Urban Z (1df)=5.58 P>.01), "Watching family members" (Rural *Vs.* Urban Z (1df)=2.29 P>.05) and "On the basis of own knowledge" (Urban *Vs.* Rural Z(1df)=6.04 P>.01). Not even one of the rural group mentioned "their own knowledge" as a criteria to decide upon the characteristics of very intelligent, less intelligent and foolish person. Similarly, none of the urban group reported the criteria of "Watching Family members". In schooled and unschooled respondents there were significant differences found on only two criteria namely "On the basis of experience" (Schooled *Vs.* Unschooled Z (1df)=2.987 P>.01) and "Watching television" (Schooled *Vs.* Unschooled Z (1df)=2.39 P>.05). For other three criteria namely watching people around, on the basis of own knowledge and watching family members both schooled and unschooled respondents were equally agree.

The respondents were also asked to describe a situation or event reflecting the intelligent behaviour. Analysing the stories showing intelligent behaviour there were eight themes found in the descriptions. These themes were shown in Table 4.3. The themes were helping behaviour, showing courage, practical intelligence, folk tales, social welfare, saving one's property, learning through mistakes and taking care of family. Two themes namely "Showing courage" [Rural *Vs.* Urban Z (1df)=3.77 P>.01] and "Saving one's property" [Rural *Vs.* Urban Z (1df)=3.77 P>.01] was mentioned significantly more by rural

Table 4.3: Free Listing of Criterion of Choosing Characteristics of Intelligent Behaviour and Description of Situations Reflecting Intelligent Behaviour, Frequencies and Z-Values

	Rural	*Urban*	*Schooled*	*Unschooled*	*Z*
Criteria for choosing characteristics of intelligent behaviour	f	f	f	f	
On the basis of experience	56	11	43	24	a=7.402** b=2.987**
Watching Television	45	5	32	18	a=6.82* b=2.39*
Watching people around	65	31	50	46	a=5.584** b=N.S.
On the basis of own knowledge	0	29	15	14	a=6.04** b=N.S.
Watching family members	9	0	5	4	a=2.29* b=N.S.
Description of situation reflecting Intelligent Behaviour					
Helping Behaviour	11	11	7	15	a=N.S. b=1.99*
Showing Courage	24	6	15	15	a=3.77** b=N.S.
Practical Intelligence	9	10	13	6	a=N.S. b=1.7*
Folk Tales	2	6	5	3	a=N.S. b=N.S.
Social Welfare	2	7	3	6	a=1.73* b=N.S.
Saving one's Property	13	0	10	3	a=3.777** b=2.04*
Learning through Mistakes	7	4	10	3	a=N.S. b=2.884**
Taking carc of family	6	11	0	17	a=3.324** b=4.372**

P>.01**
P>.05*
a=Rural *Vs.* Urban
b=Schooled *Vs.* Unschooled

participants. The theme of "Learning through mistakes" was mentioned by schooled participants significantly more [Schooled *Vs.* Unschooled Z (1df)=2.88 P>.01].

A number of questions were asked to the participants. These closed-ended type of questions had two options to answer, yes/no. The percentage was computed which have been presented in Table 4.4. Amongst these questions one is "Whether intelligence is God gifted? Among all the participants 45% agreed that intelligence is God gifted.

The next question asked to the respondents was "Whether intelligence can be increased through training"? Among all the participants 70.62% said that intelligence can be increased through training. But the percentage of separate groups reveal the difference in agreement with this statement amongst groups. The percentages of different groups are rural (50%), urban (91.25%), schooled (86.25%) and unschooled (55%).

The respondents were also asked "Whether they have ever used intelligence test"? Out of a total of 160 respondents, only 2 rural schooled female were seen intelligence test before. They said that somebody came in their school and had given intelligence test to them to fill it.

The respondents were asked "Whether intelligence increases with age or decreases with age or remains stable with age"? Among all the participants 79.37% were agreed that intelligence increased with the advancement of age but there was difference in rural (97.5%) and urban (61.25%) and schooled (91.5%) and unschooled (67.5%). So the rural and schooled respondents were agreed with this statement more than urban and unschooled respondents.

On the statement "Whether intelligence decreases with age"? Only 15.31% participants were agreed and separate groups like – rural (12.5%), urban (18.75%), schooled (10%) and unschooled (20%) agreed.

On the statement "Whether intelligence remains stable with the age"? 39.37% respondents agreed with the statement and there was no significant difference between rural (42.5%) and urban (36.25%) and schooled (42.5%) and unschooled (36.25%) groups of respondents.

Six questions were asked related with the cognitive and emotional qualities of intelligent behaviour. The questions related with the cognitive qualities of intelligent behaviour were "Whether intelligent persons plans more efficiently than other persons"?, i.e. planning capacity and "intelligent person is one who acts intelligently in one situation will also do the same in other situations", i.e. generalisability. Amongst all the participants 94.3% respondents agreed that intelligent people make plans efficiently and all four groups were equally agreed with the statement (Table 4.4). But on the second cognitive quality i.e. generalisability of intelligence only 40% respondents agreed and there was quite a bit at difference in rural (33.7%) and urban (46.2%), and schooled (26.2%) and unschooled (53.75%) groups of subjects. Unschooled participants were more in favour of the generalisability of intelligent behaviour than schooled participants.

The questions related to emotional qualities were – "Intelligent people do not excite easily" i.e., less impulsiveness, "They do not express their anger, pain or anxiety i.e. self control of emotions. "They easily understand the feelings of others" i.e. emotional sensitivity and "they are more kind-hearted or sentimental" which have been presented in Table 4.4. Amongst all the participants 93.77% were agreed that intelligent persons were less impulsive. Not much difference found in rural (97.5%), urban (90%), schooled (91.2%) and unschooled (96.2%) group of respondents. Similarly 86.87% respondents agreed that intelligent persons have self control over emotions. Amongst all the participants only 71.25% agreed that intelligent persons are more sentimental. There were difference found in rural (88.7%) and urban (53.7%) group of respondents but not much difference in schooled (71.2%) and unschooled (71.2%) participants.

DISCUSSION

"Culture is a system of interrelated values active enough to influence and condition perception, judgement, communication and behaviour in a given society" (Mazrui, 1986). These cultural variables also play an active role in formu!ating different conceptions of intellectual functioning. One major finding of the present study is that adjective "intelligent" had a positive connotation. This tendency to attribute positive qualities was even more apparent for 'very intelligent' people. Both rural and urban participants (regardless of schooling) thought that characteristics of 'very intelligent' are – good nature, respect for elders, actively helping others, patience/tolerance, less talkative and not quarrelling. All these were positively loaded qualities.

It is also found that the number of positive characteristics mentioned by each group were approximately equal in number although particular characteristics varied with setting. Two characteristics "curious and competitive" and "understand feelings of others" were stated only by urban schooled participants. Jain (1978) reported that urbanites have

Table 4.4: Percentages of Respondents Answered "YES" on theClosed-Ended Type of Questions

Questions	*Rural* N=80	*Urban* N=80	*Schooled* N=80	*Unschooled* N=80	*All Group*
Whether Intelligence God gifted	50%	40%	41.25%	48.75%	45%
Whether intelligence can be increased by training	50%	91.25%	86.25%	55%	70.62
Have you ever used intelligence test	2.5%	0	2.5%	0	1.25%
Whether intelligence increases with age	97.5%	61.25%	91.25%	67.5%	79.57
Whether intelligence decreases with age	12.5%	18.75%	10%	20%	15.31
Whether intelligence remains stable	42.5%	36.25%	42.5%	36.25%	39.37
Generalisability of intelligence	33.7%	46.2%	26.2%	53.7%	40%
Whether intelligent people plan efficiently	97.5%	91.2%	98.7%	90%	94.3%
Whether intelligent people are less impulsive	97.5%	90%	91.2%	96.2%	93.7%
Whether intelligent people easily understand feelings of others	96.2%	90%	91.2%	95%	93.12
Whether intelligent people have self control on emotions	93.7%	80%	82.5%	91.2%	86.8%
Whether intelligent people are more sentimental	88.7%	53.7%	71.2%	71.2%	71.2%

more tolerance for competition than rural people. It appears that urban people have accepted ability to compete, as a dimension of intelligent behaviour, perhaps because it is so prevalent in urban life.

India being an agricultural society and favouring joint family, the emergence of above mentioned characteristics as essentials of intelligent behaviour clearly show the influence of socio-cultural context. If intelligence comprises of the capacity to deal effectively with the environment (Weschler, 1994), then given the Indian family and social organization the above mentioned characteristics have transactional value. Culture is thought to be a socially interactive process, which has two main components. The first component is "the creation of shared activity (cultural practices)" and the second component is "the creation of shared meaning (cultural interpretation)." These two components of cultural processes are cumulative in nature. Shared activities and shared meanings are intrinsic to the human mode of adaptation for survival (Greenfield, 1997).

The emphasis on emotional intelligence e.g. good nature and social intelligence e.g. helping others as reflected in the responses of respondents in the present study especially by rural participants clearly shows the influence of cultural factors as mentioned above. Concerning the characteristics of foolish persons again the rural group emphasized the emotional characteristics e.g. quarrelling and abusing does not obey elders etc. The importance of emotional intelligence as an integral aspect of intelligence is further brought out by high consensus in all groups (90% to 96%) on characteristic of intelligent people namely, emotional sensitivity or understanding feelings of others, emotional control (80% to 94%) and sentimentality as part of intelligence (54% to 89%).

The high and low intelligent people are being distinguished on the basis of temperamental, emotional and social characteristics, as well as, work related and cognitive characteristics. The social and emotional aspects of intelligence are extremely prominent in the findings of this study. Although the schooled participants emphasized task performance related characteristics like active worker for very intelligent person and work without prior thinking for less intelligent person and cognitive characteristics like weak in studies for less intelligent person and less educated for foolish person.

The unique characteristics of less intelligent people stated only by rural participants included two positive qualities, namely, simple and gentle which is an aspect of social intelligence, and laborious. The unquestioning temperament but dedication to work are thus characteristics of less intelligent people, however, it is important to note that these characteristics are not despised. Lack of sharpness in cognitive sphere seems to be compensated by gentle and simple nature accompanied by hard work, at least for the rural people

The characteristics of foolish persons included negative characteristics in all spheres, but emphasis is on lack of emotional intelligence like quarrelling, abusive behaviour, laziness, does not obey elders. The unique characteristics of foolish people stated only by rural participants included emotional and cognitive characteristics i.e. short tempered, interfere in others work and less educated, while urban participants have stated that foolish people are unmannered which is an aspect of social intelligence. The schooled participants (regardless of rural and urban background) thought that foolish people waste time, while unschooled participants thought that foolish people use addictive drugs. Goodnow (1986) has talked about the process by which one comes to conceptualize the dimensions of intelligence. He says that during the course of daily life, both children and adults make judgements about others or themselves, labelling some actions or people as, "dumb", "slow", "stupid" or "facile" and others as "smart", "quick", "clever" or "deep".

The findings of this study show that there is a difference in the conceptualization of intelligence in rural and urban and schooled and unschooled participants. Most of the characteristics referred by the respondents were related to emotional maturity and social competence and some are to action and performance.

The specialized contribution of the educational system which emphasizes the acquisition of symbolic knowledge is apparent in the responses of schooled respondents in this study. They emphasized cognitive characteristics more often. Entering the school system provides much impetus for the development of cognitive structures. The enlarged cognitive structures enable the individual to participate in larger groups activities. So the two settings rural and urban with schooled and unschooled having different types of environmental complexities provide varied experiences hence the varied conceptualization of intelligence.

The findings of this study suggest that what lay people think of characteristics of intelligent behaviour is different from what the intelligence tests are measuring. The results of this study show the prominence of emotional and social spheres of intelligence as an integral part of intelligence, while most of the established, standardized intelligence tests only measure the cognitive and task performance related intellectual abilities e.g. a well-known intelligence tests WAIS measure the vocabulary, arithmetic, digit span, digit symbol etc. related cognitive and performance related characteristics. Only in the "picture arrangement" task there is slightly shown the emotional, intelligence and information and comprehension task pertain in part to social intelligence.

People in both rural and urban settings are aware of the importance of education and educated family. Among the factors adding the development of intelligence the rural and schooled group of respondents reported the cognitive factors like education and good schools more than urban and unschooled participants. The influence of media is also accepted by respondents in giving information about world and in discerning the intelligent behaviours. Media, however, is a double edged sword and it is too early to judge how it is going to influence the conceptualization of intelligence. In rural group more emphasis on environmental and social factors concerning the restraining factors in the development of intelligence e.g. bad company, poverty, chronic disease and unhealthy atmosphere of family, whereas, urban and schooled have emphasized acquisition of skills. They emphasized illiteracy and toxication as hazards in the development of intelligence. The emphasis on social environment by rural people comes out again when respondents were asked the criterion, the basis on which they decided the characteristics of intelligent people. Rural subjects emphasized experience, people around them and watching family members and three of these are social, whereas, urban people emphasized their own knowledge.

Psychologists have traditionally been attracted tasks stripped of context forcing the individual to work completely "in the head" (Goodnow, 1976). As a result one knows little about the intelligent use of physical and social resources. When the participants in this study were asked to narrate any event where the use of intelligence is apparent. They told stories in detailed manner. These stories generally emphasized theme of helping or altruistic behaviour by respondents themselves or to themselves by others. Some of the events were concerned with themes of house catching fire, snake bite or other animal related accidents. While the events depicted by urban subjects have themes like folktales viz. rabbit and tortoise, fox and goose, story of Newton, Nelson Mandela, freedom struggle movement and other national and international events.

They employed representations of behaviours other than those based on first hand experience. Thus their concept of intelligent behaviour is more varied and is broader. The rural group of respondents described stories about saving one's property or confronting with snake. In this group, it is the direct experience which has been quoted as an example of intelligent behaviour, whereas, the urban and schooled groups stated the fictional representation of intelligent behaviour as described in folk tales.

Nessier (1967) defines practical intelligence as intelligent performance in natural settings. Charlesworth (1976) defined practically intelligent behaviour as "behaviour under the control of cognitive processes and employed towards the solution of problems which challenge the well-being, needs, plans and survival of the individual. The occurrence of catching fire and appearance of snakes is very common in rural settings. So, a number of rural participants had personal experiences to cope with such stresses whereas urban respondents were aware and concerned with larger area. The intelligent individuals make plans about their do's and don'ts and work efficiently and in our study most of the participants agreed with the above statement. Concerning the generality of intelligent behaviour, i.e. participants agreed that an intelligent behaviour in one situation cannot be considered to be intelligent in all situations. Thus, the contextual nature of intelligent behaviour was brought out."

The analysis of cultural construction of cognitive functions indicates the need to study the nature, cause of cognitive processes in a sociocultural context (Berry and Levine, 1986; Misra and Gergan, 1983; Misra and Tripathi, 1993; Murlidharan and Srivastava, 1995). The results of this study show that social contexts are important for understanding the concept of intelligence. Results support Butterworth's (1994) contention that to understand intelligence one needs to refer to the internal representation of knowledge, external or contextual factors and the behavioural expression of intelligence.

It is interesting to note that emotional qualities of intelligent people as described here, namely, less impulsivity, emotional sensitivity and control over emotions have been found to be related with subjective well-being (Mishra and Agarwal, 2000). Furthermore, the respondents also overwhelmingly believe that planning and acting on plans is an act of intelligent behaviour. Mishra and Agarwal (2000) have reported in a completely different study that future orientation and planning is related with the social skills of social expressivity and control on the one hand

and well-being and happiness on the other. These findings are still more startling considering that these beliefs are expressed by respondents who were between the ages of 12-18 years in the present study. In Mishra and Agarwal's (2000) study such relationship between future orientation, social expressivity and emotional control and happiness and satisfaction with life was actually found to exist in women respondents who come from different socio-economic status, were either working outside home or not and were, between 25 to 45 years of age. Thus, it appears that in Indian culture intelligence is not conceived only as a set of cognitive abilities but important components of intelligence appears to be those which results in planned action socially sensitive and emotionally controlled behaviours which promotes happiness and well-being.

Reference

Berry, J.W., & Irvine, S.H. (1986). Bricolage: Saves do it daily. In R.J. Sternberg & R.K. Wagner (Eds.), *Practical Intelligence: Nature and Origins of Competence in Everyday World* (pp. 271-306). Cambridge: Cambridge University Press.

Butterworth, G. (1994), Infant intelligence. In J. Khalfan (Ed.) What is *Intelligence*? (pp.49-71). Cambridge: Cambridge University Press.

Cantor, N. and Harlow R. (1994). Social Intelligence and Personality: Flexible life task pursuit. In R.J. Sternberg and P. Ruzgis (Eds.), *Personality and Intelligence* (pp. 137-168). Cambridge: Cambridge University Press.

Charlesworth, W.R. (1976), Human Intelligence as adaptation. An ethological approach. In L.B. Reswick (Ed.). *The Nature of Intelligence*. Hillsdale, N.J. Erlbaum.

Das, J.P. and Thapa, K. (2000). Intelligence and Cognitive Processes, In *Psychology in India Revisited – Developments in Discipline*. Edited by Janak Pandey, (pp. 151-160): Sage Publications: New Delhi.

Flynn, R. (1991). *As an American Achievement beyond IQ*, Hills dale, NJ: Erlbaum.

Gergen, K.J. (1985). The social constructionist movement in modern psychology. *American Psychologist*, 40, 309-320.

Goodnow, J.J. (1976). The nature of intelligent behaviour: Questions raised by cross-cultural studies. In L.B. Reswick (Eds.). *The Nature of Intelligence*. Hillsdale, N.J.: Erlbaum.

Goodnow, J.J. (1986). Some lifelong everyday forms of intelligent behaviour: organizing and reorganizing (pp. 143-161). In Robert, J. Sternberg and Richard K. Wagner (Eds.) *Practical Intelligence: Nature and Origins Competence in the Everyday World.* Cambridge, Cambridge University Press.

Greenfield, P.M. (1997). Culture as Process: Empirical Methods for Cultural Psychology, (pp. 301-348). In John. W. Berry, Y.H. Poortinija and Janak Pandey (Ed.). *Handbook of Cross-Cultural Psychology*. Vol. I, M.A.: Allyn and Bacon.

Mazrui, A.A. (1986). The Africans: *A Triple Heritage Boston*: Little, Brown.

Misra, G. & Gergen, K.J. (1993). On the place of culture in psychological science. *International Journal of Psychology*, 28, 225-243.

Misra, G. & Tripathi, K.N. (1993). The concept and context of human development. In T.S. Saraswathi & B. Kaur (Eds.). *Human Development and Family Studies in India: An Agenda for Research and Policy*, New Delhi: Sage Publications.

Misra, M. & Agarwal, A. (2000). Future Orientation, Optimism, Social Skills and well-being in working women. Unpublished doctoral thesis. D.D.U. Gorakhpur University, Gorakhpur.

Moscovici, S. (1972). Society and theory in Social Psychology. In J. Israel and H. Tajfel (Eds.). *The Context of Social Psychology* (pp. 17-68). London : Academic Press.

Murlidharan, R. & Srivastava, A.K. (1995). Temple ecology and cognitive development: A report from South India, *Psychology and Developing Societies*, 7, 47-64.

Neisser, U. (1967). *Cognitive Psychology*. New York: Appleton-Century-Crofts.

Nessier, U. (1996). Intelligence: Knowns and Unknowns. *American Psychologist*, Vol. 51, No. 2.

Resnick, L.B.; Levine, J.M. and Teasloy, S. (1991). *Perspectives on Socially Shared Cognition*. Washington : American Psychological Association.

Schweder, R.A. & D. Andrade, R.G. (1979). Accurate reflection or systematic distortion? A reply to Block, Weiss, and Thorene, *Journal of Personality and Social Psychology*, 57, 1075-1084.

Schweder, R.A. (1991). Thinking through Cultures: Expeditions in Cultural Psychology. Cambridge: Harvard University Press.

Srivastava, A.K., Tripathi, A.M. & Misra, G. (1995 b). Western and Indian perspectives on intelligence : some reflections. *Indian Educational Review*.

Sternberg, R.J. (1997). The concept of intelligence and its role in lifelong learning and success. *American Psychologist*, 52, 1030-1037.

5

MEMORY FOR STORIES AS A FUNCTION OF CROSS CULTURAL SETTINGS AND RETENTION INTERVAL

NAZISH BANO & ANUPAM NATH TRIPATHI

INTRODUCTION

The Ebbinghaus (1885) tradition for memory is associated with S-R approach, while Bartlett (1932) followed cognitive approach, mirrored in the tradition initiated by Gestaltists. Bartlett proposed that what is remembered is not determined only by stimulus materials but by active organized pre-existent settings known as schema. Individuals have difficulty in discriminating between what was their in the text at the time of reading and what they added to the text at the time of recall (Bartlett, 1932, Zangwill, 1939, Guald & Stephenson 1967). The schemata is hierarchically organized and is used for top-down retrieval of information at the time of output. Rumelhart (1980) has proposed that, related information is organized into knowledge clustering called frames or schemata. Schema is a link between story structures and a model of cognitive processing.

It is quite natural that people are more familiar with the contents belonging to their own socio-cultural setting than different socio-cultural setting.

Stories should provide ideal materials for cross-cultural comparisons. Similar types of organisations are found in folk tales from around the world. The universality of certain kinds of schematic organisation and their control on memory process has been found in comparisons of recall of stories by the subjects of different cultures (Mandler *et al,* 1978; Johnson & Mandler 1979).

Children have already developed schemata (Pitcher & Prelinger (1963). Johnson & Mandler (1978) observed gradual formation and growth of schemata during childhood. They also found that there were qualitative and quantitative differences in recall of well formed stories by children and adults. A child is biologically programmed to develop a grammar of his own that enables him to speak and understood by others in his culture but social and psychological factors are also important. Children learn the language of their culture merely by imitation and reinforcement. Grammar generating mechanisms may be part of child's genetic equipment but the adults reinforce him to correct the grammar. Activation of schema is an inherent part of the comprehension (Rumelhart 1977) which reduces processing load by filling in details of things. We expect to see or hear and form a basis for the reconstructive aspect of memory.

The present study aims to investigate the effects of socio-cultural setting and retention interval on recall for stories.

METHOD

Design

A study in a 2 × 5 factorial design was conducted with two levels of socio-cultural setting i.e., same (Indian) and different (Foreign) and five levels of retention interval i.e., immediate, 1 day, 7 days, 15 days and 30 days.

Thus the experiment involved 10 treatment conditions.

Subject

One hundred graduate students served as subjects. They were in the age range of 18 to 20 years. Ten Ss were randomly assigned to each one of the ten treatment conditions.

Materials

Two folk stories, one belonging to same socio-cultural setting and the other belonging to different socio-cultural setting were used. Each story had seven sentences and each of the seven sentence contained approximately 10 words. Johnson and Mandler (1978) have proposed that a simple story consists of seven different essential constituents or rewrite rules (i.e. setting, beginning, simple reaction, goal, attempt, outcome and ending). These rewrite rules or grammars of the stories are universal.

Thus in all aspects the two folk stories were similar except for their socio-cultural contents.

Procedure

The study ran into two sessions, story presentation and story recall. The seven sentences of a story were presented to Ss in a systematic order one by one twice at Ss normal reading and listening rate. Subjects were again approached individually according to their retention interval and were asked to write down the previously learned story on a given sheet of paper.

Scoring Procedure

The recalled sentences having no change in meaning or form were scored as correctly recalled sentences. The maximum possible score of a subject was 7 and the minimum was zero.

RESULTS

In general, results show a consistent decrement in amount of recall with increasing length of retention interval for both types of folk stories (Table 5.1.).

Two way ANOVA for recall showed significant main effect of socio-cultural setting [$F(1,90) = 23.946$; $P<.01$] and retention interval [$F(4,90) = 56.308$; $P<.01$]. The interaction effect between the two was also found to be significant [$F(4,90) = 4.526$; $P <.01$].

Table 5.1: Mean and SD Values of Recall Scores

Socio-cultural Setting		*Retention Intervals*				
		Immediate	1 day	7 days	15 days	30 days
Same	M	5.0	4.3	4.0	2.1	0.3
	(SD)	(0.632)	(0.781)	(0.447)	(0.831)	(0.458)
Different	M	3.8	3.9	1.8	0.6	0.6
	(SD)	(1.4)	(1.3)	(1.469)	(0.663)	(1.019)

DISCUSSION

The results indicate the importance of socio-cultural contents of a story. The content of the story belonging to same socio-cultural setting facilitates the recall in comparison to different socio-cultural setting, while both of the stories have a perfect similarity in structure described by Johnson and Mandler (1977). The results puts a question mark on the hypothesis of universality of story grammar. The results strongly suggest that activation of Schema in memory for stories involves general understanding of structural properties of stories as well as familiarity with socio-cultural content of stories. The results also indicate the linear relationship between amount of recall and length of retention interval. A consistent decrement in the amount of recall is observed upto an interval of 30 days. While a considerable amount of original material is lost, the gap between amount of recall for stories from varying socio-cultural setting is considerably minimized at longer intervals. It seems that the impact of socio-cultural setting is maintained as long as central theme or length or size of the original story is retained to an extent.

References

Bartlett, F.C. (1932) *Remembering: A Study in Experimental and Social Psychology*, Cambridge University Press.

Ebbinghans, H. (1885). *Memory: A Contribution to Experimental Psychology*. Trans, by H.A. Ruger and C.E. Bussenus. New-York; Dover, Teacher College, Columbia University. 1913.

Guald, A. & Stephenson, G.M. (1967). Some experiments relating to Bartlett's theory of remembering. *British Journal of Psychology*, 58 (1,2), 39-49.

Johnson, N.S. & Mandler, J.M. (1979). *A Tale of Two Structures: Underlying and Surface Forms in Stories*: CHIP Report, 80. Centre for Human Information Processing Department of Psychology. University of California, San Diego, Lajolla, California.

Mandler, J.M. & De-Forest, M. (1978). Developmental Invariance in Story recall. Submitted for publication, University of California, Sandiego.

Pitcher, E.G. & Prelinger, E. (1963). *Children Tell Stories: An Analysis of Fantasy*. New York International University Press.

Rumelhart, D.E. (1977). Understanding and Summarizing Brief Stories in D. La Berge & J. Samuels (Eds.) *Basic Processes in Reading: Perception and Comprehension*. Hillsdale, N.J. Lawrence: Erlbaum. Associates.

Rumelhart, D.E. (1980): Schemata: The building blocks of Cognition. In R.J. Spiro, B.C. Bruce & W.F. Brewer (Eds.). *Theoretical Issues in Reading*

Comprehension: Perspectives from Cognitive Psychology. Linguistics artificial intelligence and education. Hillsdale, N.J. Erlbaum.

Zangwill. O.L. (1939). Some relations between reproducing and recognizing prose material. *British Journal of Psychology, Vol. 29*, 371-382.

6

DEVELOPMENTAL CHANGES IN ENVIRONMENTAL NEEDS, FAMILY ATMOSPHERE AND COMPETENCE IN SCHOOL-GOING CHILDREN

P.S.N. TIWARI & SHALINI SRIVASTAVA

INTRODUCTION

All human beings are social animals. There is a spirit of competence inherent in all human beings and so in society, they try to prove their competence by becoming more active and powerful than others. Competence vary from man to man because more or less it depends upon the environment and heredity. Now-a-days psychologists are trying to prove that in the development of competence the effect of environment is more than heredity. Environment means a type of surroundings the man has, such as the place or neighbourhood where he/she lives, the family in which he/she spends lots of time, the school in which he/she plays, share feelings and emotions and out of these the role of family is most significant.

Generally, these days the family is relatively a structure, usually composed of father, mother and few children. Family is a place where the child first makes his important relationships. It is also a place where the child receive his or her first education. Mother is the first teacher of the child. The first attempt to measure the family atmosphere was the development of SES indices which become more popular among researchers for long time. Soon its inadequacy was realized and the first environmental process measure was constructed by Dave (1963), Wolf (1964) which consist of three major dimensions; (1) Stimulation provided for intellectual growth. (2) Opportunities provided for and emphasis on verbal development. (3) Provision of opportunity for general type of learning in a variety of situations.

Besides many variables affect the family atmosphere such as — parental income, parental education, health and nutrition, father-mother support and rejection, socio-cultural deprivation, things available in the home, parents occupation, SES. All these influence the competence.

Privacy has a variety of meanings in everyday. Privacy means, that we try to be alone and undisturbed. All people know about the privacy we can think of having private thoughts and feelings, meanings that they are personal and that we don't want to share with anyone else. Privacy needs try from person to person, from time to time, from culture to culture. It is also very essential for intellectual competence. Generally children want to be undisturbed while studying because they cannot work properly in front of others. Privacy regulation permits people to be open to others on some occasions and to be closed off from interaction at other times. It is therefore a changing process. (Altman 1975, 77). Mentally established a desired level of privacy, a level of interaction they would like to have in a particular settings.

The term personal space was first coined by Katz (1937). The concept is not unique in area of psychology since it has roots in biology and anthropology. Personal space is the space within an invisible boundaries around people that is with them everywhere they go. People in American society typically interact with others in one of the four spatial zones – intimate zones, personal zones, social zones and public zones. Researchers have measured personal space by observing it in natural condition laboratory setting and by stimulation techniques these environmental needs interact with family atmosphere and influences the development of competence among children, competence has been conceptualised in the present investigation as a broader concept which includes the intellectual ability as well as social competence. The construct of intelligence refers to a central generalized competence. Wechsler (1975) has given a broad conception of intelligence. Intelligence is the capacity of the individual to understand the world around him and his resourcefulness to cope with its challenges. Thus taken as a totality the intelligence test constitutes as indicator of the individuals level of formal cognitive ability. Zigler and Trickett (1978) advocated the use of social competence. It tells how people face the society and how they interact with it. Against this background, the present study is planned to investigate the pattern of environmental needs and family atmosphere on one hand and development of competence among children on the other. In addition the present study also investigates the contribution of various environmental needs in the development of intellectual as well as social competence among children.

METHOD

Sample

In Gorakhpur city there are various types of schools. Some are old, some are new, some are only for boys, some are only for girls, some have co-education, some are government schools, some are semi-government, some are private, some are missionary schools. The purpose of the present research is to see the variations in various variables across medium of instruction. Therefore the schools were identified on the basis of their medium of instruction. According to their position, randomly eight schools were selected.

After selecting the school two hundred forty subjects were randomly selected from different schools. Out of two hundred forty subjects eighty were from each grade category (IV, VI and VIII). From English medium there were ninety five students. From Hindi medium there were one hundred forty five subjects. Total male subjects were one hundred fifty five whereas female subjects were eighty five only

Measures : Family Atmosphere

This questionnaire consists of three sections. First section has indices SES family size, parents education, total family educatioh, parental income, parent occupation. Second section tapped objective environment of home, books and magazines, play material, physical environment, health and nutrition. Third section yield scores on child rearing styles, parental support and child rejection, parental companionship. There are total 15 items and in each item there are five alternatives. Each alternative has its own value and students have to select anyone.

Privacy

This measure is basically based on the principle proposed by Thurstone & Chave (1929), as described by E. Edwards (1969) Varimox factor analyses yielded six factors, individuality, intimacy, anonimity, self-disclosure, reserve and commonality. It is basically attitudinal and each dimension consists of at least two or more questions. In each question there are five alternatives. Each alternative has its own value. There are total 15 items, thus the maximum score will be 75 and minimum will be 15.

Personal Space

First measure is based on self rating technique. In this students were given a plain paper on which eight geometrical designs were made, they were asked to draw line, around the figures. At what distance they will draw a line show that how much distance between themselves and others they like to keep. Second measure is based on simulation technique. In this figures or symbols are used. Subjects are given in a plain paper on which two blocks are made in which subjects have to set some human figures just to show that if they will get a space how many people they can adjust.

Intelligence Scale

For measuring intelligence, test developed by A.K.S. Cattell and R.B. Cattell (Hindi version) was used.

Academic Record

It was exact percentage of marks obtained by the students in their just previous annual examination.

Social Competence

For measuring social competence, 12 item-teacher rating was used. The dimensions covered in the scale were, verbal intelligence, introversion, considerateness, apathy, extroversion, hostility, creativity, curiosity and distractibility. On all the 12 items, the teacher has to rate each child individually on a five-point rating scale.

Procedure

After choosing the schools, the principals of the respective schools were contacted. After the permission of the principal the class teachers were contacted. After the brief orientation of the research purposes they were requested to cooperate. After an informal introduction with the children the family atmosphere questionnaire was distributed and the instruction was read loudly, which was written on the top of the questionnaire. After understanding the instruction children were advised to read each and every question and its alternatives and then put a tick to show the correct choice. After completion of this task the measure for privacy and personal space was administered in the same way.

In second session Cattell, Culture Fair Test was administered. The students were divided into small group of 10 to 12 students. The test booklets and answer-sheets were distributed. After explaining the instructions the students were asked to start the work. Since it is a speed test they have to complete it in that specified time. Same procedure was adopted in all the sub-groups belonging to various grade in different institutions. A social competence scale was introduced to the teachers. The achievement scores were obtained from the school records. Rest of the data were collected in sessions.

RESULTS

Scores obtained on various measures are subjected to 2*3*2 ANOVA with two level of medium of instructions, three levels of grade (IV, VI and VIII) and two levels of sex (male and female). To know the contribution of family atmosphere and environmental needs toward intelligence and social competence multiple regression analysis was performed. Environmental needs (privacy, personal space) and family atmosphere are used as predictors and I.Q. Academic Record and Teacher rating are used as criterion variables.

Mean scores as a function of medium of instruction, grade and sex are presented in Table 6.1 It is evident from the table that in family atmosphere the overall mean of English medium students was higher (55.44) than the Hindi medium subjects (54.0) Female subjects scored higher (55.66) than the male subjects (55.83), IV grade scored highest (56.3) followed by VIII grade (54.3) and VI grade (53.6). However more of the main effects neither any of the interactions reached significant. In case of privacy, Hindi medium scored higher (50.6) than the subjects of English medium (49.6). Mean of female scores is higher (50.2) than male (50.0). In grade the mean of VI class is highest (55.4) followed by IV (51.7) and VIII class (47.7). All the main effects are not significant. However medium of instructions and grade interaction reached the

Table 6.1: Mean Scores as a Function of Medium of Instruction, Grade and Sex

	English	*Hindi*	$F_{(7,228)}$	*IV*	*VI*	*VII*	$F_{(2, 228)}$	*Male*	*Female*	$F_{(2,228)}$
Family atmosphere	55.44	54.0	1.513	56.3	53.6	54.3	2.01	53.83	55.66	2.57
Privacy	49.6	50.6	0.36	51.7	55.4	47.7	1.93	50.0	50.2	0.01
Personal Space I	82.42	75.08	0.54	67.65	57.01	76.09	4.44*	65.05	68.74	5.32!
Personal Space II	3.5	3.4	1.78	3.75	3.35	3.35	2.53	3.6	3.3	1.88
I.Q.	93.42	89.17	2.88	88.8	93.8	91.25	1.87	94.07	88.85	5.11!
Academic Record	62.37	55.22	13.04!	56.96	60.3	59.1	0.98	60.56	57.04	3.15!
Social Competence	39.79	40.64	0.77	42.23	39.88	38.53	5.07!	40.70	38.2	1.01

*p<.05 ! p<.01

significance level F=3.60, of 2,228 p<.05. The significant interaction effect suggests that VI class student preferred maximum privacy followed by IV class and VIII class students. In case of measure I for personal space the overall mean scores of female subjects are higher (68.74) than the male subjects (65.05) (f=5.32, of 1.228 p<.01). In case of grade VIII, it scored highest (76.09) followed by IV grade (67.65) and VI grade (57.01) (f=4.44, of 2,228, p<.01). In case of measure II for personal space male subjects scored higher (3.6) than female subjects (3.3). In case of grade, subjects belonging to IV class scored 3.75 and VI class scored 3.35. All the main effects as well as interactions could not reach the significance level except grade X sex interaction which yielded significant F ratio (F=5.00, df 2,228 p<.01). Interaction effect of personal space as a function of grade and sex was found significant. It is evident from the figure that IV grade female students scored highest followed by VIII grade male students. However female students belonging to VIII grade scored lowest on measure of personal space. In case of intelligence, overall mean of English medium are higher than the subjects of Hindi medium however the main effect could not reach the significance level. The male subjects scored higher (94.07) than female (88.85) sex yielded significant main effect (F=5.11, df 1,228 p<.01). However main effect of grade as well as all the interactions were not significant. In case of academic record the overall mean of VI class is highest (60.3) followed by VIII class (59.1) and IV class (56.96) significant (F=3.15, df 1,228, p<.05) main effect of sex suggests that females scored higher (60.56) than male (57.04) and other effects were non-significant. In case of social competence the overall means of IV class is significantly higher (42.23) than VI class (39.88) and VII class (39.53) subjects (F=5.07, df 2,228 p<.01). The subjects of Hindi medium scored higher (40.64) than English medium (39.79). The overall mean of male subjects is higher (40.70) than female subjects (38.2). The main effects of medium of instruction and sex as well as medium of instruction and grade interaction could not reach the significance level. However medium of instruction and sex, grade and sex as well as medium of instruction and grade interactions were found to be significant. Results suggests that male students belonging to English scored highest followed by females belonging to Hindi medium. However female of English medium scored lowest. Significant interaction effect (F=3.26, df 2,228 p<.05) of grade suggests that VI grade male students scored highest while VII grade males scored lowest on the measure of social competence. Significant interaction effect (F=8.92 df 2,228 p<.01) suggests that IV grade English medium students were found social score competent than other groups of English medium students scored lowest on this measure.

Table 6.2: Results of Multiple Regression Analysis for the Criterion Variables I.Q., Social Competence and Academic Records

Predictors	*MR*	*RZ*	*B*	*SEB*	*Beta*	*t*	*f*	*df*
Family At	.3040	.092	.3014	.1343	.1469	2.244	12.17	2/239
Privacy	.2708	.073	.705	.1619	.270	4.358	18.99	1/240

SOCIAL COMPETENCE

Predictors	*MR*	*RZ*	*B*	*SEB*	*Beta*	*t*	*f*	*df*
Privacy	.2971	.0883	.325	.0675	.297	4.82	23.25	1/240
Family At	.3291	.1083	.269	.0711	.2463	3.795	14.52	2/239

ACADEMIC RECORD

Predictors	*MR*	*RZ*	*B*	*SEB*	*Beta*	*t*	*f*	*df*
Family Atmosphere	2.717	.0738	.4284	0.979	.2717	4.374	19.131	1/240

Regression Results

For the purpose of multiple regression analysis scores on the measures of intelligence, social competence and academic record were considered as criterion variable while family atmosphere, privacy and personal space were taken as predictor variables. As evident from Table 6.2 that, predictors-family atmosphere and privacy contributed 9% to criterion variable I.Q. However the contribution of personal space could not contribute significantly for any of the criterion variable. For the criterion variable social competence privacy and family atmosphere contributed significantly. The contribution was 8.8 per cent and 10 per cent respectively. However for the academic record the only significant predictor is family atmosphere which contributed 7.4 per cent only. In conclusion it can be said that family atmosphere and privacy are the significant determinants of competence.

DISCUSSION

The objective of this study was to find out the contribution of environmental needs and family atmosphere in the development of child's intellectual as well as social competence. There is evidence in the literature that home is a better predictor particularly during the early childhood. The result of this study also reveals that family atmosphere is the best predictor of intelligence and social competence. The present finding reveals the supremacy of the English medium is because generally the parents of Hindi medium students are less educated and their homes comparatively lack things which stimulate the cognitive functioning. The present study also reveals that female students need more privacy than males. This is because of our social structure and Indian mentality. The result also shows that generally English medium subjects need more space than Hindi medium. This is because from the beginning they get such type of training in home as well as in the school. It is based on "Hall's (1963) Proxemic Framework". Result for intelligence shows that English medium subjects and the girls of Class VII are more competent than their counterparts. This is because girls are generally from the prosperous and educated families. They give equal or better opportunity for the education to girls. Mothers give more companionship to girls, both the parents are more withdrawn towards male children. This finding really does not need any explanation because it is just reflecting the peculiarities of our Indian society. In India boys are given totally different treatments by their parents, but because the attitude are changing, the girls are also getting same or equal treatment. The male child is controlled by father because he is to inherit the familiar liabilities and responsibilities in future. It can be concluded that the family atmosphere and environmental needs influence the development of intelligence, as well as, social competence of students.

References

Altman, I. (1975) The environment and social behaviour, privacy personal space, territory, crowding, Monterey CA Brooks/Cole Altman I (1977) personal space; An analysis of E.T. Hall's proxemics framework. In I. Altman & J.F. Wohlwill (Eds.) *Human Behaviour and the Environment,* Vol. 2, Advance in theory and research, New York Plenum.

Dave, R. (1963) "The identification and measurement of environmental process variables that are related to educational achievement", Unpublished Doctoral Dissertation University of Chicago.

Edwards, D.T. (1973) A cross-cultural study of social orientation and distance schemata by the method of doll placement, *Journal of Social Psychology*, 89, 165-173.

Hall, E.T. (1963) A system for the rotation of proxemic behaviour. American Anthropologist 65, 1003-1026 Zigler, E., Trickett, P.K. (1978) I.Q. Social competence and Evaluation of early childhood intervention programs. *American Psychology*. (Sepl.) 7, 89 p.

Wechster, D. (1975) Intelligence defined and undefined. A relativistic appraisal, *American Psychologist* 30, 135-139.

Wolf, R. (1964) The identification and measurement of environment process variables related to intelligence unpublished Doctoral Dissertation, University of Chicago.

7

COPING AND SATISFACTION WITH LIFE IN WORKING WOMEN

MANJU MISHRA & ADESH AGARWAL

INTRODUCTION

The behavioural and cognitive efforts one uses in order to manage the internal and external demands of a stressful situation, have been referred to as coping (Lazarus, 1966, Lazarus and Folkman, 1984). Two forms of coping have been described by Lazarus and his colleagues. Problem focused coping strategies are directed towards the management of the problem, whereas emotion-focused coping strategies (escapism, self-blame and avoidance) are directed towards amelioration of emotional stress. In addition, there are strategies that can serve both problem and emotion focused functions. Seeking social support is one such strategy that can provide both emotional and problem related practical support. Problem focused coping strategies have been reported to have positive association with measures of psychological well-being (Folkman *et al.*, 1986). Emotion focused strategies tend to be associated with poor mental health (Aldwin and Revenson 1987; Terry, 1994). A number of researches have questioned the assumption that the use of problem focused coping will always be more adaptive than emotion focused coping (Folkman *et al.*, 1986). Recent researches have provided some evidence suggesting that to be effective, a person's coping efforts should be congruent with the controllability of the event Aldwin and Revenson (1987). This implies that problem focused strategies will be more effective if the event has some potential for control whereas emotion focused coping strategies will be adaptive in low control events. (Forsythe and Compas, 1987; Conway and Terry 1972; Vitaliano *et al.*, 1990).

Coping strategies can also be classified as approach coping and avoidance coping strategies. According to Suls and Fletcher (1985) approach coping refers to the use of strategies that focus on both source of stress and reactions to it, whereas avoidance coping refers to the use of strategies which focus away, from both source of stress and reaction to it. It has been shown that some individuals reliably cope with stressful situation by scanning for information that can be potentially threatening. In contrast, other individuals tend to ignore or distract themselves from such informations, however, approach and avoidance coping strategies are not exclusive coping classifications.

Life satisfaction is a cognitive judgemental evaluation of one's life and is considered by many psychologists as the most consistent and stable variable of well-being. Life satisfaction may be defined as a global assessment of person's quality of life according to his chosen criterion. Judgements of satisfaction are dependent upon a comparison of one's circumstances with what is thought to be an appropriate standard. It is important to mention here that the judgement of how people feel satisfied with their present state of affairs, is based on a comparison with a standard, which each individual sets for himself or herself and is not an externally imposed criterion. Health, wealth, energy and so forth may be desirable for well-being, particular individuals may place different values on them. It, therefore, becomes necessary to ask the persons for an overall evaluation of their life rather than summing across their satisfaction with specific domains.

Various factors influence the well-being and life satisfaction of a person e.g. personality, income, resources, personal goals, as well as various demographic variables (education, family, employment) etc. Personality is suggested to have an important influence on subjective well-being (Andrews and Withey, 1976). Variables like self-esteem, sociability, intelligence, optimism, etc. have consistent relationship with subjective well-being. In a recent study Schmutte and Ryff (1997) have shown that the relationship between the well-being and personality is not as simple as the existing literature suggests and, as a corrective measure they offered an alternative multidimensional model of psychological well-being which is based on the appraisals of one's life across various conceptually distinct realms of psychological functioning. Income is also an important factor which has positive relationship with subjective well-being (Andrews and Withey, 1976). Not only a person with high income can afford more services and goods but also acquires high status in soçiety. Personal goals also play an important role in a person's well-being. This links motivation to subjective well-being. (Emmons 1986, Little, 1987) and establishes that achievement of personal goals leads to heightened status of well-being (Deiner, 1984). Apart from these, some demographic variables like education, employment etc. have significant influence on well-being. Employment is positively related to well-being and, it goes beyond the obvious financial difficulties involved. Education has an influence on subjective well-being (Campbell, 1981) though there are few studies which contrasted this view but even these studies acknowledged that by interacting with other variables education becomes an important influence. Family and marriage also have significant effect on subjective well-being as number of studies (Andrews and Inglehart, 1979) indicate that married persons report greater subjective well-being.

In the present study relationship of socio-economic status, women's working status, future orientation and optimism, with her coping strategies and, satisfaction with life was investigated. After reviewing available literature following hypotheses were framed and tested in the study: Socio-economic status will influence women's coping strategies and satisfaction with life. So, women from higher socio-economic class will cope more efficiently and successfully with stressful life conditions and will be more satisfied with their lives. Women's high future orientation will facilitate better coping and result in satisfaction with life. Women having high future orientation will cope better and will be more satisfied with their lives. Optimism will facilitate coping with stress and lead to greater life satisfaction. More optimism women will cope more efficiently and experience more life satisfaction. Women's working status will also help in coping with difficult situations and increase life satisfaction. Working women will cope more efficiently and will be more satisfied with their lives.

METHOD

Sample

Subjects were 210 women between the ages of 25-40 years. They were selected from three districts of eastern U.P. viz. – Gorakhpur, Basti and Sant Kabirnagar. Half of the subjects were working outside home and half of the subjects were not employed. Subjects were selected by stratified random sampling on the basis of their socio-economic status and working status they belonged to three socio-economic classes namely, higher, middle and lower socio-economic status. Amongst the 105 working subjects, 35 subjects were from higher, 40 subjects from middle and 30 subjects from lower socio-economic status.

Higher socio-economic working group consisted of professionals like doctors, civil servants, university/college teachers and principals. In middle class working group respondents were school teachers, bank/ LIC clerks and, railway clerks. Amongst lower working class, fourth class employees of schools and offices were recruited as respondents. The non-working groups of respondents were selected from similar strata as described above but they were only home makers and were not working outside their homes.

Subjects were mostly married and Hindi speaking women, from Hindu and Muslim families. Subject's educational level ranged from fifth standard to doctoral degrees.

MEASURES

Coping

Coping was assessed by the 'COPE' scale developed by Carver, Scheier and Weintraub, (1989). COPE is a sixty item inventory with fifteen different coping scales of active coping, planning, seeking instrumental/ emotional social support, suppression of competing activities, religion, positive reinterpretation and growth, restraint coping, acceptance, focus on venting of emotions, denial, mental disengagement, behavioural disengagement, alcohol/drug use, humour.

Each scale consisted of four items. Subjects were asked to answer on four point scale ranging from 'I usually don't do this at all' (1) to 'I usually do this a lot' (4).

Internal reliability of most COPE scales was adequate, alpha values for different scales were between 0.65 to 0.90.

In the present research a shorter Hindi version of thirty items was used. Coefficient of correlation between the long sixty item scale and short thirty item scale was 0.74. Test-retest reliability of short version of COPE was 0.80 over a gap of four weeks. Coefficient of correlation between the scores of Hindi and English version of COPE was 0.78. Fifteen coping scales were merged into eight groups on the basis of Carver, Scheier and Weintraub (1989). These are, active coping, planning and restraint coping, social emotional support, mental and behavioural disengagement, positive reinterpretation and growth, acceptance, religion and humour.

Satisfaction with Life

Satisfaction with life was assessed by "The Satisfaction with Life Scale" (SWLS) developed by Diener, Emmons, Larsen and Griffin, 1985. SWLS assesses global life satisfaction. SWLS is a five item scale. The responses range from 'totally disagree' (1) to 'totally agree' (5). For example one item was "The conditions of my life are excellent". SWLS has satisfactory validity and has good psychometric properties. Test-retest reliability after two months was 0.82 and coefficient alpha was 0.87.

Future Orientation

Future orientation was measured by story writing technique, which is a variation of the technique used by Meade (1972). This technique has been successfully adapted and found to be valid and reliable by Agarwal and Tripathi (1979) and Agarwal (1980). Six cue sentences were presented to subjects who were asked to write a story to each cue sentence. Proportion of future events taking place after the event in the cue sentence, in every story were calculated and added. These proportions were converted to arc sin $\sqrt{x}$ to give the future orientation score.

Optimism

Optimism was measured by Life Orientation Test, 'LOT' developed by Scheier and Carver (1985). The LOT is an eight items scale plus four filler items. Responses are given on five-point scale answers vary from totally agree to totally disagree. Four items are scored in reverse order. LOT has adequate internal consistency Cronbach's alpha of 0.76 and test-retest reliability coefficient of 0.79 over a four-week period was found.

Procedure

Data was collected in three successive phases. In the very first phase data was collected on middle class working subjects. Prior permission of school principals was taken. When the teachers agreed to participate, the COPE inventory and Satisfaction with Life Scale and other measures were administered. Instructions were communicated properly.

Subjects took about 30 minutes to fill up the questionnaires. They worked happily and were eager to know the results of the study. Data was collected from Bank/LIC clerks and Railway clerks wherever possible in the same manner. Data was collected in groups of 3-5 subjects but sometimes subjects requested for permission to return the filled questionnaires on next day. Door to door contact was made with women from middle class localities in order to collect data on middle class non-working subjects.

In the second phase data was collected on higher socio-economic class. Subjects working outside home were contacted personally and appointments were fixed for data collection. Doctors from District Hospital were contacted and proper instructions were given, then measures were administered. The researcher was sometimes requested to collect the filled measures in a couple of days. Top civil servants were contacted and then data was collected on University/College teachers and principals. For collecting data on higher class non-working group, door to door contact was made. Women were contacted from high income and VIP areas of cities. The researcher made personal request and told the purpose of the investigation to the subjects. Most women took interest and the filled questionnaires were returned after two-three days.

In the third phase data was collected on lower class subjects. In working group, peons of schools and different offices were selected as subjects. Since most subjects of this group were illiterate, the researcher took special care in communicating the instructions and in recording the responses.

RESULTS

Simple correlations between variables were computed and separate multiple regression analyses were conducted for seven coping strategies. Predictor variables were, socio-economic status, working-nonworking status, future orientation and optimism.

Table 7.1 presents the coefficients of correlations between socio-economic status, working-nonworking status, future orientation and optimism with various coping strategies and satisfaction with life. As the table shows, SES, working-nonworking status of the respondents, F.O. and optimism have high positive and significant correlations with active coping strategy and with planning and restraint coping strategy. SES was negatively and significantly correlated with social-emotional support, disengagement, positive reinterpretation and growth and religion and positively and significantly correlated with humour.

Table 7.1: Correlation between SES, Working-non working status, FO and Optimism with Coping Strategies

Socio-Psychological Variables	*Active Coping*	*Planning and Restraint Coping*	*Support*	*Disengagement*	*Positive Interpretation*	*Religion*	*Humour*
SES	0.66***	0.71***	–0.13**	–0.32***	-0.26***	–0.39***	0.16**
W/NW Status	0.15*	0.13*	0.002	–0.13*	0.00	0.03	0.04
F.O.	0.25***	0.33***	0.04	0.003	0.008	0.02	0.01
Optimism	0.24***	0.23***	–0.03	–0.10	-0.09	–0.10	–0.02

Note : * Significant at 0.05 level
** Significant at 0.01 level
*** Significant at 0.001 level

Satisfaction with life also had significant positive correlations with three variables namely, SES, F.O. and optimism. Working status of the respondents was not significantly correlated with SWL.

Results obtained from multiple regression analyses have been presented in Table 7.2. Table 7.2 shows that the four predictors namely, SES, working status, future orientation and optimism explained 46 per cent variance in the criterion variable of active coping. Two out of the four predictors, namely, SES (β 0.66) and working-non working status (β 0.15) were the significant predictors of active coping strategy. SES explained 44 per cent and working non-working status explained 2 per cent variance in the criterion variables. Table 7.2 indicates that four predictors in combination, explained 53 per cent variance in the criterion variable of 'Planning and Restraint Coping'. Three out of four predictors namely SES (β 0.67) working-nonworking status (β 0.12) F.O. (β 0.10) significantly predicted planning and restraint coping. SES explained 50 per cent variance, working-non working status contributed 2 per cent and F.O. contributed 1 per cent in explaining the variance in the criterion variable. Table 7.2 indicates that coping strategy of, 'instrumental, social and emotional support' was significantly predicted by SES alone (β 0.13). Table 7.2 also shows that coping strategy of 'mental and behavioural disengagement' was negatively and significantly predicted by SES (β 0.15) and working-non working status (β 0.15) and positively predicted by F.O. (β 0.13). SES contributed 10 per cent working-non working status 2 per cent and F.O. 2 per cent in explaining the variance in the criterion variable. Table 7.2 indicates that coping style of 'positive reinterpretation and growth' was significantly predicted by one predictor, namely, SES (β 0.26). SES explained 7 per cent variance in the criterion variable. Use of religion was significantly predicted by F.O. (β 0.16) and SES (β 0.44). SES contributed 15 per cent and F.O. explained 3 per cent variance in the criterion variable. Coping strategy of humour was significantly predicted by only one variable of SES (β 0.16), which explained 2 per cent variance in the criterion variable (Table 7.2).

Results thus show that socio-economic status contributed significantly in explaining variances in all the seven coping strategies. Future orientation contributed in explaining variance in coping strategies of planning and restraint coping, use of religion and mental and behavioural disengagement. Working status also explained variance in the use of three coping strategies. Table 7.3 also shows the relationship of various coping techniques with satisfaction with life and happiness.

Table 7.2: Coping Strategies as Predicted by Socio-Economic Working Status and Future Orientation

Predictors	*β*	*T*		*F*
		Criterion Variable : Active Coping		
SES	0.66	13.06****	R^2=0.44	164.51****
W/NW	0.15	2.96***	R^2=.0.46	89.72****
		Criterion Variable : Planning and Restraint Coping		
SES	0.67	1348****	R^2=0.50	213.46****
W/NW	0.12	2.61***	R^2=0.52	114.27****
F.O.	0.10	2.41**	R^2=.0.53	89.03****
		Criterion Variable : Instrumental and Social Emotional Support		
SES	–0.13	–2.0*	R^2=0.01	4.06*
		Criterion Variable : Mental and Behavioural Disengagement		
SES	–0.37	–5.46****	R^2=0.10	25.11****
W/NW	–0.15	–2.35**	R^2=0.12	15.08****
F.O.	0.13	2.00*	R^2=0.14	11.54****
		Criterion Variable : Positive Representation and Growth		
SES	–0.26	–0.397***	R^2=0.07	15.77****
		Criterion Variable : Religion		
SES	–0.44	–6.74****	R^2=0.15	38.56****
F.O.	0.16	2.47**	R^2=0.18	22.80****
		Criterion Variable : Humour		
SES	0.16	2.43**	R^2=0.02	5.92**

Note:
- * Significance level 0.05
- ** Significance level 0.01
- *** Significance level 0.001
- **** Significance level 0.0001

Active coping, planning and restraint coping were positively and significantly correlated with both satisfaction with life and happiness. Humour was also positive and significantly correlated with happiness, it was positively correlated with satisfaction with life but coefficient of correlation was not significant at 0.05 level but at 0.10 level only. Use of religion was negatively and significantly correlated both with satisfaction and happiness.

Table 7.3: Coefficients of Correlations between Coping Styles and Well-being

Coping Style	*Well-being*	
	Satisfaction with life	*Happiness*
Active coping	0.23*** (P=0.001)	0.28*** (P=0.000)
Planning and Restraint Coping	0.31*** (P=0.000)	0.35*** (P=0.000)
Social, Emotional Support	–0.003	0.04
Mental and Behavioural Disengagement	–0.11	–0.04
Position Reinterpretation and growth, acceptance	–0.02	–0.05
Religion	–0.14* (P=0.03)	–0.16** (P=0.01)
Humour	0.12	0.21*** (P=0.002)

Note : Same as table 7.2.

DISCUSSION

Results have been discussed in two sections. The first section deals with relationship of socio-economic status, working status, future orientation and optimism with use of coping strategies. The second section deals with the relationship of various coping strategies, satisfaction with life and happiness.

Socio-psychological Variables and use of Coping Strategies

Table 7.1 presents the correlations between the four socio-psychological variables and usage of seven coping strategies. As Table 7.1 shows socio-economic status was highly correlated with all the seven coping strategies. Socio-economic status was negatively correlated with coping styles of mental and behavioural disengagement, positive reinterpretation and growth and, religion. These results suggest that as the socio-economic status of the individuals increased they used more problem focused coping styles, such as actively grappling with the problem and planning and made use of strategies which focus on managing emotions.

Results of regression analyses for different coping styles presented in Table 7.2 also demonstrate that four socio-psychological variables taken together, significantly predict different coping strategies. Socio-psychological variables namely, socio-economic status and working-non working status significantly predicted active coping style, planning and restraint coping, SES alone predicted rest of the coping strategies like instrumental social and emotional support, positive representation and growth and religion.

Results of this investigation strongly suggest that women from low SES, who are not working outside home and have low dispositional future orientation will be greatly handicapped when situation calls for active coping and planning, because they have not developed thesc resources.

Coping styles of seeking instrumental social emotional support, positive reinterpretation and growth and, religion were negatively and significantly predicted by only one variable of socio-economic status. These findings combined with the findings already discussed concerning role of SES in active coping and planning show that these women from low SES are doubly handicapped as they are unable to plan ahead and grapple with the problem actively, furthermore they do not try to positively reinterpret their situation and grow. These strategies cannot solve problems but may be needed for protection of ego. They disengage themselves from a problem both mentally and behaviourally. They are unable to use humour also. The importance of socio-economic status as a social fund is underscored.

Higher socio-economic status and working status helped them to cope directly and efficiently. Holahan *et al.* (1997) have proposed a resource model of coping in which coping functions as a mechanism through resources. Have been social resources conceptualised as 'social fund' which people may draw upon when handling stressors. Diener and Fujital (1995) have found that social resources can bolster coping efforts by enhancing self-efficacy, as well as, by providing informational guidance.

Coping style of mental and behavioural disengagement was significantly predicted by three socio-psychological variables, namely socio-economic status, working-nonworking status of women and future orientation.

Future orientation was positively related with and explained the use of active coping, planning and restraint coping. Individuals who have high future orientation first plan and then act. When confronted with a difficult situation, they plan in a systematic manner, suppress other competing activities and attack directly on the stressor. They have clear picture of their future plans and, therefore, they proceed to achieve those plans more actively (Brunstein, 1993). They are, however, likely to mentally and behaviourally disengage from a problem, if acting on it is not likely to solve the problem. They also use religion in such situations. It is important to note here that FO predicts actively coping on the one hand but also disengagement from a task, and recourse to religion when active coping cannot get results. It appears that future oriented person thus disengages from a problem only when active coping and planning cannot succeed. Optimism was positively correlated with two coping styles namely active coping and restraint coping. It appears that more optimistic women do not surrender to the stressor, they active grapple with stressor, they try to attack and to remove it, they suppress their other activities that may be interfering. In regression analysis, however, optimism did not emerge as a significant predictor of coping strategies. One of the reasons may be that there is overlap between FO and optimism and both of these variables were entered in multiple regression analysis. Other psychologists have found that optimism facilities in coping and enhances well-being in individuals. In a study, Scheier, *et al.*, 1989 have found that optimism in positively correlated with problem focused coping and reliance on playfulness (Carver, Scheier & Weintraub, 1989). Optimism was also positively correlated with use of positive reinterpretation and acceptance of the reality. Similar results have been found by other studies also (Chang, 1998; Taylor *et al.*, 1992; Carver *et al.*, 1993).

The results suggests that socio-economic status, working-non working status and future orientation are main predictors which explain variances in the usage of different coping styles. Optimism did not significantly predict use of any of the coping styles.

Coping Strategies Statisfaction with Life and Happiness

Results have also clearly shown that four of the seven coping strategies, namely, active coping, planning and restraint coping and humour were significantly correlated with both measures of subjective well-being namely, satisfaction and happiness. Use of religion was negatively correlated with both satisfaction and happiness. It appears that irrespective of the SES and working status, those women who actively do whatever needs to be done about the problem, concentrate on the problem and conserve their energies by leaving less important issues aside, think and try to find ways of resolving the problem are more satisfied with their life. They also control their emotions and try to look at the higher side of life when going gets tough and earn the gratification that life has not been lived in vain by making use of the above mentioned strategies. They also feel happier and have overall greater positive affect. They do not make use of religion for solution of problems. It appears that hitting the problem directly has more than one positive consequences. It can actually solve the problem but, even if it does not result in complete success, it results in a sense of accomplishment and usefulness, leading to greater satisfaction and happiness.

APPENDIX

The Cope Scale

Cope is a sixty item inventory with fifteen different coping scales. Fifteen scale were merged in eight sub-scales as follows:

(A) (i) Active coping
(ii) Suppression of Competing Activities
(B) (i) Planning
(ii) Restraint Coping
(C) (i) Seeking Instrumental Social Support
(ii) Seeking Emotional Social Support
(iii) Religion
(D) (i) Focus on and Venting of Emotions
(ii) Mental Disengagement
(iii) Behavioural Disengagement
(iv) Denial
(E) Positive Reinterpretation and Growth Acceptance
(F) Religion
(G) Alcohol/Drug use
(H) Humour

References

Agarwal, A. and Tripathi, L.B. (1979). Time perspective II : Development and empirical validation of a new tool. *Psychological Studies*, 24, 59-65.

Agarwal, A, (1980). Achievement motivation and time perspective. Agra : National Psychological Corporation.

Aldwin, C.M. & Revenson, T.A. (1987). Does coping help? A re-examination of the relation between coping and mental health. *Journal of Personality and Social Psychology*, 53, 237-248.

Andrews, F.M. and Withey, S.B. (1976). *Social Indicators of Well-being: America's Perception of Life Quality*, New York ; Plenum Press.

Andrews, F.M. and Inglehart, R.F. (1979). The structure of well-being in nine western societies. *Social Indicators Research*, 6, 73-90.

Brunstein J.C., (1993), 'Personal Goals and Subjective Well-Being: A Longitudinal Study,' *Journal of Personality and Social Psychology*, 65, 5, 1061-1070.

Campbell, A. (1981). *The Sense of Well-being in America : Recent Patterns and Trends*, New York : Mc Graw Hill.

Carver, C.S. Scheier, M.F., and Weintraub, J.K. (1989): Assessing Coping Strategies : A theoretically based approach. *Journal of Personality and Social Psychology*, 56, 267-283.

Carver, C.S. Pizo, C., Harris, Noriega, V., Schier, M.F., Robinson, D.S., Ket Cham, A.S., Moffat,F.L., Jr., and Clark, K.C., (1993). How coping mediates the effect of optimism on distress: A study of women with early stage breast cancer. *Journal of Personality and Social Psychology, 65*, 375-390.

Chang, E.C. (1998). Dispositional optimism and primary and secondary appraisal of a stressor : Controlling for confounding influences and relations to coping and psychological and physical adjustment. *Journal of Personality and Social Psychology*, 74, 4, 1109-1120.

Conway, V.J. & Terry, D.J. (1972). Appraised controllability as a moderator of life effectiveness of different coping strategies. *Australian Journal of Psychology*, 44, 1-7.

Diener, E. (1984). ' Subjective Well-Being,' *Psychological Bulletin*, 95, 3, 542-575.

Diener, E., Emmons, R., Larsen, R. & Griffin, S. (1985). The satisfaction with life scale, *Journal of Personality Assessment* 49, 71-75.

Diener, E. and Fujita, F. (1995). Resources, Personal strivings and subjective well-being: A homothetic and ideographic approach. *Journal of Personality and Social Psychology*, 68, 5, 926-935.

Emmons, R.A. (1986). Personal strivings: An approach to personality and subjective well-being. *Journal of Personality and Social Psychology*, 51, 1058-1068.

Folkman, S.; Lazarus, R.S.; Gruen, R. & Delongis, A. (1986). Appraisal, coping, health status and psychological symptoms. *Journal of Personality and Social Psychology*, 50, 571-579.

Forsythe, C.J. & Compas, B.E. (1987). Interaction of cognitive appraisals of stressful events and coping : Testing the goodness of fit hypothesis. *Cognitive Theory and Research*, 11, 473-485.

Holahan, C.J.; Moos, R.H.; Holahan, C.K. & Brennan, P.L. (1997). Social context, coping strategies and depressive symptoms : An extended model with cardiac patients. *Journal of Personality and Social Psychology* 72, 4, 918-928.

Lazarus, R.S. (1966). *Psychological Stress and Coping Proceeds.* New York : Mc Graw Hill.

Lazarus, R.S. & Folkman, S. (1984). *Stress Appraisal and Coping*, New York: Springer.

Little, B.R. (1987). Personality and environment. In D. Stobols and I. Altman (Eds.), *Handbook of Environmental Psychology*, Vol. I, 205-224. New York: Wiley.

Meade, R.R. (1972). Future time perspective of American and subcultures in India. *Journal of Cross-cultural Psychology*, 3, 93-99.

Palys, T.S. and Little, B.R. (1983). Perceived life satisfaction and the organization of personal projects system, *Journal of Personality and Social Psychology*, 44, 1221-1230.

Scheier, M.F. and Carver, C.S., (1985). 'Optimism, Coping and Health: Assessment and implications of generalised outcome expectancies.' *Health Psychology*, 4, 219-247.

Scheier, M.F.; Mittew, K.A.; Owen, J.F.; Magovers, G.J.; Srlefebvre, R.C.; Abbott; R.A. and Carver, C.S. (1989). Dispositional optimism and recovery from coronary artery bypass surgery. The beneficial effects on physical and psychological well-being. *Journal of Personality and Social Psychology*, 57, 1024-1040.

Schmutte, P.S. and Ryff, C.D., (1997), 'Personality and well-being. Re-examining methods and meanings, *Journal of Personality and Social Psychology*, 73, 3, 549-559.

Suls, J. & Fletcher, B. (1985). The relative efficacy of avoidant and non-violent coping strategies : A Meta analysis. *Health Psychology*, 4, 249-388.

Taylor, S.E.; Kemeny, M.E.; Aspinwall, L.G.; Schneider, S.G.; Rodriguez, R. and Herbert, M. (1992). Optimism, coping, psychological distress, and high-risk sexual behaviour among men at risk for Acquired Immuno Deficiency Syndrome (AIDS). *Journal of Personality and Social Psychology*, 63, 460-473.

Terry, D.J. (1994). Determinants of coping: The role of stable and situational factors. *Jorunal of Personality and Social Psychology,* 66, 895-910.

Vitaliano, P.P.; De Wolfe, D.J.; Mainro, R.D.; Russo, J. & Katon, W. (1990). Appraised changeability of a stressor as a modifier of the relationship between coping and depression : A test of hypothesis of fit. *Journal of Personality and Social Psychology*, 59, 582-592.

8

ENVIRONMENTAL STRESS AND COPING VILLAGERS HIT BY SUDDEN WHIRLWIND WITH HAILSTORM

A Case Study

A.K. SAXENA, P.S.N. TIWARI & V.C. TRIPATHI

A sudden natural unexpected calamity is more stressful than a predictable cyclic expected calamity (like flood and draught). Natural disaster includes almost a threatening event that occurs in natural environment. Natural disasters include weather of any kind e.g. heat, cold, whirlwind, floods, hailstorms blizzards. Natural disasters are generally not well predicted and are typically viewed as uncontrollable. The destructive power of a natural disaster is enormous and usually causes damage and wreck havoc the sheer magnitude of the impact of some disaster makes them unique among stressors. Natural Disasters often last only seconds or minutes and rarely persist for more than a few days. Heat waves and cold spells may persist longer, but most of them like earthquake and other mishaps are over, quickly perception of a disaster is greatest during and immediately following its occurrence.

The hazard is closely related to the well-being and resource use of a community, the inhabitancy are more aware of the danger. Frequency of disaster influences evaluative judgement of potential harm, as does personal experiences with similar disaster. Those who have lived through floods/hurricanes/drought are more aware of the risks, than those who have not had first hand experiences. Probably because each repetition of a disaster serves to preparedness to face dangers. The more frequently we experience a disaster the more conscious we are of potential risks. There are personality differences in the perceptions. Sims and Baumann

(1972) found that the Illinois residents appeared to take more precautions when storms approached such as listening for weather bulletins and warning neighbours, whereas Alabama residents paid less attention to the need to listen for radio or T.V. bulletins. Apparently then, personality plays some role in determining human perceptions of their control over hazards.

In another study of flood victims in Carman Manitoba, Canada. Simpson-Housley (1982) found that another personality characteristic of repressing was associated with efforts to minimize flood damage by activities elevating houses, installing pumps, and purchasing insurance. Individuals with a strong repressive personality type are known as repressors and they deal with threat by denying the existence of the threat and not verbalizing uneasy feelings about a potential danger. Although intuitively it seems odd that such individual would once take precautions against disaster but perhaps by doing so they feel they are in a better position to deny or avoid damage, if a disaster did occur in the area.

Lazarus (1966) suggested that cognitive appraisal is a function of individual psychological factors and cognitive aspects of the specific stimulus situation (e.g. control over the stimulus, predictability of the stimulus and immediacy or time until impact of the stimulus). Some appraisal may be oriented towards harm-loss or damage already done, that is once a disaster has struck. The appraisal is usually not that a threat is pending but a blow has already occurred. One might appraise some situations (such as climbing a mountain) as stressfully challenging but harm or loss assessments focus on damage that has already been done. For example the victims of a disaster would be expected to make harm/loss evaluations. In contrast, threat appraisals are concerned with future dangers. Attitude towards the source of stress will also mediate the responses. If we believe that a condition will cause no permanent harm our response will probably be less extreme than if it carries the threat of lasting harm. Once a stimulus has been evaluated as threatening, other cognitive factors come into play.

Most of the past research reveals that as the frequency of psychological problems increases anxiety, depression and other stress related emotional responses also increase. Disorientation and lack of connection are among the common symptoms noted in the disaster survivors when the community has been torn.

Part of the response to an aversive of stressful stimulus is automatic. General Adaption Syndrome or G.A.S consists of three stages, the alarm reaction, the stage of resistance and the stage of exhaustion. Initially there is an alarm reaction to a stressor, whereby automatic processes (heart rate, adrenaline secretion and so on) are speeded up. The second stage in the stress process, the stage of resistance, also begins with some automatic processes for coping with the stressor. In the stage of resistance many coping processes the individual must decide on a behavioural coping strategy. If the coping responses are not adequate to deal with the stressor, and all coping energies have exhausted, the organism will enter the third stage of the GAS, the stage of exhaustion. Fortunately something else usually happens before exhaustion occurs. In most situations when an aversive stimulus is presented many times, the stress reaction becomes weaker and weaker. Psychologically this process is called adaptation.

Adaptation to a stressor may occur because neuropsychological sensitivity to the stimulus becomes weaker, because uncertainty about the stressor is reduced or because the stressor is cognitively appraised as less threatening.

Coping has been defined as the process individuals use to modify adverse aspects of their environment as well as to minimize internal threat induced by the stress. The coping strategy is a function of individual and situational factors, and may consist of flight, physical or verbal attack, or some sort of compromise. A distinction is usually made between primary appraisal, which involves assessment of threat and secondary appraisal, which involves assessment of coping strategies. Lack of success in the coping process may increase the tendency to evaluate the situation as threatening. Associated with this cognitive coping process are any number of emotions including anger and fear.

Coping strategies may be classified as direct action, such as information seeking flight or attempts to remove or stop the stressor, or palliative such as employing psychological defence mechanism (denial, intellectualisation etc.), using drugs, mediating or reassessing the situation as non threatening. To the extent that direct action is not available or practical, palliative strategies become more likely [Baum Flaming and Singer (1982)].

One aspect of cognitive coping that has begun to receive attention is appraisal. It is the process of evaluating salient dimensions of the stressor event such as its threat potential, meaningfulness, predictability and controllability. Cognitive appraisals are primary components of the coping process that may interact with methods of coping to affect adjustment to stressors. Another potentially important dimension of coping is the distinction between problem focused coping strategies, defined as efforts to recognize modify or eliminate the impact of a stressor or cognitive activity and emotion associated with stress.

The present study seeks to evaluate natural disaster, a month, after, its occurrence and to understand the coping strategies of the villagers.

METHOD

Sample

The sample consisted of 100 villagers (heads of the family), living in three blocks (Chargawa, Sardarnagar and Sahjanwa) of Gorakhpur district in eastern Uttar Pradesh. They came for the study between 35 to 65 years. The most seriously affected villages were chosen. The selection of the village was determined by the characteristics classifying features of the deprivational environment.

Instruments

The villagers were interviewed with the help of a semi-structured 54 items schedule. It tapped three areas, i.e., perception of disaster, after effects (psychological problems), and coping efforts.

Procedures

The study was divided into two phases namely initial interview and stress interview. In the first phase 20 victims were taken. After establishing rapport, subjects were asked to describe about the event and to indicate their feelings of loss, anxiety and other psychological problems. After the initial interview stress related factors were studied. On the basis of these interview we made a 54 item semi-structured interview schedule.

In second phase of the study, called, stress interviews the most seriously affected villages were chosen and with the help of interview schedule, villagers were interviewed. Villagers were also asked to give their names, monthly income, age and identification information.

RESULTS AND DISCUSSIONS

The sudden natural and unexpected whirlwind with hailstorm on 25th February, 1998 destroyed the ripe harvest in some villages in the vicinity of Gorakhpur. It also resulted in the death of 6 persons. The local residents experienced feelings of anxiety, future-danger, irritation, numbness, help-lessness along with other stress related disturbances. Percentages of responses were calculated. It was found that 96 per cent indicated perceived the event as unexpected. When the villagers were asked and their views about the reason of natural calamity, there was consensus among villagers that '*ek daivi prakop hai*' (It is divine curse), 67 per cent of villagers perceived the incidence as "*Karma ka fal hai*" (The result of *Karma*), 84 per cent villagers told it was beyond their control. Most of the villagers felt that those people are lucky who have not suffered from the disaster. They were unable to speak even a word about control over such an event. 84 per cent villagers felt that only mighty force like God, fate and Government can be able to prevent such unfortunate events.

The predictability of event has also been linked to control and stress. Aversive events which are unpredictable are more difficult to control. Unpredictable stressors may also be more aversive because individuals are left without any cues. The most investigated construct mediating between environmental stressor and human outcome measures has been perceived control. It has been used as a principal mechanism for the adverse effects of environmental stressors. Chronic exposure to uncontrollable stress has been found to result in learned helplessness.

The immediate responses of the villagers are shown in Table 8.1. There was complete agreement among villagers that family feels anxious, even to think about the loss. 61 per cent showed stupefied feeling after the event. The 58 per cent subjects showed anxiety for future survival and said "*Aab kaise jiyaenge khayenge*", 24 per cent villagers said after the incident that their families did not take food on that day. 12 per cent villagers took it as a 'cruelty of God'. A stunned numb response to the immediate impact of disaster was also seen. This is consistent with researches which suggest that suddenness causes emotional numbness.

Table 8.1: Immediate Responses of Victims Family/Neighbours

S. No.	*Immediate response*	*Number in %*
1.	Stupefied feelings/Numbness	61
2.	Anxiety for future survival	58
3.	Shocked	47
4.	Abstaining from food	24
5.	Loud utterance of grief	21
6.	Some people say this is Cruelty of God	12

In regard to after effects of the event 98 per cent villagers said they felt serious anxiety when they think about their loss. 85 per cent villagers felt irritation after the disaster. 85 per cent villagers felt fear when they recalled the calamity. 35 per cent person felt sleep disturbance after the event. 85 per cent subjects believe they were unable to cope with the disaster and 84 per cent told only out side forces (Govt., God., Fate) only can control their problems. 71 per cent villagers felt helplessness after the disaster destroyed their ripe harvest. Results suggest that lack of control over the event, appear to be most disturbing.

Such differences are related to the personality dimension of internal *Vs.* external locus of control. Internals believe they are in control of their own fate, whereas, externals believe outside forces such as powerful person, Govt, God or fate control their destinies. The unpredictable, uncontrolled suddenness coupled with pre-existing faith in external forces in the Indian culture can explain these reactions.

The analysis of the pattern of responses among the victims revealed, a variety of themes. The villagers demand government help. 97 per cent villagers want to get financial assistance for the damage of crops. 47 per cent wanted to stop the rent realisation. About 35 per cent villagers wanted that government debt be waived off, 25 per cent villagers demanded permanent job for their unemployed son. Linking in terms of preference for the results revealed that 52 per cent villagers liked to take help from their relatives. 71 per cent villagers like to take loan from banks. About 17 per cent villagers liked to sell his property/wealth for compensation. Only 10 per cent villagers liked to withdraw from the area.

Table 8.2 presents the observational findings. The lower class villagers belonged to lower castes. 73 per cent villagers showed anger responses against the responsible authorities (Pradhan, Lekhpal, M.L.A. etc). 28 per cent villagers felt they will have many problems because they have no permanent employment. The most interesting observation was that 88 per cent villagers did not know about reality of environmental problems and they are not aware regarding how the environmental problems arise by technological, industrial, ecological factors.

In conclusion it may be observed that natural calamity can affect people in a number of ways. It is clearly stressful. It limits freedom and behavioural options and may cause loss of people leading to the breakdown or disruption of community life. The concept of stress, however, involves not just a simple automatic stimulus response relationship but contains a number of evaluative components. To begin

Table 8.2: Observational Findings

S. No.	*Observational ratings*	*Number in %*
1.	Caste Awareness (They want more help because they belong to lower castes)	35
2.	Angry at the responsible authority (Pradhan, Lekhpal, M.L.A.)	73
3.	They have many problems due to unemployment (self & other family members)	28
4.	They don't know about environmental problems arising by Technological and Industrial pollution.	88

with not all stressful stimuli are aversive enough in themselves to evoke the automatic alarm and resistance response. The stress process begins when a stimulus is appraised as threatening.

The study reveals that the stress was so sudden and serious that villagers were unable to evaluate the demands of the situation. However they banked heavily on Government's help and financial assistance. The results showed that the attribution of this stress was held to be external. Incidentally it was a day of worship of Lord Shiva (The *Mahashivratri*) and the event was associated with God. It was wrath of God.

The villagers held that governments contribution is more effective in such situations. It is suggested that people must be made aware of such incidents, warning signals through media be given and precautions necessary to safeguard against the disaster to be taken. If control is not possible at all then sufficient help to the people should be provided immediately after the disaster has occurred. Non-governmental organisation and voluntary help groups can help them be prepared psychologically.

The significance of the study lies in the fact that it shows how villagers react to a natural sudden disaster in a deprived setting. Keeping in view their reactions, plan for disaster management in future could be prepared.

References

Baum A. Gatchel R.J. (1981) Cognitive determinants of response to uncontrollable events. Development of reactance and learned helplessness. *Journal of Personality and Social Psychology*. Vol. 40, p. 1078-1086.

Baum, A. Flaming R, & Singer J.C. (1982) Stress at three mile island. Applying psychological impact analysis in L. Bickman (Ed) *Applied Social*

Psychology annual, Beverly Hills Sage.

Cohen, S. Evans G.W., Stokols D & Krantz, O (1986). *Behaviour, Health and Environmental Stress*, New York: Plenum.

Davidson, L.M., Baum, A, & Collins, D. (1982), Stress control-related problems at three mile island, *Journal of Applied Social Psychology*?

Fisher, J.D., Bell P.A. & Baum, A (1984) *Environmental Psychology*. C.B.S. International, New York.

Folkman's (1984) Personal control and stress and coping process : A theoretical analysis. *Journal of Personality and Social Psychology*. 46, 839-852.

Lazarus (1966) *Psychological Stress and the Coping Process*, New York. McGraw Hill.

Simpson-Housley P. Moor, R.J. Larrain P & Blair, D. (1982) Repression, sensitisation and flood hazard appraisal in Carman, Manitoba, *Psychological Reports,* Vol. 50, 839-842.

Sims J.H. & Baumann D.D. (1972). The Tornade threat: *Coping Style of the North and the South Science,* Vol. 176, 1386-1391.

Stokols, Daniel & Altman Irwin (1987) *Handbook of Environmental Psychology*, (Vol I & II) New York; John Wiley.

9

AN EMPIRICAL STUDY OF THE ROLE OF PERCEIVED CONTROL IN COPING WITH RESIDENTIAL CROWDING

SUSHMA PANDEY

An alarming increase in world population is threatening the very existence of human race. Population density has resulted in environmental pollution, depletion of natural resources, excessive demand for food and damage of quality life (Singh, 1998; Lazarus, 1974). In contemporary Psychological researches, the resurgence of interest in crowding seems to be the result of two bare realities of modern life, i.e., population explosion and revival of individualism (Jain, 1997).

The Psycho-social consequences of crowding are very natural in this overpopulated country. People try to cope with hassles related to daily life demands. Psychological resources for coping and perceived control have been found to buffer stress – health/behaviour relations (Pandey, 1999; Skinner, 1995; Pandey & Srivastava, 1995; Jain, 1997, 1984; Rodin, 1986; Pandey, 1978). In the coping process the relation between control and coping are likely to be reciprocal. Control influences coping reactions but it may also change as a function of the occurrence of negative events as well as on the extent to which stressors orient to modify it (Skinner, 1995).

Thus, personal control of people may exercise influence in perceiving and feeling of crowding related stress. Furthermore, the psychological influence of crowding and perceived control may have significant effect on people health and behaviour.

In the present study the relationship between crowding, perceived control and health is investigated and an effort is made to explain the role of perceived control between stress-health connections.

Psychologists distinguish between density and crowding. Density refers to the physical or spatial aspects of setting i.e., number. of people per spatial area. Crowding is used to refer to the psychological or subjective factors in the situation (Stokols, 1978; Rapoport, 1975). Spatial constraint is necessary for density, but for crowding it is not the sufficient condition. In order for a high density situation to be experienced as crowded additional personal and social factors need to be present. Density is the direct perception of available place while crowding is a subjective evaluation that the perceived amount of space is inadequate. A distinction is made between social density and spatial density (Saegert, 1973, 1974, Loo, 1973). Social density varies the size of a social group in a spatial setting of constant size. Spatial density is assessed by studying a social group of constant size in a setting of various size. Inside density *Vs.* outside density which is referred as social density in the broader geographic area which includes larger number of residential unit and density within the residence.

Loo (1977) presented a model of crowding which explains that person has both social needs and spatial needs. Crowding stress occurs when the individual's needs (spatial and social needs) are out of step with environmental realities, thus psychological stress may occur both in undercrowded and overcrowded settings. A state of harmony is obtained when the environment is both socially and spatially uncrowded. It is however, obvious that high density will lead to psychological stress or not, will depend on the particular characteristics of the situation whether it is perceived pleasant or unpleasant (Freedman, 1975). Stokols (1972) views crowding in two different ways. First crowding as a stressor situation and is considered as causal factor and second crowding is considered as a stress syndrome. The important aspect of crowding is a stress syndrome which consists of the ways in which people try to cope with crowding. If a person fails to control crowded situation either behaviourally (External) or cognitively (Internal) his behaviour and well-being are adversely affected. Several studies report the negative consequences of crowding on health status of people in urban environment, college dormitories and prison (Luke & Abadzi 1985, Baum *et al.,* 1978; Sundstrom, 1978; Levy & Herzog 1974). Positive correlation between inside density and mortality is reported (Coex *et al.*, 1984; Paulus, McCain & Cox, 1978; Galle *et al.*, 1972). Some of the mental problems associated with anxiety, neurosis, coronary heart diseases, hypertension, fatigue, depression, etc. are found to be associated with crowding related stress (Jain, 1997; Schaeffer *et al.*, 1988; Iwata, 1979). Nagar & Pandey (1985) reported relationship between crowding, interpersonal relation and adjustment. Psychologists remark that individual variations are found on crowding reactions as a result of age, status, power, culture and experiences (Paulus & Nagar, 1990). Therefore, effective strategies should be applied to mitigate stress-health connection. Murphy (1988) proposed that perception of control over environment has certain impact on stress-health relationship. Generally people having high sense of perceived control report less health problems than those who lack sense of control. Miller (1979) refers that controllable events hurt less than uncontrollable events.

Control refers to a 'belief' that a person has the ability to direct, regulate and manipulate events, situations and resources. The sense of control as a core construct is found in these constructs i.e. Locus of control (Rotter, 1966); self-efficacy (Bandura, 1977); Hardiness (Kabasa, Meddi & Jolla, 1983); and sense of coherence (Antonovsky, 1987). These four constructs have been found to be negatively related with distress and mediate stress-health relationship. Perceived control is an important construct, which has significant role in stress-health dynamics. Perceived control or personal control is defined as the ability to establish correspondence between cognitive and behavioural consequences of one's control. The notion of perceived control is implicit in the information overload model of crowding i.e., the experience of crowding is concerned with inability to control the level of spatial and social information faced by person in high density situation (Schmidt & Keating, 1979). The behavioural constraint model of crowding also includes the view of personal control. The experience of crowding occurs when person cannot effectively manage social and spatial interference or interruptions of one's goal directed behaviour in high density situations (Rodin *et al.*, 1978). Furthermore, 'learned helplessness model (Seligman 1975) of environmental stress explains some of the psychological consequences of loss of personal control in high density situation. This model refers that lack of perceived control leads to learned helplessness; a syndrome of cognitive, motivational and emotional deficits produced by learning that events are not one's under control (Seligman, 1975). Health is impaired or threatened if control is impaired or threatened. A close relation between crowding and illness is reported and in this regard, perceived control is beneficial to mitigate stress reactions (Pandey, 1999; Fleming *et al.*, 1987; Rodin *et al.*, 1978; Schmidt & Keating, 1979). The type of control person develop to cope with crowding is also influenced by socio-cultural factors. Rubec and Paten (1980) revealed that traditional Hindu (Indians) have belief that external forces (fate) determine behaviour (loss and gain), hence people accept things as they are. Thus perceived control over the environment should be suggested in India. The cultural variations in terms of personal control and crowding stress is also indicated in other studies (Schmidt, 1983). Baum *et al.*, (1978) evinced that the extent of personal control varies in different socio-economic groups. Prolonged exposure to crowded condition leads to loss of control over their life and outcomes.

The role of control in dealing with crowding stress is more complex. Stress reducing characteristics of control depend upon the measuring of control for individual (Averill, 1973). Worchel (1978) indicates that crowding feeling takes place only when a non-specific state of arousal is attributed to excessively close interpersonal proximity. Psychologists have suggested that density is not always perceived uncontrollable unless others are perceptually salient and unless blame for interrupting one's freedom is attributed to their presence rather than to other factors in the setting. Therefore, both social and cultural factors determine the perception of crowding (Stokols *et al.,* 1973). Investigators reasoned that perceived control influences individuals self perception, expectancies, motivations and it improves the sense of competence in dealing with environment. Crowding stress, however, can be mitigated when an individual can modify threatening events directly (behavioural control) or interpret the situation in such a way that it no longer appears threatening (Cognitive control). Crowding stress causes illness (Evans & Leopore, 1992), and perceived control buffers this stress-health relationship (Skinner, 1995).

Hypotheses

Present study aimed to investigate the relationship between crowding, perceived control and health and an attempt is made to explain the role of perceived control in coping with crowding.

Following hypotheses were put for test :

(1) It was hypothesised that there would be a close relation between crowding and illness. People residing in high dense area would express more health problems as compared to residents of low dense area. The extent of physical and mental illness would vary between both groups.

(2) It was also assumed that an inverse relation between crowding and perceived control as well as between perceived control and illness would be found. Furthermore, the extent of these relations would vary according to the behavioural and cognitive forms of perceived control in both groups.

METHOD

Respondents

A total of sixty adults aged 25-35 years (30 from high dense area and 30 from low dense area, belonging to high, middle and low socio-economic status) participated in this study. Stratified sampling technique was applied for sample selection. Two areas of Gorakhpur city were chalked out: one was a remote, old and more densely populated area and other was a more planned and well developed, low dense area. Outside density of these areas was considered according to the locality i.e., distance of roads, markets etc. from the houses.

Measures

1. *Crowding Measure* : Developed and standardised by Jain (1984), the crowding measure consists of items regarding (a) objective crowding, and (b) feeling of crowding.
   (a) *Objective Crowding* : The level of objective crowding is determined on the basis of type of house, number of rooms in the house, member of persons per room and type of locality (rated in terms of good, average and bad). Items are open ended.
   (b) *Subjective Crowding* : This questionnaire measures the feelings of crowding, insecurity, anxiety, negative attitude towards neighbours, disturbances of noise, uncleanliness and lack of space. Items are rated on five points scale.
2. *Perceived Control Scale* : Jain's (1984) perceived control scale ascertains two levels of control i.e., behavioural (External) and cognitive (Internal). Cognitive control refers to the control over self and measures the extent to which people have control over the various activities in day to day life. Behavioural control is measured in terms of environmental factors i.e., noise, neighbours, space in the house etc. Items related to cognitive

control are scored following 1, 2, 3, 4, and 5 order and for behavioural control reverse order is applied for the scoring.

3. *Health Questionnaire* : Abridged version of Cornell Medical Index (CMI) translated into Hindi by Wig, Prasad & Verma (1983) was used. CMI contains 195 questions in various sections, (a) Physical distress and (b) Emotional or Psychological distress. For the purpose of present study, 50 items were selected. These items were tested for their utility in Pilot study. The dimension of physical health (distress) has five categories of items related to common symptoms of hearing disorders, stomach problems, heart disease, joint pain and fatigue. Psychological health section consists of depression, anxiety, hesitation, frustration and other mental distress. The split half reliability of 50 items version is 0.85.

Procedure

Respondents were given booklet, containing measures of crowding, perceived control and illness. They were requested to fill up background informations and then respond on items pertaining to objective and feelings of crowding. Later on, they were asked to answer on perceived control measure and lastly, they were instructed to respond on health questionnaire.

Density (objective crowding) was considered on the basis of obtained scores on 6 items. 0-2 was considered as bad locality, 3 and 4 was put in the average and 5 and 6 in the good category.

Feeling of crowding was scored in terms of 1, 2, 3, 4 and 5 for positively used items and negatively used items were scored in reverse order. In order to determine the extent of perceived control both on cognitive and behavioural levels scoring was done differently. Cognitive control was determined following 1, 2, 3, 4 and 5 and for behavioural control reverse order i.e., 5, 4, 3, 2, 1 was applied. Since response on C.M.I. health questionnaire was obtained on Yes/No pattern hence one (1) score was provided for yes and zero (0) for no.

RESULTS

Data obtained from residents of high and low dense areas, were scored and analysed in terms of means, S.Ds and correlations. Table 9.1 presents mean and S.D. of crowding, perceived control (cognitive and behavioural) and health (physical and mental) of both groups. It appears that feeling of crowding was greater in high density group ($\bar{X}$ = 62.13) as compared to low density group ($\bar{X}$ = 40.20). The health status of high density group was poorer ($\bar{X}$ = 18.07) and compared to low density group ($\bar{X}$ = 8.27). Their mental health [$\bar{X}$ (HD)] = 10.50 $\bar{X}$ (LD) = 5.47 as compared to physical health [$\bar{X}$ (HD)] = 7.57, $\bar{X}$ (LD) = 2.8) was more affected. The mean score of perceived control (total) was greater in low density group ($\bar{X}$ = 67.6) as compared to high density group ($\bar{X}$ = 62.6). Both groups varied at cognitive and behavioural control levels. At behavioural control low density group showed better control ($\bar{X}$ = 49.8) as compared to high density ($\bar{X}$ = 41.5), but it is interesting to note that on cognitive control level, high density group reported better control ($\bar{X}$ = 20.6) as compared to low density group ($\bar{X}$ = 19.7). It is suggested that residents living in high dense areas can control stress by interpreting the situation in such a way that it no longer appears threatening (cognitive control) and thus can mitigate adverse effect of stress on health.

Table 9.1: $\bar{X}$ and S.D. of Crowding, Perceived Control and Health of High and Low Density of Groups

		High		*Low*	
		Mean	*S.D.*	*Mean*	*S.D.*
Crowding		62.13	10.32	40.20	12.42
Perceived Control :	(i) Cognitive	20.60	5.16	19.70	5.08
	(ii) Behavioural	41.50	12.96	49.80	10.60
	(iii) Total	62.20	10.94	67.60	11.60
Health :	Physical	7.57	3.18	2.8	1.10
	Mental	10.50	3.64	5.47	2.76
	Total	18.07	5.84	8.27	2.13

N = 30 in each cell.

To ascertain the direction and extent of relation between crowding, perceived control and health, correlations were computed. Correlation values displayed in Table 9.2, reveal, that in high density group, the relationships of crowding with cognitive control (r = –.42, p <.01), behavioural control (r = –.423, P <.01) and total perceived control (r = –.54, P < .001) were found to be significantly negative. Contrary to this, a positive relation between crowding and illness was reported. Crowding was found to be positively related with physical illness [r (HD) = .48, p < .01; r (LD) = .52, p < .01], mental illness [r (HD) =

.44, p < .01; r (LD) = .70, p < .01] and total illness [r (HD) = .38, p < .01; r (LD) = .79]

Apart from this, an inverse relation between perceived control and illness was found in both group. More specifically, the relations between cognitive control and illness [r (HD) = –.61, p < .01, r (LD) = –.68, p < .01] and between behavioural control and illness [r (HD) = –.42, p < .01, r (LD) = –.65, p < .01] were found to be significantly negative. It appears that persons who lack control on self and over environment feel more stress and receive poor health.

Table 9.2 Coefficient of Correlation, Computed between Crowding, Perceived Control and Health in High and Low Density Groups

	High Density	*Low Density*
Crowding & Cognitive perceived control	r= –.42**	r= .50**
Crowding & behavioural perceived control	r= –.423***	r= .63**
Crowding & Total perceived control	r= –.54**	r= .54**
Crowding & Physical illness	r= .48**	r= .52**
Crowding & Mental illness	r= .44**	r= .70**
Crowding & Total illness	r= .38**	r= .79**
Cognitive perceived Control & illness	r= –.61**	r= –.68**
Behavioural perceived Control & illness	r= –.42**	r= –.65**
Total Perceived control & Total illness	r= –.17**	r= –.26**

**p .01

Table 9.3: Chi square (X^2) Values Obtained from 2 × 2 Contingency table for Various Dimensions of Health

Dimension of Health	*x^2 Value*	*Significance*
Problems of ear, nose & throat	.064	Not significant
Problems related to heart	3.91*	P <.05
Problems related to stomach	0.137	Not significant
Fatigue	1.89	Not significant
Problems related to joints	3.98*	P <.05
Hesitation	7.44**	P <.01
Frustration	0.527	Not significant
Anxiety	3.96*	P <.05
Depression	4.44*	P <.05
Distress	0.725	Not significant

* P <.05
** P <.01

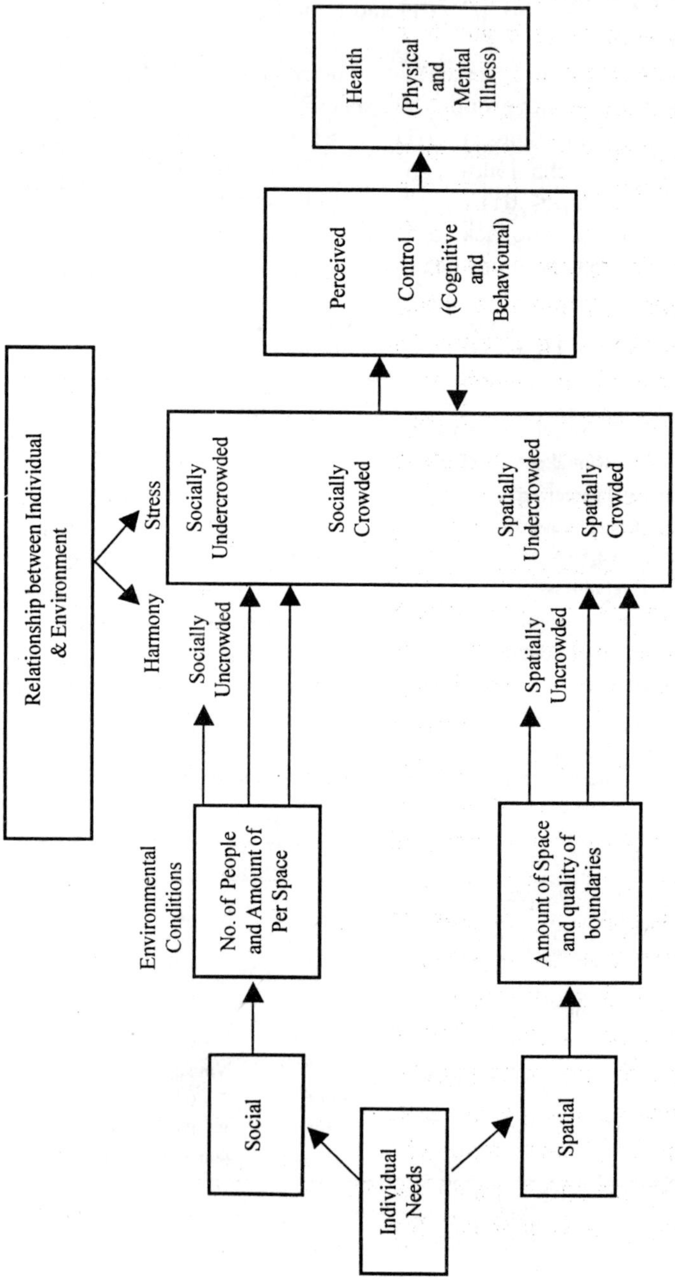

Fig. 9.1: A Model of Relationship between Crowding, Perceived Control and Health

X^2 values presented in Table 9.3 report that both groups differ significantly on some of the dimensions of health such as problems concerned with heart, joints and mental problems as hesitation, anxiety and depression ($X^2 = 3.91, 3.98, 7.44, 3.96, 4.44$) either on .05 or .01 level respectively. On the basis of findings of the present study a model (Fig. 9.1) is presented to describe the relationship between density, crowding stress, perceived control and illness.

DISCUSSION

Present study was planned to determine the relationship between crowding, perceived control and health, and effort was made to discuss the role of perceived control between stress-health connection. Discussion includes two main points. (i) Correlations between crowding and various combinations of perceived control i.e., cognitive (internal) control, behavioural (external) control and total control, report interesting facts. A negative correlation between crowding and perceived control was found in high density group. Mean scores report that pattern of cognitive and behavioural control varied among both groups, though high density group reported poorer control at behavioural level (external) but this group reported better control on self (cognitive) as compared to low density group. It seems that people residing high density condition have developed a strategy of personal control on self. Therefore, the role of perceived control can be used to cope with crowding and to mitigating illness.

Crowding has clear relation with health. As is evident from the results that high density group reported poor health, they are prone to disease, their mental health is more affected as compared to physical health, on the other hand low density group showed better health condition. Findings confirm the assumption that a clear relationship between crowding, perceived control and health is found and crowding has negative impact on physical and mental health of the resident of highly populated area. Result is consistent with earlier findings (Evan & Leepore, 1992; Jain, 1997).

The second point of discussion indicates that perceived control mediates stress-health connection. A negative correlation between crowding and perceived control is already reported. Similarly the relationship between perceived control and illness was found to be negative. Results reveal that people residing in high dense area have low level of control, therefore, their health status was more affected as compared to low density group. Mental health was adversely affected as compared to physical health.

It is apparent from Table 9.3 that some of the dimensions of health were more affected among high density group i.e. problems related to heart, joints and several psychological problems as anxiety, hesitation and depression. Since prolonged exposure of crowding helps develop incidence of poor health, however several causal factors are identified. Information overload, behavioural constraints and learned helplessness causes loss of control on environment and lead to physical and mental illness on various dimensions. Present result is consistent with other research findings, that population density characterised by stress, discomfort, arousal of personal control, evoke feeling of crowding and lead to disturbances in mental health (Jain, 1987; Cox *et al.,* 1972). Some studies reported poor correlation between stress and health in urban college dormitories. In this regard the role of cognitive factor i.e. feeling of crowding is found to be associated with illness. Findings of present study do not warrant any causal relation but support the results of studies in which health problems associated with crowding (Jain, 1997; Cox, 1984; Evans & Leopore, 1992) are reported.

Negative relation between perceived control, crowding and health indicates that in high density situation loss of control over social interaction and outcome is generally reduced due to lack of choice, and correspondence in effort to reduce crowding. The impact of cognitive control in determining reaction to crowding has been analysed (Schmidt & Keating, 1979; Valines & Baum, 1973; Jain and Mishra, 1986), Rodin *et al.*, (1978) reported significance of perceived control in coping with crowding. A model is presented to show the relationship between person and environment and also to explain the relationship between crowding, perceived control and health (Fig. 9.1). Persons have both social needs and spatial needs. The feeling of crowding takes place when the individual's needs in these areas are not fulfilled (Loo, 1977). According to this model crowding stress can be induced by the settings which are overcrowded as well as those that are undercrowded. A state of harmony is obtained if the environment is both socially and environmentally uncrowded. Whether or not high density will cause stress, will depend on the individual's social and spatial needs in a particular situation and also the particular characteristics of the situation whether it is perceived pleasant or unpleasant. Crowding is an ongoing process of human environment transaction. The feeling of stress is also mediated by perceived control. Stress causes loss of control but as a personality characteristic, it (control) diminishes stress feelings and plays important role in mitigating stress-illness relations. Findings suggest that the concept of control can be fruitfully utilised in crowded settings which help reduce distress and promote health by enhancing sense of control among residents of densely populated area. The consequences of crowding on health can be mitigated by degree of perceived control, whether people modify events directly or interpret the situation in such form that it no longer appears threatening (Cohen, Glass & Philip, 1979; Moos, 1989; Sherrod, 1974). The rapid growth of population has created a state of loss of control, hence cognitive appraisal of the negative consequences is the key to understand the significance of research on crowding. The awareness of crowding and its negative consequences, the cognition of the role of cognitive and behavioural forms of personal control in coping with crowding are relevant to town planners, architects, builders and person, in developing, maintaining and enhancing the quality of life and well-being. However, the notion of personal control is essential particularly to the information overload, behavioural constraint and diminished control theories of crowding to apply intervention strategies associating community people, administrators and planners to check the negative consequences of crowding (Jain, 1997), crowding research can also be more clearly conceptualised and thoroughly tested utilising the moderator-mediator variable distinction (Evans & Leopore, 1992).

References

Antonovsky, A. (1987). *Unravelling the Mystery of Health.* San Francisco: Jossey-Bass.

Averiel, J.R. (1973). Personal control over aversive stimuli and its relationship to stress. *Psychological Bulletin*, 80, 286-303.

Baum, A., Aiello, J. & Calesnick, L. (1978). Crowding and Perceived Control : Social density and the development of learned helplessness. *Journal of Personality and Social Psychology*, 43, 821-830.

Cohen, S., Glass, D.C. & Phillips, S. (1979). Environment and health. In H.E. Freeman, S. Levine, and L.G. Reeder (eds.), *Handbook of Medical Sociology*. Englewood Cliffs, N.J., Prentice-Hall.

Cox, V.C., Palus, P.M., McCain, G. & Karlovac, M. (1992). The relationship between crowding and health. In A. Baum and J. Singer (eds.). *Advances in Environmental Psychology*. Hillsdale, N.J. Earlbaum.

Evans, G.W. & Leopore, S.J. (1992). Conceptual and Analytical issues in crowding research. *Journal of Environmental Psychology*, 12, 163-173.

Fleming, I., Baum, A. & Weiss, L. (1987). Social density and perceived control as mediators of crowding stress in high density neighbourhood. *Journal of Personality and Social Psychology*, 52, 899-906.

Freedman, J.L. (1975). *Crowding and Behaviour*. San Francisco W.H. Freeman.

Galle, O.R., Gove, W.R., & McPherson, J.M. (1972). Population density and pathology : What are the relationships for man? *Science*, 176, 23-30.

Iwata, D. (1979) Selected personality traits as determinants of perception of crowding. *Japanese Psychological Research*, 21, 1-9.

Jain, U. (1984). Effect of inside-outside density on social behaviour. *Paper presented at U.G.C. Workshop*, Jaipur. University of Rajasthan.

Jain, U. (1987). Effect of population density and resources on the feeling of crowding and personal space. *Journal of Social Psychology*, 27, 331-338.

Jain, U. & Mishra, G. (1986). Consequences of Crowding. *Paper presented at the Workshop on Population Education*. Regional College of Education, Bhopal.

Jain, U. (1997). The feeling of crowding and its psychological consequences. New Delhi : Har Anand Publications.

Kabasa, S.C., Meddi, S.R. & Zolla, M.A. (1983). Type A and hardiness. *Journal of Behavioural Medicine*. 6, 41-51.

Lazarus, R.S. (1974). *The Riddle of Man*. Englewood Cliffs, N.J. : Prentice-Hall.

Levy, L. & Herzog, A. (1974). Effects of Population density and crowding on health and social adaptation in the Netherlands. *Journal of Health and Social Behaviour*. 15, 228-240.

Loo, C.M. (1972). The effect of spatial density on the social behaviour of children. *Journal of Applied Social Psychology*, 2, 372-381.

Loo, C.M. (1977). Beyond the effects of crowding : Situational and individual differences : In D. Stokols (ed.), *Perceptions on Environment and Behaviour*. New York : Plenum.

Miller, S.M. (1979). Controllability and human stress : Method, evidence and theory. *Behaviour Research and Therapy*, 17, 287-304.

Moos, R.H. (1979). *Evaluating Educational Environments*. San Francisco : Jossey-Bass.

Murphy, L.R. (1988). Work place intervention for stress reduction and prevention. In C.L. Cooper & R. Payne (eds.). *Causes of Coping and Consequences of Stress at Work*. New York : Wiley.

Nagar, D. (1985). Experience and Consequences of Crowding. *Unpublished Doctoral Dissertation*, Allahabad University, Allahabad.

Pandey, J. (1978). Effects of crowding on human social behaviour. *Journal of Social and Economic Studies*, 5, 85-95.

Pandey, S. & Srivastava, R. (1995). Psychological influence of crowding and perceived control on health. *Souvenir* : VII Congress of National Academy of Psychology.

Pandey, S. (1999). Role of perceived control in coping with crowding. *Psychological Studies*, 3, 86-91.

Paulus, P.B. & Nagar, D. (1990). Environmental influences on groups. In P.B. Paulus (eds.) *Psychology of Group Influences* : Hillsdale N.J. : Lawrence Erlbaum.

Paulus, P.B., McCain, G. & Cox, V.C. (1978). Death rates, psychiatric commitments, blood pressure, and perceived crowding as a function of institutional crowding. *Environmental Psychology and Non-verbal Behaviour*, 3, 107-116.

Rapoport, A. (1975). Toward a redefinition of density. *Environment and Behaviour*, 7, 133-158.

Rodin, J., Solomon, S.K. & Metcalf, J. (1978). Role of control in mediating perceptions of density. *Journal of Personality and Social Psychology*, 36, 988-999.

Rotter, J.B. (1966). Generalised expectancies for internal *Vs.* external control of reinforcement. *Psychological Monographs*, 80, 1-28.

Ruback, R.B. & Car, T.S. (1984). Crowding in Women's prison : Attitudinal and behavioural effects. *Journal of Applied Social Psychology*, 14, 57-58.

Saegert, S. (1973). Crowding : Cognitive overload and behavioural constraint. In W.F.E. Preiser (ed.), *Environmental Design Research*. Stroudsburg, Pa. Dowden, Hutchinson & Ross.

Saegert, S. (1974). Effects of Spatial and Social density on arousal, mood and social orientation. *Unpublished Doctoral Dissertation*, University of Michigan, Ann Arbor.

Schaeffer, M.A., Baum, A., Paulus, P.B. & Gaes, G.C. (1988). Architecturally mediated effects of social density in Prison. *Environment and Behaviour*, 20, 3-19.

Schmidt, D.E. & Keating, J.P. (1979). Human Crowding and Personal Control : An integration of the research. *Psychological Bulletin*, 86, 680-700.

Sherrod, D.R. (1974). Crowding, Perceived control, and behavioural after effects. *Journal of Applied Social Psychology*, 4, 171-186.

Seligman, M.E.P. (1975). *Helplessness : On depression, development and death.* San Francisco : Free Press.

Skinner, E.A. (1995). *Perceived Control, Motivation and Coping : Individual Differences and Development Series*. Volume 8, Sage Publication.

Stokols, D. (1978). A Social Psychological model of human crowding phenomena. *Journal of the American Institute of Planners*, 38, 72-84.

Stokols, D. (1978). Environmental *Psychology, Annual Review of Psychology*, 29, 253-295.

Stokols, D., Rall, M., Pinner, B. & Schopler, J. (1973). Physical, Social and Personal determinants of the perception of crowding. *Environment and Behaviour*, 5,87-115.

Sundstrom, E. (1978). Crowding as a sequential process: Review of research on the effects of Population density on humans. In A. Baum & Y.M. Epstein (eds.), *Human Response to Crowding*. Hillsdale, N.J. : Earlbaum.

Valins, S. & Baum, A. (1973). Residential group size, social interaction and crowding. *Environment and Behaviour*, 5, 421-440.

10

AWARENESS OF ENVIRONMENTAL DEGRADATION AND PERCEIVED RESPONSIBILITY FOR ITS PRESERVATION

SHEELA SINGH

Healthy environment is one of the essential prerequisites of human life. The word 'environment' refers to natural things around us, which sustain human life. It may be defined as the outer physical and biological system in which man and other organisms live with many interacting components. The usually identifiable components of environment include its rocks, minerals, soil and water, its lands and their present and potential vegetation, its animal life and potential for livestock husbandry and its climate. Earth's atmosphere, healthy air, drinkable water all are part of environment.

The problem of environmental management has become one of the greatest concerns of scientists not only in India, but all over the world. The increasing population and rapid industrialisation has resulted in the massive exploitation of natural resources, thereby, degrading the quality of environment. Deforestation, destructive of wild life and pollution have caused considerable damage to nature's renewable resources.

Pollution is, from a legal point of view, the wrongful contamination of atmosphere, or of water, or of soil or the material injury of the right of an individual. The various types of pollutions have serious consequences and pose a threat for human existence.

Unpolluted air which is so vital for life has become a rare commodity today. Pollution of air is more widespread in its effect than other forms of pollutions. The major sources of air pollution are transportation, industry and power generation. Polluted air contains solid and liquid particles, such as dust carbon, hydrocarbons etc. It also contains gases which are poisonous or obnoxious in nature e.g. sulphur dioxide, carbon monoxide, oxides of nitrogen, hydrocarbon, vapours, etc.

To control air pollution, the Government of India passed the Air (Prevention and Control of Pollution) Act 1981. Section 21(1) of the Air Pollution Act says that no person shall, without the previous consent of the state board, operate any industrial plant specified in the schedule in an air pollution control area. Section 20 of this act prescribes standards for emission of polluted air from automobiles.

The deep underground water that was once considered to be pure and pollution free and was used as safe drinking water, has now become polluted due to dump trade or sewage effluent into it. There are many sources of water pollution i.e. community wastes for human settlements, industrial effluent entering into a stream or on land, solid refuse of a mine or quarry, the use of fertilisers, pesticides etc.

For prevention and control of water pollution the Government of India passed the Water (Prevention and Control of Pollution) Act 1974 and its amendment in 1978. The act requires that no person shall knowingly cause or permit any poisonous, noxious or polluting matter defined in accordance with such standards as may be laid down by a Board, to enter in any stream or well. Further, it imposes a prohibition on a person to discharge sewage or trade effluent into a stream without consent of the board.

Noise pollution, another kind of environmental disturbance has many illeffects, such as loss of hearing, injury to ear's, internal mechanism, narrowing of vision, hypertension, vertigo, etc.

With a view to control the environmental pollution, the Government of India passed. 'The new Environmental' (Protection) Act, 1986' for providing new measures for the protection and improvement of environment and for matters connected therewith. Since all aspects of pollution are related to human and health well-being, people belonging to all walks of life i.e. scientists, academics, poets, lovers of wild life feel their concern and responsibility in this regard.

According to an estimate of WHO the impact of pollution is alarming. According to this estimate as much as 80 per cent of the world's diseases are traceable to water pollution. Jaundice, typhoid, cholera and gastro-enteric diseases are attributable to water pollution. Various respiratory problem i.e. difficulty in breathing, respiratory cancer, asthma, bronchitis, coughs, eye irritations are attributable to air pollution. Apart from health costs, air pollution corrodes buildings, shrubs, trees, etc.

Thus, it is evident that pollution of any kind may cause serious damage to man, animals, birds, aquatic life, crops and vegetation.

Realising the importance of environmental protection, centre of excellence in this area have been set up. One such centre known as Centre for Ecological Research and Training was established at Indian Institute of Science in Bangalore. Similarly Centre of Excellence on Environmental Education has been established at Nehru Foundation of Development at Ahmedabad. To boost the programme of environmental education, training and awareness, several seminars and workshops are being organised in different parts of the country.

Despite all these efforts, no phenomenal success has been achieved in this direction. People are bound to live in most of the places in an atmosphere of dirt, pollution and degraded conditions. The municipal organisations which are required to enforce existing provisions against pollution are themselves the major polluters because of their outdated methods of solid waste management, the inadequate drainage systems, polluted water sources and inadequate administrative machinery. Financial inadequacy, lack of power and authority to those who are supposed to control the agencies responsible for environmental crisis, are some of the factors responsible for unsuccessful execution of environmental protection measures.

The most important factor from Psychological point of view, in this regard is, lack of people's participation in environmental protection programmes. There is a need to bring about desirable changes in the attitude of the people towards these problems, because environmental attitudes have been found to be an important and powerful predictor of ecological behaviour (Kaiser *et al.*, 1999). In order to bring about permanent changes in people's environmentally destructive behaviour through intervention, it is essential to increase their environmental concern and knowledge about the effects and consequences of the ongoing environmental degradation (Fransson *et al.*, 1999). Unless there is mass awareness about the negative consequences of continuous and accelerating overuse and destruction of natural resources, environmentally responsible behaviour cannot be expected.

One line of research in the field of environmental psychology has, therefore, been oriented towards studying the ways in which people perceive and evaluate the various forms of environmental problems. It has been found that the type of information, people have about specific problems related with environmental degradation, serves as means of reference for structuring people's attitudes towards these problems and their endeavour to solve them.

For studying the nature of perception and evaluation of environmental problems a number of measurement scales were developed during 70s and 80s. Lounsbury and Tornatsky (1977) developed a scale for evaluating individual's position towards various environmental problems. Maloney *et al.*, (1975) developed a scale for measuring the consistency and knowledge about the environment. To study the orientations towards behaviour and actions considered ecologically responsible, a scale was developed by Antil and Bennet (1979).

Attitude towards environmental problems is found to be linked with the perception of risk about its consequences (Van der Plight and Midden, 1990). It has also been found that conditions of information uncertainty are associated with specific response strategies (Janis and Mann, 1977). Realising the importance of the nature of information the individuals have about various types of environmental problems, this survey was planned. The objective of this study was to assess the people's awareness of environmental degradation, the perceived negative consequences of environmental degradation and perceived responsibility for its preservation.

METHOD

Sample

The survey was conducted on a sample of 330 respondents of Gorakhpur District. The sample differed on various demographic characteristics i.e. educational level, age, gender, and socio-economic status. The age range of the sample was between 15 to 55 years.

Instrument

A questionnaire consisting of thirty statements was constructed to study the understanding and awareness of the respondents about various forms of environmental pollutions and problems. The respondents were required to put a tick mark on either 'True' or 'False' depending on whether they considered the statement to be True or False.

Table 10.1: Proportion Demographic Variable in the sample

Education	High School and below												Inter/B.A.												B.A.+											
Gender	M N=38						F N=60						M N=70						F N=50						M N=60						F N=52					
SES	H 15			L 23			H 22			L 38			H 30			L 40			H 20			L 30			H 30			L 30			H 32			L 20		
Age	A	B	C	A	B	C	A	B	C	A	B	C	A	B	C	A	B	C	A	B	C	A	B	C	A	B	C	A	B	C	A	B	C	A	B	C
	6	4	5	8	10	5	10	6	6	15	10	23	10	12	8	15	15	10	10	5	5	10	12	8	10	10	10	15	6	9	9	15	8	5	7	B

SES
HSES— Rs. 10000 pm or above
LSES— Rs. 3000 pm or below
Age
A— 15 to 25 Years
B— 25 to 35 Years
C— 35 to 55 years

The 'B' part of the questionnaire was used with an objective to evaluate respondents, perception of the gravity of the consequences of pollution and responsibility perceived responsibility for its preservation.

PROCEDURE

Each respondent was approached individually and was given appropriate instructions about the questionnaire. The respondents were requested to fill in the requisite information and were required to express their opinion regarding each statement.

The 'B' part of the questionnaire consisted of three questions. The first question aimed at evaluating the perceived responsibility of the individual or the government for environmental protection. The second question was framed to evaluate the respondents' perception about the awareness and knowledge about the pollution control measures to be adopted by the general public. The aim of the third question was to evaluate the perceived gravity of the negative consequences of pollution and environmental degradation. The respondents were required to respond to each of three questions as per the instructions.

RESULTS AND DISCUSSION

On the basis of the results [shown in Table 10.2 (a)] it was found that the male respondents scored higher with regard to awareness scores than the female respondents. Male respondents seemed to be better informed regarding various environmental issues, i.e. sources and causes of various types of environmental pollutions, negative impact of pollution etc. The main reason for such a finding may be that men in our society get more exposure and have more access to various sources of information. Most of the women in the traditional role in our society are still busy with their household chores and they hardly get any opportunity to address themselves to broader social issues.

Results in Table 10.2 (b) and (c) reveal that awareness regarding environmental pollution was positively correlated with educational level. The higher the education level, the more was the awareness level.

Regarding the respondents, perception of responsibility for environmental protection, it was found that 71 per cent of the respondents were of the opinion that it was government's responsibility to adopt and execute environmental protection measures. Only 21 per cent of the total number of respondents were of the opinion that individual was

Table 10.2(a): Mean, SD and t values for Awareness Scores for Male and Female Respondents

Gender	*N*	*M*	*SD*	*t*	*P*
Male	168	16.91	4.32		
				4.42	>.01
Female	162	11.46	5.17		

Table 10.2 (b): Mean, SD and t values for Awareness Scores with regard to Educational Level

Educational level	*N*	*M*	*SD*	*t*	*P*
High School & Below	98	11.18	4.03		
				4.01	>.01
Intermediate/B.A.	120	13.61	3.95		

Table 10.2 (c): Mean, SD and t values for Awareness Scores with regard to Educational Level

Educational level	*N*	*M*	*SD*	*t*	*P*
Intermediate/B.A.	120	13.61	3.95		
				6.18	>.01
B.A.+	112	17.13	4.69		

more responsible for protecting the environment and preventing it from further degradation.

These results are important in view of the fact that despite several constitutional and legal measures adopted by the government, environmental protection programmes have failed to become a mass-movement in our country, probably because as individuals we don't feel our responsibility to prevent environmental degradation and to control pollution. It has been found that felt or perceived responsibility by the individual for the environment is a promising predictor of a person's ecological behaviour (Kaiser and Simoda, 1999). In this respect discrimination has been made between moral and conventional responsibility. Feeling of moral responsibility is dependent on a person's self ascribed responsibility and guilt feeling. Conventional responsibility depends on the social expectations of which the person is aware of, and his or her readiness to fulfil it.

Environmental education and intervention, therefore, is essential for creating feeling of responsibility whether it may be moral or conventional. Ecologically responsible behaviour cannot be expected if the individual does not feel responsible for the environment. It has also been found that environmentally-related attitudes influence shopping decisions, if environmentally-relevant aspects of products are clearly recognizable (Hormuth, 1999). Environmental attitudes have also been found to be a powerful predictor of ecological behaviour (Kaiser *et al.*, 1999). Some of the other factors affecting environmental behaviour, are knowledge, internal locus of control, personal responsibility and perceived threats to personal health (Garling, 1999).

In order to know how 'serious' the problems arising out of different type of pollutions was perceived by the respondents the 'B' part of the questionnaire section of a question. "How serious are the negative consequences of various types of pollution?" The respondents were provided three alternatives i.e. 'very serious' 'undecided' and 'not very serious'. It was found that 40 per cent of the respondents rated the negative consequences as 'very serious' and 11 per cent of them rated it as 'not very serious, 49 per cent of the respondents rated it as 'undecided'.

These results clearly indicate that people are not well-informed about the serious consequences of different types of pollution and, therefore, they fail to visualise the gravity of the negative impact of pollution on the health and well-being of individuals.

The questionnaire (Part B) had another question, ''How well informed are the people about the pollution control measures?'' In response to this question, 68 per cent of the respondents expressed the opinion that people have little knowledge, or information about pollution control measures, 22 per cent were of the opinion that people have average information and 10 per cent thought that people are 'very well informed' about the pollution control measures.

These results indicate that the people lack the information about environmental problems and environmental protection measures.

Environmental knowledge and information about ecologically responsible behaviour is a prerequisite for the development of environment values and attitudes. As the results of this survey show, that most of the people are unable to visualise the ill effects of environmental pollution and are ignorant of pollution control measures, it cannot be expected from them to have positive attitude towards environment. In such a scenario, due to the lack of ecologically responsible behaviour, environmental protection programme will not bring about desirable change in people's attitudes and behaviour. Different strata of society have different cognition and evaluation of problems arising out of environmental degradation, and, therefore, different awareness programmes for various sections of society can be thought of and implemented. Inclusion of environmental education in school level curricula will help in development of knowledge and awareness about environmental issues.

References

Bonnes, M. and Secchiaroli, G. (1995) *Environmental Psychology*. New Delhi, Sage Publication.

Fransson, N. and Garling J. (1999). Environmental Concern : Conceptual Definitions, Measurement Methods and Research Findings. *Journal of Environmental Psychology, 19*, 4, 369-382.

Jenis, I.L. and Mann, L. (1977). *Decision Making*. New York :Free Press.

Kaiser, F., G. Wolfing, S. and Fuhrer, U. (1999). Environmental Attitude and Ecological Behaviour, *Journal of Environmental Psychology, 19*, 1, 1-19.

Kaiser, F.G. and Simoda, T.A. (1999) Responsibility as Predictor of Ecological Behaviour. *Journal of Environmental Psychology, 19*, 3, 243-253.

Lounsbury, J. and Tornatsky, L.G. (1977). A scale for Assessing Attitude toward Environmental Quality, *Journal of Social Psychology, 101*, 299-305.

Mohan, I. (1989). Environmental Pollution and Management, New Delhi: Ashish Publishing House.

Schulz, P.W. and Zelenzy, L. (1999). Values as Predictors of Environmental Attitudes: Evidence for Consistency across 14 Countries. *Journal of Environmental Psychology,* 19, 1,1-19.

Van der Plight, J. and Midden, C.J.H. (1990). Chernobyl. Four years later: Attitudes, Risk Management and Communication. *Journal of Environmental Psychology 10,* 91-98.

11

SAVING THE ENVIRONMENT
Cognitions and Behaviour of Urban Dwellers

NEELIMA MISRA

Environment degradation has prompted widespread concern about environmental problems and has also led to attempts at solving these problems.

Environmental concerns can be divided into three major areas: (a) physical health; (b) concern for maintenance and efficient use of available, non-renewable resources; and (c) environmental aesthetics and the quality of life.

(a) *Physical health related problems* — The detrimental effects of air and water pollution, toxic substances in the food chain, and extremely high level of noise on physical health come under this category of problems.

(b) *Resources related problems* — This category of problem includes consumption of non-renewable resources. Examples of such problems are excessive energy consumption, failure to recycle paper, metal, glass and other products, overpopulation and inadequate mass transit.

(c) *Problems of environmental aesthetics* — Both the natural and built environments impinge on our senses in ways that can be described as pleasant or unpleasant. A concern for the quality of the environment may exist quite apart from any direct concern for physical health and resource management.

It is also not uncommon to notice that a single environmental problem will have relevance in two or all the three areas of concern. For example, excessive use of automobiles produces pollution and is dangerous to health, and depletes supply of fossil fuels.

Further, it is not an exaggeration to say that virtually everything we do each day has some environmental impact — protective or destructive. And mostly, what we do is rooted in what we perceive and think. Many of our behaviours have an indirect environmental relevance and these are conceptually related to environmental problems e.g. having a certain attitude toward pollution.

The frequent occurrence of environmentally destructive or irresponsible behaviour on our part raises a number of questions such as :

(i) Is it that we are not aware of the health hazards due to unhealthy physical environment?
(ii) Is it that we do not have the foresight to see the long-term consequence of our own behaviour?
(iii) Is it that the short-term consequences overshadow the sight of long-term consequences? A housewife, for example, is freed from the garbage inside the house by throwing it on the street and making the house clean, but she probably overlooks its long-term ill consequences for health as this behaviour contributes to air pollution in the surrounding environment.
(iv) Is it "the tragedy of the commons"? Everyone feels free to use the street for throwing away the garbage. Or
(v) Is it that we are unaware of the decay of natural resources caused by our own behaviour? Probably our immediate gains are more valuable to us than having sufficient resources for our future generations also.

Indeed, researches on what people say about the environment are important, but we also find repeated demonstrations of the independence of verbal and overt motor forms of behaviour. A very common example of such contradiction is noticed regarding the use of plastic bags. Though verbal statements of people are often negative but the frequency of the usage of these bags is quite high. Psychologist know that saying does not lead to doing. Some find only a moderate overlap between the two. It was found that even when the students said "yes" when asked whether it should be "everyone's responsibility to pick up litter when they see it," however, only few students actually picked it, rest of them walked past the trash that had been deliberately planted in their path.

In some cases a stronger relationship between saying and doing exists. But even if they were strongly related in a correlation manner, one would still have to demonstrate that by directly changing environmental attitudes, one can influence the environment itself. Thus far, many attempts have been made to develop environmental attitude scales but very few studies have actually changed attitudes and then examined the effects of this change upon the environment or upon directly relevant behaviours. Until this is done, the importance of environmental attitudes will remain unknown.

It has been studied by Psychologists whether there is linkage between verbal expression of attitudes and actual behaviour. Generally speaking, the prevailing paradigm assumed a causal connection between words and deeds, first without any intervening variable, then with various overt and latent personal and situational factors mediating between attitude and behaviour, and later still with an added component for social obligation. Despite the rather cumbersome relationships evident in the later models, there remained a tacit acceptance, among most researchers, of a unidirectional relationship between attitude and subsequent response executed by a purposeful individual.

Attitudinal dispositions are the dominant force in guiding behaviour, from an exhaustive analysis of studies done. It can be concluded that taken as a whole these studies suggest that it is considerably more likely that attitudes will be unrelated or slightly related to overt behaviours than that attitudes will be closely related to actions.

The Present Study

An exploratory study was conducted by the author in 1998 to investigate some cognitions and behaviours pertaining to environmental degradation. Some residents of Lucknow were interviewed to explore (a) the meaning of environmental degradation, and environmentally responsible/irresponsible behaviour, (b) causes of environmental degradation, and (c) environmentally responsible behaviours exhibited by them.

Sample

The sample consisted of 19 residents of Lucknow city. These respondents could be divided into four subgroups : (1) Male adults, (N = 4, between 43 to 47 years in age), (2) female adults, (N = 6, between 40 to 42 years in age), (3) male students (N = 4, between 23 to 25 years in age, postgraduate students) and (4) female students (N = 5, between 21 and 22 years in age, postgraduate students).

Tool

An open-ended interview schedule.

Major Findings

Content analysis of the responses revealed that:

1. The meaning of environmental degradation was similar for all respondents. According to them, environmental degradation means deterioration in the quality of various components of air, soil and atmosphere. They added that ecological disbalance or disequilibrium is evident from acid rains, excessive rains, draughts, frequent landslides, elimination of greenery, fire in forests, and too much hot or cold weather.
2. The data revealed much awareness in the respondents regarding severity of the problem of environmental degradation. They stated that air, water and noise pollution, resource scarcity, deforestation, and vanishing greenery in cities provide sufficient evidence for deterioration in the environmental quality.

The respondents considered high level of air and water pollution to be the major environmental problems in cities. All the 19 respondents included them in their responses.

Noise pollution in cities was another much frequently mentioned problem. 5 respondents (3 male and 2 female adults) stated that nobody cares about how loudly the TVs, tape recorders, and stereos are played in the houses. Noise made by vehicles on roads is no less disturbing.

Some of the respondents stated that the greenery in cities is vanishing day-by-day. With increasing population in cities, multi-storeyed buildings are coming up very fast, and there is hardly any open space left for trees and plantation.

3. The respondents were also aware of the causes of environmental degradation. The data revealed that (i) Pollution was mentioned as the most common cause of environmental degradation. The three major sources of pollution stated by the respondents were:

(a) Increasing number of factories leading to increasing air and water pollution;
(b) Increased number and excessive use of automobiles; the

smoke emitted by vehicles especially tempos and Vikrams; and

(c) Population growth and resulting resource scarcity.

Deforestation and use of non-biodegradable materials were also mentioned as responsible for rapid deterioration in environmental quality. Throwing garbage outside the house was also mentioned as another common source of pollution.

Among the other causes of environmental degradation; two male adults referred to value system. One respondent indicated that these days instrumental values and utilitarian orientation are predominant.

He added that use of chemicals in agriculture affects the food, but farmers' desire for getting more and more money probably motivates them to shut their eyes from harmful effects of these chemicals and use them for getting larger quantity of production and thereby more money. Another respondent stated that modern man's tendency to go farther and farther away from nature is the only cause of degradation. To quote him, "In the race of modernisation today everything is artificial while previously it was natural. We are moving away from nature."

A male respondent, while referring to noise pollution, again suggested that norms and values play an important role. He said, "After all young generation gets pleasure from such music, I may add here that our family structure as well as dynamics, and the life style has changed a lot and so have values. We are concerned only with our own pleasures."

All the respondents were aware of the negative consequences of environmental degradation. A concern for health hazards was evident from their responses. For example, one respondent talked in detail about the kinds of diseases resulting from intake of foodgrains, vegetables and fruits which are grown using chemicals and/or due to polluted air and water.

Though vanishing greenery in cities was mentioned while showing awareness about environmental degradation, none of the respondents talked about the loss of the juveniating influence of the pleasant effective experiences of being with nature.

4. Some of the respondents expressed their concern over expecting more and more deterioration in future and its consequences for mankind. They stated "our very existence will be in danger if it goes on like this." "Development is necessary but not at the cost of life." "If deterioration continues like this, life will be

extinct from the planet." "It is necessary to stop this degradation by minimizing the pollutants for air, water, and soil." "To check degradation is the foremost task for us."

5. An awareness of cognitions-motivations behaviour links was also evident from the data obtained from student. For example, a male student pointed out that our materialistic attitudes are to large extent responsible for environmentally destructive behaviour. "We are more concerned about comforts. We are unable to think beyond our own comforts. We have forgotten that we are getting these comforts at the cost of degradation of our environment." He added that "environmental degradation is a problem that is created by us. We are responsible for it." Another male student also expressed the view that we can make as well as destroy our environment." Another respondent, again a male student, added that "protecting the environment is a task or goal not for a single individual only, but for everybody". Interestingly a female student pointed out the constraints in refraining from some environmentally destructive behaviours. She said that "in spite of our best intentions, things do not work as we want them to." She elaborated her point by saying that "though we know that air conditioners and refrigerators produce chloroflurocarbon which is responsible for degradation of ozone layer but our changed life style as well as limitations in cities compel us for their use."
6. Some respondents talked about what should be done to check environmental deterioration e.g. a female teacher suggested that paper and jute bags should be used in place of polythene bags. Another female suggested that one should use vehicles producing less smoke and noise, so that ozone hole may not increase further. "For another respondent, the use of filters to avoid health problems due to polluted water was thought to be necessary. A female teacher pointed out that there is need for environmental education for the survival and welfare of his species." In a previous study on whether urban women are saviours or destructors of the environment, it was suggested that urban women can do a lot in this regard by holding discussions and arranging exhibitions competitions in their clubs and kitty parties. We all know that such informal education is welcomed more than formal education. Further, as mothers they can provide role models to their children.

7. Coming to the environmentally protective behaviours on the part of the individual, the data revealed that only a few respondents indulged in such behaviour. A male adult respondent aged 48-47 years told that they do plantation in front of their house. The other two respondents, a female teacher and a female student, also said that they indulged in this activity. Two behavioural measures taken by a male adult and a housewife (aged 40 years.) were (i) not allowing children to play T.V. and music system on high volume and (ii) not allowing children to drive scooter very fast. Regular checking of their scooters was another action on the part of respondents. One male respondent stated that he does not allow accumulation of garbage around his house and keeps his office clean and dirt free. A housewife added that she does not burn wood in winters.

The data lead us to conclude that the awareness regarding the present day environment and the causes of environmental degradation is quite high in urban dwellers, and some consistent ideas regarding what can be done to check it are also prevalent in them. But when it comes to their own behavioural plane, not much actions in this regard are being taken by themselves. In the light of existing awareness, it seems that an attitude of indifference is probably responsible for it. Another attitudinal factor may be that they perceive the efforts by single individuals to be insufficient for being able to check the great extent of present day deterioration. Probably they are unable to visualise that even little effort made by each and every individual will contribute significantly to the apparently not visible pool of effort but which will be sufficient to check degradation. It is also possible that we have a tendency to view the external agencies e.g. government to be responsible for and also having the capability to take up the large scale plans for controlling and improving the environmental quality. A male adult respondent said, "Let us see what the pollution control boards can do." Therefore, it becomes imperative that programmes environmental education create awareness regarding the systemic nature of man environment relationship which emphasises mutual dependence of each unit and the system and also between units.

Briefly speaking, the findings are indicative of an inconsistency between cognitions and behaviour. Further, the sample being heterogeneous in nature, varied responses have been obtained regarding the causes and consequences of environmental degradation. Therefore, it is warranted that future researches take into account the characteristics of various subgroups of urban dwellers. Then only we would be able to enrich our knowledge regarding attitude behaviour incongruence regarding environmental degradation and thereby formulate successful action programmes in this regard.

Further, environmental awareness is a pre-requisite to environmentally responsible behaviour. But we must remember that pro-life attitudes and values as well as environmentally relevant behaviours cannot be simply taught through formal education. Informal or indirect methods of imparting environmental education, say for example, modelling or peer group discussions, are no less effective.

Therefore, attempts for environmental education are required in both forms.

Reference

Misra, N. (1998). *Cognitions and Behaviour of Urban Dwellers* : Paper presented in National Seminar on 'Environment and Cognition' U.G.C., D.S.A., Deptt. of Psychology, DDU Gorakhpur University, April 24-25, 1998.

SECTION TWO

DEVELOPMENTAL ISSUES

12

HUMAN DEVELOPMENT RESEARCH IN INDIA
Some Trends and Issues

LILA KRISHNAN*

The Department of Psychology, Gorakhpur University, deserves hearty congratulations from all of us for organising a two-day National Seminar on *Current Trends in Human Development Research.* The issue of development in its different facets is not only an active and growing area of research in Psychology, but also touches the personal life of each one of us, and thereby raises questions related to the direct application of concepts and research findings in this area. It is a matter of great pleasure and honour to me that I have been requested to present the inaugural talk on this occasion.

I would like to take this opportunity to make a comment on some noticeable trends that have been observed in Indian research related to human development, and some issues that still need to be given special attention by researchers in this area.

The Seminar has been organised in the form of several sessions which will focus on the following topics : A reconceptualisation of development, with emphasis on theoretical and methodological issues; Psychological, cognitive, language, motivational, and personality development; The development of competence and skills; Pathological problems and learning disabilities; and Changing values in the light of global challenges, modernisation and technological advances. This set

* Inaugural talk presented at the National Seminar on Current Trends in Human Development Research, Department of Psychology, DSA, Gorakhpur University: March 27-28, 1999.

of topics covers almost all the important and relevant areas within human development.

It is interesting to note that although systematic academic attention is being paid to issues of human development in contemporary psychological research, the awareness of psychological and social development was evidently present in traditional society as well, as is apparent from folk-wisdom-based *shlokas* in Sanskrit, such as: "For five years, a child should be treated with great love and affection. Upto the age of ten, he/she should be treated strictly and punitively. Upon attaining the sixteenth year the child should be treated as a friend."

There is undoubtedly the ring of a moral, religious, or spiritual prescription and injunction in such writings. But such observations cannot be set aside. This kind of wisdom would have surely been present in the tradition of all societies. So the question may be raised in some quarters : If a lay person already knows about development, what is it that a psychologist can add? What, indeed, is the concept of development? What factors influence it, and how do developmental changes get manifested? Answers to these questions are generally available in research on development, but there are still some issues that remain unexamined.

In this connection, the first trend noticeable in the reconceptualisation of development, is that in contemporary research, *a life-span approach* is adapted, as distinguished from the earlier approach that studied development from the time of birth up to the end of adolescence or the beginning of adulthood, and no further. This was true of what used to be 'child psychology' or 'developmental psychology'. Now, a study of human development is expected to include adulthood, late adulthood, and old age. Largely as a result of advances in technology and in the medical sciences, there has been an overall improvement in the quality of life worldwide, and a consequent increase in life expectancy and a reduction in mortality rates. Most societies now have a larger population of old and aged people, who cannot be ignored any more : the aged can no longer be treated like wornout goods waiting to be thrown out. Instead, they are being viewed as meaningful contributors to society. Therefore, the old and aged have a special place now in the study of human development. In this regard, Indian researchers need to pay more attention to the study of the aged, from every relevant developmental angle—personal, emotional, cognitive, as well as social.

Secondly, there is an increased emphasis on *the role of the family* in human development. The family has always been acknowledged as a significant determinant of effective development, mainly as that part of the home environment in which initial and the major part of child rearing and socialisation takes place. But now, the study of family mechanisms goes beyond this perspective. It has acquired the status of a specialised area, under the title of 'family studies'. In connection with the change in the family structure, from that of joint families to an increasing number of nuclear families, such a focused study of family influences on development is a welcome trend. At the applied level, there is a loud call for policy formulation and policy implementation with regard to family studies (Saraswathi & Kaur, 1993). Once again, although sociologists seem to have paid some attention to family studies, very few psychologists in India have taken up this area as a serious research question. Much more attention needs to be directed to systematic family studies.

Thirdly, the study of human development is becoming *increasingly inter-disciplinary.* It is not enough to know only about the *psychology of development* : a comprehensive understanding of development necessitates also an understanding of the physical developmental aspects, and related issues, such as the role of nutrition and child care. Thus the whole area of development has to be linked to other areas such as paediatrics and gerontology in the medical sciences, social work, sociology, education and law. The good news is that linkages between these diverse fields are being implemented through application (for instance, the provision of crèches, day care centres and *balwadis* for children, special care programmes and homes for the aged, where the multi-faceted needs of individuals are looked into). Community-oriented groups such as C.R.Y. (Child Relief and You) and Help Age India are examples of increasing general awareness of the need to look at the problems of both children and old people in society. What is now needed is the active participation of psychologists in the work done by community groups, both as experts and as community members. Also, specialists in different areas in psychology need to join hands and do collaborative research on development-related issues.

Fourth, attention may be pointed towards *specific theoretical issues* that have been focused on more recently, especially in the last fifteen years or so. This is not only a trend in contemporary human-development research, but is an aspect that opens up several unanswered questions. One of these questions is the following : Is human development truly cross-culturally universal, or is it more culturally specific? If the former is true, then we could deal with general developmental theories without paying too much attention to aspects such a cultural variations in socialisation and child rearing as significant determinants of development. On the other hand, if the latter is true, then it becomes imperative to pay special attention to cultural influences, and cross-cultural differences in development. In the context of cognitive-moral development, theories proposed by scholars such as Jean Piaget (1932/1965) and Lawrence Kohlberg (1969) initially gave the impression that cognitive-moral development is more or less culturally universal. These theories are now being re-interpreted in the light of evidence that such development does show some cross-cultural variation. Specific debates have been raised in this connection (for example, Gibbs & Schnell, 1985; Snarey, 1985). As a counter-argument to the developmental approach to moral reasoning, Turiel (cited in Shweder, Mahapatra and Miller, 1987) proposes the idea that concepts of morality emerge in a "social interactional" framework, and not mainly as a component of cognitive-moral development. To these two contrasting approaches, Shweder, Mahapatra and Miller (1987) add a third view, namely, the "social communication" theory, which essentially suggests that ideas of morality are culturally variant. The basic defining features of what is moral are so ingrained in the context that they become 'natural' to an individual in the same way as the 'natural' moral ideas that emerge in a developmental sequence, according to the moral developmental theorists. The view of Shweder *et al.*, becomes particularly relevant here because the evidence they cite is from the Indian context.

Within this trend, certain issues with practical implications in the social context need to be examined a little more carefully. Specifically, we may take the case of two forms of social behaviour, namely, *prosocial behaviour, and reward allocation based on distributive justice rules.* The moral developmental basis of both of these behaviours has been examined and analysed, theoretically and empirically, by researchers in the West (Damon, 1981; Hoffman, 1983). Their findings and observations have shown that there are developmental (age-related) changes in these two forms of social behaviour, but these developmental changes may not be seen in the same form in all cultures. Besides, there is also evidence from two directions. One shows that these social behaviours differ across cultures. The other evidence shows that these social behaviours are influenced by or consistently related to, certain aspects of child rearing (for instance, discipline training). If it could be shown empirically that cross-cultural differences in these behaviours are parallel to, or consistently related to, cross-cultural differences in child rearing practices (which, in turn, are related to the moral reasoning underlying these behaviours), then the conceptual picture would be more meaningful in terms of the links between the different components, namely, cultural dimensions, on one hand, specific forms of social behaviour, on the other, and the associated child rearing practices, along with developmental variations in moral reasoning, as the intervening variables.

However, clear-cut answers of the empirical kind are not yet available to many of the questions raised above. But there is sufficient incisive theoretical analysis based on observations of various cultures which strongly suggests that development alone cannot adequately account for variations in social behaviour. The role of cultural influences has been highlighted by some researchers such as Sudhir Kakar (1981) and Stanley Kurtz (1992). Both of these psychologists have adopted a Freudian/neo-Freudian approach to describe and explain personality development in the Indian cultural context, in the framework of Indian traditional thinking, reflected in the socialisation and enculturation of the Indian child. Kakar has attempted to interpret the developmental implications of traditional Hindu rituals and customs; Kurtz has presented a thorough and meticulous analysis and interpretation of the influence of the "mother-goddess" mythological figure as a socialising and child rearing agent.

Yet another possible line of exploration lies in the cognitive developmental theory proposed by Harvey, Hunt, and Schroder (1961). In this theory, an attempt is made to present the systematic relationships between the stage-wise development of *conceptual systems*, on one hand, and specific child rearing practices, on the other. The idea of conceptual systems appears to be an elaborated form of George Kelly's (1955) *personal constructs*. Conceptual systems can also be placed in a broad cultural context. To that extent, the theory proposed by Harvey *et al.*, seems to be worth exploring further in the Indian context, with specific reference to personality development from a cognitive point of view.

Once again, in the cross-cultural perspective, Miller and Bersoff (1992) have compared the U.S. and Indian cultures with regard to the role of cultural influences on moral judgements involved in prosocial and justice-related concepts. Some empirical evidence on justice rule preferences in this context has been gathered and analysed also by some Indian psychologists (Krishnan, 1999; Misra, 1991). Thus, the trend towards examining specific theoretical issues in the context of development seems to be growing stronger, and needs only to be boosted further by empirical investigations.

A fifth noticeable trend in the area of human development is that attention is being paid to *pathological aspects of development.* The impetus for this direction of developmental research seems to have come primarily from Western research. Although earlier research did contain some information about developmental problems such as retardation, disabilities, and difficulties of various kinds in childhood, now interest seems to extend beyond pathology. A more positive approach to development - related 'problems' seems to be emerging, which definitely needs to be encouraged especially from the point of view of application.

Finally, there is a trend related to changes in the *methodological approach.* Conventionally, developmental research involves observational, survey-based, and experimental methods. The intensive study of the individual was recommended and used by Piaget, and many of his followers (for example, Enright, Franklin and Manheim, 1980, in the area of distributive justice). Such methods, often combined with individual interviews, have also been used in some Indian studies. But one needs to examine the suitability of these conventional, and otherwise valid methods, in the Indian context. Some amount of tolerance is now being shown for *qualitative research methods*, such as the analysis of children's stories, folk-tales, dreams and other narratives, and the like. A dilemma that often accompanies the use of qualitative methods in psychology is that they are too subjective. This dilemma has to be ultimately resolved. For the present, the very willingness to question and modify the existing conventional methods is a positive indication of growth in the field.

In addition to the six major trends described above, it is encouraging to see researchers examining the question of development from various other perspectives, such as gender differences, deprivation and social disadvantage, language development, motivational and affective development, and so on.

Considering the total picture, then, it appears that much work has already been done in the area of human development, but even more remains to be done. Looking at the emerging trends, we can see that the area of human development research in India promises a bright future. The recent increase in publications on issues related to development is one proof of the enthusiasm being shown in this area. Endeavours like the present seminar are a second proof. So we can look forward with optimism to the presentations in this seminar.

Thank you very much!

References

Damon, W. (1981). The development of justice and self-interest during childhood. In M.J. Lerner & S.C. Lerner (Eds.). *The Justice Motive in Social Behaviour*. pp. 57-72, New York and London : Plenum Press.

Enright, R.D., Franklin, C., and Manheim, L.A. (1980). Children's distributive justice reasoning: A standardized and objective scale. *Developmental Psychology, 16(3)*, 193-202.

Gibbs, J.C. & Schnell, S.V. (1985). Moral development *versus* socialisation. *American Psychologist*, 40 (10), 1071-1080.

Harvey, O.J., Hunt, D.E., & Schroder, H.M. (1961). *Conceptual Systems and Personality Organisation*. New York : John Wiley & Sons.

Hoffman, M.L. (1983). Affective and cognitive processes in moral internalisation. In E.T. Higgins, D.N. Ruble, & W.W. Hartup (Eds.). *Social Cognition and Social Development : A Sociocultural Perspective*. pp. 236-74. Cambridge: Cambridge University Press.

Kakar, S. (1981). *The Inner World: A Psychoanalytic Study of Childhood and Society in India*. Delhi: Oxford University Press.

Kelly, G.A. (1955). *The Psychology of Personal Constructs*. New York : Norton.

Kohlberg, L. (1969). Stage and sequence: The cognitive developmental approach to socialisation. In D. Goslin (Ed.) *Handbook of Socialisation Theory and Research*, pp. 347-480. Chicago: Rand-McNally & Company.

Krishnan, L. (1999). Socialisation and cognitive-moral influences on justice rule preferences: The case of Indian culture. In T.S. Saraswathi (Ed.) *Culture, Socialisation and Human Development : Theory, Research and Applications in India*. pp. 188-212. New Delhi : Sage Publication.

Kurtz, S. (1992). *All the Mothers are One*. New York: Columbia University Press.

Miller, J.G. & Bersoff, D.M. (1992). Culture and moral judgement : How are conflicts between justice and interpersonal responsibilities resolved? *Journal of Personality and Social Psychology*; 62(4), 541-54.

Misra, G. (1991). Sociocultural influences on moral behaviour. *The Indian Journal of Social Work, LII* (2), 179-194.

Piaget, J. (1932/1965). *The Moral Judgement of the Child*. (Translated by M. Gabain). London: Routledge & Kegan Paul Ltd. (Originally published in 1932).

Saraswathi, T.S. & Kaur, B. (1993) (Eds.) *Human Development and Family Studies in India : An Agenda for Research and Policy*. New Delhi : Sage Publications.

Shweder, R.A., Mahapatra, M., & Miller, J.G. (1987). Culture and moral development. In J. Kagan & S. Lamb (Eds.). *The Emergence of Morality in young children*, pp. 130-204. Chicago: The University of Chicago Press.

Snarey, J. (1985). The cross-cultural universality of social-moral development: A critical review of Kohlbergian research. *Psychological Bulletin*, 97, 202-232.

13

CHILDHOOD IN INDIA
An Overview of Psychological Research

GIRISHWAR MISRA & ASHOK K. SRIVASTAVA

Various communities or cultural groups transmit values, skills, beliefs, motives and so forth to their new members, usually children, by way of what is called cultural transmission including the processes of enculturation and socialisation. As the term suggests, the process of *enculturation* refers to an encompassing or surrounding of the individual by one's culture. The individual acquires on his own what the culture deems to be necessary. The cultural group may not indulge into any deliberate attempt or specific teaching about its requirements. In contrast, *socialisation* refers to the process of deliberate shaping, by way of tutelage, of the individual. As a result of enculturation and socialisation behavioural similarities within cultures and behavioural differences between cultures appear. Related to enculturation is another term called *acculturation* which refers to cultural and psychological changes brought about by contact with people belonging to different cultures and exhibiting different behaviours (Berry, 1990). The present analysis is primarily concerned with the processes of enculturation and socialisation taking place in the Indian society.

In recent years beliefs about children and childhood have been explored in different cultures and historical periods (Borstelman, 1983; Brandtstadter, 1990; de Mause, 1974; Diaz-Guerrero, 1982; Gergen, Gloger-Tippelt & Berkowitz, 1990; Harkness & Super, 1983; Hess, Kushiwagi, Azuma, Price & Dickson, 1980; Kakar, 1978; Kessen & Siegel, 1983; McGillicuddy-De Lisi, 1982; Poole, 1985; Sommerville, 1982). These attempts suggest that universal and invariant characterisation of human development encompassing the developmental trajectories covered by the diverse cultural and historical contexts is almost impossible. This difficulty mainly owes to the fact that the cultural and natural aspects of human development are functionally interdependent. In this context understanding of diverse ethno-theories of development is relevant because parental behaviours toward children are often guided by and situated in the context of these theories. There is growing evidence that such beliefs are significantly related to the competence and performance displayed by children in different areas (Dweck, Chiu & Hong, 1995; Siegel, 1985). A study of such beliefs may help not only in understanding the meaning of actions of parents, and planning by educational institutions, as well as, the policy making bodies (Misra & Varma, 1994), but would also contribute to the conceptualisation of human development. Gergen *et al.*, (1990) have pointed out that the "*commonsense beliefs about the nature of the child furnish both the context for and the limits over scientific understanding. Because scientific concepts cannot be inductively derived from observation.... Developmental research must inevitably draw from the compendium of commonsense beliefs within the culture*" (*p. 110*).

The analysis of human development in the current scholarly discourse is recognising the role of culture and ethnotheories in significant ways. As Cole (1992) has pointed out, development may be viewed more appropriately as an outcome of the interaction of environmental and biological factors taking place in the medium of culture. Through artefacts, shared ideas and meanings, culture constitutes the form of interaction of biological and environmental factors and shapes their interaction. The notion of *developmental niche* articulated by Super and Harkness (1986; Harkness & Super, 1993) also emphasises an integrated eco-socio-cultural system to which a child is expected to adapt in the course of development. There are three components of the niche: (1) the physical and social settings in which the child lives, (2) customs of child-care and child rearing (i.e., cultural practices), and (3) the psychology of the caretakers or ethno-theories of caregivers. The third component is concerned with the implicit theoretical ideas that inform the decisions made by those responsible for the care and upbringing of children in a given community.

Anthropological and psychological accounts of child rearing in different parts of the world demonstrate wide range of variation in child rearing practices and goals of socialisation (Bronfenbrenner, 1958; Lytton & Romney, 1991; Maccoby & Martin 1983; Misra & Tripathi, 1993;

Sears, Maccoby & Levin, 1957; Sinha, 1981; Valsiner, 1987, 1989; Whiting, 1963; Whiting & Edwards, 1975; Whiting & Child, 1953). According to Kogan, Kersley and Zelazo (1978), there are three dimensions of these goals : (a) autonomy *Vs.* sociability, (b) sensual excitement *Vs.* serenity, and (c) potent action *Vs.* passive contemplation. Among these goals, the western cultures prefer autonomy, sensuality and action, while the eastern cultures prefer sociability, serenity and contemplation. Because of these differences in parental goals, in collectivist societies, children are socialised to accept the unquestioning authority of adults. This is evident from anthropological studies of Richards (1964) on Ganda of Uganda and Read's (1959) study of Ngoni of Central Africa. Evidence from China (Chen & Yang, 1986; Harrison, Serafica & McAdoo, 1982; Lin & Fu, 1990), Canada (Lambert, Yackley & Hein, 1971), and Mexico (Holtzman, Diaz-Guerrero, & Swartz, 1975) also lend support to this view. Despite cross-cultural variation, the process of socialisation throughout the globe does share certain common purposes. For instance, families do wish to ensure the well-being of their children. They want their children to achieve success in different domains of life, to take pride in their heritage, to be respectful towards their elders, and to live happy and healthy lives both physically and mentally.

The present chapter seeks to throw light on cultural construction of childhood through a two-pronged strategy. It utilises the available research literature and presents some of the findings of authors'on-going work in this field. However, the review of studies presented here cannot be considered exhaustive as it is largely confined to psychological studies. The contributions of indologists and anthropologists could not be included in a comprehensive manner. This chapter, thus has three inter-related goals. First, it analyses the pattern of socialisation of the Indian children as documented by various studies. Second, in the context of rapid and profound political, economic and social changes (refer Srivastava, 1995a), it attempts to understand the parental notions and beliefs about children. In particular, the values related to children, expectations from children, and the traits/characteristics desired in children are analysed. Third, the chapter documents the contemporary psychological context of socialisation as experienced by parents.

I

RESEARCH ON SOCIALISATION OF THE INDIAN CHILD: AN OVERVIEW

At the outset it may be noted that the study of childhood in India is a very complex task. Looking at the different subcultural patterns emanating from regional, religious, linguistic, racial and gender related heterogeneity in the Indian population, developing a picture of an average "Indian" child may appear a myth to many of us trained in and informed by modern cultural studies which focus more on the diversities and distinctions. To them the exercise of synthesis appears difficult. However, the tendency to seek distinctions has its own limitations. Perhaps the issue can be resolved by taking recourse to the notion of levels and purpose of analysis. At one level using the expression "Indian" can be defended on the ground of sharing in the domains of attitudes, ideals, behaviour patterns, and meanings. If culture involves meaning systems (D'Andrade, 1982), there is possibility of an Indian cultural system. At the same time there is no denial of variations within the system.

The study of psychological processes, human development and other related issues in India so far has been thoroughly grounded in the western positivist mould of scientistic exercise. Thus, Indian researchers have faithfully adopted the concepts, measures, and methodological strategies from a perspective often incongruent with the basic premises of Indian culture and its ethos. The apparently value neutral and objective categories and tools borrowed from the West were often used indiscriminately to understand everything including "childhood", "self", "personality", "values" and "motives".

Being rooted in the modernist assumptions of individualism, objectivity and rationality, the researchers have pursued the notion of a self-contained idea of person, which has been found problematic even in the Western World (Sampson, 1977, 1988). Unfortunately, this has become the normative perspective and supplies the yardstick for the practitioners of the mainstream (Euro-American?) psychology (Gergen, Lock, Gulerce & Misra, 1996). This unicultural perspective is biased in the treatment of the psychology of the people from other cultures. The descriptions of the people of India, and their values and behavioural dispositions from a Western perspective is an interesting illustration of this situation. It has created and promoted an inadequate construal and understanding of the Indian people (see Misra & Gergen, 1993; Sinha,

1998 for a detailed analysis). The cluster of values and dispositions attributed by the Western scholars and their followers (e.g., low aspiration, passivity, conformity, dependence, mistrust, lack of concern for others, emotional insecurity, subjugation of parental authority, indifference to contradictory inner conflicts, other worldliness) declares the Indian people as nothing but pathological. In contrast, the notion of Indian self as ensembled and interdependent (Markus & Kitayama, 1991; Marriott, 1976; Mines, 1988; Misra & Gergen, 1993; Misra & Giri, 1995; Obeyesekere, 1990; Ramanujam, 1986; Tripathi, 1988) suggests a different kind of identity which is situated in the group and collectivity (Misra, 1995; Roland, 1988). Dependence has a different meaning (Neki, 1973) and the socialisation context does provide scope for competence and responsibility (Anandlakashmi & Bajaj, 1981; Saraswathi & Dutta, 1990; Seymour, 1988). The indigenous values like *dharma, anasakti* and spirituality are found relevant to the contemporary functioning of organisations in India (Chakraborty, 1993; Prakash, 1995). Parents still want their children to adopt the indigenous value systems (Srivastava, Banerjee & Tripathi, 1996). In this context it must be appreciated that the Indian social reality, in spite of industrialisation, urbanisation and more recent liberalisation, has distinct features which still continue to inform the social arrangements and functioning of the cultural system. It has been observed that the response to modernisation has not been similar across cultures. The cross-cultural differences in social behaviour often persist in spite of rapid social change (Holtzman, *et al.*, 1975). The Indian social reality is also changing but it has elements of continuity too.

To combat the impact of Euro-American theories, in recent years an Indian perspective is being stressed by social scientists in a number of ways. An interesting example is the work of Misri (1986). Based on fieldwork of Kashmiri pandits, Misri, an anthropologist, observed that the conception of the child can be reconstructed on three axes which represent antithetical ideas. First, the child is seen to be simultaneously a creation of parents and gift from God, the axis of human divine. It assumes parents to be mere instruments through whom the divine will is realised. Second the child is both a collective being and a unique individual. The concept of *karma* emphasises the individual, while relationships with the family and other stress collectivity. Third, the child is born with fixed unalterable propensities, his initial nature can be transformed by *Samaskaras* and rituals. This is alterable/ transformative axis. Within this paradigm, which rests on contradictions, society attempts to simultaneously integrate and separate the new born.

While discussing the experience of childhood in India, Kakar (1981) noted that "the ego on both the individual and the collective plane, continuously responds to social change as it endeavours to synthesise its previous experience with new demands and thus to maintain the continuity of self and its integration with the outer world. In other words, there are no insurmountable psychological obstacles to the development of the modern Indian identity Vivekanand envisioned" (p. 183-184). Vivekananda's notion of a modern Indian identity integrates a rational, scientific model of inquiry and the aims of technological modernisation with the essentials of the traditional world image. Kakar (1981) noted that social change in India was gradual in the past but now its place is accelerated. He observed that "most Indians have remained true to the traditional Indian identity in which the maternal cosmos of infancy and early childhood is the inner world...in an increasingly instrumental, technocratic and rational age, India is coming under increasing political, economic and demographic pressures to abandon its cultural emphasis on the emotional, aesthetic and instinctual qualities of life, on the primacy of primary group relationships and on the communal sharing for individual lives... result in sharp discontinuities of experience." (p. 185). Such a situation may cause injuries to self-esteem and may evoke a regressive use of defences. Kakar expected that this regressive phase would in all probability be followed by the attempts at recovery. These observations of Kakar make the construction of 'childhood' in the contemporary context a pertinent issue for a detailed study.

Childhood in the Indian Context

The study of childhood in India has been undertaken from different perspectives and considerable data have been generated (see Saraswathi & Dutta, 1988; Saraswathi & Kaur, 1993, Sinha, 1981). The notions of "Indian child" and "childhood", however, are difficult to be worked out without abstraction and simplification because of regional, cultural, sub-cultural and historical variations. With these reservations in mind we may examine the trends available in research literature. Recently Krishnan (1998) has presented an insightful analysis of the major features of traditional Indian views about children and parents. She notes that the traditional view considered the child as a pure, innocent, amoral and asocial being. This innocent child required love and protection. Consistent with the idea that a person is a product of both the spiritual as well as the natural worlds (Muralidharan & Srivastava, 1995), a child was thought to be born in the image of a divine. Also, at the same time, it needed to be moulded into a social being through a number of *samaskaras* (rituals). The child rearing practices emphasised interdependence, reciprocal expectations and obligations among the family members. Children were expected to look after their parents when they grew old. They were viewed as extensions of parents (*santati*) (Misra & Gergen, 1993). Being an agrarian society it maintained a continuity between the worlds of an adult and that of a child by sharing their life spaces (Kumar, 1993).

Embedded in the spiritual context of *dharma* and *neeti*, the traditional texts are full of teachings concerning child rearing and the qualities parents should attempt to nurture in children. Children are considered as the gift of God, and having a child (preferably a male child) happens to be an essential life goal as they are considered important for continuing the family lineage (Krishnan, 1996; Srivastava 1995b), as a source of old-age security (Mamdani, 1972; Mathew, 1977; Reddy & Mahadevan, 1986), a way of enhancing the parents' sense of power, status, and personal pleasure (Singh, Bhargava, & Kumar, 1981), or as potential earning members (Mamdani, 1972; Weiner, 1990).

Parent-child tie is treated as a challenge to parental authority. The traditional view acknowledges the importance of both the parents in rearing their children, each having a distinct role in the socialisation process. Mother is considered responsible to meet child's physical needs and father the moral and intellectual needs. The importance of parental authority is also recognised. It is advised that both the parents, including the *Acharya* (teacher), should be treated as God. The practice of children touching their parents' feet, prostrating before them and receiving their blessings are also performed before the deities (Krishnan, 1996).

The traditional view focuses on stage and sex-wise differentiation in child-rearing. It is suggested that during the first-five years a child should be treated with affection; for the next ten years he should be treated with strict discipline; and upon attaining the age of 16 he should be treated like a friend. Likewise, though there is an inherent respect for the girl child as *Lakshmi* and *Annapoorna*, male children are considered essential for continuance of the family. Further, while the daughter is treated as "another one" who has to be given away in marriage to another family and the parents carry forth this rite in the act of *Kanyadaan*. In contrast, the son is brought up to be independent, courageous, and educated. He should be equipped with all the skills required by the family's occupation. Analysing the impact of this discrimination, Nandy and Kakar (1980) have observed, "despite male domination and patriarchal family pattern which ideally should lead to heightened female hostility and envy toward males among Indian women, together with the generally pronounced antagonism between the sexes, these phenomena are not the characteristics of Indian women" (p. 146). The two sexes often maintain a harmonious relationship.

The analysis of childhood in India, during modern period has been undertaken following the western perspective, particularly psychoanalysis. In this domain of scholarship, child-rearing finds a Hindu child locked in the mother's embrace; the mother's indulgent presence surrounds the child until around the age of five, when the father's discipline intervenes traumatically (see Nandy & Kakar, 1980 for a detailed analysis). At this age the Hindu boy is thrust into the orbit of his father who remains a cool and distant authority figure. Carstairs (1967) notes that this contrast between excessive early indulgence and dangerously harsh later frustration makes a child prone to regress to early infantile pleasures. He contends that what Hindu child-care lacks is the gradual training in frustration tolerance that enables the western child to cope with the demands of maturity. In his account, typical Hindu child rearing seems pathogenic than the child rearing commonly found in the western world. Similarly, Kakar (1978) stresses the child's prolonged physical contact with the mother, breast feeding on demand, and the traumatic shift to the demanding orbit of the father around age five — a period Kakar calls the "second birth". Thus a Hindu child lives in sharp contradictions. Nandy and Kakar (1980) have observed: "Given the experience of his mother's immediacy and responsiveness, one would expect an Indian child to tend to experience his mother almost totally as "good mother". The sociological and anthropological accounts do conform to this observation. However, in the deeper recess of mind, along with the protective and benign "good mother", the "bad mother" coexists (p. 142). Several explanations such as primary narcissism (Spratt, 1966), result of interrupted discontinuous mothering (Carstairs, 1967), and inversion of emotional roles (Nandy & Kakar, 1980) have been advanced.

Roland (1988) distinguishes between the Indian and Western patterns of child rearing on different grounds. He feels that to a Westerner, cultures raising children differently than their own will appear pathogenic as western child rearing norms go with psychoanalytic theory. The Indian child rearing, he notes, emphasises on the symbiotic modes of relating. Roland (1988) talks of Indian child rearing as embedded in the notion of "we self" — a kind of group ego in which a given individual is embedded. To him physical closeness stands for the early symbiotic union between the Indian mother and her child which is carefully prolonged rather than gradually transcended. He notes that the "prolonged maternal involvement with the child, with adoration of the young child to the extent of treating him or her as godlike — develops a central core of heightened narcissistic well-being in the child" (Roland, 1988, p. 148-149).

The anthropological account of Indian child rearing (Minturn & Hitchcock; 1966; Seymour, 1975, 1983) and that of other psychoanalysts (e.g., Maduro, 1976) provides a different picture sharply at variance with that of Carstairs. Minturn and Hitchcock (1966) present the emotional context of the physical care of a child (e.g., carrying the child frequently, sleeping with it, nursing on demand, little effort to control urination or defecation, and soiling accidents) offered by an Indian mother. While the child no doubt develops a strong emotional attachment to the mother as a result of the physical gratification she extends, the mother does not respond by setting up a Western-style loving and emotional partnership. Seymour's (1975, 1983) study of Bhubaneswar children and Maduro's (1976) study of Nathdwara Brahman artists lend support to Minturn's findings. Several other studies (e.g., Beals, 1962; Dube, 1955; Luschinsky, 1962; Mencher, 1963; Rohner & Chaki-Sircar, 1987; Surya, 1969; Wiser & Wiser, 1963) also document considerable consistency in child rearing across various regions of India. Seymour (1971, 1975, 1976, 1983) admits that the difference in the practices of various groups is largely of degree than of principle. However, Trawick (1990) believes that "the meaning of the weaning experience might differ greatly from child to child, according to the configuration of meaningful experiences in which it is set (e.g., the presence or absence of a younger sibling who is nursed after the older one is weaned, the quality of other kinds of food available to the child, the characteristics of other caretakers besides the mother, whether the child is male or female, and a thousand other "variables") (p. 216).

Recently Kurtz (1992) has proposed a new developmental model of Hindu child rearing practices. He is conscious of the fact that child rearing in the Indian family is the product of joint families, multiple care-takers, and rules of restraint on parent-child interaction in front of elders. The family group, and not merely the individual mother, lies at the core of this model. In his view "the Hindu mother as well as the larger group of caretakers in the Hindu joint family so arrange their care as to prompt in the child a voluntary renunciation of infantile ties to the mother" (Kurtz, 1992, p. 61). He observes that mothers and children in India berate each other with streams of threats and requests that sometimes delay and always affect the character of services rendered. This pattern of interplay has a major effect on the child's development. This is because the bargaining by play of mother and child has the effect of pushing the child away from an exclusive and dependent attachment to the mother and toward a kind of participation or immersion in the activity of the broader family group. As the child matures, the mother's response to his persistent requests slows while her emphasis on the bargain involved sharpens. The child is asked not only to abandon immature pleasures but also to join the group by carrying out various useful tasks. The group, on the other hand, offers the child a quality of attention not available from the mother. This shows a distinctive method for losening the child's attachment to pleasure. They do not withhold gratification but create conditions in which a child will abandon it without being forced to do so.

Kurtz (1992) notes that motherhood in India involves multiple mothering in types and forms. The mother occasionally frustrates but regularly gratifies the child. Further, in the joint family setting, the task of frustrating or gratifying the child is shared by the siblings, cousins, mother's sister-in-laws (the wives of her husband's brothers) and mother's mother-in-law who has a special claim on the child. Outside the home's courtyard, the task is shared by other male members of the family. The child belongs more to the family as a whole than to any one particular individual. Kurtz (1992) argues that multiple mothering can prevent the healing of the split within the image of the natural mother by spreading out the opposition between good and bad among multiple mothers.

Trawick's (1990) study of child rearing in Tamilnadu further illustrates the preceding argument. Her analysis of a Tamil (Dravidian) system of child adoption matches the basic function of multiple mothering. She presents a contrast between American and Tamil child rearing. If one asks an American what a child needs most, the answer is likely to be "love". The Tamils would respond to the same question as "clothes, jewels, books and food". Trawick (1990) observes: "On the surface of it, this contrast is ironic, since in fact Americans give their children vastly more of what can be bought with money that most Tamil parents are able to give their children, while Tamil children are the recipients of much more whole-hearted affection than American children usually get" (p. 215).

The above mentioned studies were primarily conducted by the western researchers. These studies are undoubtedly more systematic, in-depth and have used ethnographic method of inquiry. However, many of them represent an outsider's perspective about the Indian child rearing. Further, socialisation of child in the Indian cultural system is a collective responsibility of all the family members. Trying to understand it in the framework of individualistic Freudian psychoanalysis may not be a rewarding experience.

Contextual Factors in Socialization

A large number of studies have been undertaken to examine the role of subcultural and demographic factors such as residential background (rural *Vs*. urban), socio-economic class, religious groups or community, mother's age and education, mother's employment and characteristics of family in the socialisation of children. Researchers have also been interested in examining the relationship between parental practices/attitudes and specific cognitive, personality or social/behavioural characteristics in children.

Evidence indicates variation in child rearing practices, such as feeding pattern, the time of weaning and toilet training across different socio-economic classes (Aphale, 1976; Bhogle, 1978, 1981, 1983; Joshi & Daharwal, 1977; Joshi & Tiwari, 1977). These studies indicate that middle class parents are more harsh and inconsistent in their child rearing behaviour than lower or upper class parents. However, Anandlakshmy and Bajaj (1981) failed to find any consistent child rearing pattern in the weavers' community in Varanasi. With regard to rural-urban differences, the results are inconclusive. While a number of studies (e.g., Mathew, 1977; Singh & Kaur, 1981, 1990) did not find any difference, a few of them report that urban mothers are more strict and encourage dependency (Seth, Saksena & Srivastava, 1978) and more systematically administer rewards and punishments (Rai, 1979). Pandey (1977) concluded that the child rearing orientation of parents were shaped by education, occupation, urban living, and the level of economic development in the region in which they were residing. In a study of child rearing in Bhubaneswar, Seymour (1980) found no difference in child care and expectations for children in the lower status urban and rural families, these children being less dependent, more self-reliant and responsible. This has been primarily so due to the fact that the lower status mothers had to work outside the home setting. The lower status school aged children largely remained at home due to parental disregard for formal education and primarily for the reason that these children were needed at home to care younger siblings and perform other chores.

Some researchers have investigated the relationship between maternal employment and personality development of children. It has been noted that the employment *per se* has no adverse effect, but employment combined with education, age of mothers and other concomitant family factors do contribute significantly. Employed mothers display and provide greater independence to their children (Rai, 1979; Singh & Sharma, 1975), encourage vocalisation (Seth & Saksena, 1978), use greater reward and punishment (Rai, 1979), interact more with children (Singh & Kaur, 1981), and children are more adjusted and well-behaved (Juneja, 1979). The children of employed mothers show greater outgoingness, ego strength and intelligence, but are insecure and tense (Mathur & Misra, 1994). Mother's employment provides opportunities to children to explore the environment and to take independent decisions which facilitates development of psychological differentiation in children (Mathur & Misra, 1995). There is greater incidence of non-traditional sex-role among the daughters of highly educated and professional mothers (Dixit & Vishnoi, 1980; Ghadially & Kazi, 1979). Mody and Murthy (1988) have reported poor intelligence scores in children of working mothers. However, working mothers are more susceptible to marital conflict (Saksena *et al.*, 1977) and expressed maximum conflict in relation to mother's role (Gupta & Ganguli, 1982). Nanda (1991) found that though majority of the children of working mothers had a favourable opinion about their mother's employment, a small section was not happy with their mother's employment.

Child Rearing and Cognitive-Affective Development

Some studies have examined the role of child rearing practices in fostering cognitive, social, moral and personality development in children. Regarding child rearing and cognitive variables, studies have failed to show any systematic relationship. Ponuswamy (1977) found mother-child interaction to be pertinent to the cognitive style of children in American sample but not in the Indian sample. In another study (Srivastava, 1983), no significant relationship was found between the child's perceived parenting and cognitive complexity. Anandlakshmy and Bajaj (1981) showed no evidence of direct relationship between parents' efforts to socialise the child and the child's competence. S.R. Sinha (1987) found that providing encouragement and independence by mothers was positively related to child's competence.

Authoritarian, punitive and inconsistent child rearing has been associated with obedience (Joshi & Tiwari, 1977), anxiety (Hassan, Enayatullah & Khalique, 1977), authoritarianism (Ojha, 1977), negative self-esteem (Kapur & Gill, 1986) and greater inclination toward the use of defence mechanisms (Singh & Sharma, 1978). Gupta (1990) found a positive relationship between parental Machiavellianism and offspring's self-esteem. Over-protection and controlling behaviours of mothers were positively related to dependency in children (S.R. Sinha, 1987).

Agarwal and Saxena (1977) have suggested that child's emotional development is influenced by parent's child rearing attitudes and practices and parent's personality. Studies have revealed positive relationship between parental warmth and affection and a sense of competence in children (Sharma, Saraswathi & Giri, 1981), between parents rejecting attitude and anxiety in children (Ojha & Singh, 1988), nurturance of mother and emotional and social adjustment of daughters (Chatterjee & Shah, 1981), inter-parental conflict and child's adjustment (Kakar, 1970), and mother's emotional instability and hostility in children (Barlinge, 1977).

Empirical evidence relating socialisation practices to moral development reveals that the feeling of guilt in children was positively related to love-oriented parental discipline and hostility to power-assertive discipline (Singh & Sowaid, 1976). Saraswathi and Sundaresan (1979) reported that in the upper social class power assertion was negatively correlated in children of both sexes and induction positively correlated among boys with moral maturity. The use of power-assertion was frequent in both the groups (Saraswathi, Thakkar & Kaur, 1979).

The pattern of family training has been found to be associated with the development of prosocial behaviour in children (Bhargava & Gupta, 1978). Singh and Fatmi (1980) noted that the use of induction by mothers for boys was positively related with the development of social responsibility for girls, a positive relationship between social responsibility and power assertion by father and love withdrawal by mothers.

The relationship between parenting and development of motivation in children was examined in a few studies. Tiwari and Misra (1977) found that parents of children showing high achievement and low anxiety showed higher degree of independence attitude and indicated more early demands and fewer early restrictions. Parenting factors were positively associated with high internal attribution for success and low internal attribution for failure (Srivastava, 1983).

As regards children's perception of parent-child relationship, Wadekar and Palsane (1987) found that girls perceived their parents more favourably than boys. Sandhu and Bhargava (1987) have observed that perceived maternal acceptance was greater in small families than in large ones.

Gender Differences

Despite the fact that the concept of gender equality has been basic to Indian thinking for over a century, the girl child has been subjected to gross neglect. Studies have shown differences in the child rearing of male and female children. Bhogle (1991) has reported significant discrimination in feeding, weaning, and toilet training practices as well as in the parental attitudes towards the girl child. Girls have lesser access to food, health, education and recreation (Sen & Sengupta, 1983) and induced early into domestic work, marriage and motherhood (Karkal, 1991). The instances of female foeticide and sexual abuse of girl children in and out of the family have also been reported (Bhalerao, 1985). The practice of killing the baby girls has been observed in some parts of the country. The discrimination against the girl child before birth is being restrained by the protective measures being taken by the States. Work at home, such as domestic work, sibling care, helping parents in their occupation, and engagement in remunerative employment is seen as the chief reason for the dropout among girls (Nayar, 1995). Likewise, gender based division of labour and gender segregation appear to hinder girls in getting into the educational system.

Saraswathi and Dutta (1990) examined the pattern of socialisation of adolescent girls among the urban and poor of Baroda. They found that from puberty itself girl children have to bear the responsibility of house-work and child care in large families, the pains of early marriage, the anxieties of delayed marriage, and the stigma of barrenness and widowhood. They concluded that it is a man's world and woman is second in order to command, if there is any command at all.

In a nationwide study Anandlakshmy (1994) reports that birth of a girl child is desired and celebrated only by 2 per cent of the families.

Housework is an activity that about 78 per cent of the girls share with their mothers. About 28 per cent girls get skill training from mothers, about 8 per cent share time with mothers in occupational tasks, and the same proportion (8%) spend home-work time with their mothers and fathers. There is a great deal of gender segregation within the family with household tasks like sweeping and cooking being unambiguously female tasks. The girl child's life is physically and metaphorically circumscribed. School attendance of girls is influenced by the SES of the family as well as the level of development of the area. Parental attitude towards educational level to be ideally attained by boys and girls differed in favour of boys.

Ecological Factors and Socialization

Dawson's (1974) bio-social-psychological model argues that the nature of ecological subsistence environments (such as, hunting-fishing, snow-desert, islands, pastoral or agricultural jungle) determines the adaptive social organisation and selection of psychological skills needed for survival. Thus while hunting and fishing people have independent socialisation needed for survival, agricultural societies are stratified and have harsh conforming socialisation which also has survival value. Barry, Child and Bacon (1959) predicted that societies with "hunting and fishing" subsistence economies would have low food accumulation and that adults should be individualistic, assertive and venturesome. In contrast, societies with "agricultural" subsistence economies would have high food accumulation and that adults should tend to be conscientious, and conservative. Analysing 104 societies they found that agriculturists had harsher and more conforming socialisation, while hunting/fishing societies had more passive and independent socialisation. Studies (Berry, 1967; Dawson, 1963, 1969, 1974) have also shown that societies with firmer socialisation are both more susceptive to modern attitude change and have higher level of achievement motivation.

Consistent with these observations, studies on tribal children have shown them to be more independent. Dave and Takkar (1983) studied the tribals of Panchmahals in Gujarat. The general picture of the tribal child emerged as of an independent individual, capable of making demands on his parents and other caretakers for food and protection. The child was a secure and relaxed member in the family. M. Sinha (1978) observed nomadic Birhors in North India to be more independent than the sedentary Oraons. Among the tribals of North-East, Srivastava

(1987) observed rural-urban and sex differences; rural males to be significantly less conforming than other groups.

Studies showing sub-cultural variations in socialisation of children in India have essentially adopted western mode of inquiry without realising the uniqueness of the Indian culture. These have been peripheral without making an attempt to go deep in the actual socialisation process. For example, examining of the pattern of socialisation process in patrilineal and matrilineal family context is a challenging task. The values of boys and girls in patrilineal and matrilineal context are altogether different. Even within a particular context there are regional and gender variations. These cultural issues, specific to the Indian context, need to be examined carefully in order to have a full understanding of the socialisation process.

II
PARENTAL PERSPECTIVE ON CHILDREN : AN EMPIRICAL STUDY

This study (Srivastava *et al.*, 1996) explored the ideals and values that give directive focus to the socialisation of children, shaping their affective, social and cognitive development. The continuities in values across generations in the face of discontinuities introduced by factors such as rapid and profound political, economic, and social changes in the country were investigated. The primary goal of the study was to understand the pattern of value system that today's parents want their children to adopt.

The study involved 360 participants (120 mothers, 120 fathers, and 120 grandmothers of children below 10 years of age) from 3 types of residential background (rural/urban/metropolitan areas) and two levels of economic status (low/high). The mean age of mothers was 30.58 (range = 19-45) years, of fathers 34.40 (range = 24-50) years, and of grandmothers 55.05 (range = 40-88) years. The mean years of schooling for mothers was 7.76 (range = 0-21) years, for fathers 9.80 (range = 0-20) years, and for grandmothers 3.33 (range = 0-17) years. A large majority of the parents were either Brahmin (34%) or Shudras (50%) by caste. Of the Shudras, 82 per cent belonged to the low economic group. About 88 per cent Brahmins were from high economic group. The Kshatriya and Vaishya constituted about 11 per cent of the sample. About 4 per cent respondents were non-Hindus.

The rural parents were primarily Hindi speaking. The mother tongue of 89 per cent urban and 70 per cent metropolitan parents was Hindi. The rural mothers and fathers were primarily housewives and agriculturists, respectively. About half of the urban mothers were housewives and the remaining half were engaged either as domestic help or were in business and service. About 60 per cent of the urban fathers were in government service and 40 per cent in business. Similar trend was observed for metropolitan parents. Majority of the grandmothers were housewives. Some of the grandmothers were also engaged in the performance of domestic chores. Care was taken to ensure that half of the participants must have at least one boy as sex of the child has been found to play a significant role in regulating social behaviour in traditional societies like India.

Data were collected from Delhi, Allahabad city, and remote rural villages of Allahabad. Using an open-ended interview schedule parental views regarding the following issues were obtained : (a) perceived value and cost in having a child, (b) desirable human qualities and parental efforts to inculcate those qualities in children, (c) the relevance of indigenous values in the present day context, (d) the kind of solution reached at in the case of conflicting value preferences shown by the child, and (e) the rules for categorising behaviours in desirable/ undesirable categories. The obtained response were content-analysed. The results are described in the following sections.

Perceived Value and Cost of Children

The parents were asked to respond to the question that "to you personally, what are some of the advantages and disadvantages in having children as compared with not having them at all?" In a similar study of this sort, popularly known as Value of Children Study, conducted in nine countries, Indonesia, the Federal Republic of Germany, Korea, the Philippines, Singapore, Taiwan, Thailand, Turkey and the United States, two main value types — psychological and economic — were identified (Kagitcibasi, 1988). The economic value included children's material contribution to the family when they were young and when they grew up, especially as a source of old age security to their parents. However, American and German responses were in contrast to those from other countries. They found the questions regarding help expected from offspring in old age rather offensive and denied being dependent on anyone, especially their children. There was also decreased inter-generational dependency with economic development. These results, however, refer to material inter-dependencies. Other studies indicate that psychological family inter-dependencies can continue to be strong even in the absence of material inter-dependencies (Erelcin, 1988; Yang, 1988). It has also been observed that to southern European (Australian, Greek, Italian) parents, having children completes the marriage and establishes their family within the community of families (Callan, 1980).

The parental responses in the present study can also be categorised into two major value types: *Economic* and *Psychological.* The metro and urban parents considered children to be more of psychological value, such as "children make life more meaningful" (45%), "they are the source of love" (32%), "pleasure" (27%), and "provide company" (25%). Children were also of "value for extending the family lineage" (20%). In contrast, a large section of rural parents (41%) valued children for the "performance of domestic chores", followed by "psychological value of children", such as "source of love" (36%) and "pleasure" (40%). About 35 per cent of them considered children as essential for running family lineage. A comparison of parental responses in terms of social class showed that the parents from higher social class emphasised on children's psychological value. In contrast, the economic value of children such as, their performance of domestic chores (45%) followed by psychological value was emphasised by low social class parents. The patterns of responses for fathers and mothers were similar.

An analysis of the grandmothers' responses yielded an interesting trend. Irrespective of social class and locality, the grand-mothers valued children for running family lineage (50%) followed by their psychological value, such as life becomes more meaningful (23%), source of love (27%), and pleasure (24%), respectively.

Among the costs of having children, the rural parents gave primacy to the psychological cost (e.g., parents' anxiety about the child's health, and his/her future insecurity). The economic cost was assigned less importance by the rural parents. To them children were not a responsibility, sources of inconvenience and financial loss, or social obligation. About 38 per cent rural parents did not perceive any cost in having children. The urban parents gave first priority to future insecurity of children followed by "no cost" in having children. The other relatively less frequently mentioned responses were: responsibility of child rearing, concern about child's health, children as social obligation, sources of financial loss and inconvenience. It may be mentioned that while children were not viewed as causing inconvenience or social obligation by the rural parents, a small number of urban parents did perceive them as such. The responses of metropolitan parents were more diffused ranging from no cost, future insecurity and health of children, to financial losses (especially by parents belonging to the low economic status). The grandmothers were more concerned with the future insecurity of children (46%) followed by no cost (41%).

Expectations from Children

Child rearing values also reflect family relations and the changes in them. In the Value of Children Study expectations of obedience (dependence) *versus* independence and self-reliance showed a systematic variation somewhat parallel to old-age security. These were the two most desired and second most desired characteristics in children related to general developmental levels in opposite directions. The newly industrialised countries like Korea and Singapore stressed on independence. The countries like Indonesia and the Philippines, and to a lesser extent Turkey and Thailand, emphasised on expectations of dependence from children, this dependence to be reversed later on with the dependence of elderly parents on their grow-up offspring — a pattern of family interdependence through generations (Kagitcibasi, 1988).

When asked in this study what are their expectations from children, parents gave highest priority to children's success in life (73%). While metro and urban parents gave second priority to their becoming good citizens (44%), rural parents (29%) expected them to take care of their parents in old age. Relatively larger number of mothers than fathers from low economic status, expected their children to be serving in their old age. A similar pattern was observed for grandmothers, with 75 per cent of them expecting their children to be successful in life followed by children's utility in their old age (49%).

Desirable and Undesirable Characteristics

The Study of Value including the perceptions of desirable and undesirable characteristics has attracted a good deal of cross-cultural research (see for review, Jain & Singh, 1996; Srivastava, Banerjee & Tripathi, 1996). The general conclusion of these studies has been that while the western and developed countries emphasise on the development of individualistic, personal, or independent value orientation, the developing countries stress on collective, social and interdependent orientation. The developed countries focus on the development of technological intelligence (Mundy-

Castle, 1974) while social intelligence is emphasised by majority of the developing countries (Chao, 1994; Misra & Gergen, 1993; Nsamenang & Lamb, 1993).

In the present study, parents, irrespective of their residential background, wanted their children to be honest (74%) and hardworking (74%). It may be noted that the rural and urban parents gave first rank to hard work, and honesty received the second rank. The reverse was, however, true for metropolitan parents. Obedience was the third highly valued characteristics endorsed by urban (59%) and metropolitan (55%) parents while it received fifth rank in case of rural parents (34%). Further, the urban and metropolitan parents gave fifth rank to truthfulness while it received sixth rank by the rural parents. The other highly valued qualities were benevolence and humanity which were ranked third and fourth by rural parents, and fifth and sixth by the urban and metropolitan parents. The development of characteristics such as curiosity, justice and friendliness were relatively less emphasised by all the three groups of parents. Parents belonging to high economic status showed a pattern similar to that of urban and metropolitan parents.

The parents and grand-mothers gave highest priority to individual-centred characteristics such as honesty and hard work, albeit with changed priorities. While majority of the parents desired their children to be hardworking followed by honesty, the reverse was true for grandmothers. Both parents and grandparents assigned third rank to obedience, a socio-centric characteristic. Further, humanity and truthfulness turned out to be the fourth and fifth priorities, respectively, by parents while the reverse was true for grandmothers. The characteristics such as curiosity, justice and friendliness were least desired by both groups of parents.

Three individual-centred characteristics such as laziness (74%), greed (71%) and fear (70%) and two socio-centric characteristics—disobedience (64%) and quarrelsomeness (76%), were considered highly undesirable by parents of different groups. Also, within a particular group there were least variations in the frequency of parental responses. The characteristics such as stealing and arrogance were described undesirable by a few parents. A somewhat contradictory finding was that telling a lie was not deemed undesirable by parents; only a very small percentage of grandmothers described it undesirable.

In a survey conducted by *India Today* (31 December, 1995) it was observed that "perhaps the most significant way that the East and the West differ in their values system lies in the values parents wish to inculcate in their children" (p. 53). While the parents from Asian countries felt that "good manners and politeness" were most important, the "sense of responsibility" was most desired by parents from Western countries. Out of 12 values, Indians ranked the following eight values in order of importance: (1) good manners/politeness, (2) value of learning, (3) sense of responsibility, (4) tolerance and respect for others, (5) conscientiousness at work, (6) independence, (7) loyalty and (8) ability to communicate. However, the results of this study involved only the urban parents. It did not poll the views of rural India.

Children's social context is formed by adults with whom they interact. It shapes the behavioural settings which provide opportunities for children to learn and develop. In India, social and cognitive stimulation literally begins at birth. It is a common observation that Indians freely tell their babies whom they resemble, what their names should be, what they signify, and what sort of adults they are expected to become. The present study shows that to inculcate desirable characteristics there is a close correspondence in the methods adopted by parents and grandmothers: persuasion (77%), scolding (32%), induction (29%) and physical punishment (5%). Further analysis indicated that physical punishment is adopted more by parents of lower social class and that the method is preferred more by grandmothers (39%) than the parents. When asked whether the methods of child rearing adopted by today's mothers have changed, 64 per cent grandmothers answered in affirmation. They were of the opinion that this change has been for the better and is more reality oriented.

Criteria for Desirable/Undesirable Behaviours

The present study shows a close correspondence between parents and grandmothers on the criteria for deciding what is desirable for the child. Sixty eight per cent of them opined that they themselves decide what is good for the child. Other criteria were : traditional social norms (58%), family norms (28%), child's peer group (28%), and modern changes in the society. While 18 per cent parents from high social class used the child's views as criteria, only 2 per cent from the low social class gave weightage to the child's opinion. Also, while 21 per cent urban parents valued children's opinion, only 7 per cent metro and 2 per cent rural parents considered children's opinion to be of any importance.

Negotiation between Parents and Children

When asked to what extent you will make concessions to the child if she shows conflicting value patterns, two types of responses were obtained. About one-third (36%) felt that they will not allow any relaxation. In contrast, a sizeable number (58%) opted for the middle path – that they will make efforts to ensure that children must not develop undesirable behaviours. It is interesting to note that parents were of the opinion that good qualities develop in children due to parental efforts (73%). Children pick up bad qualities from friends (57%) and society (70%).

Comments

The present study explored the desirable qualities and goals that today's parents value most and would like to see them as possessed by their children. Realising the fact that the traditional Indian culture has been changing under the impact of Western education, urbanisation, and industrialisation, it was expected that modern values and beliefs — concerning child birth, early child care, for example — are rapidly substituting the traditional values. In these areas, young urban population represents the vanguard of change, whereas older, rural people cling to the most traditional beliefs. Results of the study, however, show that for the most part, traditional values are widely endorsed and appreciated by all sections of the society.

The children are valued in the Indian society primarily for psychological reasons. They are considered as source of emotional support including love, pleasure and company, and thus make life more meaningful. Though parents from rural background showed preference for economic value, the psychological value was not altogether missing. Rather, both values ran parallel. This shows that though rural parents want children for help in the performance of domestic chores and running errands, their psychological value is not diminished. A similar pattern was observed for parents belonging to the lower social class. Parental responses as compared to grandmothers show a transition from emphasis on economic value to psychological value.

Regarding the costs of children, parental responses indicated the impact of urbanisation and industrialisation. Majority of the parents were worried about children's future. In a social situation where resources are scarce, a lot of competitiveness is observed and the principle of survival of the fittest is best suited. The situation in India has gone to the extent that parents show dire anxiety from the beginning of the child's life about his/her daily school work, examination results, admission to a college, and ultimately employment and marriage (Kumar, 1993). This is probably the reason that when parents were asked about their expectations from children, majority of them wished their children to be successful in life.

The study also revealed the parental preferences for values that have been considered of importance in the Indian society. Parents want their children to be honest and hardworking, show obedience and respect for elders, be humane, truthful and benevolent, and display regard for spiritual powers. The generation gap in terms of rural grandmothers emphasising more on spiritualism and humanness was also observed. The characteristics, such as quarrelsomeness, laziness, greed, fear, and disobedience were deemed undesirable. A similar trend was noted in another study by Mathur and Misra (1995). The analyses of achievement goals by Agarwal and Misra (1986), and Singhal and Misra (1989, 1994) shows that social concern was the most salient goal for adolescents and young adolescents. Also, there was considerable overlap in the perceived importance of goals with parents and teachers.

III
THE EXPERIENCE OF SOCIALISATION: PARENTAL VOICES

As a part of our study on values some parents were interviewed in detail regarding the context and experience of socialisation. This yielded valuable hints to understand some of the practical questions faced today by the parents. In the Indian context, the expression of "socialisation" is used with different connotations. Broadly speaking it is used in an active and a passive sense. As an active process socialisation becomes a deliberate attempt on the part of socially significant others to shape the course of life of the child. This implicitly assumes the inherent potentiality of human nature. The implication is that people themselves are reasonable for the production of different types of human qualities. In contrast, the traditional Indian view holds that each and every individual is endowed with certain competencies and a pre-determined life course. It is believed that parents transfer the merits and demerits to their children. A child is an extension of his parents. The similarities between parents and children are often looked at and constructed. Fathers and mothers also consider their offsprings as self-objects, through which they (or themselves) are defined. To many of them, socialisation happens to be an occasion for self-articulation. The locus of this articulation is, therefore, often times perceived to be lying within parents themselves. The Indian parents usually find it difficult to separate and distance themselves from their children. They try to do everything possible for them. It is believed that the placement of stars at the time of birth of the child determines her fate. The horoscope or *janampatri* is often made and consulted on critical occasions (e.g., marriage, illness, job, etc.). Zodiac (*Rashiphal*) constitutes an important column in the dailies, weekly and monthly magazines. All this indicates considerable degree of pre-determination or order in the Indian belief system which delimits the scope for parental socialisation. At the same time it proves functional by reducing uncertainties and overcoming the ambiguity and indeterminacy prevailing in the life circumstances.

The parents indicated that the question of socialisation in the Indian context has to be examined in the context of country's socio-economic conditions and cultural history. Historically, the Indian society has experienced many shifts in the system of its social stratification which have been supplying the bases for personal growth and community activities. In the course of time these pre-determined role categories proved to be very rigid and did not allow freedom to change or shift one's place or position in the social hierarchy. Thus for generations *status quo* was maintained and little change could take place. The goal of socialisation was to maintain the hierarchical social order and its attendant features. People did not perceive alternatives and remained confined to the available roles and expectations. This system was reinforced by the religious sanctions, educational system and other kinds of institutional arrangements. Of course, class related differences always existed in various social categories which provided certain degree of latitude within a given category. In a way there existed a range of reactions out of which people could display different degrees of attainment.

Parents indicated that contemporaneous elements in the Indian culture are making demands for adjustment and adaptation on the part of family and other social institutions. The interplay of traditional elements and current events often demands new patterning of values which is leading to a number of contradictions and tensions. Some of them are described in this section.

Individualistic Vs. Collectivistic Goals

Traditionally the Indian ethos has been dominated by a somewhat collectivist concern in which the goals of individuality and relatedness were blended. There was relatively greater emphasis on societal functioning and order and family was the smallest social unit. One's fate was decided by the group (family) level decisions in almost all matters including family life and career (e.g., marriage, occupation and business). In this process family was chiefly responsible for taking all major decisions concerning an individual's life. During adverse circumstances the entire group extended the required support. In contemporary India, particularly in urban and metropolitan areas, the situation is, however, changing. The commitment for social security is being withdrawn and individual is held responsible for his actions; for assets as well as liabilities. In the urban and metropolitan centres life has become so complex that everybody has to look for his personal welfare. This has resulted in the narrowing of social concerns and increased concentration on the personalised and materialistic well-being. Increased individualism often coexists with the collectivist orientation. To some parents it appeared to be replacing the collectivist orientation. The parents noted increased preference for personal over the societal goals and growing disregard for the public assets. To others, the overlap and interdependence between personal and social goals experienced earlier is now vanishing very fast.

Conflict Vs. Cohesion

One of the most striking aspects of the contemporary social reality is of heightened competition, which has its root in at least three sources: increased individualistic orientation, lack of resources to accommodate the growing population, and shift towards capitalist and liberalised market economy resulting in consumerism. All of these are operating simultaneously and together tend to question the functional value or relevance of the collectivist orientation in the contemporary life. As a result cohesiveness and harmony are being replaced by the tendencies of conflict and competition. The maximisation of gains for the individual actor is becoming the core concern and legitimises all efforts to exploit others. Increased political violence, corruption and intolerance lend support to this analysis. Sharpening of the boundaries between self and others (not self), on the one hand, and ever increasing concern with celebration of individualism on the other, are culminating in disregard and hostility toward others. Thus, people often times engage in unhealthy competition which takes different forms of exploitation of others. Much of the social disorder currently evident was perceived as closely linked with these tendencies.

Insecurity and Distrust

The feeling of insecurity and lack of mutual trust were reported as two important unhealthy ingredients of the Indian social life. The sources which once upon a time were granting justice, status, prestige and place in the society and facilitated attainment of goals are now vanishing. This was attributed to the rapid social change taking place through revolution in communication and transportation. The traditional social institutions of caste, community, and religion no more assert the power which once they had enjoyed in regulating the individual and the social life of the people. The alternative systems (e.g. legal, civilian, etc.) are complicating the matter for the masses and serving the causes of the elite section in the society. In fact some parents observed that the democratic set-up with its bureaucratic jargon has become instrumental in perpetuating the social class differences and justice is often times delayed or denied to the poor. The result is widespread communal disturbance threatening the individual's trust and security-beliefs. Presently the various sections of the society are feeling insecure. This insecurity is reciprocally related to the growing mistrust. Certain groups are becoming threats for other groups and atrocities against particular communities or castes are on increase. All this point to the weakening of the social fabric of the Indian society.

Obligatory and Exchange Relationships

Being holistic in perspective the traditional approach was considered to construct relationships in terms of mutual obligation and interdependence. Caring and being cared provided a firm ground for developing strong social bonds. Such a relationship did not involve stark instrumentality in which social exchange is dictated by an appraisal of the costs involved and rewards anticipated. It is being replaced by an individualistic orientation growing within the market structure. A model of an economic man in which everything is a commodity with a certain price is gradually dominating. Now people play market games, hold exchange relationship with fellow-being, behave to maximise pleasure and materialistic gain, and avoid pain and loss. This analysis begins and ends with utility. Egoist and self-serving tactics are viewed instrumental in nourishing interpersonal interaction.

Equality based Relationship

Comparing the present day social context with the traditional or older context the parents noted that for long a vertically organised hierarchical social structure was the dominant model. It involved top-down communication and was characterised by a concentration of power and authority at higher levels in the hierarchy. The rights, obligations, and duties were determined by the hierarchical position rather than one's investment. This kind of social arrangement is being challenged and gradually replaced by more open, participative and egalitarian arrangement which has relatively greater scope for equality and equity. However, this trend has not gained momentum and is shared in different degrees. A variation of this trend is to compensate for the deprivations by engaging in socially deviant behaviours.

Short-term Goals

The consequence of uncertain future and inadequate support tend to diminish one's concern and investment into long-term goals and prolonged engagement. This is treated as a more effective survival strategy if planning is made on a short-term basis. This also gets reflected in the coordination of interpersonal interactions, and structuring of relationships. Short-term goals happen to be less demanding in terms of investment, allow scope for experimentation, and provide the feeling of contentment easily and immediately than long-term goals.

Non-committal Attitude

A large number of parents voiced the opinion that the contemporary Indian society is undergoing an ideological and attitudinal transformation. Owing to the pressures from Western education and mass-media the people are being simultaneously exposed to diverse life styles. Many of them are alien to the Indian socio-cultural ethos and uprooting of indigenous values is taking very fast. Under these circumstances it is becoming fashionable not only to question but to reject the Indian value system. Some parents remarked that an ideological vacuum is being created in which people are experimenting with different ideas and have not yet been able to formulate and crystallise their choices and preferences. The result is a non-committal attitude and a confused perspective on the values and goals of child rearing. The ambiguity is obvious in many areas such as delivery of reward and punishment, modes of interaction between parents and children, the degree of distance to be maintained between parents and children, and the extent of sharing and trust between parents and children. Taken together, today's average middle class parents are unclear and uncertain about the preferred interactional patterns with children. Children often dominate the interaction and dictate their terms and conditions.

The claims for responsibility are settled easily when a system operates in a predictable fashion. In a situation where the rules and casual order are increasingly becoming non-transparent, fixing the responsibility becomes difficult and dangerous. People know this reality and, therefore, frequently avoid accepting responsibilities by taking recourse to different tactics. The traditional pattern of social interaction provided greater open social space in which people could witness and emulate the significant behaviours of others. Most of the things happening were socially mediated. The contemporary situation questions this pattern and renders most of the things private and, therefore, invisible. Things are distanced by creating larger personal space which remains socially unshared. The norm for individuality is created and maintained. Many of the life rituals and ceremonies clearly substantiate this pattern. This situation is leading to re-arrangements and re-alignments in the social arena.

Caught between tradition and modernity, many of the parents find it difficult to stand by a consistent stance or position with reference to different but related issues. Now people take different positions depending on the kind of person involved and implications for own well-being. People compartmentalise their cognitive frame and resolve the possible contradiction across different worlds by separation and isolation. Thus their experiences are made independent and exclusive. This makes them free from the possible dissonance.

CONCLUDING COMMENTS

The study of childhood in India has many intellectual roots. In particular, the social sciences formulated according to western tradition, especially psychoanalytic theory of Freudian kind, has played a very important role. It has led the portrayals of Indians and their 'psyche' in a strange fashion which has been substantiated by subsequent researches. However, there has been certain innovations in which psychoanalytic theory has been expanded and modified to incorporate the non-western cultural perspectives. Also, there is possibility of indigenous perspectives rooted in different cultures. It seems that understanding cultures and their constructs is a multivocal enterprise. Science and non-sciences as well as the different traditions of sciences are being questioned for their legitimacy beyond certain conditions. Scientific theories are tools to facilitate understanding and there is two-way transaction between science and culture. This makes blending of theoretical innovations possible. In this regard Roland's notion of 'familial self' and 'we-self' and Kurtz's perspective on 'multiple mothering' are not dangerous rather make analysis more fruitful and authentic.

The move toward cultural-psychological interpretations and use of indigenous concepts, which is still at a nebulous stage, cannot be ruled out on account of the danger of nativism or 'west-bashing'. Similarly it will be premature to declare Roland's or Kurtz's work as white-man's guilt. In fact, the situation is quite complicated. The indigenous perspective is still very weak and many of the white psychologists' thinking that science is a western construction, as Triandis (1993) observes that "Modern science is a western construction... if there is to be an Indian science it has to follow Western patterns" (p. 249), is peculiar and pitiable. Preoccupation with the so-called non-ethnocentric western view of science, if prevails, will preclude understanding any culture in its own terms. We think that any conception of science or psychology is culturally and historically situated. This fact is forgotten because of self-reflection. Similarly, we also do not pay attention to the fact that within western cultures many alternatives exist (e.g. phenomenological, hermeneutic, feminist, etc.). Adopting the western ontology of mind, society and related things will only allow understandings framed by the western ontology and everything else will be excluded. This is a real danger and Indian social scientific studies, particularly psychological ones, have suffered from what can be called as objectification of the western construction of the world. The universalised western view is ethnocentric. Moreover, such a view dismisses the possibility of the "other". It is, therefore, necessary that indigenous perspectives rooted in different cultures to be taken up seriously. This, of course, requires conceptual and methodological innovations which are closer to the human science perspective.

The study of values presents an indigenous perspective. It emphasises on (a) the value of children to parents belonging to different sections of the society, and (b) the patterns of values parents want their children to acquire in the context of rapid and profound social changes the Indian society is undergoing. It is observed that children are valued differently by various sectors of the society. While the urban, metropolitan and high economic status parents want children for their psychological utility, the rural and lower economic status value the economic utility of the children. Notwithstanding these differences all the parents want children to be honest, sincere and hard working. Persuasion is the preferred method adopted by parents for inculcating these cherished qualities in children where children are allowed to express their feelings, but the wisdom of the elderly persons prevail. However, a large number of rural, low economic status parents as well as grandmothers also adopt the method of physical punishment, thus treating children like inanimate objects and not the human beings.

The study by Srivastava *et al.*, (1996) shows that, as compared to the traditional system of functioning, the present day Indian society is more concerned with the personalised and materialistic well-being, high level of competition, feeling of insecurity and lack of mutual trust, emphasis on equality and short term goals, non-committal attitude and so on. Since the Indian society is undergoing through the stage of transition (Srivastava, 1995a), a large section of the society finds this situation quite uncomfortable and non-palatable. People resolve the resultant conflict by compartmentalising their experiences and make them independent and exclusive.

The reports of various Commissions and Committees on Education, right from the Radhakrishnan Committee Report (1948-49), Kothari Commission Report (1964-66) onwards to the National Policy on Education (1986), the Ramamurthi Committee Report (1990) and the CABE Committee on Policy Report (1992) have emphasised the urgent need for Value Orientation of Education. The Planning Commission Five Year Plan Reports, especially in the chapters on education, have been urging the need for this important need in the Indian educational system. The question then raised is what values schools should develop in children. In any system of value education there has to be some concordance between the values proposed to be developed and the values which are energised at home by the parents. The study shows changes in the parental goals for having children across generations and residential backgrounds. Within this change, however, parents want children to develop value systems which are indigenous in nature. Thus Indian parents are in dilemma. It seems that parents, on the one hand, accept the changes the social system is undergoing. On the other hand, they are cautious of its ill-effects and want their children to adopt the long cherished indigenous values. Thus Indian parents are passing through a stage of transition where changes in the desired goals are observed, but these changes are yet to find expression in their behavioural repertoire. This is probably the right time to teach children indigenous values using diverse measures such as schools and media. Also, parents need to be oriented in their value system and teach children values that are indigenous in nature to maintain compatibility between home and school. It is hoped that these measures will go a long way in reorienting the Indian society and fight with the ill-effects of modernisation.

References

Agarwal, G., & Saksena, N.K. (1977). Emotional development of the child and role of the parents: An Overview. *Child Psychiatry Quarterly, 10*, 1-7.

Agarwal, R., & Misra, G. (1986). A factor analytic study of achievement goals and means. *International Journal of Psychology, 21*, 217-231.

Anandalakshmy, S. (1994). *The Girl Child and the Family: An Action Research Study*. New Delhi: Government of India (Deptt. of Women and Child Development, MHRD).

Anandalakshmy, S., & Bajaj, M. (1981). Childhood in the weaver's community in Varanasi: Socialisation for adult roles. In D. Sinha (Ed.), *Socialisation of the Indian Child*, New Delhi: Concept.

Aphale, C. (1976) *Growing Up in An Urban Complex*, New Delhi: National.

Barlinge, M.K. (1977). *A Study of Influence of Mother's Personality on Child's Personality*. Unpublished doctoral dissertation, Nagpur University.

Barry, H., Child, I.K., & Bacon, N.K. (1959). Relation of child training to subsistence economy. *American Anthropologists, 61*, 51-63.

Beals, A.R.C. (1962). *Gopalpur: A South Indian Village*. New York : Holt, Rinehart & Winston.

Berry, J.W. (1967). Independence and conformity in subsistence level societies. *Journal of Personality & Social Psychology, 7*, 415-418.

Bery, J.W. (1990). Psychology of acculturation: Understanding individuals moving between cultures. In R.W. Brislin (Ed.), *Applied Cross-Cultural Psychology*. Newbury Park : Sage.

Bhalerao, V.R. (1985). *Profile of Sexually Transmitted Diseases in Child*

Prostitutes in the Red Light Areas of Bombay. Bombay: UNICEF (mimeographed).

Bhargava, P., & Gupta, P. (1978). Learning to be generous or stingy: Imitation of sharing as a function of generosity and vicarious reinforcement. *Asian Journal of Psychology and Education, 3*, 46-52.

Bhogle, S. (1978). Child rearing practices among three cultures. *Social Change*, 5-13.

Bhogle, S. (1981). Socialisation among different cultures. In D. Sinha (Ed.), *Socialisation of the Indian Child*. New Delhi: Concept.

Bhogle, S. (1983). Antecedents of dependency behaviour in children of low social class. *Psychological Studies, 28*, 92-95.

Bhogle, S. (1991). Child rearing practices and behaviour development of a girl child. *The Indian Journal of Social Work, L11*, 61-70.

Borstelman, L.J. (1983). Children before psychology: Ideas about children from antiquity to the late 1800s. In P.H. Mussen (Ed.), *Handbook of Child Psychology (Vol. 1): History, Theory and Methods* (pp. 3-40). New York: John Wiley.

Brandtstadter, J. (1990). Development as a personal and cultural construction. In G.R. Semin, & K.J. Gergen (Eds.), *Everyday Understanding* (pp. 83-107). London: Sage.

Bronfenbrenner, U. (1958). Socialisation and social class through time and space. In E.E. Maccoby, T.M. Newcomb, & E.L. Hartley (Eds.), *Readings in Social Psychology*, New York : Henry Holt.

Bruner, J. (1990). *Acts of Meaning*. Cambridge, Mass : Harvard University Press.

Callan, V.J. (1980). The value and cost of children: Australian, Greek and Italian couples in Sydney, Australia. *Journal of Cross-cultural Psychology, 2*, 482-497.

Carstairs, G.M. (1967). *The Twice Born: A Study of a Community of High-Caste Hindus*. Bloomington: Indiana University Press.

Chakraborty, S.K. (1993). *Transformation of Values*. New Delhi : Sage.

Chao, Y.T. (1994). Culture and work organisations. The Chinese case. In H.S.R. Kao, D. Sinha, N. Sek-Hong (Eds.), *Effective Organisations and Social Values*. New Delhi: Sage.

Chatterjee, T.K., & Shah, V. (1981). A study of relationship between adjustment and perceived parental behaviour among male and female college students. *Our Education, 2*, 45-49.

Chen, C.L., & Yang, D.C.Y. (1986). The self image of Chinese American adolescents: A cross-cultural comparison. *International Journal of Social Psychology, 32*, 19-26.

Cole, M. (1992). Context, modularity and the cultural constitution of development. In T. Winegar & J. Valsiner (Eds.), *Children's Development within Social Context. Vol. 2: Research and Methodology*. Hillsdale, NJ : Lawrence Erlbaum Associates.

Dave, P., & Tavkar, N. (1983). *Child Care amongst the Tribals of Limkheda, Panchmahals, Gujarat.* Baroda: M.S. University (Deptt. of Child Development).

Dawson, J.L.M. (1963). *Psychological Effects of Social Change in a West African Community.* D. Phil. Thesis, University of Oxford.

Dawson, J.L.M. (1969). *Research and Theoretical Basis of Bio-social Psychology.* Inaugural lecture from the chair of Psychology: University of Hong Kong Press.

Dawson, J.L.M. (1974). Ecology, cultural pressures towards conformity and left-handedness: A bio-social-psychological approach. In J. Dawson & W.J. Lonner (Eds.), *Readings in Cross-cultural Psychology.* Hong Kong: University of Hong Kong Press.

D'Andrade, R.G. (1982). Cultural meaning systems. In R.M. Adams, N.J. Smelse, & D.J. Trieman (Eds.), *Behavioural Science Research: A National Resource.* Washington: National Academy Press.

De Mause, L. (1974). *The History of Childhood.* New York: Psychohistory Press.

Diaz-Guerrero, R. (1982). The psychology of historico-cultural premises. *Spanish Language Psychology, 2,* 283-310.

Dixit, R.C., & Vishnoi, P.L. (1980). Employment of the mothers as a determinant of mother-daughter relationship and the development of masculinity feminity among young girls. *Psychologia, 23,* 162-172.

Dube, S.C. (1955). *Indian Village.* London: Roultedge and Kegan Paul.

Dweck, C.S., Chiu, C., & Hong, Y. (1995). Implicit theories and their role in judgements and reactions: A world from two perspectives. *Psychological Inquiry, 6,* 267-285.

Erelcin, F.G. (1988). *Collectivistic Norms in Turkey: Tendency to give and receive Support.* Unpublished Master's Thesis. Istanbul, Bogazici University.

Gergen, K.J., Gloger-Tippelt, G., & Berkowitz, P. (1990). The cultural construction of the developing child. In G.R. Semin & K.J. Gergen (Eds.), *Everyday Understanding* (pp. 108-129). London : Sage.

Gergen, K.J., Lock, A., Gulerce, A., & Misra, G. (1996). Psychological Science in cultural context. *American Psychologist, 50,* 496-503.

Ghadially, R., & Kazi, K.A. (1979). Attitude towards sex roles. *Indian Journal of Social Work, 40,* 65-71.

Gupta, G.R., & Ganguly, H.C. (1982). Marriage - work interaction: A study on Indian women. *Indian Journal of Clinical Psychology, 9,* 113-123.

Gupta, M.P. (1990). Effects of parental machiavellianism on personally perceived self-esteem. *Indian Journal of Current Psychological Research, 5,* 104-108.

Harkness, S., & Super, C. (1983). The cultural construction of child development. *Ethos, 11,* 222-231.

Harkness, S., & Super, C. (1993). The development niche: Implications for children's literacy development. In L. Eldering & P. Leseman (Eds.), *Early Intervention and Culture*. Netherlands: National Commission for UNESCO: UNESCO Publishing.

Harrison, A., Serafica, F., & McAdoo, H. (1982). Ethnic families of colour. In R.D. Parket (Eds.), *Review of Child Development Research: Vol. 7, The Family*, (p. 329-371). Chicago: University of Chicago Press.

Hess, R., Kashiwagi, K., Azuma, H., Price, G., & Dickson, W. (1980). Maternal expectations for mastery of development tasks in Japan and the United States. *International Journal of Psychology, 15*, 259-271.

Holtzman, W.H., Diaz-Guerrero, R., & Swartz, J.D. (1975). *Personality Development in Two Cultures: A Cross-Cultural Longitudinal Study of School Children in Mexico and the United States*. Austin: University of Texas Press.

India Today (1995). What Indians think. *India Today*, December 31, 43-52.

Jain, U., & Singh, T. (1998). Development of attitude and values. In A.K. Srivastava (Ed.), *Child Development: The Indian Perspective* (pp. 199-227). New Delhi: NCERT.

Joshi, M.C., & Daharwal, A. (1977). Child rearing practices and personality of Satnamee children. *Indian Psychological Review, 15*, 7-12.

Joshi, M.C., & Tiwari, J. (1977). Personality development of children in relation to child rearing practices among socio-economic classes. *Indian Psychological Review, 14*, 5-16.

Juneja, R. (1979). A comparative study of working and non-working mothers with respect to practices and problems of rearing children. *Indian Psychological Review, 18*, 1-4.

Kagitcibasi, C. (1988). Family and socialisation in cross-cultural perspective: A model of change. In R.A. Dienstbier (Series Ed.), *Nebraska symposium on motivation : Cross-cultural perspectives* (pp. 135-200).

Kakar, S. (1978). *The Inner World: A psychoanalytic Study of Childhood and Society in India*. Delhi: Oxford University Press.

Kakar, S. (1981). *The Inner World*. (2nd edition), Delhi: Oxford University Press.

Kapur, R., & Gill, S. (1986), Relationship between parental acceptance – rejection and self esteem. *Indian Psychological Review, 30*, 15-21.

Karkal, M. (1991). Invisibility of the girl child in India. *The Indian Journal of Social Work, LII*, 5-12.

Kessen, F.S., & Siegel, A.W. (Eds.) (1983). *The Child and Other Cultural Inventions*. New York: Praeger.

Kogan, J., Kersley, R.B., & Zelazo, P.R. (1978). *Infancy: Its Plan in Human Development*. Cambridge: Cambridge University Press.

Krishnan, L. (1998). Child rearing: The Indian perspective. In A.K. Srivastava (Ed.), *Child Development: The Indian Perspective* (pp. 25-55) New Delhi: NCERT.

Kumar, K. (1993). Study of Childhood and Family. In T.S. Saraswathi, & B. Kaur (Eds.), *Human Development and Family Studies in India: An*

Agenda for Research and Policy. New Delhi: Sage.

Kurtz, S.J. (1992). *All Mothers are One: Hindu India and the Cultural Reshaping of Psychoanalysis*. New York. Columbia University Press.

Lambert, L.W.E., Yackley, A., & Hein, R.N. (1971). Child training values of English and French Canadian parents. *Canadian Journal of Behavioural Science, 3*, 277-306.

Luschinsky, M.S. (1962) *The Life of Women in a Village of North India: A Study of Role and Status*. Ph.D. Dissertation. Cornell University.

Lin, C.Y.C., & Fu, V.R. (1990). A comparison of child rearing practices among Chinese, immigrant Chinese, and Caucasian American parents. *Child Development, 61*, 429-433.

Lytton, H., & Romney, D.M. (1991). Parents' differential socialisation of boys and girls: A meta-analysis. *Psychological Bulletin, 109*, 267-296.

Maccoby, E.E., & Martin, J.A. (1983). Socialisation in the context of the family: Parent-child interaction. In P.H. Mussen (Ed.), *Handbook of Child Psychology* (pp. 1-101). New York: John Wiley & Sons.

Maduro, R. (1976). *Artistic Creativity in a Brahmin Painter Community*. Berkeley: Center for South and South East Asia Studies, University of California.

Mamdani, M. (1972). *The Myth of Population Control: Family, Caste and Class in an Indian Village*. New Delhi: Monthly Review Press.

Markus, H.R., & Kitayama, S. (1991). Culture and the self: Implications for cognition, emotion and motivation. *Psychological Review, 98*, 224-253.

Marriott, A.M. (1976). Hindu transactions: Diversity without dualism. In B.K. Kapferer (Ed.), *Transactions and Meaning: Direction in the Anthropology of Exchange and Symbolic Behaviour*. Philadelphia: Institute for the Study of Human Issues.

Mathew, A. (1977). Roles, responsibilities and privileges of parents and children in the rural and urban areas of Chittor in Andhra Pradesh. *Journal of Comparative Family Studies, 8*, 133-138.

Mathur, K., & Misra, G. (1994). Influence of maternal employment on children's Personality. *Indian Journal of Psychometry and Education, 25*, 11-24.

Mathur, K., & Misra, G. (1995). *Maternal Employment and Psychological Development of Children*. Unpublished manuscript, Barkatullah University, Bhopal.

McGillicuddy-DeLisi, A.V. (1982). Parental beliefs about developmental processes. *Human Development,* 25, 192-200.

Mencher, J. (1963). Growing up in south Malabar. *Human Organisation, 22*, 54-65.

Mines, M. (1988). Conceptualising the person: Hierarchical society and individual autonomy in India. *American Anthropologists, 90*, 568-578.

Minturn, L, & Hitchcock, J.T. (1966). *The Rajputs of Khalapur, India*. New York: John Wiley.

Misra, G. (1995). Reflections on continuity and change in the Indian family system. *Trends in Social Science Research, 2*, 27-30.

Misra, G., & Gergen, K.J. (1993). On the place of culture in psychological science. *International Journal of Psychology, 28*, 225-243.

Misra, G., & Giri, R.S. (1995). Is Indian self predominantly interdependent? *Journal of Indian Psychology, 13*, 16-29.

Misra, G., & Tripathi, K.N. (1993). The concept and context of human development. In T.S. Saraswathi & B. Kaur (Eds.), *Human Development and Family Studies in India: an Agenda for Research and Policy* (pp. 90-103). New Delhi: Sage.

Misra, G., & Varma, S. (1994). Social problems, psychology and social policy. *Journal of the Indian Academy of Applied Psychology, 20*, 97-105.

Misri, U. (1986). Child and childhood: A conceptual construction. In V. Das (Ed.), *The Word and the World: Fantasy, Symbol and Record.* New Delhi: Sage.

Mody, S.N., & Murthy, V.N. (1988). The study of mental health of children of working mothers. *Journal of Personality and Clinical Studies, 4*, 161-164.

Mundy-Castle, A.C. (1974). Social and technological intelligence in Western and non-western cultures. *Universities*, 4, 46-52.

Nanda, P. (1991). Opinion of children regarding their mother's employment. *Indian Journal of Behaviour, 15*, 5-12.

Nandy, A., & Kakar, S. (1980). Culture and personality. In U. Pareek (Ed.), *A Survey of Research in Psychology*, 1971-1976, Part-I (pp. 136-167). Bombay: Popular Prakashan.

Nayar, U. (1995). Planning for UEE of girls and women's empowerment: Gender studies in DPEP. Paper presented at the *International Seminar on Researches in School Effectiveness and Learning Achievement at Primary Stage*, 17-19 July, 1995 at New Delhi.

Neki, J.S. (1973). Guru-chela relationship: The possibility of a therapeutic paradigm. *American Journal of Orthopsychiatry*, 43, 755-766.

Nsamenang, A.B., & Lamb, M.E. (1993). The acquisition of socio-cognitive competence of Nso children in the Bamenda Grassfields of Northwest Cameroon. *International Journal of Behavioural Development, 16*, 429-441.

Obeyesekere, G. (1990). *The Work of Culture: Symbolic Transformation in Psychoanalysis and Anthropology*. Chicago: University of Chicago Press.

Ojha, H. (1977). Parental behaviour as perceived by authoritarian and non-authoritarian college students. *Psychologia, 20*, 49-53.

Ojha, H., & Singh R. (1988). Child rearing attitudes as related to insecurity and dependence proneness. *Psychological Studies, 33*, 75-79.

Pandey, R.S. (1977). *Child Socialisation and Modernisation.* Bombay/New Delhi: Somaiya.

Ponnuswami, S. (1977). Mother-child interactions and cognitive style. *Indian Journal of Psychology, 52*, 250-255.

Poole, F.J.P. (1985). Coming into social being: Cultural images of infants in Bimin-Kukusmin folk psychology. In G.M. White & J. Kirkpatrick (Eds.),

Person, Self and Experience: Exploring Pacific Ethnopsychologies. (pp. 168-182). Berkeley: University of California Press.

Prakash, A. (1955). Organisational functioning and values in the Indian context. In H.S.R. Kao, D. Sinha, & Ng Sek-Hong (Eds.), *Effective Organisations and Social Values* (pp. 193-201). New Delhi: Sage.

Rai, G.C. (1979). A study of certain socio-psychological dimensions of child rearing practices adopted by Indian mothers. *Psycholingua, 9*, 15-29.

Ramanujam, B.K. (1986). Social change and personal crisis: A view from an Indian practice. In M.I. White & S. Pollock (Eds.), *The Cultural Transition: Human Experience and Social Transformation in the Third World and Japan* (pp. 65-86). Boston: Routledge & Kegan Paul.

Read, M. (1959). *Children of their Fathers*. London: Methuen.

Reddy, M.M., & Mahadevan, K. (1986). Values attached to male and female children. *Social Change, 16*, 45-48.

Richards, A.I. (1964). Authority patterns in traditional Bagunda. In L.A. Faller (Ed.), *The Kingsmen*. London: Oxford University Press.

Rogoff, B. (1990). *Apprenticeship in Thinking*. New York: Oxford University Press.

Rohner, R.P., & Chaki-Sircar, M. (1987). Caste differences in perceived maternal acceptance in West-Bengal, India. *Ethos, 15*, 406-425.

Roland, A. (1988). *In Search of Self in India and Japan: Toward a Cross-Cultural Psychology*. Princeton: Princeton University Press.

Sampson, E.E. (1977). Psychology and the American ideal. *Journal of Personality and Social Psychology*, 35, 767-782.

Sampson, E.E. (1988). The debate on individualism: Indigenous psychologies of the individual and their role in personal and societal functioning. *American Psychologist, 43*, 15-22.

Sandhu, R., & Bhargava, M. (1987). Background factors as determinants of children's perception of maternal acceptance. *Indian Journal of Current Psychological Research, 2*, 124-128.

Saraswathi, T.S., & Dutta, R. (1988). Current trends in developmental psychology: A life-span perspective. In J. Pandey (Ed.), *Psychology in India: The State-of-the-Art* (Vol. 1, pp. 93-152). New Delhi: Sage.

Saraswathi, T.S., & Dutta, R. (1990). Poverty and human development: Socialisation of girls and the urban and rural poor. In G. Misra (Ed.), *Applied Social Psychology in India*. New Delhi: Sage.

Saraswathi, T.S., & Kaur, B. (Eds.) (1993). *Human Development and Family Studies in India: An Agenda for Research and Policy*. New Delhi: Sage.

Saraswathi, T.S., & Sundaresan, J. (1979). Parental disciplinary practices and development of moral judgement in children. *Social Change, 9*, 23-28.

Saraswathi, T.S., Thakkar, D., & Kaur, I. (1979). Perceived material disciplinary practices and their relation to development of moral judgement in 10-13 year old Indian children. In L. Eckenseberger, W. Lonner, & Y.H. Poortinga (Eds.) *Cross-Cultural Contribution to Psychology* (pp. 345-353. Lisse: Swets and Zeitlinger.

Sears, R.R., Maccoby, E., & Levin, H. (1957). *Patterns of Child Rearing*. Evanston, IL: Row Peterson.

Sen, A., & Sengupta, S. (1983). Malnutrition of rural children and sex bias. *Economic and Political Weekly*, Annal No. 855-864, May.

Seth, M., & Saksena, N.K. (1978). Attitudes of literate and illiterate mothers towards child rearing. *Child Psychiatric Quarterly*, *11*, 49-54.

Seth, M., Saksena, N.K., & Srivastava, R.K. (1978). Child rearing attitudes of rural and urban mothers: A comparative study. *Child Psychiatry Quarterly*, *11*, 26-30.

Seymour, S. (1971). *Patterns of Child Rearing in a Changing Indian Town: Sources and Expressions of Dependence and Independence*. Ph.D. Dissertation, Harvard University.

Seymour, S. (1975). Child rearing in India: A case study in change and modernisation. In T.R. Williams (Ed.), *Socialisation and Communication in Primary Groups* (pp. 1-58). The Hague: Mouton.

Seymour, S. (1976). Caste/class and child rearing in a changing Indian town. *American Ethnologist*, *3*, 703-706.

Seymour, S. (1983). Household structure and status of expressions of effect in India. *Ethos*, *11*, 263-277.

Seymour, S. (1988). Expressions of responsibility among Indian children: Some precursor of adult status and sex roles. *Ethos*, *16*, 335-370.

Sharma, P., Saraswathi, T.S., & Gir, S. (1981). Role of parents and teachers in promoting social competence in children. *Child Psychiatry Quarterly*, *14*, 134-137.

Sigel, I.E. (1985). *Parental Belief System*. Hillsdale, NJ: Lawrence Erlbaum.

Singh, A., & Sharma, S. (1978). Disrupted father-son relationship and its relation to delinquent behaviour. *Asian Journal of Psychology and Education*, *3*, 16-20.

Singh, L.B., & Fatmi, R.B. (1980). A relationship between social responsibility and parental discipline. *Asian Journal of Psychology and Education*, *6*, 9-11.

Singh, M.B., & Kaur, H. (1990). The selected behavioural aspect of school age children and their relationship with the rural and urban mothers. *Indian Journal of Behaviour*, *14*, 10-20.

Singh, M.B., & Kaur, S (1981). Mother-child interaction in rural and urban areas. *Indian Psychological Review*, *20*, 7-16.

Singh, S.N., & Sharma, N. (1975). Child rearing practices of working and non-working women. *Manas*, *22*, 113-119.

Singh, U.P., & Sowaid, M., (1976). The role of parental discipline in hostility, guilt and conflict over hostility. *Psychologia*, *19*, 29-34.

Singh, Y., & Bhargava, M., & Kumar, K. (1981). The value of children. *Indian Psychological Review*, *20*, 47-57.

Singhal, R., & Misra, G. (1989). Variations in achievement cognitions: Role of ecology, age and gender. *International Journal of Intercultural Relations*, *13*, 93-107.

Singhal, R., & Misra, G. (1994). Achievement goals: A situational-contextual analysis. *International Journal of Intercultural Relations, 18*, 239-258.

Sinha, D. (Ed.). (1981). *Socialisation of the Indian Child.* New Delhi. Concept.

Sinha, D. (1988). Basic Indian values and behaviour dispositions in the context of national development: An appraisal. In D. Sinha, & H.S.R. Kao (Eds.), *Social Values and Development: Asian Perspectives* (pp. 31-55). New Delhi: Sage.

Sinha, D. (1988). The family scenario of a developing country and its implications for mental health: The case of India. In P.R. Dason, J.W. Berry, & N. Sartorious (Eds.), *Health and Cross-cultural Psychology: Towards Application* (pp. 48-70). Newbury Park: Sage.

Sinha, S.R. (1987). *Indian Child Rearing Practices Relevant for the Growth of Competence and Dependence in Children.* Patna: A.N. Sinha Institute of Social Studies (Mimeographed).

Sommerville, J. (1982). *The Rise and Fall of Childhood.* London: Sage.

Spratt, P. (1966). *Hindu Culture and Personality.* Bombay: Manaktalas.

Srivastava, A.K. (1987). Incidence of left-handedness among Mizos: Examining ecology and urbanisation effects. *Personality Study and Group Behaviour, 1*, 87-93.

Srivastava, A.K. (1995a). Extent of acculturation of the Indian Society, *Social Change, 25*, 121-131.

Srivastava, A.K. (1995b). The changing place of child in Indian families: A cross-generational study. Paper presented at the *6th Congress of the National Academy of Psychology*, held at Gulbarga University, 4-6 November.

Srivastava, A.K., Banerjee, J., & Tripathi, A.M. (1996). *Role of Acculturation in the Development of Values Among Children: Maternal Views.* New Delhi: NCERT (mimeographed).

Srivastava, P. (1983). *Cognitive Complexity, Nature of Outcome, and Perceived Parenting as Determinants of Attribution.* Unpublished doctoral dissertation, Indian Institute of Technology, Kanpur.

Super, C.M., & Harkness, S. (1986). The development niche: A conceptualisation at the interface of child and culture. *International Journal of Behavioural Development, 9*, 545-569.

Surya, N.C. (1969). Ego structure in the Hindu joint family: Some considerations. In W. Caudill & Tsung-Yi Lin (Eds.), *Mental Health Research in Asia and the Pacific* (pp. 381-392). Honolulu: East-West Center Press.

Tiwari, A.N., & Misra, G. (1977). A study of achievement motive in relation to prolonged deprivation. *Psychologia, 20*, 172-179.

Trawick, M. (1990). *Notes on Love in a Tamil Family.* Berkeley: University of Berkeley Press.

Triandis, H.C. (1993). Comment on Misra and Gergen's: Place of culture in psychological science. *International Journal of Psychology, 28*, 241-250.

Tripathi, R.C. (1988). Aligning development to values in India. In D. Sinha &

H.S.R. Kao (Eds.), *Social values and development: Asian perspectives* (pp. 314-332). New Delhi: Sage.

Valsiner, J. (1987). *Culture and the Development of Children's action.* Chicester: Wiley.

Valsiner, J. (1989). *Human Development and Culture.* Lexington, MA: D.C. Heath.

Wadekar, A.J., & Palsane, M.N. (1987). Sex differences in child's perception of parent-child relations. *Journal of Psychological Researches, 31*, 160-165.

Weiner, M. (1990). *The Child and the State in India : Child Labour and Education Policy in Comparative Perspective.* Princeton, NJ : Princeton University Press.

Whiting, B. (1963). *Six Cultures : Studies in Child Rearing.* New York: John Wiley.

Whiting, B., & Edwards, C.P. (1975). A cross-cultural analysis of sex differences in the behaviour of children age three through eleven. In S. Chess & A. Thomas (Eds.), *Annual Progress in Child Psychiatry and Child Development* (pp. 32-49). New York: Brunner/Mazel.

Whiting, J.W.M., & Child, I.L. (1953). *Child Training and Personality: A Cross-Cultural Study.* New Haven, CT: Yale University Press.

Wiser, W., & Wiser, C. (1963). *Behind Mud Walls: 1930-1960.* Berkeley: University of California Press.

Yang, C. (1988). Familism and development: an examination of the role of family in contemporary China Mainland, Hong Kong, and Taiwan. In D. Sinha, & H.S.R. Kao (Eds.), *Social Values and Development: Asian Perspectives* (pp. 93-124). New Delhi: Sage.

14

ECOLOGY, COGNITIVE DEVELOPMENT AND ACADEMIC ACHIEVEMENT

A Study of Children Growing in Temple Villages of South India

ASHOK K. SRIVASTAVA & R. MURALIDHARAN

In recent years there has been a shift away from the experimental analysis of behaviour to the study of learning taking place in the social and physical environment (Ardila, 1992; Derry, 1992; Mayer, 1993). Attempts are being made to define people in terms of their context and locating their position with respect to features of the context in which they are embedded (Berry & Irvine, 1986; Bronfenbrenner, 1988; Cole, 1992; Gibson, 1982; Harkness & Super, 1993; Misra & Tripathi, 1993; Nsamenang & Lamb, 1993; Rogoff, 1994; Sinha & Sinha, 1997; Valsiner, 1994; Wagner, 1993; Wertsch, 1991). Misra and Gergen (1993) argue that "Individuals have no independent existence. Instead, they are always people in the social situation where situation and person interact to mutually define each other" (p. 235).

This chapter examines the impact of growing in the vicinity of Hindu temples on the cognitive development of children. It also analyses children's academic achievement and its relationship with parental concern by drawing participants from three varying levels of temple ecology.

The Ecological Context of Temple

Ecology, defined by geography, history, climate, and the socio-cultural system shape human development. While western cultures emphasise academic, technological, or cognitive modes of social integration (Mundy-Castle, 1974), Hindu culture places primacy on socio-affective socialization, with emphasis on the development of social individualism and contextualised relationships depending upon time, place and person (Misra & Gergen, 1993). Both social and technological intelligence (Mundy-Castle, 1974) are rooted in the eco-cultural imperatives that direct individuals to acquire specific cognitive and technical skills, right moral posture, and appropriate social graces to become an acceptable and functional member of the society. The school system "provides practice in the use of specific tools and technologies for solving particular problems" (Rogoff, 1990, p. 191).

The Indian socio-cultural scenario presents a unique challenge to the students of human development. The plurality and multiplicity of its traditions, multifaceted religious background and spiritual emphasis established distinct pattern of behavioural styles. In the Hindu philosophical-psychological perspective, a person is considered to be a product of both the spiritual and the natural worlds. The observance of various life rituals (*samskaras*), emphasis on pilgrimage, fasts (*vratas*), listening to the religious discourses, and worship of gods and goddesses, are some of the commonly shared practices in the Hindu style of living. The Hindu philosophy of life revolves around the fulfilment of four ideals, namely *Dharma* (duty), *Artha* (wealth), *Kama* (love), and *Moksha* (salvation). Of the four ideals, *dharma* has permeated Indian thinking through the ages and created a consistent pattern of thought and behaviour for the large majority of the people. Another concept which had a profound and far reaching influence on the Indian thinking is *karma* (action). It constitutes an important explanatory category in different groups of people (Keyes & Daniel, 1983).

The worship of gods and goddesses, either at home or in a temple, is a common practice of the Hindu way of life. Temples had been playing significant role in the life of men and women since early times in Hindu India. A temple is the house of God or Goddess (*devalaya*), in the womb house (*garbha-griha*) of which the emblem or the image of the God or Goddess is enshrined and regularly worshipped. The worship of the deity in a temple has become so much part and parcel of life of the people that religion cannot be conceived to be separate from the temple and the deity enshrined in it.

In addition to being a place of worship, few temples have become the centres of cultural and social life. Their structure dominates the surrounding both by its location and size. Their solidity and mass give a sense of permanence to all other institutions whose main function, like that of the temple, have been preservation of traditional values. Their influence extends beyond the purely religious and spiritual realms and make the temple an important factor in the economy of the village. The temple deity, besides being a leading landowner, receives generous gifts from a large number of visitors from different parts of the country. The daily routine of a temple, like worship of the deity, providing food (*prashad*) to visitors, recitation of holy books, management of guest houses, etc., gives assured employment to a large number of village people — priests, learned men, musicians, dancing girls, teachers, florists, cooks, tailors, clerks, accountants and functionaries of various kinds. The cultural or religious functions organised by the temple on special days are occasions of great social rejoicing.

The worship of deity in a temple is a regular activity which continues from early morning till late night. Normally a day in a temple begins with bathing and decorating the deity by the priests amidst chanting of *mantras* and *shlokas* from holy books. This is followed by the special prayer, *arati* offered during morning and evening. The offering of prayer to the God or Goddess continues throughout the day till late in the night with a little break in the afternoon. The recitation of *mantras* and holy books continues most times of the day. People from different parts of the country visit the temple. It is considered to be a great place for pilgrimage. A visitor, after having arrived in the village and made necessary lodging arrangements in one of the guest houses maintained by the temple, goes to the temple for *darshan* and offer his/her prayers. In addition, a number of rituals, such as hair shaving, marriage, etc., are also performed in the temple. Temple serves two meals of the day to the visitors. Outside the temple, activities of commercial nature, such as selling of images of deities, local handicraft items, flowers, tea and snacks, attract the attention of visitors. Temples also organise a number of cultural festivals at different times of the year in which villagers participate either as actors or spectators.

Temples thus constitute a unique context for the development of children, providing qualitatively different kinds of stimulations and experiences, and affording a variegated context for enactment of different roles. They provide opportunities to the village children and their parents to interact with different types of people and strangers (*visitors)* across different situations. A child thus tend to develop greater curiosity, concentration and attention, and engages in verbal and non-verbal interactions involving symbols, gestures, and objects of various sorts. The child at times work as an informant and a guide. The opportunities to interact with different types of people enable the child to recognise similarities and differences in their behaviour across situations which may foster the development of generalisation and discrimination abilities in them. Visiting the temple for prayer or food demands certain regularities in visitors' behaviour in terms of going in a queue at a fixed time, waiting for their turn, beginning to eat after food has been served to all, and keeping away from wasting the food. This also provides them an opportunity to compare the quantity of food served and a feeling of satisfaction that all are eating the same food. All this may be expected to develop in child a regard for social regulations. Also, the temple ecology provides practical experiences for the development of the competency of seriation, such as counting of persons, putting people/things in order, comparing the length and quantity of objects, and so on. The children get opportunities to imitate different types of behaviours in diverse situations. Temples thus supply occasions for the development of various skills and for practising them.

Growing in a temple village thus provides a contrast to the life of children in villages where these opportunities are available to a limited extent or not at all available. Since cognitive activities originate in the process of social interaction and guidance from other people (Rogoff, 1990), it was expected that temple village children would display relatively higher level of cognitive competence and show superior academic performance than children from non-temple areas. In addition, it was assumed that the quality and pattern of parental interaction would differ across different ecological settings. In particular, it was contended that the interaction of parents in temple villages will differ from parents of non-temple villages on the dimensions of child's general well-being and his/her school related activities.

The study was conducted on three groups of children and their parents having different levels of temple interaction (high, moderate and low). The groups were selected on the basis of experimental ecology provided by the temple. To validate the choice of groups, temple interaction of children and their parents in terms of their visiting and taking food in the temple was obtained. It was expected that the temple interaction of three groups would differ significantly.

METHOD

Participants

Employing a cross-sectional design, a sample of 281 children studying in Government primary schools of one of the states in southern India, Karnataka, was drawn from 3 levels of temple ecology [children from families (a) intimately associated with temple, (b) that are religious but not so intimately associated with temple, and (c) living in the non-temple villages], 2 grades (1 and 4) of both sexes. The mean age of Grade 1 children was 5 years 9 months (SD=0.91), and Grade 4 children was 9 years 3 months (SD=1.01). Since the primary education in Karnataka consists of grades 1 through 4, it was considered appropriate to study them at the beginning and at the end of the primary schooling. The schools included in the study were comparable on the grounds that these were government run schools with similar curriculum and entry requirements, and teachers with similar educational qualifications having the provision of their transfer from one school to another. The study commenced with a large number of children but due to attrition it ended with 281 children. Parents of these children also participated in the study. Table 14.1 presents the details of the sample.

Table 14.1: Details of the Sample (N=281)

Grades	*Group 1*		*Group 2*		*Group 3*	
	M	F	M	F	M	F
First	20	20	21	16	28	24
Fourth	23	20	20	22	35	32

Description of the Ecological Settings

Temple Villages (Dharmasthala and Horanadu)

Dharmasthala is one of the sacred places in south India. It attracts Jains, Hindus, Christians and Muslims too, who come there for amelioration of their ailments in some form or other. Situated in the South Canara district, the village inhabits about 6000 people and the percentage of literacy is more than 55. The climate is hot in summer and pleasantly warm during rainy season. The place is known for the temple of 'Shree Manjunatheswara Swamy'. About 5000-8000 persons visit the temple everyday, stay in the guest houses maintained by the temple, and take food in the temple's dinning hall free of cost. The villagers can also take their two meals in the temple. The school children go to the temple for their mid-day meal. Also, temple organises various cultural activities (such as, Ganesha festival, Navarathri festival, Deepavali,

Lakshadeepotsava, Shivarathri, Annual festival, mass-marriage ceremonies, etc.) throughout the year.

Providing food to a large number of persons and maintenance of guest houses in a small village are cumbersome activities which demand the cooperation of the villagers. In fact, temple provides employment to about 80 per cent of the men folk and attempts are made to meet their daily needs to the extent possible. Some people also engage in jobs of commercial nature outside the temple. An informal interview with few villagers indicated their deep faith in the temple deity and they considered it their duty to follow the norms established by the temple. Any dispute among the villagers is addressed by the temple functionaries. Temple thus provides social and economic security to the villagers.

Horanadu is a small isolated village in Chikamangalur district. The population of the village is about 1000. It is a hilly terrain situated at a distance of about 8 kms. from a place called Kalasa. There are only two buses running between Kalasa and Horanadu and timings of these buses are also adjusted according to the prayer timings in the temple at Horanadu. The place is famous for 'Annapurneshwari' temple. About 300-1000 persons visit the temple on a day depending upon the festival season. The temple provides food to all including villagers and makes stay arrangement for visitors. The school children take their mid-day meal in the temple.

Moderately Temple Dominated Village (Kalasa)

About 120 kms. from Chikamangalur, the district headquarters, Kalasa is a small town of about 12,000 population. The place is well-connected with the district headquarters. The place has a temple of Lord Shiva. Some villagers visit the temple at least once a week to offer their prayers and temple organises three to four cultural activities in a year. The children spend their time at home, in school and with friends.

Non-Temple Villages (Ujire and Puttuvedu)

Ujire is a small town, with about 15,000 people, in South Canara district, about 9 kms. from Dharmasthala. The place is gradually gaining importance for educational facilities. The town has a number of schools, a first grade college and another College of Nature Cure and Yogic Sciences. The amenities of urban life, such as availability of modern commodities, transportation to different parts of the state, and civic facilities are available at Ujire. However, the place does not have any important temple of a particular God or Goddess.

Another non-temple village included in the study was *Puttuvedu*. It is a small village located about 15 kms. away from Dharmasthala. About 2000 persons live in the village with 40% non-Hindus. The village is connected to the mainland via Dharmasthala. However, only 2-3 buses run between Dharmasthala and Puttuvedu daily. There is no temple near the village. Children usually spend their time in various activities at home, in school and with friends.

MEASURES

The Interaction Schedules

The parents (usually father) were interviewed regarding background information (e.g., monthly income, educational level, concern towards the child's education and well-being). The children and their parents were interviewed with regard to the extent of temple interaction in terms of frequency of visiting and taking meals in the temple. Since school children in temple villages take their mid-day meal in the temple, this information was not included in the analysis. The temple interaction was rated on a 5-point scale (Daily visit = 4, Weekly visit = 3, Monthly visit = 2, Occasional visit = 1, No visit = 0). Income-wise, the families were categorised into high (Rs. 2000 and above per month), middle (Rs.700-2000 per month), and low (below Rs.700 per month) groups on the basis of quartile deviations. The educational level of parents was coded on a 6 point scale (Graduate and above = 5, Pre-university courses = 4, Matric = 3, Grades 5 to 8 = 2, Grades 1 to 4 = 1, and illiterate = 0). The parental concern with regard to their children's education and well-being was recorded on a set of six 3-point scales.

Cognitive Measures

The cognitive development of children was examined by employing NCERT School Readiness Scale at grade 1, and Das, Naglieri & Kirby's Cognitive Assessment System at Grade 4.

The NCERT School Readiness Scale (Muralidharan & Banerjee, 1973) consists of two parts : Reading Readiness and Number Readiness. The reading readiness sub-scale has four components, each having 5 items: World Meaning Test (WMT), Sentence Meaning Test (SMT),

Visual Perception Test (VPT), and Auditory Discrimination Test (ADT). Due to variation in administration and scoring for different groups of children, WMT was dropped from the final analysis. A child thus could score 15, with 5 scores for each sub-test of reading readiness. The Number Readiness dealt with Pre-number Concepts (PNC), Coin Recognition and use (CR), Fractions (FR), and Seriation (SR). A child can score 20, with 5 scores for each part of number readiness.

The Cognitive Assessment System (Das, Naglieri, & Kirby, 1994) includes four major sub-scales, viz., Planning, Attention, Simultaneous and Successive information process (PASS). To this end, tasks such planned connections, expressive attention, progressive matrices, and digit span were used as a measure of planning, attention, simultaneous and successive processing, respectively (for details, Das, Naglieri & Kirby, 1994).

Measures of Academic Achievement

For measuring academic achievement in language and mathematics, separate tests were constructed in Kannada language for both grades separately keeping in view the competencies identified in Minimum Levels of Learning at Primary Stage (1991). The achievement test in mathematics (grade 1) consisted of 21 items related to the competencies such as understanding whole number, ability to add and subtract, ability to use and solve simple problems of life relating to units of money, length, mass, capacity and time, and understanding of geometrical shapes and spatial relationships. A child could score between 0-60 on this test. The achievement test in language at grade 1 consisted of 20 items related to the competencies of listening, speaking, writing and reading (maximum score 100).

The achievement test in mathematics at grade 4 consisted of 21 items, related to five competencies, such as understanding whole numbers and numerals; ability to add, subtract, multiply and divide whole numbers; ability to use and solve simple problems of daily life relating to units of money, length, mass, capacity, areas and time; ability to use fractions, decimal and percentage; and understanding of geometrical shapes and spatial relationship. The test was administered in small groups of 6-8 children at a time. The score ranged between 0-42. The achievement test in a language contained 15 items related to listening, speaking, reading, writing comprehension, self-learning, language use and vocabulary. Each competency was scored separately and the total score of these competencies, ranging from 0-21, indicated the child's score on the language test.

Procedure

After obtaining approval of the school authorities, children were asked to perform cognitive tasks individually during the school time in a separate room. The achievement tests were administered in groups of 6-8 children. The cognitive measures were administered during the beginning of the academic session and achievement tests toward the end of the academic year. Parents were interviewed either in the morning or in the evening, depending upon their availability, at their homes, after establishing proper rapport.

RESULTS

The children from Dharmasthala and Horanadu (temple villages), for convenience, will hereafter be referred to as Group 1 children; children from Kalasa (moderately temple village) as Group 2 children; and children from Ujire and Puttuvedu (non-temple villages) as Group 3 children. Analysis of income level of parents indicated that 25.3 per cent of Group 1 children belonged to high economic status, 51.8 per cent to middle economic status, and 22.9 per cent to low economic status. Likewise 30.8 per cent children in Group 2 came from high economic level, 39.24 per cent from middle economic group, and 30.38 per cent from low economic status. Of Group 3 children, 14.29 per cent came from high economic category, 48.74 per cent from middle economic group, and 36.97 per cent from low economic group. The economic status of the families of three groups varied significantly (*Chi Square* (4)=10.88, $\underline{P}<.05$). However, an informal interaction with few residents indicated that people in Dharmasthala are not discriminated as rich and poor. It is considered to be a place of charity where prosperity is a rare phenomenon. The chi square indicated that the educational level of parents of three groups was almost similar.

Temple Interaction

Based on the frequency of temple visits by children and their parents, and frequency of taking meals in the temple by parents, a temple index was computed (range = 0.20). The range of temple index for Group 1 was 7-16 (Mean = 12.19, SD = 1.74), for Group 2 it was 2-9 (Mean = 6.90, SD = 1.75), and for Group 3 it was 0-11 (Mean 6.63, SD = 4.65). ANOVA showed a significant effect of ecology {$F(2,275) = 33.096$; $P<.001$} on temple index. Further analysis showed a similar pattern of temple interaction for subjects belonging to Groups 2 and 3.

Parental Concern

Group 1 parents had a significantly greater score on parental concern (Mean = 10.40, SD = 2.18) than Group 2 (Mean = 9.27, SD = 1.84), who in turn expressed significantly greater concern than Group 3 parents (Mean = 7.76, SD = 1.93) {$F\ (1,275) = 15.28$, $P<.01$}. Also, parents showed greater concern toward girls (Mean = 9.51, SD = 1.37) than boys (Mean = 8.50, SD = 2.61) {$F\ (1,277) = 14.91$, $P<.01$}.

Cognitive Development

The details of the results on various cognitive measures for grades 1 and 4 children are presented in details elsewhere (Muralidharan & Srivastava, 1995). This section contains a brief summary of these results.

Grade 1 Children

On School Readiness Scale, Group 1 children performed significantly better than Groups 2 and 3 Children. The readiness scale had two subscales: Reading and Number readiness. Among the various indicators of Reading Readiness, Group 1 children showed superiority only on Visual Perception. However, their performance was significantly greater than Groups 2 and 3 children on all measures of number readiness, viz., Pre-number Concepts, Fractions, Seriation, and total Number Readiness.

Grade 4 Children

Group 1 children showed superior performance than Group 3 children on Planning, Attention, and Simultaneous processes. The differences between Groups 1 and 2 children were, however, not significant. Girls showed significantly better performance on Attention than boys.

Since the differences in the economic level of families was significant, it was deemed necessary to compare the performance of three groups after excluding children from low economic status families. The results, however, remained unchanged. Thus, the inferior performance of Group 3 children cannot be attributed to the difference in their economic level.

Academic Achievement

Table 14.2 shows that Group 1 children scored significantly higher on the measures of mathematics, speaking, reading, writing and total language than Groups 2 and 3 children at Grade 1. However, the performance of Groups 2 and 3 children was higher on listening than their temple counterparts. The results showed significantly superior performance of boys on mathematics {Mean (boys) = 27.91, Mean (girls) = 22.66}, {F (1,125) = 5.44, $P<.05$)} and listening (Mean (boys) = 12.23, Mean (girls) = 10.67), {F (1,125) = 15.00, $P<.01$)}. The interaction between temple ecology and sex was not significant.

Table 14.2: Mean Academic Achievement Scores by Temple Ecology and F Values for Grade 1 Children

Measures	*Group 1*	*Group 2*	*Group 3*	F *(1,125)*
Mathematics	26.80 (9-45)	27.13 (4-46)	24.52 (3-53)	4.12*
Listening	9.99 (7-16)	10.95 (2-16)	10.88 (0-17)	4.88*
Speaking	9.52 (2-14)	7.81 (0-14)	7.64 (0-14)	6.92**
Reading	8.16 (0-19)	4.59 (0-16)	3.79 (0.17)	56.17**
Writing	14.00 (1-29)	9.47 (1-26)	8.97 (1-26)	16.50**
Total Language	41.80 (18-69)	35.09 (18-60)	32.42 (18-59)	15.37**

Note : Range of scores is given in parentheses
*$P<.05$, **$P<.01$

The achievement scores for Groups 2 and 3 children were pooled together as the two were almost similar. Table 15.3 depicts the superiority of Group 1 children on the measures of mathematics, speaking, language use and vocabulary at Grade 4. Groups 2 and 3 children performed better on self-learning than their Group 1 counterparts. The performance of girls was significantly higher than boys on the competency of speaking [Mean (boys) = 3.93, Mean (girls) = 4.38), {F (1,148) = 3.33, $P<.05$)].

Table 14.3: Mean Academic Achievement Scores by Temple Ecology and F Values for Grade 4 Children

Measures	*Group 1*	*Group 3*	*F (1,148)*
Mathematics	33.07 (15-41)	14.73 (2-35)	30.62**
Listening	4.82 (2-7)	4.70 (0-7)	0.07
Speaking	4.50 (0-5)	3.79 (0-5)	4.12*
Reading	2.57 (0-3)	2.50 (0-3)	0.32
Writing	1.73 (0-2)	1.74 (0-2)	0.00
Comprehension	0.97 (0-1)	0.98 (0-2)	0.00
Self-Learning	0.54 (0-1)	0.74 (0-1)	6.71*
Language use	0.12 (0-1)	0.00 (0-0)	14.44
Vocabulary	0.80 (0-1)	0.62 (0-1)	5.17*
Total	4.83 (3-18)	4.89 (0-17)	0.00

Notes :
1. Range of scores is shown in parentheses.
2. The achievement scores for Groups 2 and 3 were pooled together since both were almost similar.

*P<.05; **P<.01

Table 14.4 shows that parental concern was positively related to performance on the following tasks: Fractions, Number Readiness, School Readiness, and Reading at Grade 1; and Attention, Simultaneous Processes, Planning and speaking at Grade 4.

DISCUSSION

The results of the study highlight the role of indigenous social institutions in promoting societal and individual development in agrarian and semi-industrialised societies. By virtue of their functioning, temples do not merely play the religious role but also promote educational, social, commercial and other cultural activities. They afford a variegated experimental context. As the temple index has established, the families from temple villages were more intimately associated with a variety of activities and practices of the temple such as participation in diverse

Table 14.4: Correlation coefficients between Parental Concern, Cognitive Development, and Academic Achievement

School Readiness (Grade 1)	*r* (n=129)	*Cognitive Measures* Cognitive Assessment (Grade 4)	*r* (n=152)	*Academic Achievement* Grade 1	(n=129)	Grade 4	*r* (n=152)
SMT	154	Attention	-192*	Maths	021	Maths	012
ADT	-049						
VPT	051	Simulta-neous		Listening	-122	Listening	009
Reading	-045	(time)	-214*			Speaking	198*
Readiness		(error)	-042	Speaking	135		
PNC	073					Reading	098
FR	283**	Successive	036	Reading	271**	Writing	011
SO	179						
CR	199	Planning	-290*	Writing	096	Compre-hension	157
Number Readiness	251*					Self Learning	003
				Total (Language)	164	Language use	135
School Readiness	384**					Vocabulary	-096
						Total (Language)	021

Notes :

1. Decimals are omitted.
2. Since time was taken as a measure in the Cognitive Assessment system, negative *r* values indicate faster response legacy.

*P<.05; **P<.01

religious, cultural and social activities. It also highlights the fact that mere presence of a structure like temple does not constitute a specific eco-cultural context. It is the activities of the temple such as eliciting and stimulating behaviours, and providing a context for cognitive and social engagement, as observed in the temple villages of Dharmasthala and Horanadu, that makes a context variegated. Temple activities provide an intervention by the community for the community.

The study revealed significant impact of temple ecology on parental concern and related behaviours. The temple village parents showed greater concern for their children's education and well-being than parents from non-temple villages. The difference in the degree of parental concern seems to be due to the differential opportunities available to parents hailing from diverse ecological settings. Participation in temple activities, listening to the readings of holy books, imbibing the related values and interaction with visitors are some of the opportunities available to the temple village parents. An analysis of the narratives in these books may suggest that a great deal of emphasis is laid on showing adequate concern towards the behaviour and education of children, development of positive values in them, and directing their activities toward helping the living beings. Constant exposure to these situations would have helped villagers to inculcate these values. Positive relationship between parental concern and some of the measures of cognitive development suggests that the greater degree of parental concern shown by temple village parents might be responsible to some extent for higher level of cognitive development displayed by their children.

It appears that schooling coupled with temple ecology transforms the child distinctly by expanding the scope and range of the use of cognitive skills and capacities. Temple village children studying in Grade 1 were better prepared for school. Prior to their entry into schools, these children were better prepared for learning of number-related concepts than with the use of words. It may be due to the fact that while visitors use different languages, temple activities provide enough opportunities for development and practice of number skills. However, one year of schooling seems to have substantially improved their language competencies.

Temple village children at grade 4 excelled other groups of children on the measures of attention, simultaneous processes, and planning. Attention is basic to all cognitive functions. Temple village children have learnt to attend to relevant aspects of a task and ignore irrelevant ones. The performance on simultaneous processing involves visual, kinetic and vestibular apparatuses responsible for orientation of the body in the space. In contrast, synthesis of stimuli in successive order (successive processing) is primarily associated with the motor system (Luria, 1966). This also partly explains the lack of difference in the younger children at Grade 1 on world Meaning and Auditory Discrimination tasks. The most pervasive impact of temple ecology was observed on tasks related to planning. This involves generation of plans, goal-setting, strategy selection or construction, and performance monitoring.

The study, to some extent, underlines the importance of socio-cultural and contextual processes in explaining the academic achievement of village children. Temple village children showed higher performance on mathematics than non-temple children at both grades. As mentioned earlier, temple provides diverse kinds of experiences which seem to have fostered the mathematical competency in children. For instance, the structure of temple provides an opportunity to the children to compare its vastness with nearby structures. Children take food in the dinning hall of the temple with a large number of other people. This enables them to count the number of persons and also compare the quantity of food served to him/her with others. The concept of time should be developed in temple children quite early as the prayer and meal timings are fixed. These children get the opportunities to analyse different geometrical shapes in the form of images of deities available in the temple and also on the shops. These opportunities are not available to children from non-temple areas which may be expected to have contributed towards their lower performance.

The religious and cultural activities which are both verbal and non-verbal in nature, and interactions with outsiders, tend to provide a rich experience for communication and language development. This is reflected in the superior performance of temple children in competencies, such as speaking, reading, writing, and total language score at Grade 1, and speaking, language use and vocabulary at Grade 4. The non-significance of the effects of temple ecology on measures of listening, reading, writing and comprehension at Grade 4, however, suggests that the effects of temple ecology are greater at the lower grade and no so high in regard to upper grade levels. Temple effects are present to a limited extent by Grade 4. Though the temple children at Grade 4 were superior on higher cognitive processes, the results of the present study suggests that academic achievement may also depend on other non-cognitive factors, such as motivation. It is also possible that social and economic security provided by the temple might make these children disinterested in studies as they grow older. However, a more detailed study of the determinants of academic achievement in temple village children would be required to isolate the specific contributions of various factors.

An examination of the ranges of scores on various measures indicates that there is no difference in the lowest scores of children from the three ecological settings. The difference is in terms of the highest scores only; a majority of non-temple children took more time for completing the cognitive tasks and performed poorly on measures of academic achievement than temple children. This implies that non-temple children were equally good on some tasks; it is the rich experience of children due to temple ecology that helped them in performing better on certain tasks.

The study thus demonstrates the importance of an ecological setting generated by the diverse temple activities by way of putting a variety of cognitive and social demands on children and their parents, and engaging them in certain types of activities. The children from temple setting have an additional advantage as compared to the school-going children from other settings which may be assumed to restructure their experiential world and help in their school related activities. The study underlines the significance of traditional social networks, the relevant components of which probably need to be incorporated in some form to foster the development of village children. The present study was, however, exploratory in nature. A more detailed study incorporating different aspects of temple ecology, cognitive and non-cognitive variables and academic achievement of children would be needed to establish the full range of the effects of temple ecology on human development.

References

Ardila, R. (1992). Towards unity in psychology: The experimental synthesis of behaviour. *International Journal of Psychology*, 27, 299-310.

Berry, J.W., & Irvine, S.H. (1986). Bricolage: Savages do it daily. In R.J. Sternberg & R.K. Wagner (Eds.), *Practical Intelligence : Nature and Origins of Competence in the Everyday World* (pp. 271-306). Cambridge: Cambridge University Press.

Bronfenbrenner, U. (1988). Interacting system in human development research paradigms: Present and Future. In N. Bolgar, A. Caspi, G. Pawney, & M. Moorehouse (Eds.), *Persons in Context : Developmental Processes* (pp. 25-49). Cambridge: Cambridge University Press.

Cole, M. (1992). Culture in Development. In M.H. Bornstein & M.E. Lamb (Eds.), *Development Psychology: An Advanced Textbook* (3rd ed., pp. 731-789). Hillsdale, NJ: Erlbaum.

Das, J.P. Naglieri, J.A., & Kirby, J.R. (1994). *Assessment of Cognitive Processes: The PASS Theory of Intelligence*. Boston, NY: Allyn & Bacon.

Derry, S.J. (1992). Beyond symbolic processing : Expanding horizons for educational psychology. *Journal of Educational Psychology*, 84-413-418.

Gibson, E.J. (1982). The concept of affordances : The renascence of functionalism. In A. Collins (Ed.), *The Concept of Development : The Minnesota Symposium on Child Development* (Vol. 15, pp. 55-81). Hillsdale, NJ : Erlbaum.

Harkness, S., & Super, C. (1993). The development niche : Implications for children's literary development. In L. Eldering & P. Leseman (Eds.), *Early Intervention and Culture : Preparation for Literacy.* Netherlands National Commission for UNESCO : UNESCO Publishing.

Keyes, C.F., & Daniel, E.V. (1983). *Karma : An Anthropological Inquiry.* Berkeley, CA : University of California Press.

Luria, A.R. (1966). *Human Brain and Psychological Processes.* New York : Harper & Row.

Mayer, R.E. (1993). Educational psychology - past and future : Comment on Derry (1992). *Journal of Educational Psychology,* 85, 551-553.

Minimum Levels of Learning at Primary Stage (1991). New Delhi : National Council of Educational Research and Training.

Misra, G., & Gergen, K.J. (1993). On the place of culture in psychological science. *International Journal of Psychology,* 28, 225-243.

Misra, G., & Tripathi, K.N. (1993). The concept and context of human development. In T.S. Saraswathi & B. Kaur (Eds.), *Human Development and Family Studies in India : An Agenda for Research and Policy* (pp. 90-103). New Delhi : Sage Publications.

Mundy-Castle, A.C. (1974). Social and technological intelligence in western and non-western cultures. *Universities, 4*, 46-52.

Muralidharan, R., & Banerjee, U. (1973). *NCERT School Readiness Scale.* New Delhi : National Council of Educational Research and Training.

Murlidharan, R., & Srivastava, A.K. (1995). Temple ecology and cognitive development : A report from south India. *Psychology and Developing Societies*, 7, 47-64.

Nsamenang, A.B., & Lamb, M.E. (1993). The acquisition of socio-cognitive competence by NSO children in the Bamenda grass fields of Northwest Cameroon. *International Journal of Behavioural Development, 16*, 429-441.

Rogoff, B. (1990). *Apprenticeship in Thinking.* New York : Oxford University Press.

Rogoff, B. (1994). Developing understanding of the idea of communities of learners. *Mind, Culture and Activity*, 1, 209-229.

Sinha, D., & Sinha, M. (1997). Orientations to psychology : Asian and Western. In H.S.R. Kao & D. Sinha (Eds.), *Asian Perspectives on Psychology* (pp. 25-39). New Delhi : Sage Publications.

Valsiner, J. (1994). *Comparative - Cultural and Constructivist Perspectives.* Norwood, NJ : Ablex.

Wagner, D.A. (1993). *Literacy, Culture and Development : Becoming Literate in Morocco.* New York : Cambridge University Press.

Wertsch, J.V. (1991). Voices of the Mind. Cambridge : Harvard University Press.

15

COPING WITH CHRONIC ILLNESS AND THE GROWING CHILD

IRA TRIPATHI & ADESH AGARWAL

Long term care of chronically ill people in India is primarily a family responsibility. Institutional care is negligible and hospital treat only critical episodes in long term illness. In developed countries, often a number of people affected by chronic diseases increase with age. The Indian scene is very different. According to National Sample Survey Report (1992) 50 per cent of all disabled were children and there were some 35 million children who were disabled (U.N. Report 1986). According to one researcher the major causes of disability in children in India are such factors as malnutrition, unhygienic living conditions, and household injuries (Dalal & Pandey, 1999). These facts highlight the magnitude of the problem. The role of parents in dealing with the problem is underscored. The fact that meaning and beliefs associated with illness influence parental reactions and coping efforts, makes it imperative to study the processes involved in the construal of meaning of illness and health (Pless and Nolan, 1991).

An important new line of enquiry in health psychology concerns the investigation of meaning and representation of health and illness and the implications of such representational processes and structures. A self-regulation/information processing model of responses to health threats, as proposed by Leventhal and his colleagues (Leventhal, 1983; Leventhal, Nerenz & Steele, 1984) helps us in understanding that (1) individual representations of health and illness vary and (2) such variations may be related with variations in health and illness related behaviours. Leventhal *et al.* (1984) identified four basic components in their representations of diseases: Identity, cause, timeline and consequences. These components determine how patients conceptualise and cope with their illness (Agarwal and Mishra, 1999).

In this chapter two cognitive variables were taken. Mother's beliefs and attitudes about health and her expectations about child's future, the relationship of these variables with her own behaviours towards her children and, her children's ability to cope with chronic illness, were examined.

In applying disease representations to self-diagnosis Bishop (1991) argued that the experience of symptoms sets off a cognitive search, resulting in the activation of disease prototype in memory. This is where the beliefs play a crucial role. The belief that if one contracts a serious illness during childhood and, even if he is cured, he will not grow up into a fully functional human being brings to mind the prototype of a disabled person due to polio or rheumatic disease.

Once a particular disease prototype is selected it provides hypotheses to a person about other related symptoms that might be present. A person may try to configure the disease and provide a label for it. A case in point is the hysteria overspreading of AIDS with casual contact. The fact that AIDS arouses the schema of contagious disease, and prototype of contagious disease is that it spreads through casual contact, hence the belief that AIDS can spread through casual contact. Similarly, mothers who have the belief system that, "serious chronic illness – if contracted in childhood – leave a person disabled", set in motion a schematic processing of symptoms. It may arouse the prototype of a disabled person conjuring up visions of a bleak future of the child. This process explains the relationship between health attitudes of mother and her expectation about her child's future, specially in those circumstances where child suffers from a chronic illness.

In an earlier study (Agarwal, 1995, 1993) we analysed the beliefs and values associated with care giving behaviours in 406 villagers from 28 villages from three states of India, i.e., U.P., M.P. and Bihar. One significant finding was that positive health attitudes and progressive health related beliefs in people successfully predicted intentions to gain more informations about healthy practices from various sources, like interpersonal interactions, print and electronic media.

In the present study the relationship between health related beliefs and values of mother with child's health related behaviours was investigated. Parental beliefs are often referred to as schemas, ideas, judgements etc. and these have been seen to influence child behaviour (McGilliccuddy-DeLisi, 1992). The present study emphasised a bi-directional influence of parent child cognitions.

METHOD

Sample

The sample consisted of 300 persons. There were two groups of children. Group I consisted of 75 chronically ill children and their mothers and Group II consisted of 75 normal healthy children and their mothers. Chronically ill children were suffering from kidney trouble, epilepsy, heart related disease, T.B., asthma etc. All children were aged between 8 to 12 years from different socio-economic classes, i.e., low socio-economic, lower middle, middle, upper middle and higher socio-economic class.

Instruments

In the present study two measures have been used to assess mother's psychological characteristics and her cognitions.

Health attitude belief questionnaire

This questionnaire developed by (Agarwal, A., 1993, 1995) was used for gathering informations about mother's health attitudes and beliefs. The questionnaire has 44 items and three categories of answers. The inventory has two types of items. One is related to value about health and another is related to belief. An example of belief item is "Children do have infectious diseases like measles, tetanus, etc. Their prevention...." The three alternative answers could be (a) is not possible (b) is possible to some extent and (c) is possible to a large extent. A corresponding value item was : "In young children prevention of infectious diseases like measles and tetanus....". The three possible answers were : (a) is useless, (b) is useful, and (c) is very essential. These were awarded scores of 1, 2 and 3 respectively. Score on each belief item is multiplied by the score on its corresponding value item. The sum of these products gives the score on attitude scale. In order to minimise the tendency to respond without thinking some of the items were reversed (Item No. 2, 20, 27, 34, 41 and 44 were reversed). So that the answer, 'not true' was awarded a score of '3' and 'completely true', a score of '1', similarly on evaluation items answer of 'useless' was awarded a score of '3' and 'very useful' was awarded a score of '1'. Although generally one belief item is paired with one item concerning the evaluation of that belief object, but four items are exceptional. Item No. 26, 36, 33 and 43 are belief related items but each of these has two corresponding evaluation items, which appear adjacent to it. For example item No. 26 is a belief item but it has two corresponding evaluation items namely nos. 25 and 27. Similarly item no. 33 is paired with both items nos. 32 and 34 and item no. 36 is paired with item no. 35 and 37 and item no. 43 is paired with item nos. 42 and 44. Thus there are twenty four products.

Test retest reliability of this measure is very high r=0.74, after fifteen days. Convergent validity of this scale is also found to be significant.

Interview Schedule

A structured interview schedule was developed by the investigator to assess mother's cognitions about their children in different areas like illness status (in chronically ill group only), health habits, parental future expectations, family relation and support, accident control and safety behaviour and, parenting style which includes granting autonomy, use of reason and use of reward/punishment. There were also some items on lack of agreeableness and some on positive agreeableness.

In this schedule all questions were predecided and fixed for both chronically ill and healthy groups. Answers were taken on this interview schedule in the form of free responses by the respondents. All responses were rated on 5 points scale ranging from 1 to 5 by the investigator.

Two measures were used on children.

PGI-HQN 1

This questionnaire was used to assess neurotic tendency and reporting of physical and psychological complaints in children. PGI-HQNI was constructed by Verma, Wig and Pershad (1985). It is a completely indigenous tool for distinguishing between neurotic/psychiatric and normal subjects having physical and psychological complaints. It consisted of 38 items divided into A (physical distress) and B (psychological distress) sections with 16 and 22 item respectively. The answers of this questionnaire were either in 'Yes' or 'No', and a score of 1 and 0 is given for each answer. The sum of these values gives the total score on this scale which shows total number of complaints, both physical and psychological as reported by the subject. Reliability of the test by using 'test-retest' and 'split half' methods is 0.88 and 0.86

respectively. It was found that the total score of PGI-HQNI was highly correlated with similar trait on other scales. Validity score with M.P.I. (N scale) was found to be 0.72.

Interview Schedule

An interview schedule was developed by the investigator to assess various behaviours of children in both groups. These behaviours include children's health related behaviours (health habit), educational behaviours, social relationships of child, future expectations of children, safety rules followed by children and, family environment as perceived by child. Self efficacy was also assessed by summation of the scores obtained in the areas of educational behaviours, social relationships and future expectations. The interview schedule was structured but responses were taken in the form of free responses by the respondent. Thereafter all responses were rated on 5 point scale, ranging from 1 to 5.

Procedure

Data were collected on specific measures, in both groups of chronically ill and normally healthy children and their mothers separately. Researcher approached many paediatricians and paediatric surgeons of the city for contacting chronically ill children. Data were collected on these chronically ill children and also on their mothers, at paediatrician's out patient clinics. Mothers and children were interrogated individually and separately and relevant informations were gathered. For normal healthy children, the investigator approached many schools of the city. Normal children were interviewed at their schools and their mothers were approached at their homes.

RESULTS

Results show that mother's positive attitude towards health is related with her own behaviours. Table 15.1 shows that those mothers who had positive beliefs about health, reported significantly lesser psychological symptoms on PGI-HQ. In Relationship between mother's attitude towards health with a number of other variables was also investigated. Table 15.2 shows coefficients of correlation between mother's attitudes towards health and her expectations about child's future, her perception

Table 15.1: Negative and Positive Beliefs amongst Mothers of Chronically ill Children who either Report more or less Pyschological Symptoms on PGI. HQ

Item No.	*Negative belief*		*Slightly positive*		*Positive belief*		*Level of Signifi-cance*
	Low Symp-toms	*High Symp-toms*	*Low Symp-toms*	*High Symp-toms*	*Low Symp-toms*	*High Symp-toms*	χ^2
2	10	16	6	6	20	17	63.28**
4	3	11	10	10	23	18	5.04 N.S.
6	4	10	13	20	19	9	7.5*
8	0	6	9	17	27	16	11.14**
10	3	9	9	19	24	11	11.27**
12	5	18	24	19	7	2	10.58**
14	11	21	18	16	7	2	5.88 N.S.
16	6	15	19	20	11	4	7.02*
18	10	19	20	16	6	4	3.49 N.S.
20	0	0	14	27	22	12	6.93*
22	7	17	17	19	12	3	9.55**
24	15	27	14	10	7	2	5.17 N.S.
26	6	14	21	22	9	3	6.09*
29	9	24	21	13	6	2	10.57**
31	5	5	28	21	3	13	7.11*
32	0	0	9	28	27	11	16.38**
34	11	14	22	24	3	1	1.31 N.S.
36	4	7	12	22	20	10	6.96*
39	23	24	8	12	5	3	1.12 N.S.
41	4	13	20	21	12	5	7.53*
43	9	19	26	20	1	0	5.22 N.S.

of family relationships and her parenting style. Table 15.2 shows that mother's expectations about child's future are positively and significantly correlated with her own attitudes towards health. This relationship was found to be significant for both, chronically ill, as well as, healthy children. It was also found that those mothers who had more positive attitude towards health perceived family relationships to be more cohesive and supportive. The coefficient of correlation for chronically ill group, however, was not found to be significant. Mother's positive attitude towards health was significantly correlated with more supportive and reward based parenting style as against punishment. This was found to be significant in the case of both, chronically ill, as well as, healthy children.

Mother's attitude towards health was also correlated with children's behaviours and results have been reported in Table 15.3. A very significant finding was that mother's health attitude was negative and

Table 15.2: Correlations between Mother's Attitudes towards Health, her Expectations about Child's Future, Family Relationship and Parenting Style

Mother's expectations about child's future			*Family relations and support*			*Parenting style*		
Chronically ill	Healthy	Total	C.I.	Healthy	Total	C.I.	Healthy	Total
0.28**	0.57**	0.43**	0.17 N.S.	0.27**	0.22**	0.24*	0.28**	0.17*

significantly correlated with the number of symptoms which her child reported. Mother's health attitude was significantly and positively correlated with academic behaviours, social relationships, future expectations and total efficacy of child and all of these correlations were significant for both chronically ill, as well as, healthy groups of children. Coefficients of Correlation varied between .27 and .51

Multiple regression analysis was also carried out with psychological symptoms reported by child as a criterion variable and predictors were education and, psychological symptoms of mother, health attitudes of mothers and scores of negative items on agreeableness scale and sex of child. 36 per cent of the variance was explained by these five predictors jointly. All these predictors significantly predicted the symptoms reported by child. Table 15.4 shows that mother's education was highly correlated with symptom reporting of children. Education of mother explained 22 per cent of variance. Psychological symptom reporting by mother explained 6 per cent variance. Sex of children reported 3 per cent, health attitude of mother explained 3 per cent and Scores of mother on negative items of agreeableness scale also explained 3 per cent of variance in psychological symptoms reported by the child.

DISCUSSION

There is a clear relationship between mother's positive attitude towards health and several behaviours of mothers. Table 15.1 and 15.2 shows that mothers positive attitude towards health was negatively and significantly related with reporting of psychological symptoms on PGI-HQ. It was positively and significantly correlated with mother's expectations about child's future, with perception of supportive and cohesive family relationships and reward based supportive parenting style. All of these relationships emerged as significant both for mothers of chronically ill, as well as, healthy children, as all but one coefficient

Table 15.3: Correlations between Mother's Attitude towards Health and Child's Symptom Reporting, Academic Behaviour, Social Relationship, Future Expectation and Efficacy of Children

Children's Symptom Reporting			*Academic behaviour*			*Social relationship*			*Future expectation*			*Total efficacy*		
Chronically ill	*Healthy*	*Total*	*Chronically ill*	*Healthy*	*Total*	*Chronically*	*Healthy*	*Total*	*Chronically ill*	*Healthy*	*Total*	*Chronically ill*	*Healthy*	*Total*
–.31**	–.43**	–.36**	.27**	.51**	.38**	.30**	.31**	.30**	.31**	.28**	.30**	.33**	.45**	.39**

Table 15.4: Predictors of Psychological Symptoms Reported by Child

Criterion: Psychological Symptoms Reported by Child

Predictors	β	*Simple*	R^2	*t value*
1. Education of mothers	–0.25**	–0.47**	0.22	2.85
2. Psychological symptom reported by mothers	0.32**	0.40**	0.28	4.31
3. Sex of children	0.18**	0.05	0.31	2.66
4. Health attitude of mothers	–0.24**	–0.44**	0.34	2.82
5. Scores of negative items on Agreeableness Scale	0.14*	0.008	0.36	2.11

Multiple R=0.6
R Square = 0.36

of correlations were found to be significant. Mothers of chronically ill children with positive health attitudes, however, did not perceive that their family relationships were cohesive and supportive.

One reason behind these relationships with mother's positive health attitude may be that this attitude includes belief concerning control. In the attitude scale some of the items were control items which expressed the belief, that mother and child care can lead to better health, prevention of diseases and long term harm. An example is "If contagious diseases result in disability like, loss of one eye or lameness then, along with physical care moral boosting and education to face his disability...(a) is not necessary (b) is somewhat necessary (c) is very much essential.

Some of the items were concerned with beliefs regarding the management of the harmful effect of chronic serious illness. These included items like, – "Treatment of diseases like, cancer.....(a) is not possible (b) is somewhat possible (c) is very much possible." A positive and high score on these items indicated an optimistic outlook, as well as, belief in controllability. Evidence suggests that these beliefs have positive impact on health.

Platt and Eisenman (1968) have related internal external control of reinforcement, time perspective and adjustment. Seeman & Evans (1962) found that internals (T.B. patient) were cognitively more clear about their conditions. Taylor, Lichtman & Wood (1984) found that breast cancer patients who believed that, they themselves, or their doctors, could control their illness, were better adjusted. Markus and Zajonic, (1986) found that in cancer patients, perception of severity of their illness and depression were markedly less severe if they believed that they could personally control their health and, for those who held positive expectations about efficacy of treatment and, about effects of complying with medical treatment. Similar patterns emerged when severity was defined in terms of prognosis for survival. In an earlier study it was seen that those mothers who perceived that health can be controlled and, had more optimistic outlook regarding consequence of illness, exhibited fewer psychological symptoms themselves (Tripathi & Agarwal, 1999).

The results of the present study show a positive and significant relationship between mother's positive health attitude and her positive expectations about her child. These findings are of immense significance because our earlier studies have revealed that a future oriented outlook helps patients in more than one ways.

We found (Agarwal & Mishra, 1999) that amongst operated patients, those patients who had high future oriented outlook, were in better affective state one week of the operation. Their physical recovery was significantly better after one to two months of the operation and, their score on quality of life scale was also significantly better after one to two months of the surgery.

Similar findings were obtained when low and high future oriented (HFO) patients suffering from chronic diseases were compared (Agarwal & Pandey, 1998). HFO patients were more optimistic and, they employed active coping strategies, planning, and acceptance, and low use of denial.

Mother's attitude and beliefs towards health were also related with parenting style. Those mothers who have positive attitude towards health, also adopted a warm nurturing parenting style, based on use of reward, as against punishment. They also gave more autonomy to children and, therefore, gave greater responsibility to children. Furthermore they used reasoning rather than order as a disciplinary technique.

Mothers attitude towards health had a week relationship with family relationship and support. It is, therefore, apparent, that a positive attitude towards health ensures that one's own and doctor's behaviour, can have positive effect for one's health beliefs and, placing high value on remaining healthy. These attitudes help mothers in taking care of their children in health and in sickness. Furthermore, mothers with these beliefs and values activity try to take care of their chronically ill children and maintain a positive outlook about child's future, supporting and disciplining the child with love. These actions in turn lead to positive behaviours in children.

Furthermore, mother's health beliefs and attitudes are related with high psychological symptom reporting in mothers on PGI-HQ on the one hand and high psychological symptom reporting by the child on the other. Eiser (1989) says that script theory (Nelson, 1986) can explain children's attitude towards health and illness. It is our contention that those mother's who report psychological symptoms to a high degree are in fact providing script like, sequential representations of everyday events like – mother has headache and, therefore, is excused from household chores and, also does not look after the child on the day when she has headache. She gets to sleep and do as she pleases. Such scripts make it easier to imitate mother's behaviours. Mothers provide powerful models and children also start reporting psychological symptoms.

In the present study mother's attitude towards health was found to be related with a number of behaviours in children. These coefficients of correlations have been presented in Table 15.3. Mother's attitude towards health was negative related with reporting of symptoms by their children. Our results show that those mothers who scored high on these beliefs had children who reported fewer psychological symptoms in spite of the fact that they were suffering from chronic illnesses (Table 15.3). Tinsley (1992) has done a number of studies in which she found clear relations among maternal attitudes concerning control, mother's perception about their children's health and, utilisation of childhood preventive health services. In our present study the results presented in Table 15.3 show that mother's health attitude was positively related with academic behaviour of child in both patient and non-patient groups.

Multiple regression analysis was carried out with symptom reporting by child as criterion variable and mother's characteristics and behaviours as predictors (Table 15.4).

Table 15.5 shows that reporting of psychological symptoms by children was significantly predicted by a number of mother's characteristics and behaviours. These included mother's education, her attitude towards health, her lack of agreeableness and, psychological symptoms of ill health reported by herself.

The mechanisms behind these linkages appear to be, (1) mother's own beliefs generate pessimism in her, regarding her child. When she feels defeated she starts reporting symptoms of ill health herself. A prospective inverse association between optimism and symptom reporting has been reported by other workers (Scheier *et al.,* 1986). (2) Such a belief system gives rise to a parenting style characterised by coldness, anger and punishment and lack of autonomy. The present

Table 15.5: Summary of Multiple Regression Analyses

Predictors	*Behaviours which were significantly predicted by parental cognitions and behaviours*		
	Chronically ill group of children	*Normal healthy group of children*	*Total group of children*
Mother's future expectations	1. Academic behaviour of child 2. Social relationship of child 3. Future expectations of child 4. Self efficacy of child	1. Academic behaviour of child 2. Social relationship of child 3. Future expectations of child 4. Self efficacy of child 5. Psychological symptom reported by child 6. Total symptom reporting of child 7. Family environment as perceived by child	1. Academic behaviour of child 2. Social relationship of child 3. Future expectations of child 4. Self efficacy of child 5. Family environment as perceived by child
Family relationship and support	1. Academic behaviour of child 2. Family environment as perceived by child	NS NS	NS NS
Parenting style	1. Social relationship of child 2. Future expectations of child 3. Family environment as perceived by child	NS NS NS	1. NS 2. Future expectations of child 3. Family environment as perceived by child

findings also show that these mothers also, are, less agreeable and have negative attitudes about health. These may lead to stress induced chemical activity in children also. Furthermore, her lack of education makes correction in these attitudes more difficult.

Mother's attitudes towards health was related with another cognitive variable, namely, her expectation about child's future. This networking of belief systems is important as their connectedness may influence the availability of particular beliefs. For example, if a mother believes that a child can be taught to cope with his disability and, by boosting the morale of disabled child, his functioning can be improved, then together these beliefs form a schema of a person who is disabled, yet functional and efficient. It is, therefore, plausible that this schema will influence other related behaviours. This can explain our another significant finding that, mother's health related attitudes are associated with child's expectations about his own future and his total efficacy score. Mother's attitude towards health was also found to be related with social relations of the child.

Furthermore, mother's future expectations about her child was a significant predictor of :

Social relationship of child.
Academic performance and related behaviours of child.
Child's expectations about his own future.
Family environment as perceived by the child.
Self efficacy of the child.

It is thus, evident that parental expectations about child's future, convey a lot more to the child, besides the specific expectation expressed by the parent. Parental expectations provide the child the glimpse into, either a rose garden or a barren, blazing void, seen through borrowed glasses of his parents.

Man has acquired the ability to develop mental schemata and meta representations about his cognitive representations. Future orientation refers to, setting future goals and planning for them and, being concerned for the future, as compared to, past or present. Goal setting and planning for the future involves cognitive representation and processing of needs.

Each of the temporal orientation accentuates its characteristic mode of experience; a focus on the past emphasises memory, history, conservation, nostalgia and tradition; one on the future on the other hand stresses anticipation, planning, saving and preparation and concern; focus on the present usually involves, a focus on experience, consumption, activity and adventure in the here and now (Hamid & James, 1973).

Those who believe in a future oriented outlook do not consider that just because something strongly affects one's life it should indefinitely have a similar effect in future. They also do not believe that it is easier to avoid than to face certain life difficulties and self-responsibilities. Future orientation is relevant for understanding many cognitive-motivational and behavioural processes. Belief systems at cultural level influence our time perspective and our expectations about future (Mischel, 1961). Similarly personal characteristics also influence our concern and prospective content of future. Unemployed groups report less structure and purpose in their future than the employed groups. It has been found that self concordant goals, proactive, self generated initiatives act for life improvements. It is seen that relative to nondepressed subjects, depressed subjects viewed their future concerns in a less positive and less active fashion. There is evidence to show that support by most important person in a person's life has important consequences for his well-being and attainment of goals (Ruchlman & Wolchik, 1988).

It is our contention that mother's positive expectations about chronically ill child's future, ensures, encouragement and suggests to the child that he is worthy. It instils a sense of self-worth in the child and gives him confidence to formulate his own plans for future and work towards them. Adaptive tasks and experiences include futurity by definition, for example retaining a belief in the future potential and productivity of patients is both future related and adaptive. Setting short and long term goals and priorities for coping efforts call for a sense of future and organised future expectations (Rakowski, 1986), it is, therefore, pertinent to point out that mother's expectations about child's future are very important, these and her health related beliefs and attitudes and, her own personality characteristics play a very important role in successful coping with chronic illness in children. It was also found to be related with social relations of the child.

Referecnes

Agarwal, A. (1989). Communication related need in a developing society with special references of eastern U.P. Report for Department of Space, Space Application Centre, ISRO, Ahmedabad.

Agarwal A. (1993). Communication related needs in a developing society Phase II, Research report for Department of Space, Space Application Centre, ISRO, Ahmedabad.

Agarwal, A. (1995). Mass media and health promotion in Indian villages. *Psychology and Developing Societies*, 7, 2, 217-236.

Agarwal, A. & Mishra, S. (1999). Some psychological factors in recovery from surgery. Paper presented at national seminar on contemporary and emerging challenges in health psychology and meeting of South Asian Association of Psychologists, Feb. 26-28, Delhi University, Delhi.

Agarwal, A. & Pandey, A. (1998). Coping with chronic disease : Role of psychological variables. *Psychological Studies* Vol. 43, No. 1 & 2. pp. 58-64.

Bishop, G.D. (1991). The understanding of illness : Lay disease representation. In J.A. Skelton, R.T. Croyle (Eds.) *Mental Representation in Health and Illness*. New York: Springer Verlag, 1991.

Dalal, A.K., & Pande, N. (1999). Cultural beliefs and family care of the children with disabilities. *Psychology and Developing Societies*, 11, 1, 55-75.

Eiser, C. (1989). Children's concepts of illness. Towards an alternative to the "stage" approach. *Psychology and Health*, 3, 93-101.

Gibson, C.H. 1995, 21,1201-1216. The process of empowerment in mothers of chronically ill children knowledge, competence and confidence.

Hamid, N. Paul & James L. (1973). Temporal perspectives and alienation. *Perceptual and Motor Skills*, 37, 139-145.

Leventhal, H. (1983). Behavioural medicine : Psychology in health care. In D. Mechanic (Eds.) *Handbook of Health Care and the Health Profession,* 709-743, New York : Free Press.

Leventhal, H., Nerenz, D. R., & Steele, D.J. (1984). Illness representations and coping with health threats. In A. Baun, S.E. Taylor & J.E. Singer (Eds.), *Handbook of Psychology and Health* : Vol. IV, *Social Psychological Aspects of Health*. 219-252, Hillsdale, N.J. : Lawrence Erlbaum Associates.

Markus, H. & Zajonic R.B. (1986). The cognitive perspective in social psychology. In G. Lindzey S.E. Aronson (Eds.) *Handbook of Social Psychology* (3rd ed. Vol. 1 PP. 137-230) Reading M.A. Addeson-Wisley.

McGillicuddy–DeLisi, A.V. (1992). Parent's belief and children's personal social development. In Sigel, I.E. McGillicuddy, DeLisi, A.V., Goodnow, J.J. (Eds.) *Parental Belief Systems : The Psychological Consequences for Children*. (Second Edition). Hillsdale, NJ : Erlbaun Associates.

Mischel, W. (1961) Delay of gratification need for achievement and acquiescence in another culture. *Journal of Social Psychology*, 62, 543-552.

National Sample Survey Report (1982). *National Sample Survey of India*, New Delhi.

Nelson, K. (1986). *Event Knowledge : Structure and Function in Development*. Hillsdale, NJ : Erlebaum.

Platt, J.J. and Eiseman, R. Internal-external control of reinforcement, time perspective, adjustment and anxiety, *Journal of General Psychology*, 1968, 79-121-128.

Pless, B. & Nolan, T. (1991). Revision, replication and neglect of research on maladjustment in chronic illness, *J. Child, Psychol. Psychiat.* 32, 2, 347-365.

Rakowski, W. (1986). Future time perspective. *American Behavioural Scientist*, Vol. 29, No. 6, 730-745.

Ruchlman, L.S., & Wolchik, S.A. (1988). Personal goals and interpersonal support and hindrance as factors in psychological distress and well-being. *Journal of Personality and Social Psychology*, 55, 293-301.

Scheier, M. F. Caroer, S., (1986). Coping with stress : Divergent strategies of optimists. *Journal of Personality and Social Psychology*, 51, 1257-1264.

Seeman, M., and Evans, J.W. (1962). Alienation and learning in a hospital setting. *American Sociological Review*, 27, 772-783.

Taylor, S.E., Lichtman, R.R., & Wood, J.V. (1984). Social comparison in adjustment to breast cancer. *Journal of Personality and Social Psychology*, 49, 1169-1183.

Tinsley, J.B. (1992). Multiple influences on the acquisition and socialisation of children's health attitudes and behaviour. An integrative review. *Child Development*, (1992), 63, 1043-1069.

Tripathi, I. & Agarwal, A. (1999). Chronic illness. Symptoms and efficacy in children in relation to some psychological characteristics of mothers.

UN Report (1986). Report of the international expert meeting on legislation for equalisation of opportunities for people with disabilities New York : UN Centre for Social Development and Humanitarian Affairs. *Pschology and Developing Societies, 12,* 31-42.

Verma, S.K., Wig, N.N. & Pershad, D. (1985). *Manual for PGI Health Questionnaire*, N. 1. Agra : National Psychological Corporation.

16

PRAGMATIC STRATEGIES IN LOCATIVE PROPOSITIONS UNDER RECEPTIVE/EXPRESSIVE CONDITIONS

Social Class Differences

BABBAN MISHRA

The main objective of the pragmatic theory is to provide an explicit account of how human beings interpret utterances. Thus, the basic purpose of pragmatic theory is the utterance interpretation and not the comprehension. In this domain the logical abilities, linguistic abilities and memory interact (Sperber & Wilson 1981). While emphasising the role of pragmatics researchers have tried to answer such questions as how disambiguation is achieved (Mohanty, 1977) and how included referents are worked out (Olson, 1970). A number of other psycholinguists have also emphasised the role of pragmatics or the context in the acquisition of language (Dale, 1980; Dore, 1974; Mey 1979; Mohanty and Mishra 1982; Mishra, 1985; Mishra and Tripathi 1991). These researchers have shown the role of context in biasing children's expression of locative relationship between two objects. The pragmatic distinctions like given-new information (Chafe, 1970; Clark & Clark, 1977; Haviland & Clark, 1974) and topic-comment (Hornby 1971) or theme-rhyme (Halliday, 1970) are considered as important parameters of language behaviour. According to Braine's (1963) open class-pivot class grammar children acquire knowledge about the position of the words or their flexibility in different directions. Such knowledge is assumed to provide important cues in comprehension of utterances. Schlesinger (1972) pointed out that the position of the words in a proposition also provide cues which act as significant aids to its interpretations. The pragmatics is sensitive to cross linguistic differences discussed as follows.

The Cross-Linguistic Differences and Theoretical Approaches

The role of word order is uniform across various languages. With regard to the interpretation of utterances cross-linguistic differences are observed in form of their relative significance of the word order. As compared to other languages, English is not affected by such pragmatic devices like contrastive stress and cleft transformation play an important role. On the other hand, in Hindi and other Indian languages flexible word order is permissible and such flexibility is based on subtle pragmatic considerations. In case of languages like Hindi and other Indian languages, where flexible word orders are permissible, pragmatic considerations like topic-comment distinctions are supposed to guide the choice of word orders. Locative propositions in Hindi can be expressed in either of the following forms to express locative relationship between two objects.

1.	Chiriya (Bird)	Gay par (on the cow)	Baithi Hai (sitting) (is)
2.	Gay par (on the cow)	Chiriya (Bird)	Baithi Hai (sitting) (is)

The subject or the main noun phrase (*Chiriya*) of the proposition appears in the beginning of the first expression followed by the adverbial phrase (*Gay par*) and the verb phrase (*Baithi Hai*). On the other hand, in the second expression, the main noun phrase occurs in between adverbial phrase and verb phrase.

In developmental psycholinguistics the issue is debated from different theoretical positions. The researchers in their theoretical approaches have tried to answer these questions as whether such variations in word orders are merely surface structural or whether there may be a pragmatic, hence, cognitive consideration in the choice of appropriate word orders. According to transformational generative grammar (Chomsky, 1965) approach, variation in word order is only surface structural variation and the meaning in surface structure provides important cues to the nature of grammatical relation in the deep structure. Thus, according to this model, variations in word order are different forms of expression of the same meaning. On the other hand, cognitive model (Bates, 1976; Macnamara, 1972; Osgood, 1971; Sinclair-Dezwart 1973; and Slobin, 1971) suggested that children are born with a processing mechanism and with the help of this mechanism, children discover linguistic patterns in the world of senses as they discover perceptual patterns. Both processes are part of general cognitive development. Slobin (1973) suggested that processes involved in children's language acquisition are the reflections of underlying cognitive development. The children are able to learn the universal feature of language only because of their capacity of processing mechanism. The process model attempts to observe how language is processed cognitively and how it is manifested behaviourally, Clark and Haviland (1974) suggested that process model is an explanatory attempt which accommodates the following informations.

(a) The moment to moment changes in the mental state of listener or speaker.
(b) The speaker's or listener's knowledge of the language as represented in the rules required for changing form one mental state to the other.
(c) The speaker's or listener's processing capacity as found in what rules can be applied, how many can be applied at one time, and how long each rule takes.
(d) The time required to say or understand an utterance.

Following the above informations, the process model deals with both competence and performance. Garden and Lakoof (1971) pointed out that the listener utilises the knowledge of the situation to get the meaning of an utterance by the speaker. While doing this, the listener goes through an inferential process. Since knowledge of the situation changes from moment to moment, thus, selecting word order in expression of locative relationship, the process model suggests that speaker's utterances are based on their perception of the situation in which the communication takes place i.e. the context. The ordering of words can be thought of as one such device indicating the role of the perceived context. The ordering of word order in case of locative proposition also depends on the nature of locative itself. Apart from the types of locatives, a number of other factors are also responsible to affect the choice of word orders especially the social class differences.

Social Class Differences and Word Orders

Bernstein (1958) has related the development of language skills to the kind of linguistic environment to which children are exposed. Findings generally support the contention that impoverished home environment hinders the adequate language development whereas the enriched home environment facilitates it. A variety of factors like socio-economic status, caste, parent-child interaction, housing parental attitude, nutrition, parental aspiration etc. have been considered to be related to the nature of language development. Shukla and Mohanty (1986); Deich and Hedges (1977); Pleh and Vargha (1992); Launerova, (1985); Shimeron, (1984); Gullo, (1981); have studied the impact of the type of family, social classes, socio-economic differences and their impact on the different types of linguistic skills. There are a number of studies opposed to each other with regard to the impact of the factors described above. In some studies the impact of social class differences is highly significant but there are other studies (Shukla and Mohanty 1986) where such effects are insignificant. Thus, the impact of class differences should not be taken without question. Now-a-days even the poorest people have the television and other facilities and they appear to be exposed to much verbalisation similar to the upper class children. As has been remarked by Devito (1970), within normal limits, the socio-economic level has no clear and proven influence on language competence and probably little on speech performance. When the environment is extremely impoverished as in case of orphanages, its influence is to delay speech and development but to exert no permanent damages. Contrary to social class differences and uniform results, individual differences in language development is highly emphasised (Nelson, 1981; Klein, 1980). The present piece of research is also an attempt to see the impact of deprivation on the choice of word order expressing locative relationships in Hindi. In the light of the studies reviewed the present investigation is an attempt to see the impact of such factors like class differences in biasing the expression of locative proposition especially the word order being used in such expression. Apart from these factors influences the word order, the nature of locative proposition itself is expected to bias the responses of the subjects either towards SF or OF order.

Development of Locatives

Locatives are described as spacio-temporal coordinates with extra linguistic cognitive considerations such as animacy, agency and dependency etc. one purpose of locative description is to narrow the domain of search for a referent. Fillmore (1971) categorised the special relations expressed by the locatives into these parts viz. local positions (Location), standing points (Source) and ending point (Goal). A number of strategies has been suggested to study children's understanding of locative propositions by Clark (1973), Bower (1974), Cooper (1968), Eve Clark (1972, 74) etc. These studies provide a sample of various directions in the study of locative propositions.

In case of children speaking languages where variant word orders are permissible, they must differ in their approaches and strategies. In case of languages permitting two different word orders in expression of locative relationship, the children have the freedom of using any one of the word orders but the question is how does a child decide which order to use? The present study, with Hindi speakers, is an attempt to seek some answers to these questions. In one of the studies Mishra (1985) used simple line drawings (Pictures) as stimulus materials. The pictorial form of stimulus material was not natural and, thus, following Miller (1975) real objects (toys) were used as stimulus material in the present investigation. A brief description of stimulus material is as follows.

Use of Toys as Stimulus Material

Following Miller (1975) toys are thought to be of great importance for children. Millar (1975) stated as

> "We have found that toys that allow the child to construct a varieties of activities elicit the most spontaneous speech from children up through Piaget's type pre-operational period, or 6-7 years" (pp 11).

Thus, following Miller (1975), toys of children's choice and fully familiar toys were used as the stimulus material in the present investigation. The toys were supposed to remove the hesitation among children and elicit the spontaneous utterances from them. The children usually treat the toys as their friends and interact with them without any hesitation. While playing with their toys children utter a number of responses and interact with them. These responses are addressed to those toys. The toys were selected on the basis of their familiarity with children and on the basis of their availability. Some of them were ready-made and some were constructed. For the purpose of selecting toys, the parents and teachers were consulted to judge their suitability for the children of younger age groups and their suggestions were taken care of. While selecting the toys some of them were rejected if they did not match with the purpose. With the help of these stimulus materials, the present study was conducted in two situations i.e. expressive and receptive conditions discussed as follows.

Receptive and Expressive Conditions

Katherene Nelson (1981) has talked about two types of linguistic abilities viz. receptive linguistic ability and expressive linguistic ability. The complete measurement of linguistic abilities of a child must reflect in both receptive and expressive conditions. For the present investigation, in receptive condition, the toys were placed in front of the subjects and they were verbally instructed either in subject first order or in object-first order to arrange the toys. The verbal instructions given to the subjects were printed and read by the investigators in front them. The instructions were given in sentential forms. These sentences were either presented with a bias towards SF order or with a bias towards OF order. The examples, of such sentences are given below.

Subject–first order (SF order)

Kitab (Book)	Gilas (Glass)	Par Hai (On) (Is)

Object–first order (OF order)

Gilas (Glass)	Par Kitab (On) (Book)	Hai (Is)

There were four sets of toys describing sentential forms of SF order and four other sets of toys for OF order and, thus, there were eight sets of toys for each locative. Since, there were five locatives hence there were 40 sets (5 × 8) of toys used in the present investigation. These toys were equally distributed on the dimension of reversibility/Non reversibility condition. In contrast to receptive condition, in expressive condition the subjects were presented with arranged toys and they had to describe them in sentential forms i.e., they had to describe the toys and the relationship in between them. For example '*Mej*' (Table) and '*Kitab*' (Book) were placed in front of the subjects to describe '*Mej Par Kitab Hai*' (The book is on the table) and the children were asked to describe them i.e. they had to name the objects and tell the relationship in between both the objects. (*Kitab Mej Par Hai*).

For each of the locative relationship there were equal number of toys arranged in front of the subject to depict a particular spatial relationship between them or equal number of toys were given to the subjects to arrange them according to instructions.

In this way receptive and expressive conditions were used to find out the choice of word order being expressed by children while narrating locative relationship between a pair of objects. For expressive condition, eight sets of toys per locative were arranged in a required manner and the reversibility/non reversibility phenomenon was equalised i.e. equal number of reversible and non-reversible sets of relations were shown to the respondents. The reversibility/non-reversibility phenomenon was balanced for receptive condition keeping in view the impact of impoverished conditions on language development. The subjects were categorised as low deprived or high deprived on the basis of their scores on Prolonged Deprivation Scale (Mishra & Tripathi 1977) and details of the methodology used is given below:

METHOD

Study-I : Receptive Condition

Stimulus Design

Five locatives in Hindi namely *Par* (on), *Samaney* (Front), *Nechey* (Under), *Uper* (Above) and *Peechchey* (Behind) were used in this study. The toys common in nature, were selected (Some readymade and some prepared according to the need were used as stimulus materials like, cat, dog, table, chair, monkey etc.). Forty sets of (eight per locative out of which four reversible and four non-reversible) were used for the present investigation. The selection of toys for all locatives was predetermined. The reversible/non-reversible order in case of locative *Par* (on), for example, was as follows:

Reversible order:

Kitab (Book)	Par (on)	Gilas (Glass)	Hai (is)

Non-reversible order:

Chiriya (Bird)	Gutkey (wooden cube)	Par (on)	Hai (is)

Thus, in case of reversible order both the objects were used by putting the main object (Topic) first and it was not possible to use the item interchangeably. In other words, *Gilas* and *Kitab* can be placed on each other but this is not possible in case of *Chiriya* and *Gutka*. On the other hand, in non reversible order both the objects could not be used interchangeably. Reversibility/Non-reversibility was balanced so that they do not bias the responses of the subjects.

Subject Selection

Four hundred and twenty subjects were individually tested for their choice of word order while expressing spatial (locative) relationship between a pair of objects. The subjects belonged to seven different age groups viz. 24, 30, 36, 42, 48, 54 and 60 months. There were 60 subjects from each age group with equal number of male and female subjects. All the subjects, on the basis of their scores on Prolonged Deprivation Scale, by Mishra and Tripathi (1977), were categorised either as highly deprived (HD) or low deprived (LD) ones. There were 105 LD male subjects and 105 LD females. Similarly 105 HD males and 105 HD female subjects were also tested. Thus, the total number of subjects (60 per age group i.e. 60×7) were 420 (210 LD subjects and 210 HD subjects).

All the subjects belonged to Eastern part of UP i.e. Gorakhpur, Deoria and Basti districts. These subjects were Hindi speaking monolinguals and were also fluent in their regional language Bhojpuri.

Procedure

After an initial warming up period investigator placed two toys in front of the subjects and they had to arrange them according to the verbal instruction given by the investigator i.e. according to the sentences uttered by the investigator. The instructions were given either in SF order or in OF order. In other words, the sentences uttered by the investigator were written either in SF order or in OF order. For example, when the subject was given the toys like *Kursi* and *Mej* (Table and Chair) the subjects were requested to arrange them either *Kursi Mej Par Hai* or as *Mej Par Kursi Hai* i.e. the subjects either picked up *Kursi* first or *Mej* first. In other words the subjects had to arrange the toys as:

Subject–first order (Picking up subject, Kursi, first)

Kursi	Mej	Par	Hai
(Chair)	(Table)	(on)	(is)

Object–first order (Picking up object, Mej, first)

Mej	Par	Kursi	Hai
(Table)	(on)	(Chair)	(is)

The instruction given to the subjects were in both the forms i.e. reversible and non-reversible and the arrangement of toys were made as per the example. The selection of toys for the subjects was based on the reversibility non-reversibility dimension. Some sets of toys were reversible and other sets were non-reversible. The number of reversible/ non reversible toys was equal for each locative. For example, the arrangement of toys for locative 'on' was like as follows :

Subject–first order (Reversible order)

Gilas	Par	Kitab	Hai
(Glass)	(on)	(Book)	(is)
Kursi	Mej	Par	Hai
(Chair)	(Table)	(on)	(is)

Subject–first (Non-reversible order)

Chiriya	Gutke	Par	Hai
(Bird)	(wooden cube)	(on)	(is)
Chiriya	Khambhey	Par	Hai
(Bird)	(pole)	(on)	(is)

Object first (Reversible order)

Kitab	Par	Chasma	Hai
(Book)	(on)	(Goggle)	(is)
Kursi	Mej	Par	Hai
(Chair)	(Table)	(on)	(is)

Objective first (Non-reversible order)

Kursi	Par	Billi	Hai
(Chair)	(on)	(Cat)	(is)

The subjects were individually tested in their family context and other member of the families were not allowed to speak or indicate anything i.e. they did not participate in the testing session. Children who made no attempt to arrange the toys were dropped from the study. At the end of the testing session the subjects were given some incentive in the form of chocolates/toffees. Full length responses as well as broken responses were accepted both in Khari Boli Hindi and in local dialect called

Bhojpuri and each session lasted for 40 approximately minutes but the subjects were free to take as much time as they needed for arranging toys according to the instruction.

RESULTS

The responses of the subjects were scored either as SF order or as OF order and for each correct responses a score of one was given. For example, when the investigator uttered a sentence like *Mej Par Kursi Hai'* and placed two objects i.e. '*Mej*' and '*Kursi*' it in front of the subjects and the subjects picked up '*Kursi*' to place it on '*Mej*' indicated the choice of SF order and a score of one was given in favour of SF order responses. On the other hand, if the subjects picked up '*Mej*' first and then took '*Kursi*' to place on the '*Mej*' a score of one was assigned to the subjects in favour of OF order. Thus, the total number of SF order and OF order responses were computed and the proportion of SF/OF order responses was then computed for further analysis. The proportion of SF order responses were computed and following Winer (1971) these proportion scores were transformed in Arcsin scores. The means and SDs were computed on the basis of transformed scores in Arcsin and presented in Table 16.4. The total number of obtained scores i.e. transformed scores were analysed in a 2 (level of deprivation) × 7 (Age groups) × 5 (locatives) repeated measure ANOVA design with the last factor being repeated. For the present investigation proportion of SF order responses were used as dependent measure. The findings obtained were discussed under the general discussion, in combination with the findings of the second study.

Study-II : Expressive Condition

Stimulus Design

In expressive condition, contrary to the receptive condition, the investigator arranged two toys to depict the spatial relationship between a pair of objects (Toys) in front the subjects and they had to describe the spatial relationship between toys. The basic aim of this part of study was to find out the natural word order being used by the subjects while expressing the spatial relationship between two objects. In case of receptive condition the word order was predetermined by the investigator and the subjects were required to act accordingly. And, on the basis of correct responses, the preference of subjects for a particular word order has been determined. But, in expressive condition, the subjects were free to use a particular kind of word order while describing the spatial relationship between two objects provided to them in an arranged manner. For example, the investigator placed a '*Gilas*' on the '*Mej*' (this arrangement was made behind the wooden curtain first) and asked the subjects to describe the relationship between both the objects i.e. '*Gilas*' and '*Mej*' (Table). In this case the subjects either uttered Gilas first or Mej first and then, after again being questioned, they described the relationship. Their responses here, are scored as SF order when they uttered Gilas first and on the other hand if they said '*Mej Par Gilas Hai*' the responses were scored as object first (OF) order. Thus, the number of SF/OF order responses were counted for each the categories i.e. age, level of deprivation and locatives. The details of the subjects and the procedure is discussed as follows.

Subjects

The subjects remained same as in receptive condition. The procedure of testing was a bit different in expressive condition. In receptive condition, as contrary to expressive condition, the subjects arranged the toys according to the instructions (in the form of verbal instructions printed on a sheet of paper) given by the investigator. But, in expressive condition, the investigator arranged the toys in front of the subjects in a manner predetermined by the investigator. For example, the investigator, behind a wooden curtain, placed a small '*Kursi*' on the '*Mej*' and then asked the subject to narrate the whole scene i.e. to narrate the objects and the relationship between them. The verbal description of the objects and the relationship between the objects were recorded. From the responses of the subjects i.e. on the basis of utterances of the objects (verbatim recording) it was decided whether the subjects were biased towards SF order responses or towards OF order. SF/OF order responses were scored.

The children who made no verbal expression in five testing sessions, were dropped. The testing session generally lasted for 40 minutes and the testing session was made very informal. For this to achieve, frequent visits to children were made by the investigators to establish the rapport. All the subjects were given chocolates/toffees in the form of incentives and thanked for their participations in the present study. The responses in 'Khari Boli' and 'Bhojpuri' were accepted and recorded for analysis.

The investigates were also very fluent in both linguistic expressions which enabled them to compute the responses of the subjects for further analysis. The reversibility/non-reversibility phenomenon was balanced for equalising the stimulus materials related with their reversibility/ non-versibility nature. In other words, equal number of pairs of objects were provided to the subjects for their choice of word order being used in locative propositions.

The responses were scored as they were scored in receptive condition. The SF order/OF order responses were computed. In describing the relationship behaviour, for example, '*Mej*' and '*Kursi*' if the subjects uttered '*Kursi*' first, the responses were scored as SF order responses and a score of one was given to each of them. Later, on the proportion of SF order responses were computed and put for further analysis.

Procedure

After an initial warming up period investigator placed two toys in front of the subjects (behind the wooden curtain) and they had to arrange them according to the verbal instruction given by the investigator i.e. according to the sentences uttered by the investigator. The instructions were given either in SF order or in OF order. In other words, the sentences uttered by the investigator, were printed on a proforma, either in SF order in OF order. For example, when the subject was given the toys like '*Kursi*' and '*Mej*' (Table and Chair) the subjects were requested to arrange them either '*Kursi Mej Par Hai*' or as '*Mej Par Kursi Hai*' i.e. the subjects either picked up '*Kursi*' first or '*Mej*' first. In other words the subjects had to arrange the toys as :

Subject–first order

Kursi	Mej	Par	Hai
(Chair)	(Table)	(on)	(is)

Object–first order

Mej	Par	Kursi	Hai
(Table)	(on)	(chair)	(is)

The instructions given to the subjects were in both the forms i.e. reversible and non-reversible. The arrangement of toys were made as per the example. The selection of toys for the subjects was based on the reversibility/non-reversibility dimension. Some sets of toys were reversible and other sets were non-reversible. The number of reversible/ non reversible toys was equal for each locative. For example, the arrangement of toys for locative 'on' was as follows :

Subject–first order (Reversible order)

Gilas	Par	Kitab	Hai
(Glass)	(on)	(Book)	(is)
Kursi	Mej	Par	Hai
(Chair)	(Table)	(on)	(is)

Subject–first (Non-reversible order)

Chiriya	Gutke	Par	Hai
(Bird)	(wooden	(on)	(is)
Chiriya	cube)	Par	Hai
(Bird)	Khambhey	(on)	(is)
	(pole)		

Object first (Reversible order)

Kitab	Par	Chasma	Hai
(Book)	(on)	(Goggle)	(is)
Kursi	Mej	Par	Hai
(Chair)	(Table)	(on)	(is)

Objective first (Non-reversible order)

Kursi	Par	Billi	Hai
(Chair)	(on)	(Cat)	(is)
Mer	Par	Gudiya	Hai
(Table)	(on)	(Doll)	(is)

The subjects were individually tested in their family context and other members of the families were not allowed to speak or indicate anything i.e. they did not participate directly in the testing session. Children who made no attempt to arrange the toys were dropped from the study. At the end of the testing session the subjects were given some incentive in the form of chocolates/toffees. Full length responses as well as broken responses were accepted both in Khari Boli Hindi and in local dialect called Bhojpuri and each session lasted for approximately 40 minutes but the subjects were free to take as much time as they needed for arranging toys according to the instruction.

RESULTS

The responses of the subjects were scored either as SF or OF order as was done in the receptive condition. When, for example, the subjects uttered the relationship as '*Gilas Mej Par Hai*' (the glass is on the table) their responses were scored as SF order responses. On the other hand, the responses like, '*Mej Par Gilas Hai*'. (On the table there is a glass) the responses were scored as OF order. The proportion of SF order responses were analysed after they were transformed in Arcsin score as suggested by Winer (1971). The means and SDs were computed from these proportion scores being transformed into Arcsin transformation. Howell (1994) suggests that the significant F-ratios reveal these differences of transformed mean scores not the raw score means. It is also suggested that the anti-transformation should be done before reporting the means. However, transformed scores mean reporting is better on the place of raw score mean when anti-transformation is not done. The SF order responses, in receptive condition, were analysed in a 2 (level of Deprivation) × 7 (Age groups) × 5 (locatives) with the last factor being repeated. The means and SDs are presented in Table 16.1. The obtained results are discussed under general discussions.

INTEGRATED DISCUSSION

The main aim of the present investigation was to see the impact of level of deprivation on the choice of word order being used by the children while expressing the spatial relationship between a pair of objects. After the scores were analysed in a 2 (level of deprivation) × 7 (Age groups) × 5 (Locatives) with the last factor being repeated, the impact of level of deprivation [$F(1,406) = 59.10$ $P<.01$]; age [$F(6,406) = 16.84$; $P<.01$] and the locatives [$F(4,1624 = 1384.09$ $P<.01$] was found significant. It shows the independent and significant impact of these factors on the choice of SF order responses taking place in the expression of locative relationship between a pair of objects in receptive condition. The variation caused by age shows the developmental trends in selecting the word order i.e. SF order responses. The significant impact of locatives on choice of SF order responses suggests that the uniform selection of SF order responses are not possible and the SF order/OF order's choice depends heavily on the nature of locative relationship. In other words, the choice of word order is affected by the nature of locatives. For example, in case of locative *Par* (On) the total number of SF order

Table 16.1: Means and SDs of SF Order Responses in Receptive Condition

	LD					*HD*				
Age	*On*	*In front*	*Under*	*Behind*	*Above*	*On*	*In front*	*Under*	*Behind*	*Above*
(Maths)										.93
24 $\overline{X}$	3.03	2.00	1.13	1.60	1.10	2.43	1.96	.79	1.59	
SD	.82	.97	.87	.99	.96	.98	1.02	.74	.92	.92
										1.16
30 $\overline{X}$	2.56	2.40	1.0	1.60	0.86	2.49	1.61	1.63	1.39	
SD	.90	.92	1.03	.83	1.01	1.05	1.06	.94	.76	1
										1.36
36 $\overline{X}$	2.97	2.33	1.53	2.06	1.59	2.43	2.26	1.59	1.73	
SD	0.70	.96	.99	.95	1.07	.91	.87	1.05	1.10	.87
										1.03
42 $\overline{X}$	3.13	2.73	1.73	2.43	1.40	2.53	1.39	1.63	1.83	
SD	.64	.82	1.26	.81	.55	.75	1.04	.97	.87	.86
										1.23
48 $\overline{X}$	1.89	3.29	2.46	2.73	2.29	2.89	2.03	1.66	1.76	
SD	.57	.66	1.00	.83	.75	.79	.97	1.04	1.05	1.17
										1.53
54 $\overline{X}$	3.19	3.19	2.26	3.03	2.00	2.66	2.16	1.96	1.83	
SD	.68	.53	.95	.75	.99	.93	.88	1.07	1.06	1.10
										1.73
60 $\overline{X}$	3.53	3.09	2.79	2.86	2.66	3.13	1.09	1.8	1.83	
SD	.55	1	1.12	.98	1.1	.87	1.00	.89	1.18	1.07

responses from the children of low level of deprivation (LD) were = 91, 78, 89, 94, 100, 96, 107 and for HD = 73, 75, 73, 76, 87, 80, 94) were quite different from each other across seven different age groups. Apart from the significance of major factors like deprivation and locatives, the interactions between level of deprivation and age [F(6,406) = 4.04; P<.01] and between locatives and level of deprivations [F(4, 1624) = 52.28 P<.01] were also found significant. This fact becomes clear through the dissimilar trend of mean scores which is supposed to be the cause of the significant interaction. It also shows that the deprivation does not affect all the locatives in a similar manner across different age groups. It is evident that perhaps because of the frequent uses of some type of locatives and less frequent use of some other kind of locative relationship might have caused significant interaction effect as the SF order responses for locative 'on' is the best example. Apart from these interactions, the interactions between all the three variables (Age, Level of Deprivation and Locative) was also found significant which shows the independent status of all the variables and this fact can easily be noticed from dissimilar trend of means for each factor.

The means and SDs of SF order responses in expressive condition is presented in Table 16.2. The obtained scores analysed in a 2 (Level of deprivation × 7 (Age groups) × 5 (Locative) repeated measure analysis of variance. The impact of deprivation on choice of word order, expressive condition, was found significant, [F(1, 406 = 2.73 P<.05]. Similarly the impact of age on choice of SF order responses was also found significant [F(6,406) = 12.73 P<.01]. This shows that the selection of word order for different locatives varied from different age levels i.e. seven age levels in this study. It is again noticed that the type of order of words for some type of locatives for example, locative '*Par*' is highly preferred as compared to other locatives. It means there is no uniform trend in preference of SF order for all locatives. The interaction between age and locatives was found significant [F(24, 1324) = 2.39 P<.05]. It indicates that at different age levels the choice of SF order responses for different locatives are quite different from each other. Any uniform trend of SF order responses across different age levels is not visible. Perhaps because of these trends the interaction between level of deprivation, locatives and age was found significant in case of expressive condition. It is evident from these findings that perhaps children in expressive condition found it difficult to follow the instructions as they were not very decisive. Both the objects (stimulus materials) were presented in front of the subjects and it was at their will to select any of the object. It

Table 16.2: Means and SDs of SF Order Responses in Expressive Condition

	LD					HD				
Age	*On*	*In front*	*Under*	*Behind*	*Above*	*On*	*In front*	*Under*	*Behind*	*Above*
(Maths)										
24 $\overline{X}$	1.32	0.66	0.30	0.38	0.34	1.16	0.47	0.35	0.43	0.67
SD	0.24	0.48	0.38	0.43	0.50	0.38	0.50	0.41	0.52	0.56
30 $\overline{X}$	1.36	0.89	0.34	0.71	0.28	1.22	0.80	0.56	0.74	0.45
SD	0.20	0.36	0.36	0.43	0.37	0.25	0.37	0.39	0.43	0.53
36 $\overline{X}$	1.17	0.92	0.59	0.80	0.72	1.38	0.85	0.52	0.59	0.54
SD	0.42	0.47	0.46	0.45	0.54	0.18	0.42	0.39	0.53	0.56
42 $\overline{X}$	1.32	0.99	0.58	0.85	0.67	1.27	0.79	0.51	0.61	0.51
SD	0.24	0.34	0.41	0.49	0.45	0.22	0.44	0.41	0.50	0.48
48 $\overline{X}$	1.33	0.87	0.55	0.79	0.39	1.32	0.59	0.65	0.56	0.73
SD	0.25	0.44	0.45	0.48	0.52	0.20	0.55	0.45	0.39	0.55
54 $\overline{X}$	1.34	0.85	0.59	0.60	0.80	1.16	0.82	0.59	0.76	0.61
SD	0.21	0.37	0.35	0.56	0.54	0.40	0.44	0.46	0.50	0.60
60 $\overline{X}$	9.18	6.50	3.80	5.19	4.14	8.86	5.20	3.92	4.41	4.48
SD	1.31	0.92	0.54	0.74	0.59	1.29	0.74	0.56	0.63	0.64

must have caused score variation in selecting the word order. The trend of the mean scores are also indicating fluctuation in the choice of word order.

Table 16.3: ANOVA Summary of SF Order Responses in Expressive Conditions

Source of variation	*Ss*	*df*	*MS*	*F*
Between Ss	163.945	419		
A (Level of Deprivation)	0.907	1	0.907	2.73*
B (Age)	25.340	6	4.223	12.73*
A × B	3.026	6	0.504	1.52
Error term	134.672	406	0.332	
C (Locatives)	146.178	4	36.55	189.35**
A × C	4.051	4	1.012	5.24**
B × C	11.098	24	0.462	2.39*
A × B × C	9.105	24	0.376	1.95*
Error term	255.126	1324	0.193	

Table 16.4: ANOVA Summary of SF Order Responses in Receptive Conditions

Source of variation	*Ss*	*df*	*MS*	*F*
Between Ss	1349.88	419		
A (Level of Deprivation)	134.77	1	134.77	59.10**
B (Age)	230.50	6	38.41	16.84**
A × B	55.37	6	9.22	4.04
Error term	929.24	406	2.28	
C (Locatives)	497.75	4	124.43	1384.09**
A × C	16.38	4	4.70	52.28**
B × C	36.06	24	1.72	19.13**
A × B × C	40.98	24	1.95	21.63**
Error term	146.03	1624	0.0899	

A number of views were suggested regarding the pragmatic strategies being used by children regarding their choice of word order in describing spatial relationship between a pair of objects. Among these are the Topic-Comment (Subject first order) by Gruber (1967) and Comment-Topic (Objects first order) by Bates (1976). On the basis of present investigation it seems that children's choice of selecting a pragmatic strategy for ordering the words in describing spatial relationship depends on types of locatives, age level and level of deprivation, that is why, for some locatives and at certain level of age and deprivation they select one strategy and at some other level, their choice is changed. Thus, the selection of SF order responses depends on these factors and selection of Topic-Comment (Gruber, 1967) and comment-Topic (Bates, 1976) cannot be generalised rather it depends on such variables like type of locative relationship, level of age and the type of environmental conditions the subjects come from. In the light of Gruber (1967) and Bates (1976) controversy the present investigation clearly indicates the possibility of separate identity of locatives, age and level of deprivation with regard to the selection of word order used in describing spatial relationship and, thus, there is no universal pragmatic strategy for describing locative relationship between a pair of objects rather these strategies depend on the nature of locative proposition, age and the environmental conditions the subjects belong to.

References

Bates, B. (1976) *'Language and Context'* : *The Acquisition of Pragmatics*, New York, Academic Press.

Bennett, D.C. (1972) Some observation concerning the locative directional distinction, *Semiotica*, 5, 58-88.

Bernstein, B (1958) Some sociological determinants of perception : An enquiry into subcultural differences, BTS, 9, 159-74.

Braine, M.D.S. (1963) On learning the grammatical order of words, *Psychological Review*, 76, 232-346.

Clark, V. (1972) On the child's acquisition of Antonyms in two semantic fields : *Journal of Verbal Learning and Verbal Behaviours*, 11, 750-758.

Clark, H. and Clark, E. (1977) *Psychology and Language*, New York : Hare Court Brace, Jovanovich.

Clark, E.V. (1973) What's in a word? On the child's acquisition of semantics in his first language. In T.E. Moore (Ed) *Cognitive Development and the Acquisition of Language.*, New York, Academic Press.

Cooper, G.S. (1968) *A Semantic Analysis of English Locative Proposition*,

Bolt Beraneck & New Deprt, 587.

Chomsky, N (1965) *Aspects of the Theory of Syntax*, Cambridge M.A. MIT Press.

Dale, P (1980) Is early pragmatic development measurable?, *Journal of Child Language*, 7, 1-12.

Devaki, L. (1986) *Learning of Morphological Rules in Children* : Doctoral Dissertation University of Mysore, Mysore.

Dore, F.A. (1974) Pragmatic Description of Early Language Development. *Journal of Psycholinguistic Research*, 4, 423-430.

Fillmore, S. (1974) Pragmatic Normalisation : Further Results for some conjunctive and disjunctive sentences; *Journal of Experimental Psychology*, 102, 574-578.

Gordan, D. and Lakoff G. (1971) Conversational postulates. In papers from seventh Regional Meeting, *Chicago Linguistic Society*, 63-84.

Gruber, J. (1967) Topicalisation in child language. *Foundation of Language*, 3, 57-65.

Halliday, M.A.K. (1970), Language structure and language, function, Inds. J. Lyons (Ed) *New Horizons in Linguistics*, Baltimore, Pelicon, 140-165.

Haviland, S. and Clark, H. (1974) What's new? Acquiring new informations as a process in comprehension. *Journal of Verbal Learning and Verbal Behaviour*, 123, 512-521.

Homby, P. (1972) The psychological subject and predicate. *Cognitive Psychology*, 3, 632.

Howell, D.C. (1994) *Statistical Methods for Psychology*, Belmount, California, Duxbury Press.

Mey, J.L. (1979) (Ed) *Pragmatics; Theory and Practice*. The Hague, Mounton.

Miller, G. (1975) Pragmatic constraints on the linguistic realisation of semantic interaction in early child language (Telegraphic speech). *Paper Presented at Third International Child Language Symposium*, London.

Misra, B (1984) *Development of Pragmatic Strategy in Word Order of Hindi Locative Proposition*. Doctoral Dissertation, Utkal University, Bhubaneswar.

Misra, B. and Tripathi, L.B. (1991). *Some Aspects of Language Development among Hindi Speaking Children in Deprivational/Non-deprivational Environment : A Psycholinguistic Study*, NCERT, New Delhi.

Misra, G. and Tripathi, L.B. (1977) *Prolonged Deprivation Scale*, National Psychological Corporation, Agra, India.

Mohanty, A.K. and Misra, B. (1982) Effect of context on word order in children's expression of locative proposition. *Psychological Report*, 50, 1163-1166.

McNamara F. (1972) Cognitive Basis of Language Learning in Infants *Psychological Review*, 79, 1-14.

Nelson, K. (1981) Individual Differences in Language Development Implications for Development and Language. *Developmental Psychology*, 17, (2) 170-187.

Winer, B.J. (1971). Statistical Principles in Experimental Design,New York: McGraw Hill Book Company, pp. 514-518.

17

SELF-EFFICACY AND MATHEMATICAL COMPETENCE AS A FUNCTION OF ATTRIBUTIONAL FEEDBACK

PUSHPA MISRA & NAMITA SRIVASTAVA

People have a tendency for making causal attribution to their own psychosocial functioning through the mechanisms of personal agency. Bandura (1997) has explicitly stated that among the mechanisms of personal agency, "none is more central or pervasive than beliefs of personal efficacy". Our actions are based more on what we believe rather than what is objectively true. Thus, it is a sense of control which leads to the desired effects through appropriate actions and we observe our behaviour being guided by the beliefs of self efficacy. Self efficacy can be understood as a component of the self concept that deals with one's perceived abilities and competencies to deal with a given task. This personal influence may be exercised differently by people to influence their motivations, thought processes, affective states and even actions with the result that the impact of their efficacy beliefs may be seen on the action chosen by them, how much effort they put in the task and how long they will persist in the face of obstacles/failure. What is important in the context of efficacy beliefs is to what extent the thought patterns of a person are self hindering or self aiding. This entire mechanism seems to be associated with the level of accomplishments achieved by us. Researches conducted in the area of self efficacy suggest that students' poor performance may be either due to lack of skills or because they have skills but lack the perceived efficacy to make optimal use of them (Collins, 1982). Schunk (1989) believes that efficacy beliefs though are influenced by acquisition of cognitive skills, are not merely a reflection of them. Showing the independent contribution of efficacy beliefs to cognitive performance, Bouffard *et al.* (1991) concluded that regardless of whether children were of superior or average cognitive ability, those having high self efficacy were more successful in conceptual problem solving than children having equal ability but lower perceived efficacy. The unique contribution of efficacy beliefs has been shown through direct as well as mediated effect (Pajares & Kranzler, 1995; Pajares & Miller, 1994; Bouffard, 1990).

Conducting a series of experiments Schunk (1983-84, 1989) employed an informative experimental paradigm and tried to explain the predictive superiority of efficacy beliefs over acquired skills. Schunk suggested that children vary in how they interpret, store and recall their success and failure and, therefore, they derive self efficacy differentially from similar attainments. Moreover, in judging their capabilities, social influence has its impact on efficacy beliefs independently of skills. Thus Schunk's work suggested that in the self efficacy framework, attributional feedback constitutes a valuable source of information and influence performance by affecting efficacy expectations. In this context the present study made an attempt to see the effect of different types of attributional feedback on the self-efficacy judgements and mathematical competence of children belonging to VIII grade. VIII graders were selected on the basis of the work of Nicholls (1978), which showed that the concepts of ability and effort begins to emerge around the age of 9 and is almost complete by the age of 13 years.

Three different types of feedback used in this research were effort, ability and effort-ability combined. Specific expectancies (self efficacy) constitutes, theoretically a crucial link between attributional feedback and subsequent behaviour change, therefore, providing attributional feedback was expected to enhance children's mathematical skills. Within the framework of Weiner's (1986) theory it was expected that effort feedback would be more effective for enhancing self efficacy judgements and mathematical competence as compared to ability feedback.

METHOD

Design

The study employed a 2 × 4 factorial design.

The independent and dependent variables of the study are given below :

Independent Variables

1. Sex-boys and girls
2. Attributional feedback
   a. Ability feedback
   b. Effort feedback
   c. Ability + Effort feedback
   A. Control group was taken besides three experimental groups

Dependent Variables

1. Self efficacy
2. Mathematical competence

Age and grade were controlled while seeing the effect of independent variables on the dependent variable.

Sample : The sample consisted of 192 children of 8th grade, belonging to middle socio-economic status and ranging in age from 12 to 14 years. The sample was chosen from the schools of Lakhimpur Kheri, U.P., India.

The children selected for the study were deficient in mathematical ability. Mathematical deficiency was assessed on the basis of marks obtained in their previous examination. Those children who failed in the last examination or obtained only 45% marks were selected as subjects. Besides, teachers were also asked to indicate children who were weak in mathematical ability. All doubtful cases (where teachers assessment did not agree with the school records were discarded).

Out of the total sample of 192, 96 were boys and 96 were girls. These children were assigned to four treatment groups, each group consisted of 24 boys and 24 girls.

Tools

In the present research following tools were used:

Self Efficacy Scale

The self efficacy scale used in the present research, was similar to that developed by Bandura and Schunk (1981).

The efficacy scale ranged from 10 to 100, with an interval of 10 units, with verbal description occurring at the following points, 10 = not sure, 40 = may be, 70 = pretty sure, 100 = real sure. Children were given practice for rating of self efficacy judgement. Thus children learned to assign the different numerical values. After this children were shown 24 mathematical problems. These problems were different from those used by Bandura and Schunk (1981) for the simple reason that the subjects of this study were 8th graders while the subjects of Bandura and Schunk's study were 3rd graders (8.4 years). The description of the mathematical problems is given in the test of mathematical achievement.

In measuring strength of mathematical self efficacy, each problem was shown to children only for 2 seconds. This brief exposure was sufficient to portray the nature of the task but much shorter to even attempt any solution. After each sample exposure, children judged their capability to solve the type of problem depicted and rated privately the strength of their perceived efficacy on a 100 point rating scale.

The measure of strength of self efficacy was obtained by dividing the summed magnitude scores by the total number of problems.

Test of Mathematical Achievement

To measure mathematical achievement of children, a test was constructed. The test consisted of 24 arithmetic problems, selected from the text book of class 7th. Out of these 24 problems some were of addition, subtractions, divisions and multiplications. Other problems were of LCM, GCM, Fractions, Decimals, Percentage, Interest, etc. Since the interest of the study was in having problems of average difficulty, problems selected for the test of mathematical ability were separately pretested on a group of 20 children and only those problems were finally selected which were solved by 50 to 51% of children. Rest of the problems were discarded either as easy or as difficult. Following this procedure 24 mathematical problems could be taken for the study, out of which 8 problems were given everyday to children in the training session. Two parallel sets of 8 problems, involving different mathematical concepts used in the above said 24 problems were also prepared for the pre-test, post-test of mathematical achievement. The r found between the 2 parallel sets of problems was .80 ($N = 50$; $P<.01$).

Scoring

For each correct problem a score of 12.50 was given. Thus for all 8 problems, if done correctly a child could get a score of 100. Scores were given only when the problem was fully correct. No score was given for the problems which were correct partially.

Procedure

First of all children from Class VIII who were deficient in mathematical ability were selected according to the procedure described earlier. Then children were assigned to four treatment conditions. Children were shown 24 problems of the mathematical test for about 2 seconds each, and given the scale of self efficacy for which the following instructions were given. "Circle the number on the line that matches how sure you are that you could work problems like these standards. Get the right answer, remember that higher the number the more sure you are. Please be honest and mark how you really feel right now."

After taking self efficacy ratings from children, they were given 8 problems to solve which were selected for the pre-test. The time limit for the 8 problems was 45 minutes. The time limit was decided on the basis of the pilot study.

After completing this procedure subjects were given 3 days training sessions. On each day 8 problems were given to children to solve. The time limit was 45 minutes for every training session. In these training sessions children were given attributional feedbacks. Feedback was given individually to the children for only two times per training sessions. Data was collected in small groups. Eight children were taken at a time. The seating arrangement was quite spacious so that children were unable to see each other papers and hear their voices. In each group two children were given four different treatments or feedback. All feedbacks were given by the same experimenter. The description of the feedback is given below:

Ability Attributional Feedback

Giving ability feedback investigator asked the child what page are you working on. After child's reply with the page number the investigator linked child's prior achievement to ability by remarking "you are good at this."

Effort Attributional Feedback

The treatment was identical to ability feedback condition except that following the child's reply the investigator linked the child's prior achievement with effort by remarking "you have been working hard."

Ability + Effort Attributional Feedback

These children received both forms of feedback. The procedure was similar to those of previous conditions. Following the child's reply the investigator either remarked "you are good at this and you have been working hard" or you are working hard and you are good at this".

No Attributional Feedback

These children were monitored in the same fashion as the feedback treatment except that after the child's reply the investigator remarked 'OK' and departed. This group was control group.

Social reinforcers such as smiles or pats were not given in any condition with a view to manipulate only verbal reinforcement. Immediately following the last training session, children were asked to rate the amount of effort expended during the training session on a scale of effort expenditure to ensure that the instructions really worked.

After three-day training session, on the fourth day, post-test was conducted in which self efficacy ratings were taken and mathematical achievement was measured as it was done in pre-testing.

RESULTS

Results showed a significant improvement in self-efficacy scores of children after attributional feedback was given. A significant sex differences was also observed with boys having higher efficacy scores than girls. (Tables 17.1 to 17.3).

Table 17.1: Mean Self-efficacy Scores of Children before (pre-test) and after (post-test) Attributional Feedback was given (N = 48 in each Condition)

Conditions		*Effort Att.*	*Ability Att.*	*A+E Att.*	*No Att.*
Pre-test	Mean	52.42	51.67	47.39	48.93
	SD	11.16	15.57	15.05	14.76
Post-test	Mean	77.63	69.89	62.16	46.37
	SD	9.44	12.49	13.54	11.33

Table 17.2: Sex Difference on Self-efficacy Judgements (post-test)

	Subjects	*N*	*Mean*	*SD*
1.	Boys	96	67.06	17.94
2.	Girls	96	62.28	15.35

Table 17.3: 2 × 4 Analysis of Variance – Showing the Effect of Attributional Feedback on Self Efficacy Judgements of Boys & Girls

Source of Variation	*Sum of Squares*	*Degrees of freedom*	*Variance Estimate*	*F*
Rows (Sex)	1413.67	1	1413.67	8.74*
Columns (feedback conditions)	27180.30	3	9060.10	55.99*
Interaction	238.75	3	79.58	.49
Within cells	29768.60	184	161.79	

* Significant at .01 level

However, a differential effect of feedback for efficacy scores was found with effort feedback showing maximum impact followed by ability feedback and ability+effort feedback (Table 17.4).

Table 17.4: Duncon's Multiple Comparison Test – Showing Significance of Difference among Different Types of Attributional Feedback Conditions (self efficacy judgements).

Mean	*A* 46.37	*B* 62.16	*C* 69.89	*D* 77.63	*Shortest significance range*
A-46.37	X	15.79*	23.52*	31.26*	R_2 6.66
B-62.16		X	7.13*	15.45*	R_3 6.95
C-69.89			X	7.74*	R^4 7.13

* Significant at .01 level
Here
A = No attributional feedback
B = A+E attributional feedback
C = Ability attributional feedback
D = Effort attributional feedback

The mean scores on mathematical achievement also significantly increased as a function of attributional feedback, though no sex difference was found. (Table 17.5 and 17.6).

Table 17.5: Mean Mathematical Achievement Scores of Children before (pre-test) and after (post-test) Attributional Feedback was given (N = 48 in each condition)

Conditions		*Effort Att.*	*Ability Att.*	*A+E Att*	*No Att*
Pre-test	Mean	26.82	28.12	23.95	20.57
	SD	9.52	9.81	10.58	11.03
Post-Test	Mean	51.64	53.64	47.12	20.83
	SD	20.43	19.96	19.51	13.96

Table 17.6: Sex Difference on Mathematical Achievement (post-test)

Subject	*N*	*Mean*	*SD*
Boys	96	42.57	21.73
Girls	96	43.75	23.37

Differential effect of different feedback conditions on mathematical achievement was not observed (Table 17.7).

Table 17.7: 2 × 4 Analysis of Variance – showing the Effect of Attributional Feedback on Achievement of Boys and Girls

Source of variation	*Sum of squares*	*df*	*Variance estimate*	*F*
Rows (Sex)	66.50	1	66.50	.29
Columns (feedback condition)	22928.29	3	10976.06	32.23*
Interaction	402.64	3	139.21	.39
Within cells	62652.69	194	340.50	

*Significant at .01 level

Table 17.8: Duncon's Multiple Comparison Test – showing Significance of Difference among Different Types of Attributional Feedback Conditions with Regard to Mathematical Achievement

Mean	*A* *20.83*	*B* *47.12*	*C* *51.04*	*D* *53.64*	*Shortest significance range*
A 20.83	X	26.29*	30.21*	32.81*	$R_2 = 9.68$
B 47.12		X	3.92	6.52	$R_3 = 10.10$
C 51.04			X	2.60	$R_4 = 10.37$
D 53.64				X	

*Significant at .01 level.

Here — A = No attributional feedback; B = A+E attributional feedback; C = Effort attributional feedback; D = Ability attributional feedback

DISCUSSION

The present study demonstrated that in the context of competency development, providing attributional feedback constitutes an effective means of promoting self efficacy and mathematical achievement. Before feedbacks were given, four groups of children did not differ significantly on the pre-test scores of self efficacy (F=1.18, ns, df 3, 188) and mathematical competence (F=2.57, ns, df=3,188). The results revealed that after attributional feedback was given, efficacy judgements significantly improved. Comparison of different types of feedback demonstrated that effort feedback was most effective in enhancing efficacy scores, next was ability feedback followed by ability and effort combined. Telling children that they had been working hard conveys them that they were efficacious enough to succeed and could actualise their capabilities through sustained effort and thus raising their self efficacy judgements. It seems that the approval given to subjects who were weak in mathematics was more believable and readily acceptable in effort feedback condition. Working with younger children (second grades) Schunk (1983) found ability feedback to be most effective and this was explained in terms of greater social reinforcement value of ability feedback. This discrepancy in results raises an important issue of exploring the differential impact of attributional feedback in developmental perspective. Since the subjects of this study were old enough to understand the concepts of effort/ability, they could be aware of effort as being under volitional control and as an unstable property. Furthermore for greater effectiveness of effort feedback another plausible explanation, as suggested by other researches (Kukla, 1972) could be that effort feedback is most effective for tasks having intermediate difficulty level which was applicable for this study too.

Highlighting the importance of effort feedback should not undermine the impact of ability feedback which also significantly enhanced efficacy judgements. This suggests that ability feedback too motivates the person to be highly persistent and task oriented. Among the three feedback conditions, the lowest but significant impact was observed when ability and effort feedbacks were combined. The finding suggests that in this condition, efficacy was not promoted in an additive manner, and children might have discounted the ability information in favour of effort. They might have wondered how good at mathematics they really were if they had to work hard to succeed. In other words, they must have questioned the validity of the ability feedback.

The results obtained for mathematical achievement showed that different attributional feedback affected performance in a positive manner. This improvement is expected to be mediated through enhanced self efficacy (the value of r between self efficacy and mathematical achievement obtained in this study is .81, $p<.01$). The finding substantiates the role of efficacy beliefs by suggesting that academic performance is not only a product of cognitive capabilities, but is also influenced by motivational and other self regulatory skills for instance, it may influence how consistently and effectively children apply what they know.

No differential effect of various feedback conditions was observed for mathematical competence though logically one would expect it to be as performance changes are expected through enhanced self efficacy judgements. The overall gain in mathematical skills suggested that probably feedback conditions did enhance the motivational levels of the SS but we need to examine some of the mechanisms operating in the context of self efficacy to have better insights, though some of these have been suggested by a few researchers (Bouffard *et al.*, 1991), in terms of more efficacious students being better at time management while solving problems and are more persistent and less likely to reject correct solutions prematurely.

In the present study significant sex differences were observed only with regard to self efficacy. The boys perception of efficacy was greater than girls. It appears that sex differences in efficacy judgements are likely to vary according to the task for which it is judged. Cobb (1957) observed that boys perceived efficacy was more than girls in the areas of personal achievement and possessions, whereas girls had stronger wishes than boys in matters pertaining to social and family relationships. In some other researches too, success expectancies were found to be higher in males than females (Lenney, 1977; Stein & Bailey, 1973).

In conclusion, it may be stated that attributional feedbacks are important for enhancing efficacy beliefs which are expected to influence the actual performance. In this context, the perceived credibility of the persuaders will play a significant role. Having great significance for teachers and parents, this area needs further probing especially with regard to the specific mechanisms which mediate this improvement. In the efficacy framework, the developmental status of the SS and the area of performance may also be looked into to provide better understanding of human performance.

References

Bandura A. (1997) Self efficacy; *The Exercise of Control*, Freeman and Company, New York.

Bouffard-Bouchard, T. (1990) Influence of self efficacy on performance in a cognitive task, *Journal of Social Psychology*, 130, 353-363.

Bouffard-Bouchard, T., Parent, S., & Larivee, S. (1991) Influence of self efficacy on self regulation and performance among junior and senior high school age students. *International Journal of Behavioural Development*, 14, 153-164.

Bandura, A. & Schunk, D.H. (1981). Cultivating competence, self efficacy and intrinsic interest through proximal self motivation. *Journal of Personality and Social Psychology*, 41, 586-598.

Collins J.L. (1982 March) self efficacy and ability in achievement behaviour. Paper presented at the annual meeting of the American Educational Research Association, New York.

Cobb, H. V. (1954). Role wishes and general wishes of children and adolescents. *Child Development*, 25, 173-183.

Kukla, A. (1972) Foundations of an attribution theory of performance. *Psychological Preview*, 79, 454-470.

Lenney, E. (1977). Woman's self confidence in achievement settings. *Psychological Bulletin*, 84, 1-13.

Miller, R.L., Brickman, P. & Bolen D. (1975) Attribution *versus* persuasion as a means for modifying behaviour. *Journal of Personality and Social Psychology*, 31, 430-441.

Nicholls, J.G. (1978). The development of the concepts of effort and ability perception of academic attainment, and the understanding that difficult task requires more ability. *Child Development*, 49, 800-814.

Pajares, F., & Kranzler, J., (1995). Self efficacy beliefs and general mental ability in mathematical problem solving contemporary, *Educational Psychology*, 20, 426-443.

Pajares, F., & Miller, M.D. (1994). Role of self efficacy and self concept beliefs in mathematical problem solving. A path analysis. *Journal of Educational Psychology*, 86, 193-203.

Schunk, D.H. (1983) Ability *versus* effort attributional feedback; differential effects on self efficacy and achievement. *Journal of Educational Psychology*, 75, 848-856.

Schunk, D.H. (1984) Enhancing self efficacy and achievement through rewards and goals: Motivational and informational effects. *Journal of Educational Research*, 78, 29-34.

Schunk, D.H. (1989) Self efficacy and cognitive skill learning. In C. Ames and R. Ames (eds). *Research on Motivation in Education*, Vol. 3, Goals and Cognitions (pp. 13-44) San Diego Academic.

Stein, A.M. & Bailey, M.M. (1973). The socialisation of achievement orientation in females. *Psychological Bulletin*, 80, 345-366.

Weiner, B. (1986). *An Attribution Theory Motivation and Emotion*. New York, Springer-Verlag.

18

VERBAL, NUMERICAL AND ATTENTIONAL PROBLEMS OF LEARNING DISABLED CHILDREN

ACHAL NANDINI SRIVASTAVA & SHEETLA PRASAD

The term 'learning disabilities' emerged from a need to identify and help children who, despite having average or above average intelligence level, experience continuous school failure in one or more academic, and also non-academic areas and yet, these children elude the traditional categories of retarded or deprived. Medicine, psychology, education and even sociology have contributed to the development of this new area of children's problems. Due to these multi-disciplinary contributions, a certain amount of confusion was inevitable. During the early developmental years, many terms were being used synonymously for the same behavioural problems; terms such as, 'learning handicaps', 'educational underachievement', 'minimal brain injury', 'minimal brain dysfunction', 'psycho neurological disabilities', 'perceptual disabilities', 'educational handicaps', etc. etc. Cruickshank (1972) has listed more than 40 English terms used to refer to the same types of problems with same meanings.

During late 1950s and early 1960s teachers were referring many children to special education centres (which had sprung up primarily for retarded or handicapped children) because these children were not learning. But the crux of the matter was that these children were not diagnosed as retarded, blind, deaf, dumb or crippled. Then in 1963, several regional parents' associations planned a national conference at New York City in which Samuel Kirk suggested that any term describing these children should be educationally based, and not etiologically. He proposed the term "learning disabilities" for such children and this term was accepted and registered. In 1964, the Association for Children with Learning Disabilities (ACLD) was formally established in the U.S.A. Very soon, a *Journal of Learning Disabilities* was also started.

Historically, the roots of this new area may be traced to some different type of work. Kurt Goldstein (1927) started his longitudinal study with head-injured soldiers of World War I, and observed that generally they displayed five behavioural characteristics : forced responsiveness to stimuli, figure-ground confusion, hyperactivity, slow meticulosity, and catastrophic reaction. These observations of Goldstein led Alfred Strauss, a neuro-psychiatrist, and Heinz Werner, a developmental psychologist, to investigate brain-injured and mentally retarded children. Werner and Strauss (1930a) found that Goldstein's five adult behaviour manifestations could also be observed in children with brain damage. These authors also noted that children with exogenous brain-damage (neurological damage not caused by genetic factors) could be clearly differentiated from children with endogenic (genetic) brain-damage problems. In addition to behavioural characteristics observed by Goldstein (1927), Strauss and Werner (1942) also found in their brain-damaged and retarded children "behavioural and visual preservation, and an inability to organise and deal with abstract concepts". Kephart and Strauss (1940) in a longitudinal remedial programme for such children found that after special remedial training, the inteligence levels of endogenous children increased over the years, but the exogenous children not only did not improve, but their condition deteriorated as time went on.

William Cruickshank, recognised as the leader in the field of special education, also contributed significantly to the new and growing area of learning disabilities of children. He replicated the works of Goldstein, Strauss, and Werner with cerebral palsied children of near-normal, normal, and above normal intelligence (Cruickshank, Bice & Wallen, 1957). It was found that cerebral palsied children of normal intelligence exhibited behavioural characteristics similar to exogenous mentally retarded children of Werner and Strauss. This was the first major research on children who had normal intelligence, yet, also exhibited learning problems.

Numerous attempts have been made to define learning disabilities. Despite having many commonalities, each definition has a certain bias. Most definitions have at least these four factors :

1. A discrepancy between the I.Q. and the educational achievement.

2. Possibility of some nervous system dysfunction.
3. Psychological processing problems
4. Learning problems not attributable to mental retardation, or environmental deprivation.

The Potential-Achievement Discrepancy

Many researchers consider the discrepancy component, popularised by Bateman (1964), as the commonest denominator of learning disabilities. When a child's academic performance is significantly lower than the estimated potential, and continues to be so, it is considered to be an almost undebatable characteristic of learning disability.

There are several view-points as to how to measure this discrepancy. These view-points consider the child's age, years spent in school, level of intelligence, level of educational achievement etc. Lerner (1976) has summarised these approaches by advising the researchers to consider 3 questions before labelling a child as learning disabled :

(a) What is the child's potential for learning, as tested by standard intelligence tests?
(b) What is the child's present achievement level, as assessed by standardised achievement tests?
(c) What degree of discrepancy between potential and achievement is significant?

There are several viewpoints regarding this third query. Myklebust (1968) proposed a Learning Quotient method, whereas Prasad and Srivastava (1980) devised a Learning Disability Quotient (LDQ) method.

Dysfunction of Central Nervous System

This is the most debatable area of learning disability, and also the earliest. Many concepts of learning disability grew out of the work done with brain-injured persons and it was noted that many characteristics observed in learning disabled children, such as distractibility, perceptual problems, attention, general orientation deficits etc., were also noted in brain-injured children. But a child diagnosed as learning disabled on the basis of psychological tests cannot be labelled as brain-damaged without neurological tests. Moreover, a child with brain-injury or brain damage may not necessarily suffer from brain dysfunction.

Problems related with Psychological Processing

Most learning disabled children exhibit a handicap in one or more of the basic psychological processes essential for the reception, integration and expression abilities in perceptual-motor, psycholinguistic, and cognitive tasks. The United States Office of Education (USOE, 1968) clearly stated that :

> "Children with special learning disabilities exhibit a disorder in one or more of the basic psychological processes involved in understanding or in using spoken or written languages. These may be manifested in disorders of listening, thinking, talking, reading, writing, spelling, or arithmetic. They include conditions which have been referred to as perceptual handicaps, brain injury, minimal brain dysfunction, dyslexia, developmental aphasia etc. They do not include learning problems which are due primarily to visual, learning, or motor handicaps, to mental retardation, emotional disturbance or to environmental disadvantage".

Exclusion Variables

Mental retardation, emotional disturbance and environmental deprivation are excluded from learning disabled category. A mentally retarded child has a significant subaverage intellectual functioning with impairments in adaptive behaviour. A learning disabled child is of an average or above average I.Q. level, yet, may manifest some socially adaptive problems. Hallahan and Kauffman (1977), and Hallahan, Kauffman, and Lloyd (1985), point out that many mildly emotionally disturbed children and mildly mentally retarded children also exhibit an IQ-achievement discrepancy similar to learning disabled children, and also many behavioural similarities. Cullinan and Epstein (1985) point out that remedial teaching techniques and teaching materials for learning disabled and mildly mentally retarded children are quite similar.

Many early researchers maintained that a learning problem attributable to environmental deprivation cannot be categorised as a learning disability of the child. These researchers worked with the presumption that the cause of the learning problem is within the child. The information processing functions of the child, which are essential to academic learning, suffer from impairments. These processes, such as, perceptual-motor ability, language processing and attentional ability, memory and thinking abilities, etc., underlie academic functions. Any impairment in one or more of these areas may cause learning problems. These are inner abilities and capacities of a child. They are not caused by environment, though environment may enhance or inhibit them.

In contrast to this ability model, there are researchers who follow the skill model which is a behavioural approach to identify learning disabled children. These researchers believe in the existence of an environmental or experience deficit. They state that the locus of the handicap is outside the child, and the researcher must focus upon the immediate antecedents of the problem behaviour. Thus, this view point maintains that environmentally disadvantaged children may also have learning problems similar to non-disadvantaged ones (Hallahan and Cruickshank, 1973; Hallahan, Kauffman and Lloyd, 1985).

Keeping these various view points under consideration, in 1981, the National Joint Committee for Learning Disabilities (NJCLD) in the U.S.A., studied various definitions put forward by Bateman (1965) introducing the discrepancy clause; by Task Force 1 in which Clements (1966) introduced the minimal brain dysfunction factor; by USOE in which Kirk (1968) emphasised the psychological process disorders, and which is a widely accepted definition, and by the Federal Register of USOE (1977) which combines the discrepancy clause and the exclusion of mental retardation, sensory handicaps and environmental disadvantage. After mulling over all the above definitional approaches, and after consulting with the American Speech Language Hearing Association, the Association for Children and Adults with Learning Disabilities, the Council for Learning Disabilities, the Orton Dyslexia Society, and many such institutions, the NJCLD issued the following definition of learning disability :

> "Learning disabilities is a generic term that refers to a heterogeneous group of disorders manifested by significant difficulties in the acquisition and use of listening, speaking, reading, writing, reasoning, or mathematical abilities. These disorders are intrinsic to the individual and presumed to be due to central nervous system dysfunction. Even though a learning disability may occur concomitantly with other handicapping conditions (e.g., sensory impairment, mental retardation, social and emotional disturbance) or environmental influences (e.g., cultural differences, and

insufficient-inappropriate instruction, psychogenic factors), it is not the direct result of those conditions or influences". (Hammill, Leigh, McNutt, and Larsen, 1981).

Psychological and Behavioural Characteristics

Researches in learning disabilities have attributed a variety of characteristics to such children. These characteristics are so numerous and sometimes synonymous and overlapping that a National Task Force in the U.S.A., under the leadership of Clements (1966) took up the challenge of enumerating them. They found twenty nine characteristics reported by various authors. Clements also pointed out the ten most frequently found symptoms which were organised in the following six groups by Hallahan and Kauffman (1988).

Perceptual, Perceptual-Motor, and General Coordination Problems

These include visual and auditory perceptual disabilities, whole-part and figure-ground perceptual problems, haptic perceptual problems, kinesthetic problems, perceptual-motor-match problems, motor problems such as balance, maintenance of posture, locomotion, contact skills, grasping, releasing, manipulating etc. (Prasad and Srivastava, 1992; Prasad, 1994).

Attentional and Hyperactivity Problems

Cruickshank (1961), while working with Werner and Strauss, focused upon the attentional and hyperactivity problems displayed by several learning disabled children. Shaywitz and Shaywitz (1987) have documented a range of 33 to 80 per cent learning disabled children being hyperactive as well.

Hyperactivity and attentional problems are often used synonymously. But in 1980 the American Psychiatric Association's "Diagnostic and Statistical Manual of Mental Disorders" (DSM-III) included in its list of mental disorders the categories of :

(a) Attention Deficit Disorder with Hyperactivity (ADDH), and
(b) Attention Deficit Disorder without Hyperactivity ADD.

Shaywitz & Shaywitz (1987) suggested a combined name for both of these : "Attention Deficit Hyperactivity Disorder", thus making attention the primary problem. DSM-IV refers to these disorders as "clinical attentional problem."

Disorders of Memory and Thinking

In general, learning disabled children display memory deficits for both auditory and visual material (Hallahan, 1975). Torgessen and Kail (1980) maintain that the major reason for such memory deficits in learning disabled children is their inability to use learning strategies.

Thinking problems involve metacognition problems of learning disabled children. They are not aware which skills and strategies are required for a particular task, they are unable to plan their moves, they cannot remedy their difficulties, and they cannot monitor the comprehension meaningfully.

Social Adjustment Problems

Socially, learning disabled children find it difficult to interact with others and to be friendly. They have frequent mood changes and may not like to participate in group discussions. They usually get socially rejected peer ratings. Teachers often rate them as not trying sufficiently. Learning disabled children do have negative self concepts regarding their academic abilities, but they do not suffer from poor self-esteem concerning non-academic performances (Bryan and Bryan, 1986). They lack social comprehension and have difficulties in reading and interpreting social cues.

Neurological Disorders

These disorders must be approached with extreme caution. The "hard neurological symptoms" such as cerebral palsy, epilepsy etc. cannot be ascertained without detailed neurological diagnostic tests and their very careful interpretations. But some learning disabled children do exhibit the "soft signs" such as problems in fine motor coordination, poor balance, general clumsiness, certain uncontrollable movements etc. But the presence of these symptoms does not necessarily mean a brain-injury. A brain-injury dysfunction is almost irreversible, whereas a learning disability is very often remediable.

Academic Achievement Problems

This is one symptom about which there are no doubts. A learning disabled child is one who is unable to learn, which means low academic achievement. This may be exhibited in a variety of ways. There may be spoken and written language problems with poor syntax and semantics. Learning disabled children often do not know how to use language in social settings. They also show reading problems such as dyslexia, word recognition errors, errors of omissions or insertions, etc. There are written language problems of slow and illegible handwriting, of lack of phoneme-grapheme correspondence leading to faulty spellings, or grammatical errors in composition.

Besides language problems, the next basic academic disorder is arithmetical disability. McLeod and Armstrong (1982) report that two out of three learning disabled children receive special instruction in arithmetic and more than one in four have to have special education services mainly due to problems in mathematics. Many of these problems are caused by attentional and reading problems, some by memory and thinking disorders. These, and other behavioural problems are also exhibited by mentally retarded children with greater intensity. Hyperlexia is one example. Learning disabled children sometimes are hyperlexic, but retarded children manifest more language or emotional problems (Prasad & Srivastava, 1992).

Statement of the Objectives of the Present Research

The present investigation has two major objectives : to identify and diagnose learning disabled (LD) children in a given population; and to investigate their linguistic and numerical abilities, and disabilities, and to compare them with the linguistic and numerical levels of normal, or, non-learning disabled (NLD) children.

The first problem is how to identify and diagnose learning disabled children. How can learning disability be measured? Who are the children that are learning disabled? Are they retarded? Are they educationally backward? Are they stupid? Are they dumb? Are all learning disabled (LD) children alike? Are they all disabled in the same area, to the same extent? Diagnosis here does not mean the determination of a condition (e.g. typhoid, or schizophrenia). Here it refers to the extent of the existence of a problem behaviour, e.g., language problem. Screening the children with the help of adequate psychological tests furnishes the investigators with information regarding their potential and their achievements, thus providing an index of learning disabilities, and abilities (Prasad & Srivastava, 1980).

The second objective is to explore the dissimilarities and similarities between learning disabled and other children. The LD and the NLD children are compared on several linguistic, numerical and attentional tasks. In all the definitions of learning disabilities, language problem is the first one to be mentioned and it is categorised in a variety of ways. But arithmetic and attention problems are no less important.

Many language disabled children exhibit phonological problems such as confusing the sounds p/b/d/t etc. They also have problems involving blends such as confusion with br/bl (break/black), fr/fl (frock/flock), and pr/pl (pray/play) etc. Often, one is pronounced instead of the other, and the meaning is also overlooked. Wiig, Semel and Crouse (1973) report that many LD children confuse time related verb tenses. They go on using only the present tense even if the use of past or future tense is required. When auxiliary verbs are added to the sentences, e.g., 'I am reading', 'I was playing', then the confusion increases even more. Wiig and Semel (1976) also point out that LD children assign a very narrow set of attributes to each word resulting in the problem that each word has a very limited meaning for them. Children with such problem persist in confusing dual-meaning words such as 'right', 'ball', 'watch' etc. Phrases that carry the same meaning, such as, 'the dog is chasing the cat', and 'the cat is being chased by the dog', are often not understood by LD children as having the same meaning. They also have difficulties in processing oral syntax and negative sentences. They show problems in auditory figure-ground perception, auditory and visual reception of simple words or questions, and visual and auditory sequential memory and verbal expression. Then there are pragmatic problems. They move inappropriately in space, stand too close to others, talk at wrong moments, talk very loudly and abruptly. Obviously, these manners irritate others and as a consequence, LD children are rejected by their peers, and many times by teachers and other elders too. The situation becomes truly pathetic when they are rejected by youngsters as well.

Traditionally, arithmetic consists of both verbal and written symbols. The purpose of these symbols is to communicate concepts such as size, order, space, form, distance, relationships, and time. Also, arithmetic requires logical and non-verbal thinking. According to Mercer (1979), reading may be the most common academic disability, but for numerous LD children the primary academic problem is numerical disability.

It has been found in several studies that LD children are poor performers at both concrete and representational levels of arithmetic. Many researchers relate mathematics to cognitive developmental stages. The developmental stages of Piaget (1969) are often incorporated in arithmetic workbooks, and a specified degree of logical quantitative thinking is essential at each level. Kaliski (1967) notes that many of the characteristics attributed to LD children are related to numerical problems. For example, problems related with perception, direction, reading, memory, and abstract thinking are very often attributed to LD children. Each of these problems has also been related to numerical disabilities.

Kaliski (1967) has observed that problems with spatial relationship and directionality, such as, confusions with 'first-last', 'up-down', 'upon-below', 'left-right' etc., have an adverse effect upon doing simple numerical problems. Reading proceeds from left to right; addition, subtraction and multiplication proceed from right to left; division again proceeds from left to right. All this is taken for granted by the normal child, but it is sufficient to confuse the LD child.

Numerical disabilities exist at all age levels. During the kindergarten and primary years, children with such problems cannot sort objects by shape, size etc. Later, they get confused by fractions, decimals, percentages and proportions. Roherst (1968) identified four primary error categories in such children :

(1) *Wrong operation.* LD Students add, when they should subtract.
(2) *Obvious computational error.* Very often, LD children apply correct operation, such as subtraction, but do the calculation wrong e.g., 30-9=39.
(3) *Defective algorithm.* This is a problem-solving pattern which includes specific steps to calculate a problem. But LD children are confused by this. For example $6 \times (2+4)$ may be calculated as $6 \times 2 = 12 + 4 = 16$ while the correct answer should be 36.
(4) *Random response.* When the LD children find themselves utterly helpless and confused, they start guessing and giving random responses which are not at all related with the problem given. For example, 7623+345 is given the answer of 7777777; and 345+124 may become 333333.

A knowledge of simple arithmetic is essential for smooth daily routine and adjustment. Similarly, using the language correctly is required for learning, expressing, understanding and interacting. Paying adequate attention makes it easier to approach any type of task. An early identification and diagnosis of children suffering from language and numerical disabilities as well as attentional problems may improve relations with peers, may stop further deterioration, may make the parents more understanding. It may, with careful remedial training, improve the child's academic performance.

There is a general consensus that children with learning problems very often suffer from attentional problems. Not only the problem children exhibit were attentional problems than unhandicapped children, but different types of handicapped children exhibit different types of attentional problems. Sustained attention tasks like vigilance, reaction time, etc. have been shown to have different amounts of cognitive demands. In tasks of minimum cognitive demands such as to detect a change in the brightness of light or loudness of tone, hyperactive, learning-disabled and retarded children have been reported to make more errors of omission than the non-handicapped matched groups (Goldberg and Konstantareas, 1981; Swanson, 1980, 1983; Aman, 1979). In tasks requiring greater punitive demands such as Continuous Performance Tasks which requires children not only to in memory for several seconds, hyperactive children exhibit more problems than learning disabled children (Douglas & Peters, 1979).

In the area of selective attention, two of the most popular tasks used with learning problem children are types selected to incidental learning and distraction. Distractible children are over-sensitive to the multitude of stimuli at any given time, and thus they tend to respond to task-irrelevant stimuli to a greater extent than the central subjects. The distracters themselves may be distal, proximal or embedded characteristics.

The main purpose of the present investigation was to compare the performance of LD and NLD children on learning and recall of linguistic and numerical stimuli, and also their attentional processes. Generally speaking, most of the studies in this field have already concluded that LD children's performance.

Considering the nature of the two objectives of this research, the investigation was carried out in two phases. In the first phase learning disabled children were identified. In the second phase, these children, along with a comparison group, were subjected to various linguistic, numerical and attentional tasks.

A perusal of literature suggests that differences between LD and

NLD children on language and number tasks are virtually limitless. LD children are very often characterised by many off-task behaviours such as faulty reproduction of verbal information in serial learning, poor organisation of material in free recall, inadequacy of retrieval from storage in recognition memory tasks, inability to make use of strategies such as clustering etc., not being able to recognise helpful patterns in number sequences, having difficulty in Norinder type arithmetical tasks where one has to do at least two or three, or even more steps of mental calculations and remember them all. They are also unable to concentrate upon the task for adequate amount of time, and are easily distracted.

The concept of subjective organisation in verbal or numerical tasks consists of many different operations that the concept can only be loosely defined. Tulving (1968), defining primary and secondary organisation, suggested that in tasks involving free-recall, one must distinguish category clustering from subjective organisation even though both exhibit strong organisational elements. Category clustering occurs when items of the same category as prepared by the experimenters are recalled together. In subjective organisation subjects impose their own organisation upon unrelated items on the basis of their previous experience and familiarity with the material. This distinction is useful, but it can be applied to only certain types of subjects and certain types of materials. Researches with handicapped children of various types indicate some other types of organisation. For instance, autistic children very often impose their own unique organisation on the material, be it linguistic or numerical. Frith (1970) presented word sequences to autistic, subnormal and normal children. She observed that the normal and subnormal children tended to recall the items according to the presentation pattern, but the autistic children very often imposed their own organisation. It was difficult to find any logical pattern in these organisations. Spitz, Goettler, and Webreck (1972) visually presented various types of pre-organised number sequences to subnormal children (mean I.Q. 62). They wanted to see whether these children could detect these patterns and make use of them in recall. They found that these children most often did not recognise the repetitive characteristics of the stimuli. Several studies have explored the sustained and selective attention processes in learning-handicapped children. Dainers *et al.* (1981) and Swanson (1980, 1981, 1983) examined vigilance performance in LD and NLD youngsters and all four studies reported significant differences between both the groups with LD children making significantly more errors of omission. Copeland and Wisniewski (1981) administered a speeded classification test to LD & NLD children in low, high and medium distraction conditions. Overall, LD children took longer to complete the tasks and made more errors.

The main purpose of the present investigation was to compare the performance of LD and NLD children on learning and recall of linguistic and numerical stimuli and to explore their attentional problems. Generally speaking most of the studies in this field have already concluded that LD children's performance is inferior to that of NLD children. Indeed, the very definition of LD children indicates that they are educationally underachievers; otherwise, being of average or above average intelligence, they would not be labelled as LD. Why then investigate an obvious fact where results are predictable? The reason is that the present authors were also interested to find out the sort of processing the LD and NLD children apply to serial recall and free recall. Of course, we were interested in their amount of recall in the correct order as well as correct recall irrespective of order. But we were also interested in exploring their errors of omission, errors of intrusion, and errors of importation. We also wished to find out about their sensitivity to proactive and retroactive interference.

Talking of sensitivity, recognition is generally considered to be more sensitive than recall. This alleged distinction was classified by Kinstsch (1970) who stated that recall involves a search process whereas recognition does not. But Tulving asserted that under specific test conditions, recall may be significantly superior to recognition (Tulving, 1968, Tulving and Thompson, 1971). Recognition has often been regarded as a sensitive measure of storage since subjects find it difficult to recall an item which they cannot recognise in their memory store. But Tulving maintains that recognition is not just passively identifying an item as 'new' or 'old'. In fact, contextual biasing and cue-dependent forgetting phenomena can demonstrate that retrieval has an active role in recognition tasks too. Mandler (1972) also concedes that some items may be recognised on the basis of familiarity but other items which might not be sufficiently familiar are subjected to a retrieval check by the subject. This familiarity factor also permitted us to treat the recognition responses in a non-traditional way.

According to Piaget, the general principles applicable to cognitive development of children, are also generally applicable to the development of arithmetical concepts as well. Even before children can deal meaningfully with numbers and computations, they have to have the comprehension of the meaning of numbers and computations. When the children learn operations, they can carry out these operations in thought as well as action. They also learn that operations are reversible. For instance, addition and subtraction are the same operations carried out in opposite directions. Inhelder (1968) stated that experiential deprivation early in life may lead to retardation or dyslexia, or aphasia, and this may hinder the proper development of logic structures. Inhelder was very much on the right track since very many learning disabled children are dyslexics and two major characteristics of dyslexia are reading problems and mental arithmetic problems. In the present investigation, the researchers employed simple arithmetical tasks which required mental calculations and memory of these calculations so that the mathematical skills of the LD children could be investigated and compared to those of the NLD Children. The present study also investigated the distractibility phenomenon in LD children. If the experimental task consists of certain irrelevant stimuli embedded in the task, do they recognise the irrelevance and ignore such cues, or do they get distracted by it and hence take longer time to complete their work? Also, does the presence of irrelevant stimuli increase their error count as compared to no-distraction tasks as well as compared with NLD children?

The major hypotheses of this investigation are as follows :

Hypothesis 1

The first, and the general hypothesis was that on all the tasks LD children shall give inferior performance than the NLD children. This, of course, is a rather expected result and there would be small chance of committing a Type II error.

Hypothesis 2

Conceding the assumption that LD children do poorly compared to the NLD children, our next hypothesis was that in serial recall (both written and oral) a primary effect should emerge; where as in free recall (both written and oral), a recency effect should emerge. These effects should be more prominent in the NLD group. But the LD group may exhibit different, more extreme, or random pattern. Also, the middle of the list items should be sensitive to both proaction and retroaction.

Hypothesis 3

Both LD and NLD children shall do better on a recognition task than on a recall task, but the NLD children shall have a higher level of performance.

Hypothesis 4

LD children would make less use of verbal learning strategies such as category clustering.

Hypothesis 5

LD children shall exhibit inferior performance on pattern recognition in number sequences in both visual and auditory conditions.

Hypothesis 6

LD children shall do poorly on mental arithmetic tasks, taking more time and making more errors.

Hypothesis 7

LD children's attention shall be easily distracted resulting in poorer performance compared with NLD children.

METHOD

PHASE I

Sample

Five Primary schools of Gorakhpur City were selected according to approachability. Two were superior and advantaged schools while three were of medium or average type. In these schools 15 class teachers of different sections of Class IV rated 606 children of their respective classes.

Step 1 : Ability and Potential Rating

The class teachers were requested to fill up LARS-I, i.e., Learning

Abilities Rating Scales-I (Prasad and Srivastava, 1992) for each child in the class. This is a very short 3-point, 15 item scale, each item relating to one area of ability (such as verbal, numerical, general knowledge etc.), of psychological processes (such as attention, memory, etc.) and social-emotional adjustment. The score range is from 0 to 45. The higher the score, the greater the ability. Of all the ratings, those below Q_1 (N = 151) were separated and the rest were discarded.

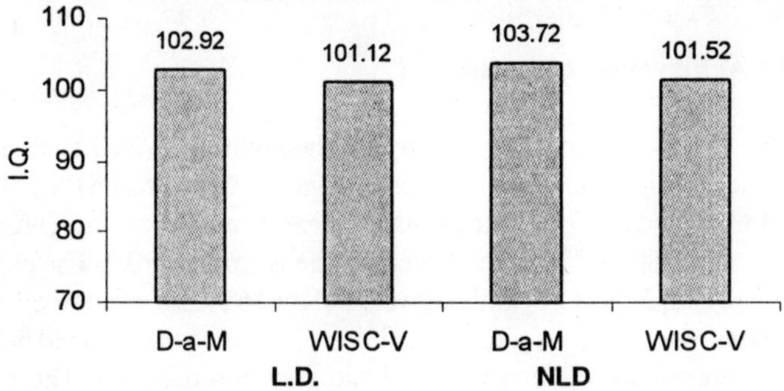

Fig. 18.1a : I.Q. of LD and NLD Children on Draw-a-Man and WISC-Verbal

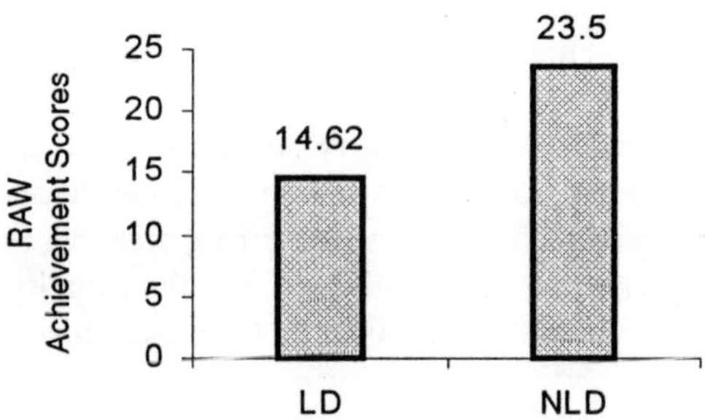

Fig. 18.1b : Average RAW Achievement Scores of LD and NLD Children

The teachers were then requested to rate these 151 children on LARS-II (Prasad and Srivastava, 1992), a 3-point, 45 items rating scale with randomly distributed 3 items for each of the 15 areas of LARS-II. Out of these ratings, children below the median point (N=75) were taken for further investigation and the rest were dropped.

Step 2: Intelligence Testing

The 75 children, 32 girls and 43 boys were given the Draw-a-Man

Performance Test of Intelligence originally devised by Goodenough (1926) and Indianised by Pramila Pathak (1956). The children within the normal I.Q. range (N = 65) were separated and rest were discarded.

The remaining 65 children, 28 girls and 37 boys were then given 4 tests of WISC-Verbal (Indianised by Srivastava and Prasad), and the scores were perorated according to the Manual and I.Q. obtained. Again, the children within the WISC-Verbal average range (85 to 115 I.Q.) were taken (N = 61) and the rest were dropped.

Step 3 : Achievement Assessment

These 61 children were then given the class-wise RAW, i.e. Reading-Arithmetic-Writing Achievement Test (Srivastava and Prasad) based upon the National Council of Educational Research and Training (NCERT) text books for Class IV. The total score range is from 0 to 30. The children scoring above Q3 (N = 17) and below Q1 (N = 16) were separated and the middle ones discarded. Of these 33 children 3 were again dropped because 2 and 1 were in two different schools situated at a distance. The rest 30 (15 above Q3 and 15 below Q1) were taken up for further investigation. They belonged to 3 schools, one superior, two average.

Step 4 : Clinical Information

Parents of these 30 children were approached to fill up a Clinical History Rating Scale (Srivastava and Prasad) requiring detailed information concerning with any specific occurrences during prenatal, perinatal and postnatal periods regarding their children. No abnormality was found anywhere and none of the children suffered from any sensory or organic handicaps.

Sample Selection Procedure

The sample selection criteria had been decided upon, after consulting a large amount of literature and before starting the actual investigation. The lengthy four-step process of sample selection was conducted in order to fulfil these criteria which are stated below :

1. The children must not be suffering from any sensory-motor problem, physical deformity, or mental retardation, or having an I.Q. below one standard deviation from average.

2. The children must not have suffered any fever and illness of serious consequence, or any traumatic accidents.
3. There must not be significant difference between the I.Q. of the LD and the NLD group. On Draw-a-Man, the average I.Q. of the NLD group was 103.72. Similarly, on WISC-Verbal, the LD children's average I.Q. was 101.2 and the NLD children's average I.Q. was 101.52 (Fig. 18.1a).
4. There must be a significant difference between the achievement scores of the LD and NLD children. The RAW (Reading, Arithmetic and Writing) average scores for LD youngsters were 14.12, 10.73 and 16.34; while for the NLD, they were 19.73, 15.67 and 19.74 respectively. The composite RAW average scores for LD and NLD groups were 13.73 and 18.38, in that order (Fig. 18.1b).

METHOD

PHASE II

Sample

The 15 LD students and 15 NLD students culled out after the lengthy screening of Phase I took part in this study (see Fig. 18.2).

Tasks

This investigation is concerned with the problems that LD children face while performing simple verbal and numerical learning tasks. The children have to learn as early as during elementary school years to receive, attend, comprehend, categorise, store, recognise, retrieve, repeat and operate upon all sorts of language and number stimuli. The tasks had to be such that these processes could be studied with their help. The selection of tasks was made keeping these objectives in mind. Some of the tasks are standard procedures, such as tasks of serial and free-recall, recognition and clustering. Some were modified and adapted, such as, pattern recognition in number series, or arithmetical tasks of 2 and 3 step mental calculations, or attention distraction tasks.

Materials

1. From the Hindi language text book of Class IV, 100 words of

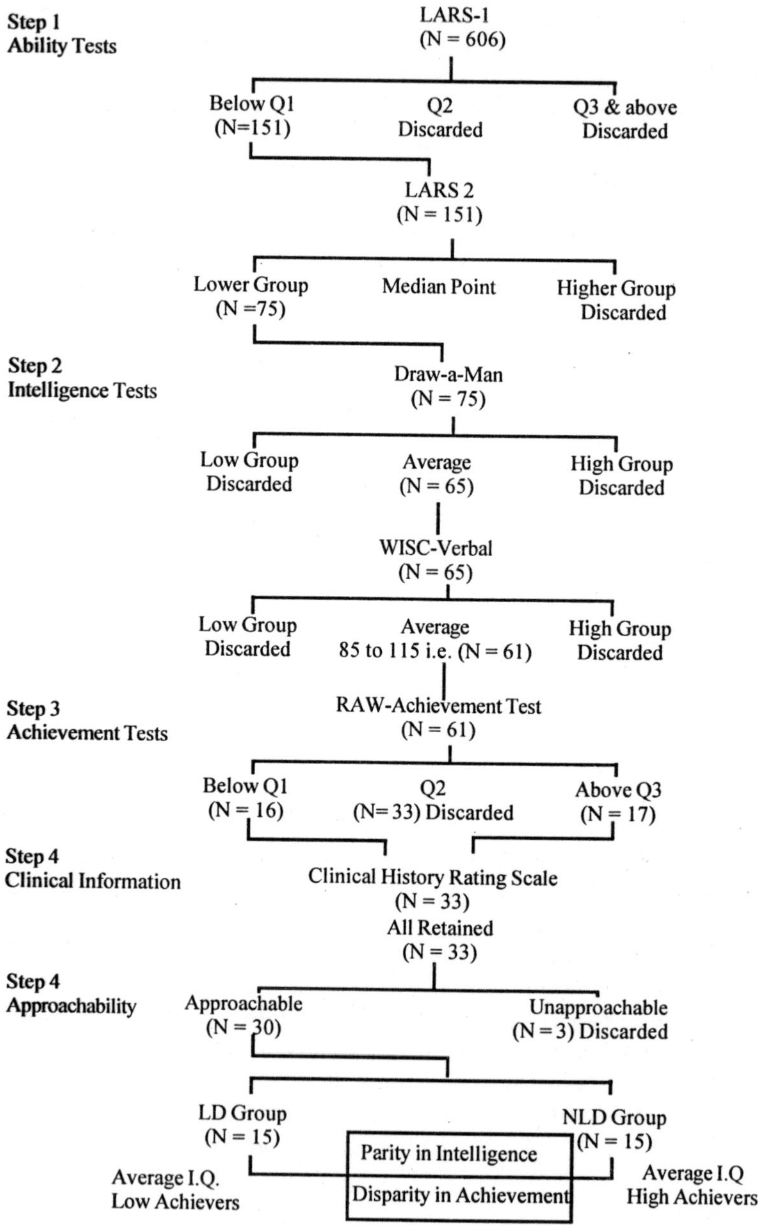

Fig. 18.2: Culling Out of the Sample

3 to 5 letters were selected out of first seven lessons. Each word was written with thick black pen on a 2 × 3 inches white card. Ten words packets were made, and their order was noted so that each subject may be presented with the words in the same order. From this repertoire words were taken as required.

2. A 20 words list was especially prepared which consisted of 5 words per category which were : fruits, birds, rivers and professions. These categories were selected with the purpose that one may not be confused with the other. Each word was written on separate cards as before. The cards were mixed in a random order, and this order was noted on answer sheets. The same words were also written on one inch square piece of paper. Then the papers were neatly folded twice.

3. This material consisted of 6 types of 6 digit numbers all written by thick black pen on white cards. Following 6 types of structures were used :

Structure type	*Example*
Same digit, all	444444
Same digit, pairs	449966
Couplet repetition	494949
Triplet repetition	496496
Mirror	496694
Random	495863

Five cards of each category, 30 in all were prepared and mixed randomly. The experimenters noted this order on answer sheet so that each subject could get the same order presentation. Another set of 30 was made similarly. One set was for auditory presentation, other for visual presentation.

4. Simple and small Norinder type fifteen arithmetical tasks were made according to the standard of Class III, plus the added task of keeping the result of one calculation in memory, then carrying out another calculation, then operating upon two products of the two tasks. For example

	9		7		82		61		187		240	
	– 3		+ 4		– 6		+ 3		+ 2		– 8	
=	____	+	= ____	= ?	= ____		– ____	= ?	= ____	+	= ____	= ?

5. Twelve simple arithmetical addition sums were prepared. Each sum was of two 5-digit numbers which the child had to add. These sums were written in black ink in the centre of 2×3 inches white cards. On any one corner of 3 of these cards, an attractive colourful picture of a flower, fruit, butterfly, bird, or any such thing was stuck. This was low external distraction condition. On 3 other cards, two attractive pictures were stuck on any two different corners. This was medium external distraction condition. On 3 other cards, these pictures were stuck on any three different corners. This was high external distraction condition, three cards were without any pictures, with only the sums upon them. This was the zero or no distraction condition. All these tasks were proximal external distracters tasks. All the cards were mixed to a random order and that order was noted on the response sheet.

For internal or embedded distracter tasks the same type of twelve 5-digit addition sums were prepared. In high distraction condition, four different colours were used in both the lines on three cards. Similarly, in medium and low distraction conditions respectively, three and two colours were interspersed randomly while writing the sums on three cards for each condition. In the zero or no distraction condition only black felt pen was used to write the sums on three cards. All these tasks were proximal internal distracters tasks. All the tasks were mixed to a random order and that order was noted on the response sheet.

Procedure

Study 1 : Serial Recall

Four conditions were generated by two variables, LD *vs.* NLD, and written *vs.* oral. Each subject was run in both written and oral conditions. All subjects were presented with the same list, in the same order. All subjects went through a practice session with 10 words. These words and data were then discarded.

Subjects were given a blank answer sheet which they initialled and dated. They were shown 10 new words at the rate of 4 seconds per word with the help of a metronome. Immediately after the list was over, the subjects wrote down as many words as they could, trying to follow the same order. They were allowed 3 minutes for this.

Then a new 10-word list was presented. This time the subjects orally recalled the words, in the serial order of presentation. Their responses were noted by one Experimenter in such a way that the subjects may not be able to see it. The subjects were given 5 minutes for it.

Study 2 : Free Recall

Again four conditions were generated as in Study 1. Two new lists were used, one for written, the other for oral responses, plus the 10 words list for practice trial. The study was conducted in the same way as Study 1 except that this time the subjects were free to recall in any order.

Study 3 : Recognition Memory

From the word bank, 20 new words were taken out, and 10 were presented to the subjects as previously. Then the remaining 10 words were included in the pack and mixed randomly. Now this 20 words list was presented as previously. The subjects were instructed that for each word the question was the same, "was this word present in the list just now shown to you first?" The subjects had to answer in "Yes" or "No". One experimenter presented the words, while the other noted the response.

Study 4 : Category Clustering

Specially prepared 4 category, 20 words list was presented both visually and aurally simultaneously, and written responses were taken.

Study 5 : Pattern Recognition

Two practice cards were aurally presented to the subjects and two visually. They were asked to repeat the number in exactly the same order. This data was discarded.

Of each of the 6 categories, 5 cards were prepared, 30 in all. Two such sets were made. The first set, in random order, was presented aurally, the second visually. The subjects repeated the stimuli. One experimenter did the presentation, the other noted the responses.

Study 6 : Mental Arithmetic

The subjects were given two practice trials. They were told that they have to do the first calculation mentally beginning with the first step. The answer of that had to be kept in mind while the second sum was calculated, also mentally. Then the answers of both were to be operated upon according to the sign given.

When the children understood the instructions, they were shown sums cards one-by-one. After doing the mental arithmetic covertly, the subjects vocalised their answers, and one experimenter noted it while the other changed the stimulus card. The subjects were given 3 minutes for each card. The subjects were not permitted to count on their fingers since that way they could hold first answer on the fingers. But they were not interrupted if they made lip movements as long it was done silently.

Study 7 : Attention

All the randomised sum-cards were pencilled at the back serially. First, the external distracters set was presented, then the internal distracters set. All the cards were presented to all the children in the same order. For each child a separate answer sheet was prepared on which the answers were to be written. There were no instructions or cues on the answer sheet except the serial numbers. The only verbal instructions given to the children were that they had to do some addition sums, quickly but carefully. In the end, all children wrote their names on the answer sheet.

Precaution

All these studies were carried out at intervals of some days so that the children may not become overtired, and also to minimise practice effect. Each child was tested individually.

RESULT AND DISCUSSION

This section is organised into three parts according to the type of abilities investigated, verbal, numerical and attentional. The tasks used herein are more or less traditional since the researchers' aim was to tap the very basic core of the problems faced by learning disabled children.

Verbal Learning and Memory

All the materials used in these experiments consisted of meaningful Hindi words from the text books of the subjects. Four types of tasks were given: serial recall, free recall, recognition memory and category clustering.

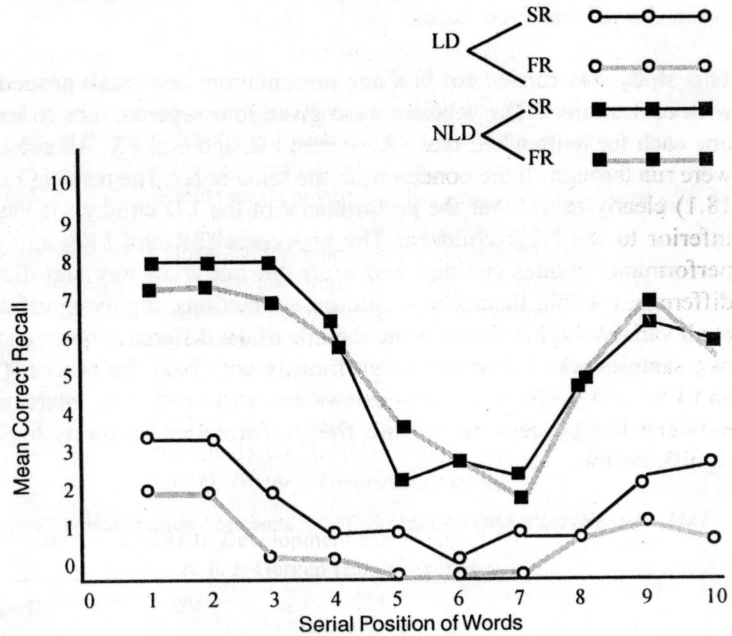

Fig. 18.3a : LD and NLD Children's WRITTEN responses on Serial Position of words in SR and FR conditions

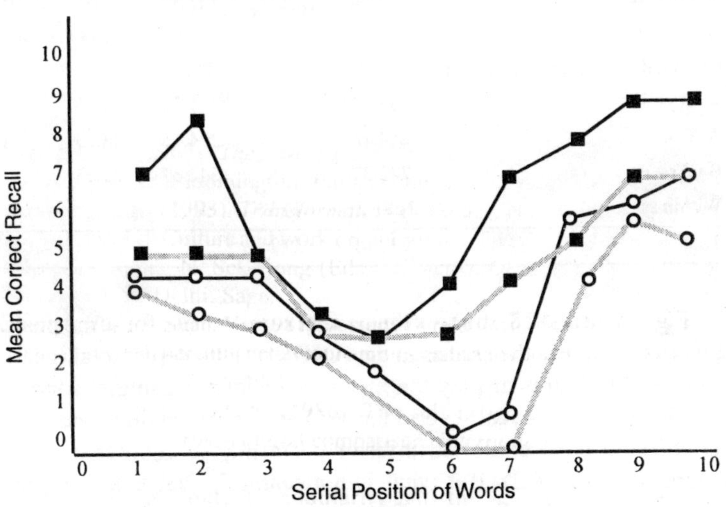

Fig. 18.3b : LD and NLD Children's ORAL responses on serial position of words in SR and FR conditions

Serial Recall and Free Recall

This study was carried out in a one presentation, one recall procedure with each subject. The subjects were given four separate lists to learn, one each for written SR, oral SR, written FR, and oral FR. All subjects were run through all the conditions in the same order. The results (Table 18.1) clearly reveal that the performance of the LD children is vastly inferior to the NLD children. The processes (SR and FR), and the performance modes (written and oral) did not show any significant differences within themselves. But the interactions, highly significant at all variables again demonstrate the role of the difference between the two samples which interacted significantly with both the process (SR and FR) and performance modes (written and oral). The interaction between the process factor and the performance factor is highly significant too.

Table 18.1: Summary ANOVA Table for 2×2×2 Repeated Measure Factorial Design

Source of Variance	*SS*	*df*	*Mss*	*F*	*Significance*
Source Variance					
Ass (LD & NLD)	234.92	1	234.92	21.85	.01
Bss (SR & FR)	37.29	1	37.29	3.48	n.s.
Css (Oral & Written Interaction)	16.21	1	16.29	1.51	n.s.
A×B ss	332.34	1	332.34	41.03	.01
A×C ss	254.16	1	254.16	23.73	.01
B×C ss	242.37	1	242.37	22.63	.01
Within ss	1211.21	113	10.7		
Total ss	2328.5	119			

Fig. 18.3a and 18.3b show the correct recall means for serial position of words. Whereas the results in the ANOVA table depict total recall by subjects, the figures display the mean recall for each single words.

These results reveal several factors besides the obvious one that the LD children have exhibited inferior performance compared to NLD children (Table 18.2). But what is noticeable is that both the groups have given better performance in written responses than oral ones. The reasons may be manifold. It may be the rather autocratic atmosphere of the classroom where children neither get much opportunity nor encouragement to vocalise. A harassed teacher trying to cope with a large number of children in a small and inadequately equipped classroom is more concerned with completing the assignment in the given time, and any participation from the students is bound to delay it. Besides, a classroom where children chatter lively may be interpreted as an unruly class by the administration whereas a classroom full of dumb children may be praised as orderly and disciplined. Another important reason may be that while writing the responses, children may have felt that they are working without interruption. They can quickly write three words, then nibble at their pencil for a while, then write another one or two words. But while speaking, they may have felt that they have to go on speaking without stopping, and any pause, short or long, may be interpreted not as an effort at retrieval but as forgetfulness or worse still, ignorance. This is sure to make the children nervous and tense, causing mental blocks or blankness, hence a poorer performance in oral conditions.

As is clear from Fig. 18.3a and 18.3b there is a marked difference between the serial recall and free recall response of LD children, but it is not so with the NLD children. One reason may be that the LD children are reported to be lacking in long-term-memory ability. As Faigel (1979), a clinical paediatrician, has stated, short- and long-term memory work like storing of valuables in an almirah in another room. First, the information is shifted to the room which is analogous to STM, and then to the almirah which represents the LTM. Retrieval takes the data of the almirah of LTM into the room of STM from where it is taken out and used. But if there is a block in LTM or STM due to lack of attention, inadequate learning, interference by new stimuli and many such variables, then this block acts as a lock and retrieval is hindered. Since the LD children very often exhibit lack of understanding and problem in comprehending the sequence of arrangements, it seems logical that their serial recall is poor.

The serial position effects as shown in Fig. 18.3a and 18.3b are another clear indication that serial learning is problematic for LD children. As the theory of serial learning goes, even the normal children show better performance on free recall. But the present data are not absolutely smooth. In written condition, the tail-end of correct retrieval in SR and FR shows highly significant difference, but very little difference at the beginning. The serial instructions probably forced the children to concentrate hard upon the sequence as well as the words themselves. Since the LD children are generally unable to attend to more than one or two instructions simultaneously, the effort to maintain the sequence is at the cost of creating blocks at comprehension, storage or retrieval. The NLD children also show better recall of the tail-end items in FR condition, but their SR is not so vastly inferior. The difference between the recall of early items in SR and FR conditions is also negligible for NLD children, that is, that when they paid more attention to words and less to sequence in the FR condition, even then the early items did not suffer from much forgetting compared to SR. But in oral response condition the story is somewhat different. The LD children exhibited a performance which is conducive to theory, that is, more recall of early items in SR condition, and more recall of tail-end items in FR condition, and significantly so. But with NLD children, better recall of early items in SR condition is there, but there is not much difference between SR and FR of tail-end items. Perhaps their better vocalising capacity, or better memory processing may have been the reason behind it. As expected, the middle items in all conditions by all groups have showed very poor recall.

Besides general correct recall, the researchers also looked into the types of errors. The omission errors represent the number of words from the stimulus list missing from the recall. The intrusion errors are the number of words recalled from the practice list. The importation errors show the number of words nowhere presented in the experiment but put in by the subjects from their vocabulary repertoire.

When one looks at the error factor (Table 18.2) all conditions reveal omission errors to be maximum. In SR conditions, omission errors show not much difference between written and oral conditions for both LD and NLD groups. But in FR condition there are more omission errors in oral conditions, again, may be due to children's inhibition while vocalising. The intrusion errors, though less than omission errors, show a similar pattern. The subjects produced words from practice list which was given them at the beginning of the experiment. As for the importation errors. LD children have shown very many such errors in all conditions than NLD children. Since these errors come from the children's personal vocabulary store and not from experimental material, one may be deceived in thinking that LD children at least have a vast storage of vocabulary. But a close perusal of the response sheets quickly dispels any such idea since a lot of words were repeated in LD children's response sheets, and some imported words were totally irrelevant such as 'yes', 'no', etc. (Fig. 18.4a, Fig. 18.4b and Fig. 18.4c).

Table 18.2: Mean of Three Types of Errors in Serial and Free Recall Conditions by LD and NLD Subjects

Types of errors	*LD (N=15)*				*NLD (N=15)*			
	SR		*FR*		*SR*		*FR*	
	Written	*Oral*	*Written*	*Oral*	*Written*	*Oral*	*Written*	*Oral*
Omission	4.17	4.15	2.82	3.50	2.50	2.67	2.00	2.83
Intrusion	2.50	2.52	1.85	2.50	1.50	1.33	1.05	1.50
Importation	1.53	2.48	1.48	0.90	0.40	0.50	0.50	0.82
$\bar{X}$ Total Errors	8.20	9.15	6.15	6.90	4.40	4.50	3.55	5.15

Recognition Memory

This study too, was carried out with the subject's familiar text book as source for stimulus words. The presentation order of words on the original list (10 words) and the test list (10 old+10 new words) was same for all the subjects.

The first *prima facie* analysis of the data consisted of frequency of correct and error responses, and a chi-square value of 0.758 which was not significant gave an impression that both the LD and NLD youngsters were rather homogeneous, at least on this variable. Downie and Starry (1977) declare that the assumption behind the use of chi-square is that cell frequencies are 'mutually exclusive and exhaustive', that is, each score may be assigned to only one cell. These authors specifically forbid the use of chi-square for data such as this one where a 'yes' response may be 'correct' if it is given to an old list word, and incorrect if it is given to a new list word. Conversely, a 'No' response is incorrect if it is given to an old list word, but correct if it is given to a new list word.

During recent years many authors have advocated the application of signal detection theory (SDT) for recognition memory experiments (Banks, 1970; Egan, 1958; Lockhart and Murdock, 1970; Wickelgren and Norman, 1966). Snodgrass, Volvovitz, and Walfish (1972) have reviewed many such studies and have come to the conclusion of the appropriateness of these approaches. According to them, the applicability of signal detection model for recognition memory data is determined by whether or not these data follow the characteristic shape of the receiver operating characteristic (ROC) curve predicted by the SDT. This may be done by placing the hit rates (saying 'yes' or 'old' to an old item)

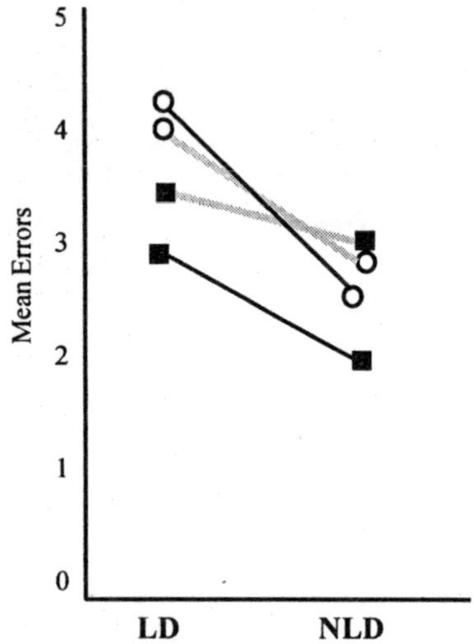

Fig. 18.4a : Written & Oral <u>Omission</u> errors by LD & NLD subjects in SR & FR conditions

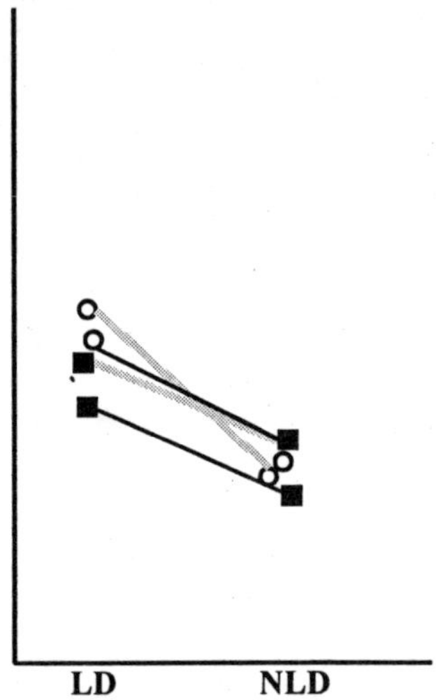

Fig. 18.4b : Written & Oral <u>Intrusion</u> errors by LD & NLD subjects in SR & FR conditions

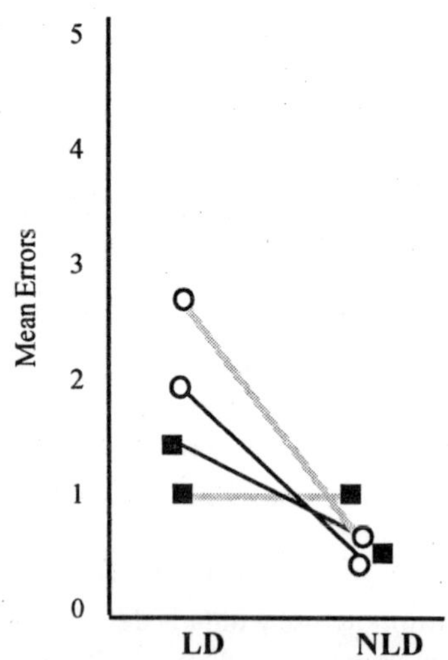

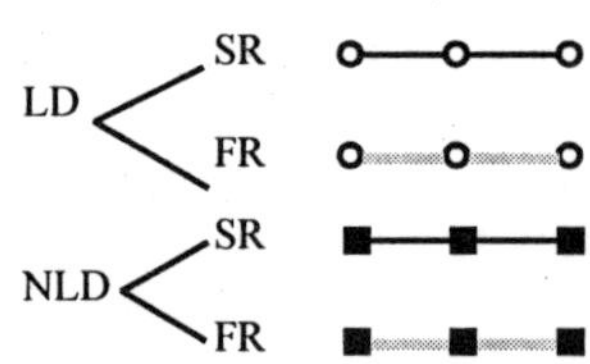

Fig. 18.4c : Written & Oral <u>Importation</u> errors by LD & NLD subjects in SR & FR conditions

against false alarm rates (saying 'yes' or 'old' to a new item). The curve obtained by such plottings have come to be known as memory operating characteristics (MOC) curves.

Because it is difficult to run the same subjects repeatedly in a memory experiment, MOC curves are usually derived from confidence rating data. But our subjects were not able to follow the confidence rating instructions correctly, so we had to abandon that data, wait for some days and start again with fresh word lists, Because of this, instead of combining the data across subjects, we had to plot individual subjects. And if the subjects gave only one of the two responses, 'yes' (old) or 'no' (new), then their response bias also had to be considered. Because, only the hit rate (the probability of correctly saying YES to an old item from first list) or the false alarm rate (the probability of incorrectly saying YES to a new item) is not sufficient. Subjects who have a YES response bias will have a high hit rate, but also a high false alarm rate, whereas subjects having a No response bias will have a low false alarm rate but also a low hit rate (see Fig. 18.5a and 18.5b).

To correct such bias difference, Woodworth (1938) advised to

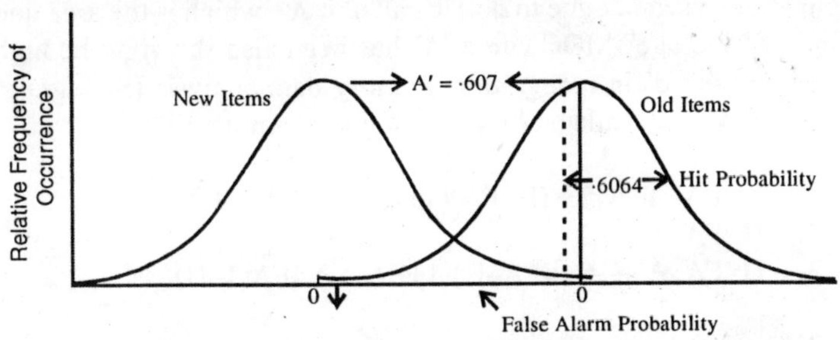

Fig. 18.5a : Distribution of hit and false alarm probabilities of LD subjects

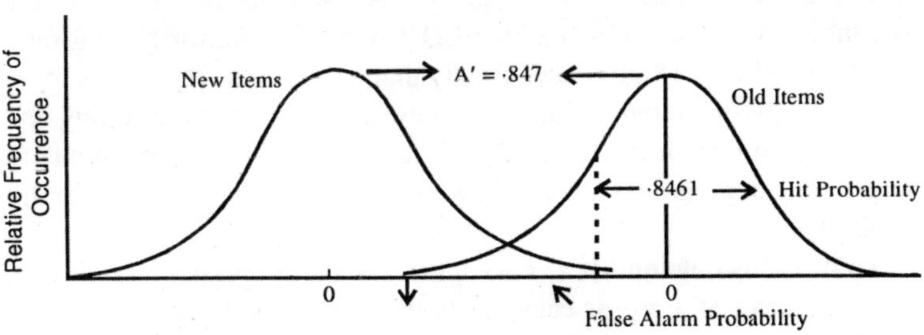

Fig. 18.5b : Distribution of hit and false alarm probabilities of NLD subjects

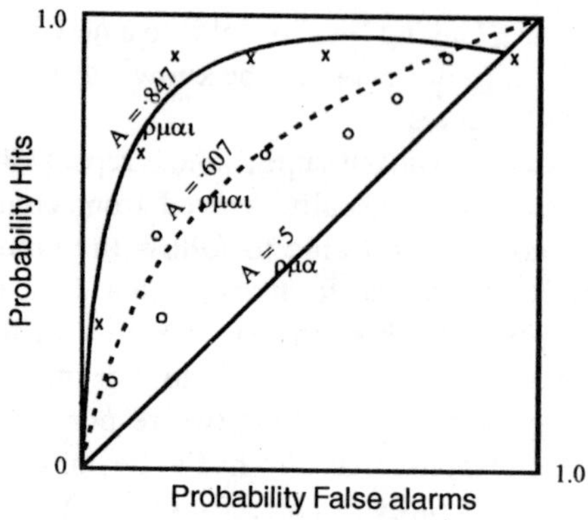

Fig. 18.6 : MDC curves for LD (---) and NLD (—) subjects constructed from the cumulated probabilities and ratings for old and new stimulus words.

subtract the false alarm rate (FA) from the hit rate (H). This technique remained classic for several years. But since some subjects produce a hit rate of 1.0, and a false alarm rate of 0, a, d′ score cannot be calculated by this method. Pollock (1970) devised an alternative measure which is a nonparametric analogue to d′. He called it A′, which is the area under a kind of "average" MOC curve. A′ has been also shown to be highly correlated with d′ in recognition memory data analysis (Snodgrass *et al.*, 1972). A′ is calculated by the following formula :

1. H>FA, A′ = .5 + (H–FA)(1+H–FA)/4H(1–FA)
2. H=FA, A′ = .5
3. H<FA, A′ = .5 – (FA–H)(1+FA–H)/4FA(1–H)

This formula was adopted for analysing the individual data in this study, and the A′ for LD group was .607, whereas for NLD group it was .847. As the YES and NO responses are assumed to be normally distributed, the Z-scores pertaining to these A′s were located in the normal curve table and found to be 0.27 for LD group and 1.02 for NLD group. Fig. 18.5a and Fig. 18.5b depict clearly that a smaller a′ represents more uncertainty about an item being old or new, hence more overlapping and less hit probability for the LD group. Whereas the NLD group which has a larger A′, depicts less uncertainty comparatively, and a higher hit probability.

To plot this data on MOC curve, the 20-words test list was divided into five blocks of 4 words each for both the groups. Each block's hits and false alarms were socialised and cumulated and then were converted into proportions by dividing each cumulated frequencies by the total number of each cumulated frequency (20 in each case). When the frequencies are cumulated and converted into probabilities, the last set for hits and false alarms always equalled 1.00 for both the LD and the NLD group. These probabilities are then used to plot the MOC curve as shown in Fig. 18.6 The area under the MOC curve matches the theoretical probability of a correct response in a two-alternative forced-choice experiment (Green & Sweets, 1974).

Category Clustering

The results of this study surprisingly showed near normal distribution in both LD and NLD groups with the LD group of course, showing inferior performance. But the authors were more interested in the clustering phenomena rather than in total recall. Bousfield and Sedgewick's (1944) first study depicted the cluster phenomena but posed several quantification problems. Some years later, Bousfield (1951, 1953) again studied the phenomena and this time found a unique way of quantifying the data. The present study follows his techniques.

The items (20 in all, 5 per category) were arranged in random order and presented both aurally and visually one at a time. This single input phase was immediately followed by a recall period for which the subjects were given seven minutes each.

The results showed that the total number of recall varied widely from subject to subject. The range for LD group was from 5 to 11 with a mean of 6.73. The NLD group's range was from 6 to 17 and the mean was 11.47. Now obviously, the more the number of items recalled by a subject, the higher the probability of clustering. Therefore each subject's total number of item repetitions within a category was divided by the total number of items recalled by that subject. This cluster ratio formula follows:

$$CR = r/N$$

where,

CR = Cluster ratio

r = total number of repetition within a category

N = total number of items recalled

This Bousfield formula was used for all LD and NLD subjects individually. The range of CR for LD group was from .28 to .67, the mean CR being .49. For the NLD group the range was tremendously high, from .28 to .91, and the mean was .67. Even though there are obvious differences between the two groups, the researchers also wanted to find out that on the chance basis of random-order sequences of output from N items what extent of clustering might be expected, because in the absence of this theoretical chance ratio, it is impossible to interpret either .49 or .67.

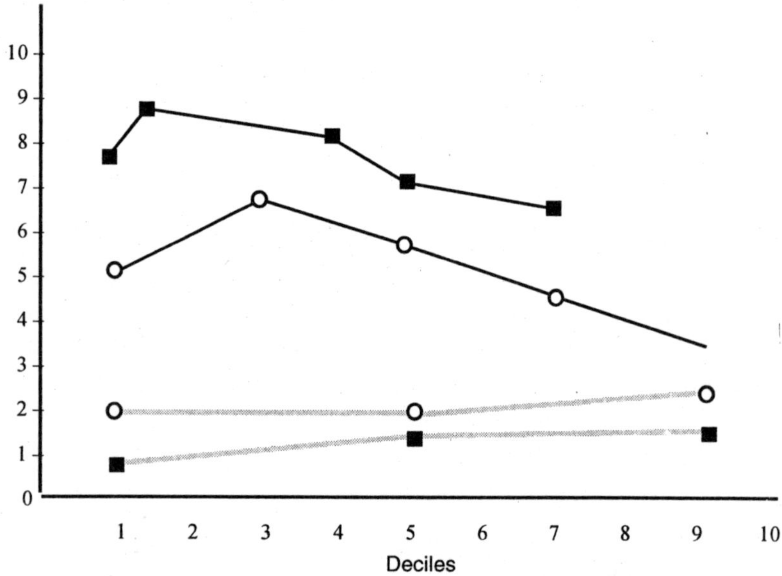

Fig. 18.7 : Clustering for "real" LD (O—O), "artificial" LD (O—O) real NLD (■—■), and "artificial" NLD (■—■) subjects successive tenths of response outputs

Therefore, the authors again applied Bousfield's idea of an artificial experiment. The 10 old and 10 new words that were written on separate bowl and thoroughly shaken. Then for each subject, the same-size slips of paper and neatly folded twice, were put in an empty bowl. Again same number of slips were drawn one by one and their contents noted against the responses of that very subject. The slips were again neatly folded, mixed, and the process was repeated for the second, third and all the subjects in both the groups. Thus, each real subject was yoked with an artificial subject. The critical ratio for every single repetition case was calculated for the artificial subjects whenever there was a repetitive clustering. In fact, there was very little clustering in this chance artificial experiment. For artificial subjects yoked with LD subjects the range of CR was from .16 to .22, and the mean was .19. For the NLD subject's artificial counterpart, the range of CR was from .11 to .23, and the mean was .17 (Table 18.4).

It was also clear from the raw data that the clustering responses were high in early phase of the response outputs of individual subjects and slowed down later. In order to compare this with the artificial data all 30 (15LD+15NLD) response output cluster ratio were fractionated into decides and plotted with deciles of artificial data (Fig. 18.7).

The curves in the graph clearly demonstrate that the real subjects,

Table 18.3: Cluster Ratio of Real and Artificial LD and NLD Subjects

No. of clusters	*LD*		*NLD*	
	Real	*Artificial*	*Real*	*Artificial*
1.	.50	.18	.77	.08
2.	.64	.22	.91	.23
3.	.67	.18	.91	.13
4.	.55	.16	.88	.11
5.	.55	.22	.87	.22
6.	.44		.80	.13
7.	.45		.82	
8.	.33		.70	
9.	.28		.67	
10.			.60	
11.			.63	
12.			.44	
13.			.44	
14.			.28	
15.			.33	

Table 18.4: Mean Cluster Ratios for Real LD Group and Artificially Yoked LD Group, and Real NLD Group and Artificially Yoked NLD Group

	LD		*NLD*	
	Real (Empirical)	*Artificial* (Chance)	*Real* (Empirical)	*Artificial* (Chance)
Mean	.49	.19	.67	.17

both LD and NLD, have exhibited more clustering during the early output phase and show a gradual decrease at tail ends, whereas the chance artificial curves do not show any logical pattern at all.

NUMERICAL ABILITIES

Pattern Recognition

In all conditions, all the response sequences were recorded by one experimenter while the other presented the stimuli. Total correct recall percentages are shown in Table 18.5. It is clear that not only the LD youngsters again have given poorer performance, both LD and NLD have done not so well in auditory conditions.

Table 18.5: Per cent Correct Recall of Pattern Recognition in Number Stimuli by LD and NLD Children

Stimulus Patterns	*LD*		*NLD*	
	Auditory	*Visual*	*Auditory*	*Visual*
1. Same	90	95	95	100
2. Pair	70	90	75	100
3. Couplet	60	80	60	85
4. Triplet	42	80	40	88
5. Mirror	30	55	35	60
6. Random	16	50	15	55

Besides correct recall, three other types errors were also calculated: omissions, substitutions, and wrong order. The LD group has omitted a large number of digits. It would seem that they have been unable to grasp that all stimuli consist of 6 digits. The NLD children have made much less omission errors, grasping the size of the stimuli. Specially in the visual condition the NLD children have committed significantly few omission errors. In the substitution errors the LD children have committed almost as much errors in auditory condition as in visual condition. But the NLD children have exhibited a surprisingly high rate of errors in auditory condition. This may have been due to their paying more attention to visual stimuli. In the wrong order errors, the LD children have committed somewhat more errors in auditory condition than in visual condition, but the NLD group again has committed a remarkably higher rate of errors in the auditory condition.

Table 18.6: Pattern Recognition — Percent Errors

Stimulus Pattern	*LD Group*					
	Omission		*Substitution*		*Wrong order*	
	Aud.	*Vis.*	*Aud.*	*Vis.*	*Aud.*	*Vis.*
1. Same	4	2	3	1	3	2
2. Pair	17	3	6	3	7	4
3. Couplet	27	13	5	4	8	3
4. Triplet	28	14	12	3	18	3
5. Mirror	42	18	15	12	13	15
6. Random	58	23	14	15	12	12
	NLD Group					
	Omission		*Substitution*		*Wrong order*	
	Aud.	*Vis.*	*Aud.*	*Vis.*	*Aud.*	*Vis.*
1. Same	1	0	2	0	2	0
2. Pair	5	0	9	0	11	0
3. Couplet	6	2	19	5	15	8
4. Triplet	8	4	22	2	30	6
5. Mirror	9	4	32	17	24	19
6. Random	12	5	35	23	38	17

Mental Arithmetic

The aim of this task was not primarily to judge the simple numerical ability only, but also the ability to do a piece of arithmetical task, keep them all in memory, and do all this mentally without the help of paper and pencil or even fingers. Though the sums were simple but three difficulty levels were created by using 2-digit, 3-digit and 4-digit numbers. The results are in Table 18.7.

Table 18.8: Percent Correct Responses on Three Levels of Arithmetical Tasks by LD and NLD Students

Groups	*LD*			*NLD*		
Difficulty levels	*Low*	*Medium*	*High*	*Low*	*Medium*	*High*
% Correct	20	12	7	65	30	18

As these data were in percentages, after calculating the chi-square the resultant had to be multiplied by 15/100 since there were 15 sums in all, 3 of each difficulty level. At the low difficulty level the obtained chi-sq. was 0.378, just below the criterion level of 0.384 at .05 level. The other two, 0.155 and 0.283, were not significant. One can only deduce that the simple arithmetical sums enabled the NLD to score higher, but the rest were quite difficult for them also even though they were somewhat ahead of their LD counterparts.

ATTENTIONAL PROBLEMS

Proximal External and Embedded Distraction

Two types of tasks were presented. The tasks themselves required the same amount of cognitive demand but they were presented with two types of distracters : proximal external, and proximal embedded; and with four levels of distraction : zero, low, medium and high. The first dependent variable was whether the answers were right or wrong (Table 18.8). After that the answer sheets were scanned for four major types of arithmetical errors : (i) wrong operation, (ii) computational error, (iii) defective algorithm, and (iv) random response. None of the children in either group committed a wrong operation, that is, they all recognised the plus sign correctly and did the addition work. The distribution of the rest of the errors is in Table 18.9.

Table 18.8: Percent Correct Solutions to Arithmetical Sums with Four Types Each of External and Internal Distractors by LD and NLD Subjects

Levels of Distraction	*LD*		*NLD*	
	Extnl. Distr.	*Intnl. Distr.*	*Extnl. Distr.*	*Intnl. Distr.*
Zero	66	66	100	100
Low	66	33	66	66
Med	33	33	33	66
High	0	33	33	33

To find out whether the groups were homogeneous in their performance, a chi-square test was applied resulting into chi-sq. p>68.09 at 9df which was significant at .001 level. Presence of distractors definitely hindered a task for both the LD and the NLD children. The more the distractors, the more the errors. Besides this, the role of external distractors has been more disturbing than embedded distractors.

Table 18.10: Percent Errors of Calculation, Algorithm and Random Mistakes on External-Internal Distractional Arithmetic Tasks by LD and NLD

Types of Random / Dis-tractors	*LD*						*NLD*					
	Extnl. Distr.			*Intnl. Distr.*			*Extnl. Distr.*			*Intnl. Distr.*		
	Calcu-lation	*Algo-rithm*	*Random*	*Calcul-ation*	*Algo-rithm*	*Random*	*Calcula-tion*	*Algori-thm*	*Random*	*Calcula-tion*	*Algorithm*	*Random*
Zero	17	9	8	18	10	6	0	0	0	0	0	0
Low	19	10	5	44	13	10	18	10	6	16	9	9
Med	41	16	10	48	12	7	40	16	11	16	10	8
High	62	24	14	53	8	6	47	11	9	45	12	10

There is a general consensus that learning-problems children very often suffer from attentional problems as well. Not only these children display more problem in attention demanding task, but different types of handicapped children exhibit different types of attentional problems. Sustained attention tasks like vigilance, reaction time etc. have been shown to have different amounts of cognitive demands. In tasks of minimum cognitive demands such as to detect a change in the brightness of light or loudness of tone LD children have been reported to make more errors (Goldberg and Konstantareas, 1981; Swanson, 1980, 1993). In tasks requiring greater cognitive demands, such as Continuous Performance Tasks which require children not only to recognise the letter, or word, or numbers, but to understand its meaning and operation, and to retain in memory for several records, at the same time paying attention to another stimulus, normal children also have been found to have some problems, LD children more than them, and hyperactive children most of all (Douglas and Peters, 1979).

In the area of selective attention, two of the most popular tasks used with problem children are tasks related to incidental learning and distraction. Distractible children are over-sensitive to the multitude of stimuli at any given time, and thus they tend to respond to task-irrelevant stimuli to a greater extent than the control subjects.

CONCLUSIONS

The major objective of this study was to gain more insight into the learning styles of LD youngsters as compared to their NLD counterparts. The children were tested upon several types of tasks and the researchers tried to make out some meaning of the results.

Besides the very much expected result about the poorer performance of the LD children, it was revealed that NLD children also were rather behind where oral responses were concerned though not as much as the LD children. To integrate the concept of learning disability with verbal skills is rather a perplexing task. However, it is a task of great importance since a vast majority of learning disabled children are labelled so because of their verbal and language disabilities. Stanovich (1986) pointed out the correlations obtained between I.Q. and reading ability. In primary classes this correlation is from .3 to .5, but by the time the children reach the secondary classes, the correlation between I.Q. and reading ability increase to from .6 to .75. But to learning disabled children these relationships do not apply because they have severely depressed performance on reading ability and virtually normal I.Q. scores. Why is it so?

There is some research in the reading literature that suggests that LD subjects are deficient in naming various stimuli such as letters, words, figures, pictures, etc. (Denckla and Rudel, 1976). The other problem is the type of task, whether it is continuous or discrete, serial or free. According to Stanovich (1983) continuous tasks that involve serial naming of a list of items yield less accuracy in comparison to discrete tasks.

Stanovich (1986) advances two general explanations. First is that learning disabled children are deficient in phonological processes. They take longer time in mapping letters into phonetic segments and then combine them to make a word. This slow process hinders their acquisition, and also storage and recall. Stanovitch's other hypothesis is that learning disabled children are "less prone to employ the active, playful, memorisation strategies (e.g., verbal rehearsal, imagery, and elaboration) that have been shown to facilitate memory performance". Torgesen (1978-1979) has also suggested that LD children display inferior short-term-memory performance due to deficits in "both phonological processing and strategic planning".

Other researchers have also shown that learning disabled children while performing a verbal task, are less likely to employ a variety of cognitive strategies that facilitate memory performance (Bauer, 1972; Torgesen, 1978-1979, 1980; Wong, 1978). For instance research findings such as depressed primary effects in the serial-position-curves of LD children indicate that they are less likely to use a verbal rehearsal strategy properly. But Torgesen also opines that in several cases all that these LD children require is very clear and detailed instruction alongwith some practice, because to some extent the strategies have been found to be within their capabilities, only if they are properly taught to use them.

The factor of strategies brings us to the strategy of category clustering in free recall. Learning disabled subjects have been reported to display marked performance deficits on such memory tasks. In a study by Foster and Gavelek (1983), learning disabled children, compared to nondisabled children displayed strong indicators of not making use of strategic functioning on several measures including item differentiation and category clustering. Such tasks minimally require maintenance rehearsal while the cue is processed and differential encoding is being carried out. Freston & Drew (1974) and Parker, Freston, and Drew (1976) have found that learning disabled children do not employ the category-clustering strategy. Though LD children are not to be equalled with unschooled children but a very detailed and complex study by Cole *et al.* (1971), as quoted by Dash & Mohan (1996) states, besides many other results, that all age groups of Liberian children whose language is Kpelle, whether they were educated or uneducated, learned clusterable lists fairly easily, why the schooled LD children are unable to do show poses a problem for further research.

The pervasive verbal deficit of LD children could also be the result of a very general lack of linguistic awareness. They also have problem in dealing with complex syntactic structures in a spoken language. Vogel (1974) found that LD children performed poorly in comparison to NLD children on seven out of nine measures of oral language syntactic ability. Newcomer and Magee (1977) examined seven different aspects of oral verbal behaviour. All seven revealed that LD children's performance was inferior to NLD children, and significantly so on six of them. Siegel and Ryan (1984) also administered a series of language tasks to LD and NLD children and found the group to be inferior on oral-cloze, oral sentence-error location and many others. Thus, the research in this area has now gone beyond merely the "holding" operation in memory to areas of study strategy and cognitive planning.

Recognition memory tasks with learning disabled children do not seem to be very popular with the researchers. Dash and Mohanty (1996) present a detailed review of recognition-memory cross-cultural experiments using schooled *versus* non-schooled children of various age-groups but most of these studies have used pictorial stimuli. Cole *et al.* (1977) used for their stimulus material orally presented words and visually presented objects to their Kpelle-speaking Liberian subjects of 6-8, 10-14 years old and adults. The overall correct recognition was almost identical between the schooled and non-schooled all age groups, but the schooled subjects recognised more words whereas the non-schooled subjects recognised more subjects. Rogoff (1977a) also found that sixty children of Guatemala school aged nine years, when presented with four memory tests of recognition and recall, displayed better performance on visual stimuli and lower on verbal stimuli. Hall (1972) found that Columbian school children easily recognised the old words while the unschooled children falsely recognised the new words as old.

The signal detection model for recognition memory starts with an assumption that the stimulus items lie along a continuum of memory strength or familiarity. Some old items are highly familiar, some have medium familiarity, and some are only slightly familiar. It is the same with the new items, some are of high familiarity, some of medium, and some are of low familiarity. It is also assumed that both the new and old items' familiarity distribution will overlap. The old items distribution corresponds to the signal plus noise distribution, the new items distribution corresponds to the noise alone distribution.

Of course, the average familiarity of old items is expected to be higher than average familiarity of the new items. Since the subjects are intrinsically uncertain whether a particular word is old or new, they base their decision upon the degree of familiarity. They decide upon a high threshold for old items and a high threshold for new items and respond as OLD or NEW only when the items cross any of these thresholds. But when an item crosses neither old nor new threshold, the subjects guess according to their bias towards YES or NO responses. This bias is influenced by subject's liberal or conservative criteria, experimenter manipulated schedules of payoff, and the type of task. Thus, it may be said with justification (Snodgrass, 1983) that the data of a recognition memory task should be analysed by the signal detection method.

The results of pattern-detection study are somewhat disturbing. The easiest of the stimuli, same numbers (e.g. 666666, or 444444) was expected to obtain a hundred per cent correct response but the LD group did not display as much. Either they did not correctly guess that in each case the number. of digits was always 6, and they stopped after 4 or 5 repetitions, or they were counting wrong internally. In occasional subjects there was also a tendency to introduce a new digit such as 6667 or 88889. The remarkable thing was that this new digit was always at the tail-end, and it was the number after the previous ones. Probably the subjects, due to their conditioning with counting numbers serially, made this error.

When the stimulus item was a difficult one, such as a random order number, the LD children performed really poorly in both visual and aural conditions. But that was expected. In pairs the LD children did somewhat better than in couplet or triplet. The reason probably was that in pairs the chunks were 22-55-33, in couplets they were of same size but the chunk had two different digits : 25-25-25; whereas triplets had extra difficulty level : there were though only two chunks, but they were of larger size, and the chunk had 3 different digits 253-253. Since the learning disabled children are also deficient in left-right, first-last perception, even the visual presentation was also not of much help.

Particular weakness in arithmetic techniques is another weak nerve of the LD children. Reasoning tasks have been found to be difficult for them in several studies. They can compute a simple arithmetic sum, but to do it mentally, and then to hold its product in memory, then go on to do another calculation, and then do a third operation with the products of both the calculations was expecting rather too much from them. If they could "hold" the one in memory, the other slipped. In short, their memory capacity was not sufficient. But surprisingly, there was not much difference as to whether the first computational result had slipped off, or the second one.

None of them did any wrong operations, but many did miscalculations. They also followed wrong algorithms. Instead of adding the summations of the two sums, they sometimes added the first rows of the two sums, then the second rows of the two sums. There were also times when after a wrong algorithm, they probably became confused, and started giving random responses as if they have to get it over with.

The NLD children also made mistakes but much less in comparison to the LD ones. Their pattern detection performance was vastly superior, though in mental arithmetic they also stumbled occasionally.

The proximal distractors of a task are close at hand. A large number of studies have been done in this area. Radosh and Gittelman (1981) gave 300 arithmetic sums on a teaching machine to normal and hyperactive children. The sums on the screen were surrounded with none, one, two or three distractive pictures. Results showed that the two groups did not differ in total number of correct responses, but the normal group made most of their mistakes in high distraction condition whereas the hyperactive group showed a progressive increase of errors with increase in distraction. Samuels (1967) had groups of poor and good reading ability children read a story which contained 50 different words. Half of the children in each group read only the story, whereas the other half had the story illustrated with pictures related with the text. Upon good readers these two conditions did not make any significant difference. But poor readers were distracted with picture and read less words.

If the distractor is embedded in the task, the results depend upon the type of the distractor. Zentall and Colleagues (1978) used colour distractions in learning spelling, but did not find any significant deteriorating effect. The tasks that are more cognitively demanding, such as arithmetical sums or concept formation, sowed different results. Copeland and Wisniewiski (1981) presented cards with different figures in different colours or numbers, and the children were asked to sort them on some particular attribute. In this long and complex study, overall the LD children took longer time and made more errors relative to the NLD group.

These studies indicate that LD children are not distractible under all conditions, but the distractibility episodes are mainly task or situation specific.

To integrate the concept of learning disability with psychological theories of learning, memory and attention is a difficult and complex task. Attempts are being made to explore all the possible variables, and a plethora of studies are being carried out. The areas is full of new research ideas, interesting and instructive.

The main purpose of the present investigation was to compare the performance of LD and NLD children on several types of curriculum-related tasks and to gain more insight into their strengths and weakness. But the final goal is not reached yet. The researchers shall feel that they have really done some service to society, when they are able to diagnose LD children early in life, since the sooner they are given special attention, the better it is; and also when special remedial curriculum and individual education programmes can be developed for such children who are of average intelligence but low achievers.

Acknowledgements

The authors wish to thank all the headmasters, teachers and most specifically the students of the schools where data were collected. Arun Kumar Singh, Sunita Yadav and Zaintunnishan are also thanked for their help in data collection and scoring.

References

Brayan, T.H. (1978). *Learning Disabilities.* Paediatric Annuals, 7, 31-44.

Clement, S.D. (1974). *A New Look a Learning Disabilities, "Introduction to Educational & Medical Management"*, (Ed.) Tarnopol, L., Springfield, Illinois, Charles C. Thomas.

Cruickshank, W. (1972). Some Issues facing the Field of Learning Disabilities, *Journal of Learning Disabilities*, 5, 330-338.

Dash, U.N. and Mohanty, M.M. (1996). *Schooling and Cognition*, Centre of Advanced Study in Psychology, Bhubaneswar, Shovan.

Goldstein, K. (1936). The Modification of Behaviour Consequent to Cerebral Lesions. *Psychiatric Quarterly*, 10, 586-610.

Gottlieb, M.I., Zinkus, P.N. Bradford, L.J. (1979), *Current Issues in Developmental Paediatrics and Learning Disabled Children*, Grune & Stratton Inc., New York.

Hallanhan, D.P. and Kaufman, J.M. (1976). *Exceptional Children : Introduction to Special Education*, (2nd Edn.), Englewood Cliffs, N.J., Prenticehall.

Hulse, S.H., Deese, J. & Egeth, H., (1975). *The Psychology of Learning*, N.D., McGraw-Hill Koga Kusha Ltd.

Johnson, D. & Myklebust, H., (1967). *Learning Disabilities : Educational Principles and Prachies*, N.Y. Grune & Stratton.

Kephart, N.C. (1960). *The Slow Learner in the Class-Room*, Columbus, Ohio, Charles E. Merri II.

Kirk, S.A. (1962). *Educating Exceptional Children* (3rd Edn.), Boston, Houghton Mifflin Co.

Kirk, S.A. and Bateman, B. (1962). *Diagnosis and Remediation of Learning Disabilities*. Exceptional children, 29, 73-78.

Lerner, J.W., (1981), *Children with Learning Disabilities : Theories, Diagnosis, and Teaching Strategies*, Boston, Houghton Mifflin.

McDonald, G. and Mackay, D.N., (1977). Pattern Detection by Mongol & Non-Mongol Subnormals, *Br. J. Psychol.*, 68, 223-228.

Mercer, C.D. (1979). *Children and Adolescents with Learning Disabilities*, Columbus, Charles E. Merri II.

Myklebust, H. (1968). Learning Disabilities : Definition and Overview, In H. Myklebust (Ed.), *Progress in Learning Disabilities*, (Vol. I), N.Y., Grune & Stratton.

Piaget, J. and Inheljer, B. (1956). *The Child's Conception of Space*, Routledge and Kegan Paul.

Prasad, S. (1991). Identification of Learning Disabled Children and their Behavioural Correlates, Unpublished Doctoral Dissertation, D.D.U. Gorakhpur University, Gorakhpur, India.

Prasad, S. and Srivastava, A.N. (1992). *Perpetual-Motor Problems in Learning Disabled and Non-Learning Disabled Children*, Disabilities and Impairments, Vol. 6(1&2), 15-24.

Prasad, S. and Srivastava, A.N. (1992), Psychogenic Disorders in Hyperlexics and Mentally Retarded Children, *Psycholingua*, 22(2), 105-144.

Prasad S. and Srivastava, A.N. (1992), Development of Learning Abilities Rating Scale to identify Learning Disabled Children. *Ind. J. of Psychometry and Education*, 23 (1) 1-15.

Prasad, S. and Srivastava, A.N. (1992). *Application of Psychometric Formula for Assessment of Learning Disabled Children*. Paper presented at National Workshop on Learning Problems of Children, NCERT, New Delhi.

Prasad, S. and Srivstava, A.N. (1993). Effect of Distance and Colour Background upon Attention of LD and NLD Children, *Disabilities and Impairment*, Vol. 7.

Prasad, S. and Srivastava, A.N. (1994). Hypoxican Characteristics of LD and NLD children. *J. of the Indian Academy of Applied Psychology*, Vol. 20 (1).

Prasad, S. and Srivstava, A.N. (1995). *The Cognitive Clarity Test as a Measure of Learning Disabilities*, Paper presented at the 82nd Annual Conference of Indian Science Congress Association, Jadavpur University, Calcutta.

Prasad, S. and Srivastava, A.N. (1995). *The Able but not Well in Performance: A Challenge for the Psychologist*, Paper presented at the VI Annual Conference of National Academy of Psychology, Gulbarga University, Gulbarga, Karnataka, India.

Prasad, S. and Srivastava, A.N. (1996). STOP Strategy of Language Cueing for LD Children, *Psycholingua*, Vol. 26 (1).

Prasad, S. and Srivastava, A.N. (1996) *Unheard Cry of LD Child : Projection by Rorschach Inkblot Test*, Paper presented at the 3rd International Conference of SIS and 23rd Conference of Clinical Psychologists Association of India, Chandigarh, India.

Prasad, S. and Srivastava, A.N. (1997). *Plastic Dreams of Reserachers of LD.* Paper presented at the 84th Annual Conference of Indian Science Congress Association, Delhi University, Delhi.

Prasad, S. and Srivastava, A.N. (1997). Learning Index : Eyes for MR Training, 3rd National Conference, S.V. University, Tirupati, India.

Prasad, S. and Srivastava, A.N. (1997). *Diagnosing and Helping Learning Disabled Children to I Prove and Save from Wasting National Potential*, Paper presented at the 85th Annual Conference of India Science Congress Association, Osmania University, Hyderabad, India.

Prasad, S. and Srivastava, A.N. (1998). *Environment versus Process Approach to Learning Disability*, Paper presented at UGC National Seminar on Environment and Cognition, D.D.U. Gorakhpur University, Gorakhpur, India.

Prasad, S. and Srivastava, A.N. (1998). Learning Disabled Children : Diagnostic and Remedial Measures, *Psycholingua*. Vol. 28(1), 81-87.

Prasad, S. and Srivastava, A.N. (1999). Psychogenic Symptoms of Learning Disabled Children, SIS *J. of Projective Psychology and Mental Health*, Vol. 6(2), 45-50.

Shepard, I., Smith M. and Vojir, C. (1983). Characteristics of Pupils identified as Learning Disabled, *American Educational Research Journal*, 20, 309-327.

Snodgrass, J.G., (1975). Psychophysics, In B. Scharg (Ed.), *Experimental Sensory Psychology*, Scotts, Foreman.

Strauss, A.A. and Werner H. (1942). Disorders of Conceptual Thinking in the Brain-Injured Child, N.Y., *Journal of Nervous Mental Disease*, 69, 153-172.

Torgessen, J.K. and Wong, B.Y.L., (1986) *Psychological and Educational Perspectives on Learning Disabilities*, Florida, Academic Press Inc.

19

EDUCATION AND SES AS RISK FACTORS IN COGNITIVE IMPAIRMENT IN MILDLY DEMENTED ALZHEIMER'S PATIENTS

RAKESH PANDEY, SATYA GOPAL JEE, C.B. DWIVEDI & RAJENDRA MISHRA

Dementia of the Alzheimer's type (DAT) is a neurological disease accounting for 55 per cent or more of all demented patients in which all domains of cognitive functioning are adversely affected. It is a global impairment of higher cortical functions, including memory, the capacity to solve the problems of everyday living, the performance of learned perceptual motor skills and the correct use of social skills and control of emotional reactions, in the absence of gross clouding of consciousness (Anon, 1981). DAT is characterised neuropathologically by neocortical atrophy and neuronal loss (Terry, Peck, De Teresa, Schechter & Horoupian, 1981), and by the presence of neurofibrillary tangles and plaques (Blessed, Tomlinson & Roth, 1968; Terry & Katzman, 1983; Tomlinson, 1977; Tomlinson, Blessed & Roth, 1970; Wilcock & Esiri, 1982). Plaques and tangles have been found to be most extensive in the association cortices particularly in the parietal and temporal regions, with a relative sparing of primary sensory cortical areas (Brun, 1983). It is primarily an affliction of the elderly, with the prevalence increasing dramatically with age to include almost a third of the population over the age of 85. In the wake of the increased life expectancy in recent years, DAT has instigated considerably research interest among the cognitive scientists.

Memory impairments are a major component of the cognitive decline seen both in normal ageing and in the dementia associated with Alzheimer's disease (Poon, 1985). The memory impairment in

Alzheimer's patients, however, is not only much more severe than that found in the normal old but also may be more extensive involving aspects of memory that are relatively spared by ageing. Morris and Kopelman (1986) have suggested the memory deficit to be one of the earliest and most pronounced symptoms of the DAT. Memory deficits in the long-term and secondary memory components are very severe in the DAT patients and much less in the recency effect (Spinnler, Della Sala, Bandera & Baddeley, 1988; Wilson, Becon, Fox & Kaszniak, 1983). In this chapter an attempt has been made to highlight the deterministic role of education and socio-economic status in cognitive impairments in the mildly demented patients.

Education as a risk factor in the prevalence of Dementia of the Alzheimer's Type

A number of community surveys on the prevalence of dementia have reported that education exerts some sort of a protection against the development of the symptoms of dementia (Dartigues, Gagnon, Michel *et al.*, 1991; Evans, 1990; Rocca, Banaiuto, Lippi *et al.*, 1990; Sulkava, Wikstrom, Aromaa *et al.*, 1985; Zhang, Katzman, Salmon Jin, Cai, Wang, Qu, Grant, Levy, Klauber & Liu, 1990). In this regard Mortimer (1989) has analysed data from various sources to highlight that "psychosocial factors act primarily to reduce the margin of intellectual reserve to a level where a more modest level of brain pathology results in a diagnosable dementia (p. 39)". It has been fairly well-established that otherwise normal subjects with low education may do poorly on mental status tests (Fillenbaum, Hughes, Heyman *et al.*, 1988; Folstein, Anthony, Parhad *et al.*, 1985; Gurland, 1981; Jorm, Scott, Henderson *et al.*, 1988), it is still not clear whether lack of or low education works as a confounder or whether education actually delays the onset or prevalence of dementia. Zhang, Katzman, Salmon *et al.* (1990) reported the prevalence rates for dementia and Alzheimer's disease on a probability sample survey of 5,055 noninstitutionalised older persons in Shanghai, China. A two stage procedure was used for case finding and case identification. Three different cutoff points on the Chinese version of Mini Mental Status (CMMS) test were used depending on the respondent's level of education. The clinical diagnoses of dementia and Alzheimer's disease were done following the D.S.M. III and NINCDS-ADRDA criteria. The prevalence rate of dementia in 65 years and older persons was 4.60 per cent and it was found that clinically diagnosed Alzheimer's disease accounted for 65 per cent of the demented patients. Bonaito (1990) also reported that 73 per cent subjects with low education showed a higher prevalence of DAT. Hill, Klauber, Salmon *et al.*, (1993) examined the relationship of culturally adapted Chinese version of the Mini-Mental Status Examination (CMMS) and several functional measures to the effect of education on the clinical diagnosis of dementia in 554 subjects, who had undergone intensive evaluation during the Shanghai survey of dementia. Low education was associated with increased prevalence of clinically diagnosed dementia.

Indian studies conducted in Tamil Nadu and Kerala (Rajkumar & Kumar, 1996; Rajkumar, Kumar & Thara, 1997; Shaji, Promodi, Abraham, Roy & Verghese, 1996) have also reported higher prevalence of dementia in the illiterates. However, contrary findings have also been reported in a recent Indo-US survey conducted on 5000 rural elderly in Ballabhgarh, Haryana (Chandra, Ganguli, Pandav, Johnston, Belle & Dekosky, 1998). DAT was not found associated either with gender or literacy, though increased age was significantly associated with its higher prevalence. In a recent editorial (*Times of India*, 1999), Indians were reported to be less susceptible to Alzheimer's disease than those in the West, presumably because of their lower cholesterol levels. Unverzagt, Hui, Farlow, Hall & Hendrie, (1998) also reported lesser cognitive decline in their low educated demented group. Apparently any decisive role of education can only be partly true because merely some schooling might be fraught with over generalisation. Besides this, unless the continuous use of learned material is practiced the hypothesis of an intellectual reserve cannot be adequately tested. In the present study this aspect was analysed statistically to test whether intellectual reserve as a blanket concept or whether there occurs some specification in this aspect also.

Age and SES as risk factors in the prevalence of DAT

Review of studies using global measures of SES suggest that low SES during adult life is associated with a wide range of risk factors (such as infectious diseases, chronic illnesses, poor nutrition, and high risk behaviours and health practices) any one of which may increase the risk of dementing illness (Mortimer, 1988). Low SES during early life may also increase the risk of cognitive impairment in general and dementia in particular (Mortimer & Graves, 1993). Early life low SES is associated with reduced body size which in turn is associated with reduced brain size (Nystrom & Vagero, 1987). These research evidences suggest that low SES in early life increases the risk of impaired brain development which lowers the cognitive capacity and increases the risk of dementia late in life. The low SES in early life increases the risk of dementia in late life by reducing the 'brain reserve' capacity (Mortimer & Graves, 1993).

Besides SES, age is another most important risk factor for DAT (Rocca, Amaducci & Schoenberg, 1986; Zhang *et al.*, 1990). Alzheimer originally described this disorder as a form of accelerated ageing (Prick, Amaducci & Pepeu, 1987), however, no specific age-related change has been established as mechanistically important in the causation of DAT. Error theories of ageing postulate that ageing is caused by an accumulation of damage and invoke a variety of sources of damage. Random events have also been postulated to be the trigger for activating "age" or "killer" genes (Blass, Chermak & Weksler, 1992).

Hendrie, (1997) found that prevalence rates in aged 65 years and older ranged from 3.67 per cent to 10.30 per cent. Age specific prevalence rate for DAT and other dementia get doubled approximately every five years. It has been estimated that 59 per cent of the world population aged 65 years and older in the year 2000 will be in developing countries like India. According to a recent estimate (*Times of India*, 1998), in India there are over three million elderly with dementia. Zhang and associates (1990) in a survey of dementia in Sanghai, China have obtained increased age as a highly significant and independent risk factor for DAT. They reported that age specific prevalence curve climbs after the age of 75 and increases geometrically after 80 years of age.

Semantic Memory Impairment in the DAT

Tulving (1972, 1983, 1984) has differentiated three components of the long-term memory and has labelled them as episodic memory, semantic memory and procedural memory. The episodic memory is an autobiographical record of unique events in an individual's experience encoded in relation to spatial-temporal context. Semantic memory, on the other hand, is a mental thesaurus which contains the permanent representation of knowledge of concepts, words and their meanings. Many researchers have shown that impairment in semantic memory is much more prominent in the Alzheimer's patients while it remains essentially intact in normal aged persons. Salthouse (1982) has reported that the vocabulary, information and comprehension sub-scales of the Wechsler Adult Intelligence Scale (WAIS) showed little or no change over the course of normal ageing while there is a considerable loss for variety of semantic memory tasks of DAT patients. Nebes (1989) has evaluated the studies to conclude that the semantic memory impairments in Alzheimer's patients are severely visible but they are not found in normal olds. He has examined the semantic deficits of word findings, awareness of attributes, association, category membership, semantic priming, sentence completion, semantic correlation, and homophone disambiguation. The decline in primary memory functioning in Alzheimer's disease is substantial, but not as striking as for memory over longer periods. This may be partly due to the differential sensitivity of the tests, rather than a genuine dissociation. DAT patients have been found to show deficits in free recall, story recall (logical memory), paired associate learning, pictorial recognition and facial recognition (Corkin, 1982; Kopelman, 1986; Wilson, Bacon, Kramer, Fox & Kaszniak, 1983b; Wilson, Kaszniak, Bacon, Fox & Kelly, 1982).

Studies have also shown that DAT is associated with a progressive anomia, but the cause of the naming deficit remains unclear (Hart 1988). Whilst a number of studies have suggested a primary perceptual deficit as the major cause of the naming disorder (Barker & Lawson, 1968; Kirshner, Webb & Kelly, 1984; Rochford, 1971), other investigators have favoured a central semantic defect (Bayles & Tomoeda, 1983; Huff, Corkin & Growdon, 1986; Martin & Fedio, 1983; Smith, Murdoch & Chenery, 1989). Word finding difficulty in every day speech can be an early sign of the Alzheimer's disease. To test this problem, patients are often asked to describe either an object or a picture which reveals a speech which is vague, repetitive, fairly empty of content words, full of pronouns without antecedents, empty phrases, indefinite and semantically related but incorrect words, and circumlocutions (Nicholas, Obler, Albert & Helm-Estabrooks, 1985). Hier, Hagenlocker and Shindler (1985) examined a spontaneous speech sample of normal and DAT patients and reported that both speeches were very similar in their use of prepositional phrases and subordinate clauses and in the length and grammatical complexity of their utterances. However, the speech of the demented patients contained many more empty words and instances of indefinite anaphora than did the normals.

A difficulty in naming objects is considered to be a sensitive marker for language impairment due to brain injury (Benson, 1979). Normal ageing produces relatively slight change in the accuracy of object naming (Labarge, Edwards & Knesevich, 1986). Contrarily, the DAT patients show a substantial problem in naming objects, the severity of which is strongly correlated with the severity of their overall dementia (Barker & Lawson, 1968; Kirshner, Webb & Kelly, 1984). Rochford (1971) argued that demented patients misnamed objects because they misperceived them. He based his conclusions on the finding that many incorrect responses of the DAT patients' were names of the items that were visually similar to the presented objects and the DAT patients reported lesser difficulty in naming the body parts. The demented patients are more likely to name an object if they are allowed to handle it or if its use is demonstrated to them, thus providing them with additional sensory cues to aid their identification (Barker & Lawson, 1968).

Impairment in lexical access in which the semantic representation of the object concept is intact, but the connection from this representation to the corresponding lexical representation is disrupted has been proposed as a reason for the naming deficit. This mechanism has been suggested to underlie the minor naming problems in the normal olds (Albert *et al.*, 1988). One common finding (Barker & Lawson, 1968; Kirshner *et al.*, 1984; Skelton-Robinson & Jones, 1984) supporting this model is that the severity of naming deficit in demented patients varies with frequency of the name in a language. The less frequent a name, the less success demented patients had in producing the name of a pictured object. Martin and Fedio (1983) found that on the Boston Naming Test, phonemic cues were effective in helping demented patients 60 per cent of the time to name an object which they had apparently failed to name when its picture was shown. One line of evidence against a lexical access deficit is the poor performance of demented patients on a name-recognition paradigm (Flicker *et al.*, 1987; Huff *et al.*, 1986; Skelton-Robinson & Jones, 1984). Conflicting results were, however, found by Harold (1988), who used a three choice paradigm with both semantic and phonemic distractors. She found that demented patients performed quite well on the recognition task, and on those tasks, on which they did make a mistake, they were quite likely to choose the phonemic as the semantic distractor. Analysis of naming errors suggest that high level visuo-perceptual impairment is typically a major contributor only in the late stage of the disease, although occasional atypical cases presenting with prominent visual deficits have also been reported (Levine, Lee & Fisher, 1993; Mendez, Martin, Smyth & Whitehouse, 1990). Most of the evidence point to a breakdown at the level of detailed, specific semantic processing : the majority of object naming errors by patients with DAT are category co-ordinate, associative, or super ordinate responses (Bayles & Tomoeda, 1983; Chertkow & Bub, 1990; Chertkow,

Bub & Caplan, 1992; Hodges, Salmon & Butters, 1991; Huff, Corkin & Growdon, 1986).

Although impairment in new learning is the earliest and most pervasive cognitive deficit in patients with dementia of the Alzheimer's type (Brandt & Rich, 1994; Grady, Haxby, Horwitz, Sundaram, Berg, Schapiro, Friedland & Rapoport, 1988; Heindel, Salmon & Butters, 1993; Parasuraman & Haxby, 1993; Welsh, Butters, Hughes, Mohs & Heyman, 1991), the ability to produce familiar nominal terms is also compromised at a fairly early stage and frequently becomes a major problem as the disease progresses. There has been considerable debate regarding the relative contribution of perceptual, semantic and lexical-retrieval deficits to the naming disorder. Matthews, Ralph, Patterson and Hodges (1997) studied naming and semantic memory relationship in a group of 10 patients with DAT. The results showed that the successful naming relied one subset of critical semantic features only which vary somewhat across different categories of semantic knowledge. Hodges and Patterson (1995) also reported impairment in category fluency, naming of the drawing, naming to verbal description, answering semantic feature questions and a non-verbal picture task in the minimal DAT patients whereas mild and moderate DAT groups showed additional deficit in picture sorting and word to picture matching tests.

However, it is still not clear, whether and to what extent the deficit found on test of semantic memory reflects impaired access to semantic memory. Similarly, there is still a controversy regarding semantic memory deficit occurring due to a breakdown in the storage of structure of semantic memory (Chan, Butters, Paulson, Salmon, Swenson & Maloney, 1993; Chertkow & Bub, 1990; Hodges & Patterson, 1995; Hodges, Salmon & Butters, 1992). Apart from this the foregoing discussion also brings to fore the possibility that level of education and socio-economic status (SES) may moderate atleast partly the observed semantic memory deficits in demented patients. Low level of education and SES may become a risk factor in DAT, while a considerable higher level of these variables may *per se* obviate cognitive impairments including impairment of semantic memory in the DAT patients.

This chapter addressed these issues in a two phase study and attempted to analyse the role of psycho-social risk factors of education and socio-economic status in mental status and prevalence of DAT followed by the semantic memory impairments in mild demented and matched controls.

Role of Risk Factors of Education and SES in Mental Status and Dementia : The first phase of the present study

In the first phase of the present study we individually tested 200 elderly adults above 60 years of age (age range 60 to 82 years, mean = 73 years, SD = 6.06 years) on a Hindi version of the Folestein, Folestein & McHugh's (1975) Mini-Mental Status Examination (HMMS; Dwivedi, Pandey & Gopaljee, 1996), Mattis Dementia Rating Scale (1992) (HMDS; Dwivedi, Gopaljee & Pandey, 1998), and on two subtests of Weschler Memory Scale (1995) (HWMS, Dwivedi, Pandey, Gopaljee, Pathak & Mandal, 1997)* The HMMS presented an assessment of time orientation, the ability of registration of information, attention, calculation, recall of previously registered information, object naming, repetition of words, following of the multi-stage commands, reading/ writing a sentence and copying geometrical figures. The HMDS evaluated the subjects on 5 cognitive dimensions using verbal and pictorial materials-attention, initiation and preservation, construction, conceptualisation, and memory. The two subtests of HWMS assessed the visual reproductive memory and logical memory.

Obtained results (See Table 19.1) revealed that literate subjects (N=116) unequivocally scored significantly higher on all of the aforesaid semantic measures ($p<0.001$). The HMMS scores of illiterate subjects showed higher range (8-25) and SD (4.48) as compared to those of the literate subjects. An obverse pattern was, however, found for the HMDS and HWMS scores (See Table 19.1). These results extend the theory that literacy lowers the risk of cognitive impairment in elderly subjects and provides a protection against deterioration of registration, attention, storage, retrieval and other cognitive components as assessed by HMMS, HWMS and HMDS. Most evidences show that the cognitive capacity of encoding, storage and retrieval is relatively less in the illiterates than is seen in the literate subjects.

Similar trend was visible for the criterion of socio-economic status (SES), where low SES subjects performed poorer than did their middle SES counterparts. The obtained differences on all the three measures have consistently shown that significantly lesser mean HMMS, HMDS and HWMS scores were obtained by the low SES subjects. It appears that education and socio-economic status have strong association with

*These tests are commercially available from M/s Rupa Psychological Centre, Varanasi.

Table 19.1: Mean HMMS, HMDS and HWMS Scores and SDs relative to the Education and Socio-Economic Status of Subjects

Screening Tools		*Education*			*Socio-economic status*		
		Literate *N=116*	*Illiterate* *N=84*	*t-value*	*Middle SES* *N=101*	*Low SES* *N=99*	*t-value*
	M	25.29	17.71		24.29	18.52	
HMMS	SD	2.97	4.48	13.53	3.94	4.56	9.62
	Range	14-30	8-25	P<0.001	14-25	8-25	P<0.00
	M	116.69	90.02	–	122.32	89.67	
HMMS	SD	18.65	17.36	10.42	11.98	15.24	16.82
	Range	81-138	57.124	P<0.001	81-138	57-120	P<0.00
	M	47.98	23.22		51.00	23.79	
HMMS	SD	15.40	8.01	14.82	13.68	8.13	17.22
	Range	17-98	3-40	P<0.001	21-98	3-43	P<0.00

cognitive performance which cannot be attributed entirely to the impaired test taking ability of the illiterates or low SES subjects. These results extend the theory that illiteracy and low SES deprive the subjects from many cognitive avenues and their stunted growth of cognitive domains adversely affects their higher mental functions. Although the present results suggest that illiteracy and low SES increase the risk of global cognitive impairment and also the onset of dementia, it does not provide any convincing information whether and to what extent education and higher SES resist protect against rapid and severe cognitive decline after the disease has set in. Moreover, the present findings also do not provide any definitive information regarding the role of education and SES in DAT specific impairments such as semantic memory impairment.

To address these specific research questions, in the second phase of the present study we conducted an experiment with three semantic memory tasks of increasing difficulty (viz. word to picture matching, picture naming, and picture recognition) on a group of 25 mildly demented patients (age range = 60-76 years, mean age = 68.75 years, SD = 3.35 years) and matched control group (age range = 60-75 years, mean age = 68.13 years, SD = 3.15 years). Out of the 25 demented patients, 7 were literates and 18 were illiterates, 13 belonged to middle SES and 12 belonged to low SES group. In the control group 11 subjects were literates and 14 were illiterates, 15 belonged to middle SES and

10 belonged to low SES group. The selection of the 25 probable DAT patients was done on the basis of the inclusion-exclusion criteria of NINCDS-ADRDA (McKhann *et al.*, 1984) as well as on the basis of their obtained scores on HMMS, HWMS, and HMDS tests. Figures 19.1 & 19.2 display the sample CT scans of two patients of the present study.

Stimulus materials were 100 pictures prepared on 3×5 inch card having concrete picturable nouns belonging to 8 semantic categories (10 items each, plus 20 miscellaneous objects). The 8 semantic categories used in this phase of the present study were vehicles, clothings, furnitures, tools, fruits, vegetables, animals, and body part (Snodgrass & Vanderwart, 1980). All items were prescreened such that 95 per cent at normal age matched control subjects could correctly name each picture.

Subjects were tested individually for picture naming, who were asked to name each of the line drawn 100 pictures without the aid of any semantic or phonemic cueing. The pictures were presented as single stimuli drawn on a 3 × 5 inch card and the subjects were instructed to name each picture as quickly as possible. All responses were noted verbatim without any comment about their accuracy. The procedure for word to picture matching comprised a set of cards containing five items on each card from within the same semantic category, which were arranged vertically in a column. The subjects were asked to match each picture with appropriate label which was noted without any comment about its accuracy. The picture recognition test was also conducted, similarly, in which the set of picture cards comprised five items each belonging to different categories and the subjects were asked to correctly recognise each of the pictures.

Table 19.2 shows the mean HMMS, HMDS and HWMS scores along with SDs and range relative to the education and SES of DAT patients and matched controls of phase-2 of the present study.

Mean HMMS scores of literate subjects was significantly higher than that of the illiterates ($t = 4.42$, $df = 23$, $p<0.01$). Similarly, the literate subjects score significantly higher on HWMS and HMDS measures. Poorer input and storage capacity in the illiterates have been reflected in significantly lesser mean scores by the illiterates on HMDS and HWMS measures. Similar pattern of responses was visible for low SES patients who have scored significantly lesser on HMMS, HMDS and HWMS as compared to DAT patients of middle SES. The corresponding scores of matched controls did not show such a clear indication where illiterates scored slightly lesser on HMMS and HMDS measures compared to their literate counterparts ($p<0.05$). However, on

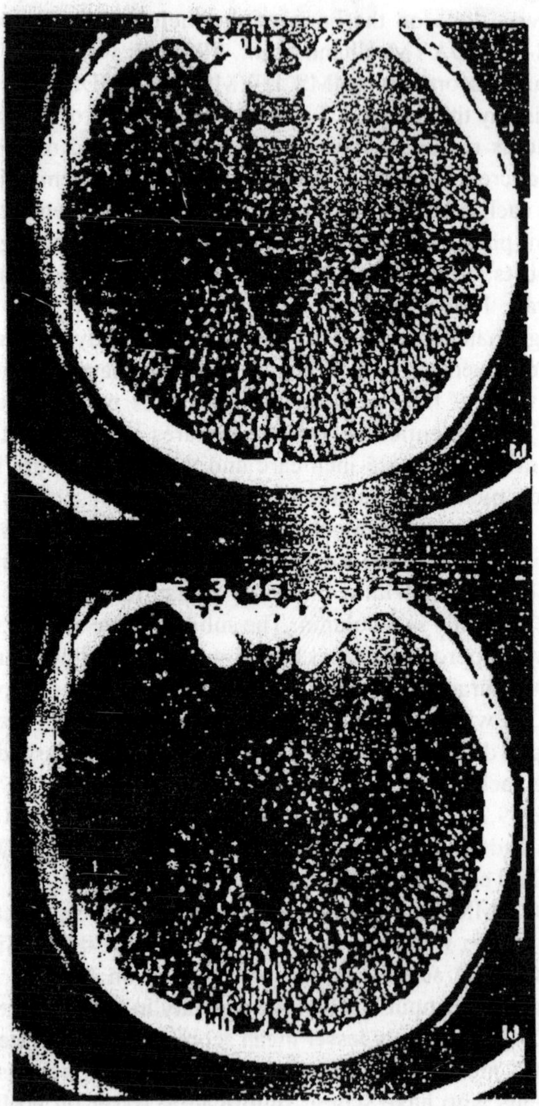

Fig. 19.1 CT scan images in moderately demented patients: two sequential cuts orientated through the temporal lobes at the level of the midbrain showing focal left neocortical atrophy.

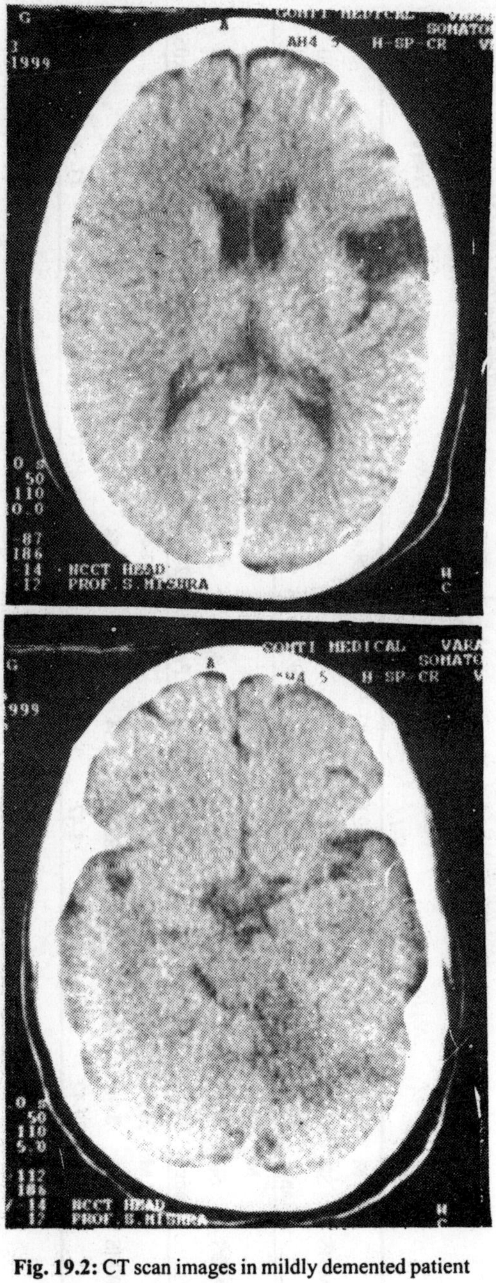

Fig. 19.2: CT scan images in mildly demented patient

Table 19.2: Mean HMMS, HMDS, HWMS Scores and SDs Relative to the Education Level and Socio-Economic Status of DAT Patients and Matched Controls

		DAT patients (N=25)						Matched Controls (N=25)					
		Literate N=7	*Illiterate N=18*	*t-value*	*Middle SES N-13*	*Low SES N=12*	*t-value*	*Literate N=11*	*Illiterate N=14*	*t-value*	*Middle SES N-15*	*Low SES N=10*	*t-value*
	M	16.57	13.17	-	16.23	11.83	-	28.45	28.29	-	28.53	28.10	-
HMMS	SD	0.90	2.91	4.42	1.19	2.54	5.43	1.08	0.88	0.39	0.96	0.94	1.10
	Range	15-18	8-18	P<0.01	14.18	8-16	P<0.01	28-30	27-30	NS	27-30	26-30	NS
	M	93.14	65.72	-	83.23	62.75	-	131.72	127.57	-	131.6	126.1	-
HMDS	SD	14.68	7.99	4.69	15.56	7.53	4.24	5.64	6.52	1.70	4.99	7.05	2.14
	Range	77-124	57-86	P<0.01	67-124	57-86	P<0.01	124-140	119-139	NS	124-140	119-139	P<0.05
	M	33.71	16.56	-	28.0	14.17	-	69.45	55.93	-	64.8	51.5	-
HWMS	SD	8.01	5.13	5.28	8.62	4.54	5.08	11.54	9.41	3.15	20.17	5.89	2.41
	Range	29-42	3-13	P<0.01	18-42	3-21	P<0.01	55-98	43-70	P<0.01	55-98	43-58	P<0.05

HWMS illiterate controls scored significantly less than did their literate counterparts (t = 3.15, df = 23, p<0.01). SES also extended almost a similar picture.

These observations corroborated the theory that education and SES work as protective factors which reduce also the severity of cognitive impairment after the onset of the DAT. Variations in SES and education have little impact on the cognitive performance (as assessed by the HMMS, HWMS and HMDS) of normal elderly subjects. Low level of education and SES, however significantly reduced the performance on HWMS in matched controls. This pattern of findings indicates that SES and education are relatively more important after the onset than before the onset of DAT.

The Role of Psychosocial Risk Factors in Semantic Memory Impairments : The Second Phase of the Present Study

Table 19.3 shows the mean word-to-picture matching, picture naming and picture recognition scores along with SDs and ranges relative to the education and SES of DAT patients and matched control subjects.

The mean scores in word-to-picture matching are more that of picture naming and picture recognition conditions which relate to the increased levels of complexity involved in the three tasks. However, even the illiterates have obtained mean scores of 72.66, SD = 1.60 on word-to-picture matching task. The literates on the other hand, obtained significantly higher mean scores on this task (mean = 75.57, SD = 2.56). The difference of mean scores on this measure between literates and illiterates was statistically reliable (t = 4.85, p<0.01). The mean scores on picture naming task, which are a little more complex than are the word-to-picture matching have also shown the effect of illiteracy. The mean scores of illiterates (mean = 62.11, SD = 4.43) have been found to be significantly less (t = 2.94, p<0.01) than that of the literates (mean = 66.14, SD = 2.36). The most complex among the three experimental tasks was the picture recognition where literates (mean = 53.71, SD = 2.12) have scored significantly higher (t = 3.84, df = 23, p<0.01) than that of the illiterates (mean = 51.44, SD = 3.22).

These observations were corroborated in the same proportion by the SES. The DAT patients of the middle SES scored significantly more than did the low SES patients on all the three experimental tasks. The effect of literacy and SES was also visible in the matched controls. Literates outperformed illiterates on all the three measures, relative to

Table 19.3: Mean Word to Picture Matching, Picture Naming and Picture Recognition Scores and SDs as Related to the Education Level and Socio-Economic Status of DAT Patients and Controls

		DAT patients (N=25)						*Matched Controls (N=25)*					
		Literate N=7	*Illiterate N=18*	*t-value*	*Middle SES N-13*	*Low SES N=12*	*t-value*	*Literate N=11*	*Illiterate N=14*	*t-value*	*Middle SES N-15*	*Low SES N=10*	*t-value*
Word to picture matching	M	75.57	72.66		74.54	72.33	3.88	89.9	88.07		89.80	88.90	
	SD	2.56	1.60	4.85	2.31	1.69	P<0.01	1.38	2.91	2.07	1.83	2.98	1.30
	Range	73-81	71-77	P<0.01	72-81	71-77	89.9	88-93	85-94	P<0.05	87-94	85-93	NS
Picture Naming	M	66.14	62.11		66.08	60.16		87.36	85.79		86.33	85.90	
	SD	2.36	4.43	2.94	1.82	4.21	6.43	2.90	3.57	1.70	3.28	3.36	0.32
	Range	63-70	53-67	P<0.01	64-70	53-65	P<0.01	83-92	82-92	NS	80-92	82-92	NS
Picture Recognition	M	53.71	51.44		53.07	51.00		71.45	71.14		71.40	71.10	
	SD	2.12	3.22	3.84	2.70	3.19	2.46	2.46	2.13	0.47	2.03	2.62	0.45
	Range	51-56	48-56	P<0.01	50-56	42-55	P<0.05	69-76	65-74	NS	69-76	65-74	NS

level of complexity involved in the task. Similarly, the middle SES matched controls scored higher on all the three measures than did the low SES subjects. However, these differences were not statistically reliable for all possible comparisons except on word-to-picture matching where literates scored significantly higher than did the illiterates. These observations suggest that low SES and illiteracy have deleterious effect on semantic memory impairments after the onset of DAT but not before it which is evident in statistically significant effect of these variables in DAT patients.

The findings of the present study extend the theory that cognitive impairment is more in illiterates as well as in low SES DAT patients. These findings do not support the prevalence study of Chandra *et al.* (1998) who have not found any association of DAT with literacy. One of the reasons cited by Chandra *et al.* was that approximately half of the study population was younger than 55 years of age whereas mild demented subjects of the present study were aged 63 to 82 years (mean = 68.44 years). Three earlier Indian studies conducted in Tamil Nadu and Kerala (Rajkumar & Kumar, 1996; Rajkumar, Kumar & Thara, 1997; Shaji, Pramodi, Abraham, Roy & Verghese, 1996) have reported higher prevalence of dementia in the illiterates. The present study corroborates their findings insofar as higher prevalence of DAT in illiterates is concerned.

The findings of the present study have shown unequivocally lower mean score on all three experimental tasks which were varied in the level of complexity, and irrespective of complexity, the illiterates and low SES subjects scored poorly on all the three tasks. This finding extends the theory that psycho-social risk factors of education and socio-economic status are potent indicators of dementia and education works as an umbrella for protecting the probable onset of dementia in the elderly. The contentions of Mortimer and Graves (1993) that low education level and low SES adult life are associated with a wide variety of infectious diseases, chronic illness, poor nutrition and high risk behaviour and health practices, one or more of which might increase the risk of dementia are corroborated by the present study. Though reliable information of subjects on some indicators, for example, childhood nutrition, was not available in the present study, yet the fact that illiterates and low SES subjects score poorly on screening instruments as well as on all the three types of cognitive task support the contention that early life exposure to the psycho-social risk factors of education and SES is related to the brain development of the patients (Mortimer & Graves, 1993).

The 'intellectual (or cognitive) reserve' hypothesis proposed by Mortimer (1988) which suggests that education brings about a remarkable difference in the patients because they constantly rehearse and reproduce the available information is corroborated by the findings of the present study. Ronchi and associates (1998) have also reported that the first decade of life in which education starts works as a critical period for the onset of dementia during later decades. All the literate subjects of the present study obtained their educational inputs during the first decade of their life and none of them acquired literacy through adult education programmes in the later decades of their life. All these factors appear responsible for better performance of literate subjects compared to that of the illiterates.

Though the sample size of the present study was relatively small and any generalisation based on such a drastically small sample of DAT patients is always fraught with oversimplifications, yet it appears that illiteracy and low SES during early life are associated with physique, brain size and other functions of the DAT patients. In all probability, the findings of the present study support the theory that there is a strong correlation between brain size and body size. The present study has also shown that illiteracy and low SES are likely to be related to impairment of brain development which would be reflected in lower cognitive ability and increase the risk of dementia in such subjects. Based on the present finding it is suggested that effective and improved health programmes should be undertaken by educating the masses in general, and elderly in particular, towards the pathogenic role of these psycho-social risk factors on the onset of dementia of Alzheimer's type.

References

Albert, M.S., Heller, H.S. & Milberg, W. (1988). Changes in naming ability with age. *Psychology and Ageing*, 3, 173-178.

Anon (1981). Organic mental impairment of the elderly. *Journal of the Royal College of Physicians of London*, 15, 142-167.

Bayles, K.A. & Tomoeda, C.K. (1983). Confrontation naming impairment in dementia. *Brain and Language*, 9, 98-114.

Benson, D.F. (1979). Aphasia : In K.M. Heilman & E. Valenstein (Eds.), *Clinical Neuropsychology*, 22-58. New York : Oxford University Press.

Bick, K. Amaducci, L., Pepeu, G (1987). *The Early Story of Alzheimer's Disease*. Padua : Livinia Press.

Blass, J.P., Cherniak, E.P., Weksler, M.F. (1992). Theories of ageing. In :

Clakins, E., Davis, P.J., Ford, A.B., *et al.* Eds. *Practice of Geriatrics*, 2nd edition. New York : W.B. Saunders 10-28.

Blessed, G, Tomlinson, B.E., and Roth, M. (1968). The association between quantitative measures of dementia and of senile change in the cerebral gray matter of elderly subjects. *British Journal of Psychiatry*, 114, 797-811.

Bonaito, S., Rocca, E., Lippi, A. (1990). Impact of education and occupation on the prevalence of Alzheimer's disease and multi-infarct dementia in Appignano, Macerata province, Italy. *Neurology*, 40 (Suppl. 1) : 346.

Brandt, J. & Rich, J.B. (1994). Memory disorders in the dementias. In A.D. Baddeley, B.A. Wilson and F. Watts (Eds.), *Handbook of Memory Disorders*. Chichester : Wiley.

Brun, A. (1983). An overview of light and electron microscopic changes. In B. Reisberg (Ed.), A*lzheimer's Disease* (pp. 37-47). New York : Free Press.

Chan, A.S., Butters, N., Paulson, J.S., Salmon, D.P., Swenson, M. & Maloney, L. (1993). An assessment of the semantic network in patients with Alzheimer's disease. *Journal of Cognitive Neuroscience*, 5, 254-261.

Chandra, V., Ganguli, M., Pandav, R., Johnston, J., Belle, S. & DeKosky, S.T. (1998). Prevalence of Alzheimer's disease and other dementia's in rural India : The Indo-US study. *Neurology*, 51, 1000-1008.

Chertkow, H. & Bub, D. (1990). Semantic memory loss in dementia of Alzheimer's type. *Brain*, 133, 397-417.

Chertkow, H., Bub, D. & Caplan, D. (1992). Constraining theories of semantic memory processing : evidence from dementia. *Cognitive Neuropsychology*, 9, 327-365.

Dartigues, J.F., Gagnon, M., Michel, P. *et al.* (1991). Le Programme de recherché paquid sur I. epidemiologic dela demence methods et resultants initiaux. *Review of Neurology*, (Paris), 147, 225-230.

Dwivedi, C.B., Pandey, R. & Gopal Jee, S. (1996). *Hindi adaptation of Folstein, Folstein & McHugh's Mini Mental Status Examination*. Varanasi : Rupa Psychological Centre.

Dwivedi, C.B., Pandey, R., Gopal Jee S., Pathak, K.S., & Mandal, M.K. (1997). *Hindi Adaptation of Two Subscale of Wechster Memory Scale*. Unpublished manuscript, Department of Psychology, B.H.U.

Dwivedi, C.B., Gopal Jee, S. & Pandey, R. (1998). *Hindi adaptation of Mattis Dementia Rating Scale*. Varanasi. Rupa Psychological Centre.

Evans, D.A. (1990). Estimated prevalence of Alzheimer's disease in the United States. Milbank, Q., 68, 267-289.

Fillenbaum, G.G., Hughes, D.C., Heyman, A., George, L.K., Blazer, D.G. (1988). Relationship of health and demographic characteristics of mini-mental state examination score among community residents. *Psychological Medicine*, 18, 719-726.

Flicker, C., Ferris, S.H., Crook, T. & Bartus, R.T. (1987). Implications of memory and language dysfunction in the naming deficit of senile dementia. *Brain and Language*, 31, 187-200.

Folstein, M., Anthony, J.C., Parhad, I., Duffy, B. & Gruenberg, E.M. (1985). The meaning of cognitive impairment in the elderly. *Journal of American Geriatric Society*, 33, 228-235.

Folstein, M.F., Folstein, S.E. & McHugh, P.R. (1975). Mini-mental state : A practical guide for grading the mental state of patients for the clinician. *Journal of Psychiatric Research*, 12, 189-198.

Grady, C.L., Haxby, J.V., Horwitz, B., Sundaram, N., Berg, G., Schapiro, M., Friedland, R.P. & Rapoport, S.I., (1988). Longitudinal study of the early neuropsychological and cerebral metabolic changes in dementia of the Alzheimer type. *Journal of Clinical and Experimental Neuropsychology*, 10, 576-596.

Gurland, B.J. (1981). The borderlands of dementia : the influence of sociocultural characteristics on rates of dementia occurring in the senium. In : Miller NE, Cohen GD, eds. *Clinical Aspects of Alzheimer's Disease and Senile Dementia*. New York : Raven Press, 61-84.

Harrold, R.M. (1988). Object naming in Alzheimer's disease : What is the cognitive deficit? Paper presented at the 96th Annual Meeting of the American Psychological Association, Atlanta, GA.

Hart, S.A. (1988). Language and dementia : A review. *Psychological Medicine*, 18, 99-112.

Heindel, W.C., Salmon, D.P. & Butters, N. (1993). Cognitive approaches to the memory disorders of demented patients. In : Sutker PB, Adams, HE, editors. *Comprehensive Handbook of Psychopathology*, 2nd ed. New York : Plenum Press, 735-761.

Hendrie, H.C. (1997). Epidemiology of Alzheimer's disease. *Geriatrics*, 52 (Suppl. 2), 54-58.

Hier, D.B. Hagenlocker, K. & Shindler, A.G. (1985). Language disintegration in dementia : effects of etiology and severity. *Brain and Language*, 25, 117-133.

Hill, L.R., Klauber, M.R., Salmon, D.P. *et al.* (1993). Functional status, education and the diagnosis of dementia in the Shanghai survey. *Neurology*, 43, 138-145.

Hodges, J.R., Salmon, D.P. & Butters, N. (1991). The nature of the naming deficit in Alzheimer's and Huntington's disease. *Brain*, 114, 1547-1558.

Hodges, J.R., Salmon, D.P. & Butters, N. (1992). Semantic memory impairment in Alzheimer's disease : Failure of access or degraded knowledge? *Neuropsychologia*, 30, 310-314.

Hodges, J.R. & Patterson, K. (1995). Is semantic memory consistently impaired early in the course of Alzheimer's disease? Neuroanatomical and diagnostic implications. *Neuropsychologia*, 33, 441-459.

Huff, F.J. & Corkin, S. (1984). Recent advances in the neuropsychology of Alzheimer's disease. *Progress Neuropsychopharmacology, Biology and Psychiatric*, 8, 643-648.

Huff, F.J., Corkin, S. & Growdon, J.H. (1986). Semantic impairment and anomia in Alzheimer's disease. *Brain and Language*, 28, 235-239.

Jorm, A.F., Scott, R. Henderson, A.S., Kay, D.W.K. (1988). Educational level differences on the mini-mental state : the role of test bias. *Psychological Medicine*, 18, 727-731.

Kirshner, H.S., Webb, W.G. & Kelly, M.P. (1984). The naming disorder of dementia. *Neuropsychologia*, 22, 23-30.

Kopelman, M.D. (1986). Clinical tests of memory. *British Journal of Psychiatry*, 148, 517-525.

LaBarge, E., Edwards, D. & Knesevich, J.W. (1986). Performance of normal elderly on the Boston Naming Test. *Brain and Language*, 27, 380-384.

Levine, D.N., Lee, J.M. & Fisher, C.M. (1993). The visual variant of Alzheimer's disease : A clinicopathologic case study. *Neurology*, 43, 305-313.

Martin, A. & Fedio, P. (1983). Word Production and comprehension in Alzheimer's disease. *The Breakdown of Semantic Knowledge*, 19, 124-141.

Matthew, A., Ralph, L., Patterson, K. & Hodges, J.R. (1997). The relationship between naming and semantic knowledge for different categories in dementia of Alzheimer's type. *Neuropsychologia*, Vol. 35, No. 9, 1251-1260.

Mattis, S. (1992). *Dementia Rating Scale*. NFER-Nelson, Windsor.

McKhann, G., Drachman, D., Folstein, M., Katzman, R., Price, D. & Stradlan, E.M. (1984). Clinical diagnosis of Alzheimer's disease. *Neurology*, 34, 939-944.

Mendez, M.F., Mendez, M.A., Martin, R., Smyth, R.A. & Whitehouse, P.J. (1990). Complex visual disturbances in Alzheimer's disease. *Neurology*, 40, 439-443.

Morris, R. G. and Kopelman, M.D. (1986). The memory deficit in Alzheimer type dementia : a review. *Quarterly Journal of Experimental Psychology*, 38A, 575-602.

Mortimer, J.A. (1988). Do psychosocial risk factors contribute to Alzheimer's disease? In: Henderson A.S., Henderson J. II., eds. *Etiology of Dementia of Alzheimer's Type*. Chichester : John Wiley & Sons, 39-52.

Mortimer, J.A. & Graves, A.B. (1993). Education on other socio-economic determinants of dementia and Alzheimer's disease. *Neurology*, 43 (Supp 4) 539-544.

Nebes, R.B. (1989). Semantic memory in Alzheimer's disease. *Psychological Bulletin*, 106, 377-394.

Nicholas, M., Obler, L.K., Albert, M.L. & Helm-Estarbrooks N. (1985). Empty speech in Alzheimer's disease and fluent aphasia. *Journal of Speech and Hearing Research*, 28, 405-410.

Nystrom Peck A.M., Vagero D.H. (1987) Adult body height and childhood socioeconomic group in the Swedish population. *J. Epidemiol Community Health*; 41, 333-337.

Parasuraman, R. & Haxby, J.V. (1993). Attention and brain function in Alzheimer's disease : A review. *Neuropsychology*, 7, 242-272.

Poon, L.W. (1985). Differences in human memory with ageing: *Nature, Causes and Clinical Implications*. In J.E. Poon and K.W. Schaic (Eds.), (pp. 427-462). New York : Van Nostrand Reinhold.

Rajkumar, S. & Kumar, S. (1996). Prevalence of dementia in the community : a rural-urban comparison from Madras, India. *Australia Journal of Ageing*, 15, 9-13.

Rajkumar, S., Kumar, S. & Thara, R. (1997). Prevalence of dementia in a rural setting : a report from India. *Internatonal Journal of Geriatric Psychiatry*, 12, 702-707.

Rocca, W.A., Banaiuto, S., Lippi A. *et al.* (1990). Prevalence of clinically diagnosed Alzheimer's disease and other dementing disorders : a door to door survey in Appignano, Macerata province, Italy. *Neurology*, 40, 626-631.

Ronchi, D.D., Fratiglioni, L., Rucci, P., Peternico, D.A., Graziani, S.O. & Dalmonte, E. (1998). The effect of education on dementia occurrence in an Italian population with middle to high socio-economic status. *Neurology*, 50, 1231-1238.

Salthouse, T.A. (1982). *Adult Cognition*. New York : Springer-verlag.

Shaji, S., Promodu, K., Abraham, T., Roy, K.J. & Verghese, A. (1996). An epidemiological study of dementia in a rural community in Kerala, India. *British Journal of Psychiatry*, 168, 745-749.

Skelton-Robinson, M. & Jones, S. (1984). Nominal aphasia and the severity of senile dementia. *British Journal of Psychiatry*, 145, 168-171.

Smith, S.R., Murdoch, B.E. & Chenery, H.J. (1989). Semantic abilities in dementia of the Alzheimer type : 1 Lexical semantics. *Brain and Language*, 36, 314-324.

Snodgrass, J.G. and Vanderwart, M.A. (1980). A standardised set of 260 pictures : Norms for name agreement, familiarity and visual complexity. *Journal of Experimental Psychology: General*, 6, 174-215.

Spinnler, H; Della Sala, S., Bandera, R., & Baddeley, A. (1988). Dementia, ageing and the structure of human memory. *Cognitive Neuropsychology*, 5, 193-211.

Sulkava, R., Wikstrom, J., Aromaa, A. *et al.* (1985). Prevalence of severe dementia in Finland. *Neurology*, 35, 1025-1029.

Terry, R.D., Peck, A., De Teresa, R., Schechter, R., & Horoupian, D.S. (1981). Some morphometric aspects of the brain in senile dementia of the Alzheimer type. *Annals of Neurology*, 10, 184-192.

Terry, R.D., and Katzman, R. (1983). Senile dementia of the Alzheimer type. *Annals of Neurology*, 14, 397-506.

The Times of India. (1998, July 27). Three million people have Alzheimer's disease in India. New Delhi Edition.

The Times of India (1999 Sept.) Age of unreason. New Delhi Edition.

Tomlinson, B.E. (1977). The pathology of dementia. In C.E. Well and (Ed.) *Dementia* (2nd Ed., pp. 13-153). Philadelphia : Davis.

Tomlinson, B.E.; Blessed, G; and Roth M. (1970). Observations of the brains of demented old people. *Journal of Neurological Science*, 11, 205-242.

Tulving, E. (1972). Episodic and semantic memory. In E. Tulving & W.

Donaldson (Eds.) *Organisation of Memory.* New York: Academic Press, pp. 381-403.

Tulving, E (1983). *Elements of Episodic Memory*. Oxford England : Clarendon press.

Tulving, E. (1984). Precis of elements of episodic memory. *Behavioural and Brain Science*, 7, 223-268.

Unverzagt, P.W., Hui, S.L., Farlow, M.R., Hall, K.S. & Hendrie, H.C. (1998). Cognitive decline and education in mild dementia. *Neu. ology*, 50, 181-185.

Wechsler, D. (1945). A standardised memory scale for clinical use. *Journal of Psychology*, 19, 87-95.

Welsh, K., Butters, N., Hughes, J., Mohs. R. & Heyman, A. (1991). Detection of abnormal memory decline in mild cases of Alzheimer's disease using CERAD neuropsychological measures. *Archives of Neurology*, 48, 278-281.

Wilcock, G.K.; and Esiri, M.M. (1982). Plaques, tangles and dementia: A quantitative study. *Journal of Neurological Science*, 56, 343-356.

Wilson, R.S., Bacon, L.D., Fox, J.H. & Kaszniak, A.W. (1983). Primary memory and secondary memory in dementia of the Alzheimer type. *Journal of Clinical Neuropsychology*, 5, 337-344.

Wilson, R.S. C. Bacon, L.D., Kramer, R.L., Fox, J.H. & Kaszniak, A.W. (1983b). Word frequency effect and recognition memory in dementia of the Alzheimer's type. *Journal of Clinical Neuropsychology*, 5, 97-104.

Wilson, R.S.; Kaszniak, A.W.; Bacon, L.D.; Fox, J.H. & Kelly, M.P. (1982). Facial recognition memory in dementia. *Cortex*, 18, 329-336.

Zhang, M., Katzman, R., Salmon, D., Jin, H., Cai, G., Wang, Z., Qu, G., Grant, L., Yu, E., Levy, P., Klauber, M. & Liu W. (1990). The prevalence of dementia and Alzheimer's disease in Shanghai, China : Impact of age, Gender and Education. *Annals of Neurology*, 27, 428-437.

INDEX